CHRISTMAS 1959.

With all best wishes for enjoyable hours of reading.

Wynn, Mabel & Siân. *(The most interesting pages)*

```
D1493325
```

SCRAMBLES AMONGST THE ALPS

By the same Author

HOW TO USE THE ANEROID BAROMETER

EDWARD WHYMPER, AT THE AGE OF 25.

SCRAMBLES
AMONGST THE ALPS

EDWARD WHYMPER

With Additional Illustrations and
Material from the Author's
Unpublished Diaries

REVISED AND EDITED BY H. E. G. TYNDALE

*Toil and pleasure, in their natures opposite, are yet linked
together in a kind of necessary connection.—*LIVY.

LONDON: JOHN MURRAY, ALBEMARLE STREET

First Edition	. . . . . .	June 1871
Second Edition	. . . . . .	November 1871
Third Edition (The Ascent of the Matterhorn)	.	November 1879
Fourth Edition	. . . . . .	December 1893
Fifth Edition	. . . . . .	August 1900
Sixth Edition	. . . . . .	November 1936
Reprinted	. . . . . .	May 1948
Reprinted	. . . . . .	July 1954

Made and Printed in Great Britain by Butler & Tanner Ltd., Frome and London,
and Published by John Murray (Publishers) Ltd.

EDITOR'S PREFACE

THE ascent of the Wetterhorn on September 17, 1854, is generally regarded as the birthday of modern mountaineering, with the classic encounter of Mr. Alfred Wills and Christian Almer beneath the final snowslope. Six years later, when these two apostles of a new faith were finding fresh converts year by year, Edward Whymper paid his first visit to the Alps. It was a fortunate chance for him that his instructions took him to Zermatt, for here a new world was opened to him : a world not merely of snow and high pasturage beneath the mountain whose destiny was to be knit so close with his own, but one where a new-born enthusiasm was now bringing with each summer to the Alps the leaders of intellectual life among his fellow-countrymen. To the young man of twenty, escaped from the monotony of an engraver's life, association with such men as Leslie Stephen and Hinchliff, Tyndall and John Ball, Alfred Wills and A. W. Moore, was like a vision of some unexplored country into which he was now privileged to enter.

Whymper's diary of 1860 gives some picture of his first impressions. He is travelling alone, armed only with sketch-book and a reasonable knowledge of French ; a stranger among his compatriots at Zermatt, with their peeling faces and scarce comprehensible jargon. Gradually the spirit of their enthusiasm enters into his being : the dinner-table at Zermatt among " Alpine men, very plucky fellows, the talk continually interesting " ; Hinchliff and Stephen returning " wet as water-dogs " from the Riffelberg in 35 minutes, " rather a contrast to my four hours of last night " ; an offer of coaching in rockwork from Hinchliff, "which offer was gratefully accepted"; a chance encounter near Saas with his hero Imseng, the famous climbing *curé*, when "I immediately extended a paw and we gave each other a gripe"; the grave bearded faces of guides on the low wall before the hotel, as he looks with reverence on these stewards of the mysteries of the mountains—through all these influences the dreams already forming take shape, and find their fulfilment in a short career of unexampled brilliance, until he learned the bitter lesson with which he closes his narrative, that "a momentary negligence may destroy the happiness of a lifetime."

The story of Whymper's repeated attempts to ascend the Matterhorn is one of the great epics of Alpine history; indeed, the third edition of his book dealt almost entirely with this mountain. It is, however, noteworthy that the two following editions restored the original text. The Alps meant to him far more than the conquest of a mountain reputed inaccessible; though he might linger rejected at the foot of the Matterhorn "as a foolish lover," his two concluding campaigns mark him out as a mountaineer of wide experience and unfeigned devotion. If his abandonment of mountaineering as a recreation after the disaster of 1865 be considered evidence that he was never wholeheartedly devoted to mountain travel; if the record of his Alpine days, here told with Homeric simplicity, be not sufficient proof that he had other ideals than the conquest of one peak, let it be remembered that when abruptly recalled to England in 1864 he advised his friend Adams-Reilly to try the Matterhorn himself, offering him the services of Michel Croz. Furthermore, this book was first published in 1871, six years after the accident, but it is not alone for the Matterhorn chapters that it remains a classic to this day; it breathes that spirit of the pioneers which Whymper himself first learned from such men as Stephen and Wills. From 1865 his practice changes, but not his outlook; his faith is unshaken; only, after so grievous a blow, there was "never glad confident morning again."

Concerning the accident of July 14, 1865, there would be no further occasion to write here, were it not that even now it is sometimes said that the full story of that day has never been told.[1] Immediately after the accident, Whymper entrusted the relation of the day's events to the chaplain at Zermatt, whose letter to *The Times* is dated July 17. Had he realized how greatly feeling in England was stirred by the disaster—he did not leave Switzerland for home until July 26—he would assuredly have made public his own story at the earliest possible moment. There was as yet in England little understanding of the ideals which drew men to the mountains. "Well," says *The Times* of July 27 in a leading article, "it is magnificent. But is it life ? Is it duty ? Is it common sense ? " Scholars and divines, seeking the mountains, are here pictured as " accepting the equal alternative of an idle boast and a horrible death." Before such an attitude of mind, Whymper's reluctance is intelligible. His original resolution was to write nothing for public consumption, but to put the whole matter before the consideration of the Alpine Club. "I cannot bring myself to write to the newspapers," he writes to Herr von Fellenberg on July 26, in forwarding an account which he is prepared for Fellenberg to publish in Switzerland. His friends in England took a different view. "Let me implore you not to delay," writes the editor of the *Alpine Journal* on July 24, "as I think it absolutely necessary such a narrative should appear." "Give your own account," writes Mr. Wills, then President of the Alpine Club, on August 6 ; " let it be truthful, manly and unflinching—wherever blame is due (if blame there be) let it rest—but do not let people go

---

[1] There is the rumour, which has found its way into print, that the full story was told by Whymper in confidence to Dr. G. F. Browne, Bishop of Stepney (later, of Bristol). In this connexion, I may quote from Whymper's diary of 1895 : "*Aug.* 30. . . . At dinner (at Riffelalp) Browne, Bishop of Stepney, came up and spoke to me. Said he could recognize me, although he hadn't seen me for 31 years." Apart from a note that they attended a funeral together five days later, the diaries from 1895 to 1911 contain no further reference to Bishop Browne.

on conjecturing the worst, when you could silence the greater part of it by your utterance. To some extent also the Club is on its trial. People are daily writing to abuse us and our doings." In response to such urgence, Whymper wrote his story for *The Times* of August 8, with an accompanying letter from Mr. Wills. Nothing which has since been published, whether by Whymper himself or by others, no statement in Whymper's collected papers or in the account dictated in 1917 by " young " Peter Taugwalder (the document is in the possession of the Alpine Club, and it contains many inaccuracies of fact) show any sign that the story given in these pages is anything but the whole truth.

I am greatly indebted to Mrs. Woodgate, niece of Edward Whymper, for her courtesy in placing all relevant documents and diaries at my disposal ; to Miss Ethel Whymper, who has happily inherited the author's love of mountains ; to the *Alpine Journal* ; to Colonel E. L. Strutt, President of the Alpine Club, and to Mr. John Grey Murray, for their friendly advice and interest. The maps in the text and at the end are as printed in the 1900 edition ; elsewhere I have endeavoured to give names according to modern spelling.

H. E. G. TYNDALE.

WINCHESTER COLLEGE,
July 23, 1936.

AUTHOR'S PREFACE TO THE FIFTH EDITION

In the year 1860, shortly before leaving England for a long continental tour, a certain eminent London publisher requested me to make for him some sketches of the great Alpine peaks. At that time I had only a literary acquaintance with mountain-climbing, and had not even seen—much less set foot upon—a mountain. Amongst the peaks which were upon the list was Mont Pelvoux, in Dauphiné. The sketches that were required of it were to celebrate the triumph of some Englishmen who intended to make its ascent. They came—they saw—but they did not conquer. By a mere chance I fell in with a very agreeable Frenchman who accompanied this party, and was pressed by him to return to the assault. In 1861 we did so, with my friend Macdonald—and we conquered. This was the origin of my Scrambles amongst the Alps.

The ascent of Mont Pelvoux (including the disagreeables) was a very delightful scramble. The mountain air did *not* act as an emetic ; the sky did *not* look black, instead of blue ; nor did I feel tempted to throw myself over precipices. I hastened to enlarge my experience, and went to the Matterhorn. I was urged towards Mont Pelvoux by those mysterious impulses which cause men to peer into the unknown. This mountain was reputed to be the highest in France, and on that account was worthy of attention ; and it was believed to be the culminating point of a picturesque district of great interest, which was then almost entirely unexplored ! The Matterhorn attracted me simply by its grandeur. It was considered to be the most completely inaccessible of all mountains, even by those who ought to have known better. Stimulated to make fresh exertions by one repulse after another, I returned, year after year, as I had opportunity, more and more determined to find a way up it, or to *prove* it to be really inaccessible.

A considerable portion of this volume is occupied by the history of these attacks on the Matterhorn, and the other excursions that are described have generally some connection, more or less remote, with that mountain or with Mont Pelvoux. All are new excursions (that is, excursions made for the first time), unless the contrary is pointed out. Some have been passed over very briefly, and entire ascents or descents have been disposed of in a single line. If they had been worked out at full length, three volumes, instead of one, would have been required. Generally speaking, the salient points alone have been dwelt upon, and the rest has been left to the imagination. This treatment spares the reader from much useless repetition.

In endeavouring to make the book of some use to those who may wish to go mountain-scrambling, whether in the Alps or elsewhere, undue prominence, perhaps, has been given to our mistakes and failures ; and it will doubtless be pointed out that our practice must have been bad if the principles which are laid down are sound, or that the principles must be unsound if the practice was good. We were not immaculate. Our blunders are not held up to be admired, or to be imitated, but to be avoided.

These scrambles amongst the Alps were holiday excursions, and as such they should be judged. They are spoken of as sport, and nothing more. The pleasure that they gave me cannot be transferred to others. The ablest pens have failed, and I think must always fail, to give a true idea of the grandeur of the Alps. The most minute descriptions of the greatest writers do nothing more than convey impressions that are entirely erroneous—the reader conjures up visions, it may be magnificent ones, but they are infinitely inferior to the reality. I have dealt sparingly in descriptions, and have employed illustrations freely, in the hope that the pencil may perhaps succeed where the pen must inevitably have failed.

About fifty of the subjects were drawn on the wood by the late Mr. James Mahoney, and I am much indebted to that artist for the care and fidelity with which he followed my slight memoranda, and for the spirit he put into his admirable designs. Most of his drawings will be identified by his monogram. Twenty of the remainder are the work of Mr. Cyrus Johnson.

It is now my pleasant duty to acknowledge assistance rendered, directly or indirectly, by friends and strangers, at home and abroad. First of all, my thanks are due to my companions for having placed their journals and sketches freely at my disposal. From Prof. T. G. Bonney, F.R.S., and Mr. Robert H. Scott, F.R.S., I have received many friendly hints and much valued criticism ; and aid, in a variety of ways, from Mr. Budden, Prof. Gastaldi, and Sig. Giordano, in Italy ; from M. Emile Templier and the Maréchal Canrobert, in France ; and from Mr. Gosset of Berne. I am indebted to the Messrs. Longman for the use of a portion of their Map of the Western Alps. The other Maps are original.

LONDON, *June*, 1900.

CONTENTS

1860

CHAPTER I

INTRODUCTORY

1861

CHAPTER II

THE ASCENT OF MONT PELVOUX

CHAPTER III

MY FIRST SCRAMBLE ON THE MATTERHORN

xiii

xiv

CONTENTS

1862

CHAPTER IV

RENEWED ATTEMPTS TO ASCEND THE MATTERHORN

1863

CHAPTER V

THE VAL TOURNANCHE—THE BREUILJOCH—ZERMATT—THE FIRST ASCENT OF THE GRAND TOURNALIN

CHAPTER VI

OUR SIXTH ATTEMPT TO ASCEND THE MATTERHORN

1864

CHAPTER VII

FROM ST. MICHEL TO LA BERARDE BY THE COL DES AIGUILLES D'ARVES, COL DE MARTIGNARE, AND THE BRECHE DE LA MEIJE

CHAPTER VIII

THE FIRST ASCENT OF THE POINTE DES ECRINS

CHAPTER IX

ON THE FIRST PASSAGE OF THE COL DE LA PILATTE

CHAPTER X

IN THE MONT BLANC RANGE—PASSAGE OF THE COL DE TRIOLET, AND ASCENTS OF MONT DOLENT, AIGUILLE DE TRELATETE, AND AIGUILLE D'ARGENTIERE

CHAPTER XI

FIRST PASSAGE OF THE MOMING PASS—ZERMATT

CONTENTS

1865

CHAPTER XII

THE FIRST ASCENT OF THE GRAND CORNIER

CHAPTER XIII

THE ASCENT OF THE DENT BLANCHE

CHAPTER XIV

LOST ON THE COL D'HERENS—MY SEVENTH ATTEMPT TO ASCEND THE MATTERHORN

CHAPTER XV

ON THE VALLEY OF AOSTA AND THE FIRST ASCENT OF THE GRANDES JORASSES

CHAPTER XVI

THE FIRST PASSAGE OF THE COL DOLENT

CHAPTER XVII

THE FIRST ASCENT OF THE AIGUILLE VERTE

CONTENTS

CHAPTER XVIII
THE FIRST PASSAGE OF THE COL DE TALEFRE

CHAPTER XIX
THE FIRST ASCENT OF THE RUINETTE—THE MATTERHORN

CHAPTER XX
THE FIRST ASCENT OF THE MATTERHORN

CHAPTER XXI
THE DESCENT OF THE MATTERHORN

APPENDIX

S.A.A.   B

CONTENTS

LIST OF ILLUSTRATIONS

FULL PAGE

IN THE TEXT

LIST OF ILLUSTRATIONS

The Drawings were made on the Wood by
H. J. BOOT, C. JOHNSON, W. LAPWORTH, J. MAHONEY, J. W. NORTH, A.R.A.,
T. D. SCOTT, P. SKELTON, W. G. SMITH, and C. J. STANILAND; and were
Engraved by J. W. and EDWARD WHYMPER.

* From Photographs.   ** Designs.

MAPS

To be placed at the end of the Volume.

GENERAL ROUTE MAP.
THE VALLEY OF ZERMATT, AND THE CENTRAL PENNINE ALPS.
THE VALPELLINE, THE VALTOURNANCHE, AND THE CENTRAL PENNINE ALPS.
THE CHAIN OF MONT BLANC.
THE MATTERHORN AND ITS GLACIERS.

SCRAMBLES AMONGST THE ALPS

BEACHY HEAD.

CHAPTER I

INTRODUCTORY

On the 23rd of July 1860, I started for my first tour in the Alps. As we steamed out into the Channel, Beachy Head came into view, and recalled a scramble of many years ago. With the impudence of ignorance, my brother [1] and I, schoolboys both, had tried to scale that great chalk cliff. Not the head itself— where sea-birds circle, and where the flints are ranged in orderly parallel lines—but at a place more to the east, where a pinnacle called the Devil's Chimney had fallen down. Since then we have been often in dangers of different kinds, but never have we more nearly broken our necks than upon that occasion.

In Paris I made two ascents. The first to the seventh floor of a house in the Quartier Latin—to an artist friend, who was

[1] The author of *Travels in Alaska*.

3

engaged, at the moment of my entry, in combat with a little Jew. He hurled him with great good-will, and with considerable force, into some crockery, and then recommended me to go up the towers of Notre Dame. Half an hour later I stood on a parapet of the west front, by the side of the leering fiend which for centuries has looked down upon the great city, and then took rail to Switzerland ; saw the sunlight lingering on the giants of the Oberland ; heard the echoes from the cowhorns in the Lauterbrunnen valley and the avalanches rattling off the Jungfrau ; and crossed the Gemmi into the Valais, resting for a time by the beautiful Oeschinen See, and getting a forcible illustration of glacier-motion in a neighbouring valley —the Gasterental. The upper end of this valley is crowned by the Tschingel Glacier, which, as it descends, passes over an abrupt cliff that is in the centre of its course.

THE DEVIL OF NOTRE DAME.

On each side the continuity of the glacier is maintained, but in the centre it is cleft in twain by the cliff. Lower down it is consolidated again. I scrambled on to this lower portion, advanced towards the cliff, and then stopped to admire the contrast of the brilliant pinnacles of ice with the blue sky. Without warning, a huge slice of the glacier broke away, and fell over the cliff on to the lower portion, with a thundering crash. Fragments rolled beyond me, although, fortunately, not in my direction. I fled, and did not stop until off the glacier ; but before it was quitted learned another lesson in glacial matters. The terminal moraine, which seemed to be a solid mound, broke away underneath me, and showed that it was only a superficial covering resting upon a slope of glassy ice.

On the steep path over the Gemmi there were opportunities

for observing the manners and customs of the Swiss mule. Though it is not perhaps in revenge for generations of ill-treatment that the mule grinds one's legs against fences and  stone walls, and pretends to stumble in awkward places (particularly when coming round corners and on the brinks of precipices), their evil habit of walking on the outside edges of paths (even in the most unguarded positions) is one that is distinctly the result of association with man. The transport of wood from the mountains into the valleys occupies most of the mules during a considerable portion of the year. The faggots into which the wood is made up project some distance on each side of the beast, and it is said that they walk intuitively to the outside of paths having rocks on the other side to avoid the collisions which would otherwise occur. When they carry tourists they behave in a similar manner; and, no doubt, when the good time for mules arrives, and they no longer carry burdens, they will still continue to do the same. This habit frequently gives rise to scenes. Two mules meet; each wishes to pass on the outside, and neither will give way. It requires considerable persuasion, through the medium of the tail, before such difficulties are arranged.

I visited the baths of Leuk, and saw the queer assemblage of men, women, and children, attired in bathing-gowns, chatting, drinking, and playing at chess in the water. The company did not seem to be perfectly sure whether it was decorous for elderly men to chase young females from one corner to another, but it was unanimous in howling at the advent of a stranger who remained covered, and literally yelled when I departed without exhibiting my sketch.

I trudged up the Rhone valley, and turned aside at Visp to go up the Visptal, where one would expect to see greater traces of glacial action, if a glacier formerly filled it, as one is said to have done.

I was bound for the valley of Saas, and my work took me high up the Alps on either side ; far beyond the limit of trees and the tracks of tourists. The view from the slopes of the Weissmies, on the eastern side of the valley, 5,000 or 6,000 feet above the village of Saas, is perhaps the finest of its kind in the Alps. The full height of the three-peaked Mischabelhörner (the loftiest mountain in Switzerland) is seen at one glance ; 11,000 feet of dense forests, green alps, rocky pinnacles, and glittering glaciers. The summits seemed to me then to be hopelessly inaccessible from this direction.

I descended the valley to the village of Stalden, and then went up the Visptal to Zermatt, and stopped there several days. Numerous traces of the formidable earthquake-shocks of five years before still remained ; particularly at St. Niklaus, where the inhabitants had been terrified beyond measure at the destruction of their churches and houses. At this place, as well as at Visp, a large part of the population was obliged to live under canvas for several months. It is remarkable that there was hardly a life lost on this occasion, although there were about fifty shocks, some of which were very severe.

At Zermatt I wandered in many directions, but the weather was bad, and my work was much retarded. One day, after spending a long time in attempts to sketch near the Hörnli, and in futile endeavours to seize the forms of the peaks as they peered out for a few seconds above the dense banks of woolly clouds, I determined not to return to Zermatt by the usual path, and to cross the Gorner Glacier to the Riffel hotel. After a rapid scramble over the polished rocks and snow-beds which skirt the base of the Théodule Glacier, and wading through some of the streams which flow from it (at that time much swollen by the late rains), the first difficulty was arrived at, in the shape of a precipice about 300 feet high. It seemed that it would be easy enough to cross the glacier if the cliff could be descended ; though higher up, and lower down, the ice appeared, to my inexperienced eyes, to be impassable for a single person. The general contour of the cliff was nearly perpendicular, but it was a good deal broken up, and there was little difficulty in descending by zigzagging from one mass to another. At length there was a long slab, nearly smooth, fixed at an angle of about forty degrees between two wall-sided pieces of rock. Nothing, except the glacier, could be seen below. It was an awkward place, but being doubtful if return were possible, as I had been dropping from one ledge to another, I passed it at length by lying across the slab, putting the shoulder stiffly against one side, and the feet against the other, and gradually wriggling down, by first moving the legs and then the back. When the bottom of the slab was gained a friendly crack was seen, into which the point of the bâton could be stuck, and I dropped down to the next piece. It took a long time coming down that little bit of cliff, and for a few seconds it was satisfactory to see the ice close at hand. In another moment a second difficulty presented itself. The glacier swept round an angle of the cliff, and as the ice was not of the nature of treacle or thin putty, it kept away from the little bay, on the edge of which I stood. We were not widely separated, but the edge of the ice was higher than the opposite edge of rock ; and worse, the rock was covered with loose earth and stones which had fallen from above. All along the side of the cliff, as far as could be seen in both directions, the ice did not touch it, and there was a marginal crevasse, seven feet wide, and of unknown depth.

All this was seen at a glance, and almost at once I concluded that I could not jump the crevasse, and began to try along the cliff lower down ; though without success, for the ice rose higher and higher, until at last further progress was stopped by the cliffs becoming perfectly smooth. With an axe it would have been possible to cut up the side of the ice ; without one I saw there was no alternative but to return and face the jump.

Night was approaching, and the solemn stillness of the High Alps was broken only by the sound of rushing water or of falling rocks. If the jump should be successful—well ; if not, I fell into that horrible chasm, to be frozen in, or drowned in that gurgling, rushing water. Everything depended on that jump. Again I asked myself, " Can it be done ? " It *must* be. So, finding my stick was useless, I threw it and the sketch-book to the ice, and first retreating as far as possible, ran forward with all my might, took the leap, barely reached the other side, and fell awkwardly on my knees. Almost at the same moment a shower of stones fell on the spot from which I had jumped.

The glacier was crossed without further trouble, but the Riffel,[1] which was then a very small building, was crammed with tourists, and could not take me in. As the way down was unknown to me, some of the people obligingly suggested getting a man at the chalets, otherwise the path would be certainly lost in the forest. On arriving at the chalets no man could be found, and the lights of Zermatt, shining through the trees, seemed to say, " Never mind a guide, but come along down, I'll show you the way " ; so off I went through the forest, going straight towards them. The path was lost in a moment, and was never recovered. I was tripped up by pine-roots, tumbled into rhododendron bushes, and fell over rocks. The night was pitch dark, and after a time the lights of Zermatt became obscure, or went out altogether. By a series of slides, or falls, or evolutions more or less disagreeable, the descent through the forest was at length accomplished ; but torrents of a formidable character had still to be passed before one could arrive at Zermatt. I felt my way about for hours, almost

---

[1] The Riffelhaus hotel (the starting-point for the ascent of Monte Rosa), a deservedly popular inn, is placed at a height of 3,100 feet above Zermatt (8,429 above the sea), and commands a superb panoramic view.

hopelessly ; by an exhaustive process at last discovering a bridge, and about midnight, covered with dirt and scratches, re-entered the inn which I had quitted in the morning.

Others besides tourists get into difficulties. A day or two afterwards, when on the way to my old station, near the Hörnli, I met a stout curé who had essayed to cross the Théodule

pass. His strength or his wind had failed, and he was being carried down, a helpless bundle and a ridiculous spectacle, on the back of a lanky guide ; while the peasants stood by, with folded hands, their reverence for the Church almost overcome by their sense of the ludicrous.

I descended the valley, diverging from the path at Randa to mount the slopes of the Dom,[1] in order to see the Weisshorn face to face. The latter mountain is the noblest in Switzerland, and from this direction it looks especially magnificent. On its north there is a large snowy plateau that feeds the glacier of which a portion is seen from Randa, and which on more than one occasion has destroyed that village. From the direction of the Dom (that is, immediately opposite) this Bies Glacier seems to descend nearly vertically. It does not do so, although it is very steep. Its size is much less than formerly, and the lower portion, now divided into three tails, clings in a strange, weird-like manner to the cliffs, to which it seems scarcely possible that it can remain attached.

Unwillingly I parted from the sight of this glorious mountain, and went down to Visp. A party of English tourists had passed up the valley a short time before with a mule. The party numbered nine—eight young women and a governess. The mule carried their luggage, and was ridden by each in turn. The peasants—themselves not unaccustomed to overload their beasts—were struck with astonishment at the unwonted sight ;

[1] The highest of the Mischabelhörner.

and made comments, more free than welcome to English ears, on the nonchalance with which young miss sat, calm and collected, on the miserable beast, while it was struggling under her weight, combined with that of the luggage.

Arriving once more in the Rhone Valley, I proceeded to Fiesch, and ascended the Eggishorn ; on which unpleasant eminence I lost my way in a fog, and my temper shortly afterwards. Then, after crossing the Grimsel in a severe thunderstorm, passed on to Brienz, Interlaken, and Berne ; and thence to Fribourg and Morat, Neuchâtel, Martigny, and the St. Bernard. The massive walls of the convent were a welcome sight as I waded through the snow-beds near the summit of the pass, and pleasant also was the courteous salutation of the brother who bade me enter. He wondered at the weight of my knapsack, and I at the hardness of their bread. The saying that the monks make the toast in the winter that they give to tourists in the following season is not founded on truth ; the winter is their most busy time of the year. But it *is* true they have exercised so much hospitality that at times they have not possessed the means to furnish the fuel for heating their chapel in the winter.[1]

---

[1] The temperature at the St. Bernard in the winter is frequently 40° Fahr. below freezing-point. January is their coldest month. See Dollfus-Ausset's *Matériaux pour l'étude des Glaciers*, vols. vi. and vii.

Instead of descending to Aosta, I turned aside into the Valpelline, in order to obtain views of the Dent d'Hérens. The night had come on before Bionaz was gained, and I had to knock long and loud upon the door of the curé's house before it was opened. An old woman, with querulous voice, and with a large goître, answered the summons, and demanded rather sharply what was wanted ; but became pacific—almost good-natured—when a five-franc piece was held in her face, and she heard that lodging and supper were requested in exchange.

My directions asserted that a passage existed from Prarayé, at the head of this valley, to Breuil, in the Val Tournanche, and the old woman, now convinced of my respectability, busied herself to find a guide. Presently she introduced a native, picturesquely attired in high-peaked hat, braided jacket, scarlet waistcoat, and indigo pantaloons, who agreed to take me to the village of Valtournanche. We set off early on the next morning, and got to the summit of the pass without difficulty. It gave me my first experience of considerable slopes of hard steep snow, and, like all beginners, I endeavoured to prop myself up with my stick, and kept it *outside*, instead of holding it between myself and the slope, and leaning upon it, as should have been done. The man enlightened me ; but he had, possibly, a very small opinion of his employer, and it is probably on that account that, a few minutes after we had passed the summit, he said he would not go any farther and would return to Bionaz. All argument was useless : he stood still, and to everything that was said answered nothing but that he would go back. Being rather nervous about descending some long snow-slopes, which still intervened between us and the head of the valley, I offered more pay, and he went on a little way.

AT THE ST. BERNARD.

Presently there were some cliffs down which we had to scramble.
He called to me to stop, then shouted that he would go back,
and beckoned to me to come up.   On the contrary, I waited
for him to come down ; but instead of doing so, in a second

THE VILLAGE OF BIONAZ.

or two he turned round, clambered deliberately up the cliff,
and vanished.   I supposed it was only a ruse to extort offers
of more money, and waited for half-an-hour, but he did not
appear again.   This was rather embarrassing, for he carried off
my knapsack.   The choice of action lay between chasing him
and going on to Breuil, risking the loss of the knapsack.   I
chose the latter course, and got to Breuil the same evening.

The landlord of the inn, suspicious of a person destitute of luggage, was doubtful if he could admit me, and eventually thrust me into a kind of loft, which was already occupied by guides and by hay. In later years we became good friends, and he did not hesitate to give credit and even to advance considerable sums.

My sketches from Breuil were made under difficulties, for my materials had been carried off. Nothing better than sugar-paper could be obtained, and the pencils seemed to contain more silica than plumbago. However, they *were* made, and the pass [1] was again crossed, this time alone. By the following evening the old woman of Bionaz again produced the faithless guide. The knapsack was recovered after the lapse of several hours, and then I poured forth all the terms of abuse and reproach of which I was master.

The following night was spent at Courmayeur, and the day after I crossed the Col Ferret to Orsières, and on the next the Tête Noire to Chamonix.[2] The Emperor Napoleon arrived on the same day, and access to the Mer de Glace was refused to tourists ; but, by scrambling along the Plan des Aiguilles, I managed to outwit the guards, and to arrive at the Montenvers as the Imperial party was leaving : the same afternoon failing to get to the Jardin, and very nearly succeeding in breaking a leg by dislodging great rocks on the moraine of the glacier.

From Chamonix I went to Geneva, and thence by the Mont Cenis to Turin and to the Vaudois valleys. A long and weary day had ended when Paesana was reached. The inn was full, and I was tired, and about to go to bed, when some village stragglers entered and began to sing. They sang to Garibaldi !

[1] This pass is usually called the Valcournera. It is also known as the Gra Cornère ; which is, I believe, patois for Grand Cornier.

[2] In 1860, the name of this village was frequently, or usually, written Chamounix or Chamouni. Inquiry has, however, satisfied me that Chamonix is the official and correct form. See my *Guide to Chamonix and Mont Blanc,* p. 79.

The tenor, a ragged fellow, whose clothes were not worth a shilling, took the lead with wonderful expression and feeling. The others kept their places, and sang in admirable time. For hours I sat enchanted ; and, long after I retired, the sound of their melody could be heard, relieved at times by the treble of the girl who belonged to the inn.

" GARIBALDI ! "

The next morning I passed the little lakes, which are the sources of the Po, on my way into France. The weather was stormy, and misinterpreting the patois of some natives—who in reality pointed out the right way—I missed the track, and found myself under the cliffs of Monte Viso. A gap that was occasionally seen, in the ridge connecting it with the mountains to the east, tempted me up ; and, after a battle with a snow-slope of excessive steepness, I reached the summit. To the north there was not a particle of mist, and the violent wind coming from that direction blew one back staggering ; while on the side of Italy, the valleys were completely filled with dense masses of cloud to a certain level, and there—where they felt the influence of the wind—they were cut off as level as the top of a table, the ridges appearing above them.

I raced down to Abriès, and went on through the gorge of the Guil to Montdauphin. The next day found me at La Bessée, at the junction of the Vallouise with the valley of the

Durance, in full view of Mont Pelvoux ; and by chance I walked into a cabaret where a Frenchman was breakfasting, who, a few days before, had made an unsuccessful attempt to ascend that mountain with three Englishmen and the guide Michel Croz of Chamonix ; [1] a right good fellow, by name Jean Reynaud.

The same night I slept at Briançon, intending to take the courier on the following day to Grenoble ; but all places had been secured several days beforehand, so I set out at 2 p.m. on the next day for a seventy-mile walk. The weather was again bad ; and on the summit of the Col de Lautaret I was forced to seek shelter in the wretched little hospice. It was filled with workmen who were employed on the road, and with noxious vapours proceeding from them. The inclemency of the weather was preferable to the inhospitality of the interior. Outside, it was disagreeable, but grand ; inside, it was disagreeable and mean. [2] The walk was continued under a deluge of rain, and I felt the way down—so intense was the darkness—to the village of La Grave, where the people of the inn detained me forcibly. It was perhaps fortunate that they did so ; for, during that night, blocks of rock fell at several places from the cliffs on to the road with such force that they made large pits in the macadam. I resumed the walk at half-past five the next morning, and proceeded, under steady rain, through Bourg d'Oisans to Grenoble, arriving at the latter place soon after 7 p.m.

This was the end of the Alpine portion of my tour of 1860, on which I was introduced to some of the great peaks, and acquired the passion for mountain-scrambling, the development of which is described in the following chapters.

[1] I had been sent to the Vallouise, to illustrate this ascent.

[2] Since that time a decent house has been built on the summit of this pass. The old vaulted hospice was erected for the benefit of the pilgrims who formerly crossed the pass *en route* for Rome.—Joanne's *Itinéraire du Dauphiné.*

BRIANÇON.

CHAPTER II

THE ASCENT OF MONT PELVOUX

" Thus fortune on our first endeavour smiles."
VIRGIL.

THE district of which Mont Pelvoux and the neighbouring summits are the culminating points, is, both historically and topographically, one of the most interesting in the Alps.   As the nursery and the home of the Vaudois, it has claims to permanent attention.   The names of Waldo and of Neff will be remembered when men more famous in their time will be

16

forgotten ; and the memory of the heroic courage and the simple piety of their disciples will endure as long as history lasts.

This district contains the highest summits in France, and some of its finest scenery. It has not perhaps the beauties of Switzerland, but has charms of its own. Its cliffs, torrents, and gorges are unsurpassed ; its deep and savage valleys present pictures of grandeur, and even sublimity, and it is second to none in the boldness of its mountain forms.

The district includes a mass of valleys which vie with each other in singularity of character and dissimilarity of climate. Some the rays of the sun can never reach, they are so deep and narrow.[1] In others the very antipodes may be found ; with temperature more like that of the plains of Italy than of Alpine France. This great range of climate has a marked effect on the flora of these valleys. Sterility reigns in some ; stones take the place of trees ; débris and mud replace plants and flowers : while in others, in a few miles, one passes vines, apple, pear, and cherry trees, the birch, alder, walnut, ash, larch, and pine, alternating with fields of rye, barley, oats, beans, and potatoes.

The valleys are for the most part short and erratic. They are not, apparently, arranged on any definite plan. They are not disposed, as is frequently the case elsewhere, either at right angles to, or parallel with, the highest summits ; but they wander hither and thither, take one direction for a few miles, then double back, and then perhaps resume their original course. Thus, long perspectives are rarely to be seen, and it is difficult to form a general idea of the disposition of the peaks.

The highest summits are arranged almost in a horse-shoe form. The loftiest of all, which occupies a central position, is the Pointe des Ecrins ; the second in height, the

---

[1] The depth of the valleys is so great that the sun not only is not seen for more than a few hours per day during the greater portion of the year, but in some places—at Villard d'Arène and at Andrieux for example—it is not seen at all for one hundred days.—Ladoucette's *Hautes-Alpes*, p. 599.

Meije,[1] is on the north ; and Mont Pelvoux, which gives its name to the entire block, stands almost detached by itself on the outside.

The district is still very imperfectly known ; there are probably many valleys, and there are certainly many summits which have never been trodden by the feet of tourists or travellers ; but in 1861 it was even less known. Until quite recently there was, practically, no map of it ; General Bourcet's, which was the best that was published, was completely wrong in its delineation of the mountains, and was frequently incorrect in regard to paths or roads.

The mountainous regions of Dauphiné, moreover, are not supplied, like Switzerland, Tyrol, or even the Italian valleys, with accommodation for travellers. The inns, when they exist, are often filthy beyond description. Rest is seldom obtained in their beds, or decent food found in their kitchens, and guides there are none. The tourist is thrown very much on his own resources, and it is not therefore surprising that these districts are less visited and less known than the rest of the Alps.[2]

Most of the statements current in 1861 respecting these mountains had been derived from two authors [3]—M. Elie de

[1] Sometimes called the Aiguille du Midi de la Grave, or the Aiguille de la Medje.

[2] By the lapse of time, some of the remarks in the above paragraphs have become inaccurate. Since the first publication of *Scrambles amongst the Alps*, Dauphiné has been more frequently visited, and at several of the places that are mentioned in this and in other chapters there is now tolerable accommodation for travellers. A railway has been opened from Embrun to Briançon, with a station at La Bessée, whence a good carriage-road leads up the Vallouise. There are now two hotels at La Ville de Vallouise. The high mountains of Dauphiné are pretty completely explored, and the principal peaks are frequently ascended by tourists.

[3] " Faits pour servir à l'Histoire des Montagnes de l'Oisans," by Elie de Beaumont in the *Annales des Mines* ; and *Norway and its Glaciers, followed by Excursions in the High Alps of Dauphiné*, by J. D. Forbes.

The following works also treat more or less of the districts referred to in this chapter :—*Outline Sketches in the High Alps of Dauphiné*, by Prof. T. G. Bonney ;

Beaumont and the late Principal J. D. Forbes. Their works, however, contained numerous errors in regard to the identification of the peaks, and, amongst others, they referred the supremacy to Mont Pelvoux, the highest point of which they termed the Pointe des Arcines, or des Ecrins. Principal Forbes erroneously identified the high peak seen from the valley of St. Christophe, with that seen from the valley of the Durance, and spoke of both as the Mont Pelvoux, and M. de Beaumont committed similar mistakes. In point of fact, at the time when M. de Beaumont and Forbes wrote their respective memoirs, the proper relation of Mont Pelvoux to the neighbouring summits had been determined by the engineers employed on the survey for the map of France ; but their observations were not then accessible to the public, although they had evidently been seen by M. de Beaumont. This party of surveyors, led by Captain Durand, made an ascent of Mont Pelvoux from the side of the Val d'Ailefroide—that is, from the direction of Vallouise—in 1828. According to the natives of the Vallouise, they got to the top of the second peak in height, and remained upon it, lodged in a tent for several days, at a height of 12,904 feet. They took numerous porters to carry wood for fires, and erected a large cairn on the summit, which has caused the name of Pic de la Pyramide to be given to their summit.

In 1848, M. Puiseux made an ascent from the same direction, but his Vallouisan guide stopped short of the summit, and allowed this courageous astronomer to proceed by himself.[1]

Histoire des Hautes-Alpes, by J. C. F. Ladoucette ; *Itinéraire du Dauphiné*, by Adolphe Joanne (2nd part) ; *Tour du Monde*, 1860, edited by Ed. Charton ; *The Israel of the Alps*, by Alexis Muston ; *A Memoir of Felix Neff*, by W. S. Gilly. Engravings of Dauphiné scenery are to be found in *Voyages Pittoresques dans l'ancienne France*, by Ch. Nodier, J. Taylor, and A. de Cailleux, and in Lord Monson's *Views in the Departments of the Isère and the High Alps*.

[1] M. Puiseux took for guide a man named Pierre Bornéoud, of Claux in the Vallouise, who had accompanied Captain Durand in 1828. In 1861, the expedition of M. Puiseux was quite forgotten in the Vallouise. I am indebted to M. Puiseux for the above and other details.

In the middle of August 1860, Messrs. Bonney, Hawkshaw, and Mathews, with Michel Croz of Chamonix, tried to ascend the Pelvoux, likewise from the same direction. These gentlemen spent several days and nights upon the mountain ; and, encountering bad weather, only attained a height of 10,430 feet.

M. Jean Reynaud, of whom mention has been made in the preceding chapter, accompanied the party of Mr. Mathews, and he was of opinion that the attempt had been made too late in the season. He said that the weather was usually good enough for high mountain ascents *only* during the last few days of July, and the first ones of August,[1] and suggested that we should attempt to ascend the mountain the following year at that time. The proposition was a tempting one, and Reynaud's cordial and modest manner made it irresistible, although there seemed small chance that we should succeed where a party such as that of Mr. Mathews had been beaten.

At the beginning of July, 1861, I dispatched to Reynaud from Havre, blankets (which were taxed as " prohibited fabrics"), rope, and other things desirable for the excursion, and set out on the tour of France ; but, four weeks later, at Nîmes, found myself collapsed by the heat, then 94° F. in the shade, and took train at once to Grenoble.

I lost my way in the streets of this picturesque but noisome town,[2] and having only a half-hour left in which to get a dinner and take a place in the diligence, was not well pleased to hear that an Englishman wished to see me. It turned out to be my friend Macdonald, who confided to me that he was going to try to ascend a mountain called Mont Pelvoux in the course of ten days ; but, on hearing of my intentions, he agreed to put

[1] This is a common saying in Dauphiné. It means that there is usually less snow on the mountains during these days than at any other time of the year. The natives have an almost childish dread of venturing upon snow or glaciers, and hence the period of minimum snow seems to them to be the most favourable time for excursions.

[2] In the last thirty years, Grenoble has been greatly improved and extended, and it is now one of the finest towns in France.

in an appearance at La Bessée on the 3rd of August. In a few moments more I was perched in the banquette *en route* for Bourg d'Oisans, in a miserable vehicle which took nearly eight hours to accomplish less than thirty miles.

At five on a lovely morning I shouldered my knapsack and started for Briançon. Gauzy mists clung to the mountains, but melted away when touched by the sun, and disappeared by jerks (in the manner of views when focussed in a magic lantern), revealing the wonderfully bent and folded strata in the lime-stone cliffs behind the town. Then I entered the Combe de Malval, and heard the Romanche eating its way through that wonderful gorge, and passed on to Le Dauphin, where the first glacier came into view, tailing over the mountain side on the right. From this place until the summit of the Col de Lautaret was passed, every gap in the mountains showed a glittering glacier or a soaring peak. The finest view was at La Grave, where the Meije rises by a series of tremendous precipices 8,000 feet above the road.[1] The finest distant view of the pass is seen after crossing the Col, near Monêtier. A mountain, commonly supposed to be Monte Viso, appears at the end of the vista, shooting into the sky ;[2] in the middle distance, but still ten miles off, is Briançon, with its interminable forts, and in the foreground, leading down to the Guisane, and rising high up the neighbouring slopes, are fertile fields, studded with villages and church spires. The next day I walked over from Briançon to La Bessée, to my worthy friend Jean Reynaud, the surveyor of roads of his district.

All the peaks of Mont Pelvoux are well seen from La Bessée, the highest point, as well as that upon which the engineers erected their cairn. Neither Reynaud nor anyone else knew this. The natives knew only that the engineers had ascended

[1] See Chapter VII.

[2] Monte Viso is not seen from the Lautaret Road. That this is so is seen when one crosses the Col du Galibier, on the south side of which pass Monte Viso is visible for a short time.

a peak, and had seen from that a still higher point, which they called the Pointe des Arcines or des Ecrins. They could not say whether this latter could be seen from La Bessée, nor could they tell the peak upon which the cairn had been erected. They knew nothing of the ascent of Monsieur Puiseux, and they confidently asserted that the highest point of Mont Pelvoux had not been attained by anyone. It was this point we wished to reach, and we were under the impression that the highest point was concealed by the peaks we saw, and would be gained by passing over them.

Nothing prevented our starting at once but the absence of Macdonald and the want of a bâton. Reynaud suggested a visit to the postmaster, who possessed a weapon of local celebrity. Down we went to the bureau, but it was closed ; we halloed through the slits, but no answer. At last the postmaster was discovered endeavouring (with very fair success) to make himself intoxicated. He was just able to ejaculate, " France ! 'tis the first nation in the world ! " which is a phrase used by a Frenchman at times that a Briton begins to shout, " We won't go home till morning "—national glory being uppermost in the thoughts of one, and home in those of the other. The bâton was produced ; it was a branch of a young oak, about five feet long, gnarled and twisted in several directions. " Sir," said the postmaster, as he presented it, " France! 'tis the first— the first nation in the world, by its "—he stuck. " Bâtons ? " I suggested. " Yes, yes, sir ; by its bâtons, by its—its," and here he could not get on at all. As I looked at this young limb, I thought of my own ; but Reynaud, who knew everything about everybody in the village, said there was not a better one, and we went off with it, leaving the official staggering in the road, muttering, " France! 'tis the first nation in the world ! "

The 3rd of August came, and as Macdonald did not appear, we started for the Vallouise ; our party consisting of Reynaud, myself, and a porter, Jean Casimir Giraud, nicknamed " little nails," the shoemaker of the place. An hour and a half's smart

walking took us to La Ville de Vallouise, our hearts gladdened
by the glorious peaks of Pelvoux shining out without a cloud
around them. I renewed acquaintance with the mayor of La
Ville. His aspect was original, and his manners were gracious,

MONT PELVOUX FROM ABOVE LA BESSÉE.

but the odour which proceeded from him was dreadful. The
same may be said of many of the inhabitants of these valleys.[1]

[1] Their late préfet shall tell why. " The men and women dress in sheepskins,—which have been dried and scoured with salt, of which the feet are used
as clasps, the fore feet going round the neck, and the hinder ones round the loins.
Their arms are naked, and the men are only distinguished from the women by
the former wearing wretched drawers, and the latter a sort of gown, which
only covers them to just below the knees. They sleep without undressing
upon straw, and have only sheepskins for coverings. . . . The nature of their
food, combined with their dirtiness, makes them exhale a strong odour from
their bodies, which is smelt from afar, and is almost insupportable to strangers.
. . . They live in a most indifferent manner, or rather they linger in dreadful
misery ; their filthy and hideous countenances announce their slovenlineas and
their stink."—Ladoucette's *Histoire des Hautes-Alpes.* pp. 656–7.

At La Ville the Vallouise splits into two branches—the Val d'Entraigues on the left and the Vallon d'Ailefroide on the right. Our route was up the latter, and we moved steadily forwards to the village of La Pisse, where a certain Pierre Sémiond lived, who was reputed to know more about Mont Pelvoux than any other man. He looked an honest fellow, but unfortunately he was ill and could not come. He recommended his brother, an aged creature, whose furrowed and wrinkled face hardly seemed to announce the man we wanted. Having no choice, we engaged him and again set forth.

Walnut and a great variety of other trees gave shadow to our path and fresh vigour to our limbs; while below, in a sublime

IN THE VAL D'AILEFROIDE.

gorge, thundered the torrent, whose waters took their rise from the snows we hoped to tread on the morrow.

The mountain could not be seen at La Ville, owing to a high intervening ridge. We were now moving along the foot of this to get to the chalets of Ailefroide, where the mountain actually commences. From this direction the subordinate, but more proximate peaks appear considerably higher than the loftier ones behind, and sometimes completely conceal them. But the whole height of the peak which in these valleys goes under the name of the " Grand Pelvoux " is seen at one glance from summit to base, six or seven thousand feet of nearly perpendicular cliffs.

THE GRAND PELVOUX DE VALLOUISE.

The chalets of Ailefroide are a cluster of wooden huts at the foot of the Grand Pelvoux, and are close to the junction of the streams which descend from the Glacier de Sapenière (or du Sélé) on the left, and the Glaciers Blanc and Noir on the right. We rested a minute to purchase some butter and milk, and Sémiond picked up a disreputable-looking lad to assist in transporting our stores.

Our route now turned sharply to the left, and all were glad that the day was drawing to a close, so that we had shade from the mountains. A more cheerless and desolate valley it is scarcely possible to imagine. It contains miles of boulders, débris, stones, sand, and mud ; few trees, and they placed so high as to be almost out of sight. Not a soul inhabits it. The mountains are too steep for the chamois, too inhospitable for the marmot, and too repulsive for the eagle. We did not see a single living thing in this sterile and savage valley during four days, except some few poor goats which had been driven there against their will.

It was a scene in keeping with the diabolical deed perpetrated here about four hundred years ago—the murder of the Vaudois of Vallouise, in the cavern which was now in sight, though high above us. Their story is very sad. Peaceful and industrious, for more than three centuries they had inhabited these retired valleys in tranquil obscurity. The Archbishops of Embrun endeavoured, though with little success, to get them within the pale of their church ; their efforts were aided by others, who commenced by imprisonments and torture,[1] and at last adopted the method of burning them by hundreds at the stake.[2]

In the year 1488, Albert Cattanée, Archdeacon of Cremona and legate of Pope Innocent VIII, would have anticipated the barbarities which at a later date roused the indignation of Milton and the fears of Cromwell ;[3] but, driven everywhere back by the Waldenses of Piedmont, he left their valleys and crossed the Mont Genèvre to attack the weaker and more thinly populated valleys of the Vaudois in Dauphiné. At the head of an army which is said to have been composed of vagabonds, robbers, and assassins (who had been tempted to his banner by promises of absolution beforehand, of being set free from the obligation of vows which they might have made, and by the confirmation of property to them which they might have wrongfully acquired), as well as regular troops, Cattanée poured

[1] It became a regular business. " We find amongst the current accounts of the Bailiff of Embrun this singular article—' *Item, for persecuting the Vaudois, eight sols and thirty deniers of gold.*' "—Muston, vol. i., p. 38.

[2] On the 22nd of May 1393, eighty persons of the valleys of Freissinières and Argentière, and one hundred and fifty persons of the Vallouise, were burnt at Embrun.—Muston, vol. i., p. 41.

[3] See Morland's *History of the Evangelical Churches of Piedmont*, 1658 ; Cromwell's *Acts*, 1658 ; and Burton's *Diary*, 1828.

down the valley of the Durance. The inhabitants of the Vallouise fled before a host that was ten times their number, and took up their abode in this cavern, where they had collected provisions sufficient for two years. But intolerance is ever painstaking ; their retreat was discovered. Cattanée had a captain who combined the resources of a Herod with the cruelty of a Pelissier, and, lowering his men by ropes, fired piles of brushwood at the entrance to the cavern, suffocated the majority, and slew the remainder. The Vaudois were relentlessly exterminated, without distinction of age or sex. More than three thousand persons, it is said, perished in this massacre ; the growth of three hundred and fifty years was destroyed at one blow, and the valley was completely depopulated. Louis XII caused it to be re-peopled, and after another three centuries and a half, behold the result—a race of monkeys.[1]

We rested a little at a small spring, and then hastened onwards till we nearly arrived at the foot of the Sapenière Glacier, when Sémiond said we must turn to the right, up the slopes. This we did, and clambered for half an hour through scattered trees and fallen boulders. Then evening began to close in rapidly, and it was time to look for a resting-place. There was no difficulty in getting one, for all around there was a chaotic assemblage of rocks. We selected the under side of a boulder which was more than 50 feet long by 20 high, cleared out the rubbish, and then collected wood for a fire.

That camp-fire is a pleasant reminiscence. The wine-cask had got through all its troubles ; it was tapped, and the French-

[1] The commune of the Vallouise contains at the present time between three and four thousand inhabitants. This cretin population was described by M. Elisée Reclus in the *Tour du Monde*, 1860. He said—" They attain the highest possible development of their intelligence in their infancy, and—abundantly provided with majestic goîtres, which are lengthened and swollen by age—are in this respect like ourang-outangs, who have nothing more to acquire after the age of three years. At the age of five years the little crétins have already the placid and mature expression which they keep all their lives. . . . They wear trousers, and coats with tails, and a large black hat."

men seemed to derive some consolation from its execrable contents. Reynaud chanted scraps of French songs, and each contributed his share of joke, story, or verse. The weather was perfect, and our prospects for the morrow were good. My companions' joy culminated when some red fire was thrown into the flames. It hissed and bubbled for a moment or two, and then broke out into a grand flare. The effect of the momentary light was magnificent; the mountains all around were illuminated for a second, and then relapsed into their solemn gloom. One by one our party dropped off to sleep, and at last I got into my blanket bag. It was hardly necessary, for, although we were at a height of about 7,000 feet, the minimum temperature was above 40° Fahrenheit.

We roused at three, and made a start at half-past four. Giraud had been engaged as far as this rock only, but as he wished to go on, we allowed him to accompany us. We mounted the slopes and quickly got above the trees, then had a couple of hours' clambering over bits of precipitous rock and banks of débris, and, at a quarter to seven, got to a narrow glacier—Clot de l'Homme—which streamed out of the plateau on the summit, and nearly reached the Glacier de Sapenière. We worked as much as possible to the right, in hopes that we should not have to cross it, but were continually driven back, and found that it could not be avoided. Old Sémiond had a strong objection to travel on the ice, and made explorations on his own account to endeavour to escape it; but Reynaud and I preferred to cross, and Giraud stuck to us. This glacier was narrow—in fact, one could throw a stone across it—and it was easily mounted on the side; but in the centre it swelled into a steep dome, up which we were obliged to cut. Giraud stepped forward and said he should like to try his hand, and having got hold of the axe, would not give it up; and here, as well as afterwards when it was necessary to cross the gullies filled with hard snow, which abound on the higher part of the mountain, he did all the work, and did it efficiently.

Old Sémiond of course came after us when we got across. We then zigzagged up some snow-slopes, and shortly afterwards commenced to ascend the interminable array of buttresses which are the great peculiarity of Mont Pelvoux. The rocks were very steep in many places, yet on the whole afforded good hold, and no climbing should be called difficult which does that. Gullies abounded among them, sometimes of great length and depth. *They* were frequently rotten, and would have been difficult for a single man to pass. The uppermost men were continually abused for dislodging rocks and for harpooning those below with their bâtons. However, without these incidents the climbing would have been dull—they helped to break the monotony.

We went up chimneys and gullies by the hour together, and always seemed to be coming to something, although we never got to it. The outline sketch will help to explain the situation. We stood at the foot of a great buttress — perhaps

BUTTRESSES OF MONT PELVOUX.

about 200 feet high—and looked up. It did not go to a point as in the diagram, because we could not see the top ; although we felt convinced that behind the fringe of pinnacles we did see there was a top, and that *it* was the edge of the plateau we so much desired to attain. Up we mounted, and reached the pinnacles ; but, lo ! another set was seen,—and another,—and yet more— till at last we reached the top, and found it was only a buttress, and that we had to descend 40 or 50 feet before we could commence to mount again. When this operation had been performed a few dozen times it began to be wearisome, especially as we were somewhat in the dark as to our whereabouts. Sémiond, however, encouraged us, and said he knew we were on the right route,—so away we went once more.

It was now nearly midday, and we seemed no nearer the summit of the Pelvoux than when we started. At last we all joined together and held a council. " Sémiond, old friend, do you know where we are now ? " " Oh yes, perfectly, to a yard and a half." " Well, then, how much are we below this plateau ? " He affirmed we were not half an hour from the edge of the snow. " Very good ; let us proceed." Half an hour passed, and then another, but we were still in the same state,—pinnacles, buttresses, and gullies were in profusion, but the plateau was not in sight. Then we called him again—for he had been staring about latterly, as if in doubt—and repeated the question. " How far below are we now ? " Well, he thought it might be half an hour more. " But you said that just now ! Are you sure we are going right ? " Yes, he believed we were. Believed ! that would not do. " Are you sure we are going right for the Pic des Arcines ? " " Pic des Arcines ! " he ejaculated in astonishment, as if he had heard the words for the first time. " Pic des Arcines ; no ! but for the pyramid, the celebrated pyramid he had helped the great Capitaine Durand," etc.

Here was a fix ;—we had been talking about it to him for a whole day, and now he confessed he knew nothing about it. I turned to Reynaud, who seemed thunderstruck. " What did he suggest ? " He shrugged his shoulders. " Well," we said, after expressing our minds pretty freely to Sémiond, " the sooner we turn back the better, for we have no wish to see your pyramid."

We halted for an hour, and then commenced the descent. It took us nearly seven hours to come down to our rock ; but I paid no heed to the distance, and do not remember anything about it. When we got down we made a discovery which affected us as much as the footprint in the sand did Robinson Crusoe : a blue silk veil lay by our fireside. There was but one explanation,—Macdonald had arrived ; but where was he ? The baggage was soon packed, and we tramped in the dusk, through the stony desert, to Ailefroide, where we arrived about half-past nine. " Where is the Englishman ? " was the first question. He was gone to sleep at La Ville.

We passed that night in a hay-loft, and in the morning, after settling with Sémiond, posted down to catch Macdonald. We had already determined on the plan of operation, which was to get him to join us, return, and be independent of all guides, simply taking the best man we could get as a porter. I set my heart on Giraud,—a good fellow, with no pretence, although well up to the work. We were disappointed ; he was obliged to go to Briançon.

The walk soon became exciting. The natives inquired the result of our expedition, and common civility obliged us to stop. But I was afraid of losing my man, for it was said he would wait only till ten o'clock, and that time was near at hand. At last I dashed over the bridge,—time from Ailefroide an hour and a quarter. A cantonnier stopped me, saying that the Englishman had just started for La Bessée. I rushed after him, turned angle after angle of the road, but could not see him ; at last, as I came round a corner, he was also just turning another, going very fast. I shouted, and luckily he heard me. We returned, reprovisioned ourselves at La Ville, and the same evening saw us passing our first rock, *en route* for another. I have said we determined to take no guide ; but, on passing La Pisse, old Sémiond turned out and offered his services. He went well, in spite of his years and disregard of truth. " Why not take him ? " said my friend. So we offered him a fifth of his previous pay, and in a few seconds he closed with the offer. This time he came in an inferior position,—we were to lead, he to follow. Our second porter was a youth of twenty-seven years, who was not all that could be desired. He drank Reynaud's wine, smoked our cigars, and quietly secreted the provisions when we were nearly starving. Discovery of his proceedings did not at all disconcert him, and he finished up by getting several items added to our bill at La Ville, which, not a little to his disgust, we disallowed.

This night we fixed our camp high above the tree-line, and indulged ourselves in the healthy employment of carrying our fuel up to it. The present rock was not so comfortable as the first, and, before we could settle down, we were obliged to turn out a large mass which was in the way. It was very obstinate, but moved at length ; slowly and gently at first, then faster and faster, at last taking great jumps in the air, striking a stream of fire at every touch, which shone out brightly as it entered the gloomy valley below, and long after it was out of sight we heard it bounding downwards, and then settle with a sub-dued crash on the glacier beneath. As we turned back from this curious sight, Reynaud asked if we had ever seen a torrent on fire, and said that in the spring, the Durance, swollen by the melting of the snow, sometimes brings down so many rocks, that, where it passes through a narrow gorge at La Bessée, no water whatever is seen, but only boulders rolling over and over, grinding each other into powder, and striking so many sparks that the stream looks as if it were on fire.

We had another merry evening with nothing to mar it ; the weather was perfect, and we lay backward in luxurious repose, looking at the sky spangled with its ten thousand brilliant lights.

> . . . " The ranges stood
> Transfigured in the silver flood,
> Their snows were flashing cold and keen,
> Dead white, save where some sharp ravine
> Took shadow, or the sombre green
> Of hemlocks turned to pitchy black,
> Against the whiteness at their back." [1]

Macdonald related his experiences over the *café noir*. He had travelled day and night for several days in order to join us, but had failed to find our first bivouac, and had camped a few hundred yards from us under another rock, higher up the mountain. The next morning he discerned us going along a

[1] J. G. Whittier, *Snow-Bound*.

ridge at a great height above him, and as it was useless to endeavour to overtake us, he lay down and watched with a heavy heart until we had turned the corner of a buttress, and vanished out of sight.

Nothing but the heavy breathing of our already sound asleep comrades broke the solemn stillness of the night. It was a silence to be felt. Nothing ? Hark ! what is that dull booming sound above us ? Is that nothing ? There it is again, plainer— on it comes, nearer, clearer ; 'tis a crag escaped from the heights above ! What a fearful crash ! We jump to our feet. Down it comes with awful fury ; what power can withstand its violence ? Dancing, leaping, flying ; dashing against others ; roaring as it descends. Ah, it has passed ! No ; there it is again, and we hold our breath, as, with resistless force and explosions like artillery, it darts past, with an avalanche of shattered fragments trailing in its rear ! 'Tis gone, and we breathe more freely as we hear the finale on the glacier below.[1]

We retired at last, but I was too excited to sleep. At a quarter-past four every man once more shouldered his pack and started. This time we agreed to keep more to the right, to see if it were not possible to get to the plateau without losing any time by crossing the glacier. To describe our route would be to repeat what has been said before. We mounted steadily for an hour and a half, sometimes walking, though more frequently climbing, and then found, after all, that it was necessary to cross the glacier. The part on which we struck came down a very steep slope, and was much crevassed. The word crevassed hardly expresses its appearance—it was a mass of

[1] M. Puiseux, on his expedition of 1848, was surprised, when at breakfast on the side of the mountain, by a mass of rock of more than a cubic yard falling like a bomb at his side, which threw up splinters in all directions.

formidable *séracs*. We found, however, more difficulty in getting on than across it ; and, thanks to the rope, it was passed
in safety. Then the interminable buttresses began again. Hour
after hour we proceeded upwards, frequently at fault, and obliged
to descend. The ridge behind us had sunk long ago, and we
looked over it, and all others, till our eyes rested on the majestic
Viso. Hour after hour passed, and monotony was the order
of the day. When twelve o'clock came we contemplated the

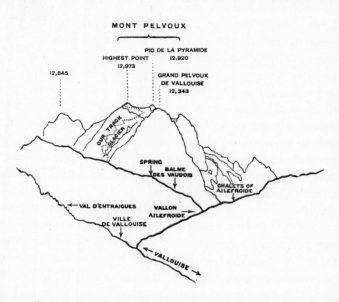

scene with satisfaction. All the summits in sight, with the
single exception of the Viso, had given in, and we looked over
an immense expanse of peaks and snowfields. Still the pinnacles
rose above us, and opinions were freely uttered that we should
see no summit of Pelvoux that day. Old Sémiond had become
a perfect bore. Whenever one rested for a moment to look
about, he would say, with a complacent chuckle, " Don't be
afraid, follow *me*." We came at last to a very bad piece, rotten
and steep, and giving no hold. Here Reynaud and Macdonald

confessed to being tired, and talked of going to sleep. A way was discovered out of the difficulty ; then someone called out, " Look at the Viso," and we saw that we almost looked over it. We worked away with redoubled energy, and at length caught sight of the head of the glacier as it streamed out of the plateau. This gave us fresh hopes ; we were not deceived ; and with a simultaneous shout we greeted the appearance of our long-wished-for snows. A large crevasse separated us from them, but a bridge was found ; we tied ourselves in line, and moved safely over it. Directly we got across there rose before us a fine snow-capped summit. Old Sémiond cried, " The pyramid ! I see the pyramid ! " " Where, Sémiond, where ? " " There ; on the top of that peak."

There, sure enough, was the cairn he had helped to erect more than thirty years before. But where was the Pic des Arcines which we were to see ? It was invisible, and somewhat sadly we moved towards the pyramid, sighing that there was nothing to conquer. Hardly had we gone two hundred paces, before there rose a superb white cone on the left, which had been hidden before by a slope of snow. We shouted—" The Pic des Arcines ! " and inquired of Sémiond if he knew whether that peak had been ascended. As for him, he knew nothing, except that the summit before us was called the pyramid, from the cairn he had, etc. etc., and that it had not been ascended since. " All right then—face about," and we immediately turned at right angles for the cone, the porter making faint struggles for his beloved pyramid. Our progress was stopped, in the sixth of a mile, by the edge of the ridge connecting the two peaks, and we perceived that it curled over in a lovely volute. We involuntarily retreated. Sémiond, who was last in the line, took the opportunity to untie himself, and refused to come on ; said we were running dangerous risks, and talked vaguely of crevasses. We tied him up again, and proceeded. The snow was very soft ; we were always knee-deep, and sometimes floundered in up to the waist ; but a simultaneous jerk before and behind always released one. By this time we had arrived at the foot of the final peak. Its left-hand ridge seemed easier than that upon which we stood, so we curved round to get to it. Some rocks peeped out 150 feet below the summit, and up these we crawled, leaving our porter behind, as he said he was afraid. I could not resist the temptation, as we went off, to turn round and beckon him onwards, saying, "Don't be afraid —follow *me*," but he did not answer to the appeal, and never went to the top. The rocks led to a short ridge of ice—our plateau on one side, and a nearly vertical precipice on the other. Macdonald cut up it, and at a quarter to two we stood shaking hands on the loftiest summit of the conquered Pelvoux.

The day still continued all that could be desired, and, far and near, countless peaks burst into sight, without a cloud to hide them. The mighty Mont Blanc, full seventy miles away, first caught our eyes, and then, still farther off, the Monte Rosa group; while, rolling away to the east, one unknown range after another succeeded in unveiled splendour; fainter and fainter in tone, though still perfectly defined, till at last the eye was unable to distinguish sky from mountain, and they died away in the far-off horizon. Monte Viso rose up grandly, but it was less than forty miles away, and we looked over it to a hazy mass we knew must be the plains of Piedmont. Southwards a blue mist seemed to indicate the existence of the distant Mediterranean, and to the west we looked over to the mountains of Auvergne. Such was the panorama; a view extending in nearly every direction for more than one hundred miles. It was with some difficulty we wrenched our eyes from the more distant objects to contemplate the nearer ones. Montdauphin was very conspicuous, but La Bessée was not readily perceived. Elsewhere not a human habitation could be seen; all was rock, snow, or ice; and, large as we knew were the snow-fields of Dauphiné, we were surprised to find that they very far surpassed our most ardent imagination. Nearly in a line between us and Monte Viso, immediately to the south of

AILEFROIDE   PIC SANS NOM   MONT PELVOUX
(12,878)   (12,845)   (12,973)   (12,920)

THE DURANCE

MONT PELVOUX AND THE AILEFROIDE, FROM NEAR MONTDAUPHIN, IN THE VALLEY OF THE DURANCE.

Château Queyras, was a splendid group of mountains of great height. More to the south an unknown peak seemed still higher ; while close to us we were astonished to discover that there was a mountain which appeared even loftier than that on which we stood. At least this was my opinion. Macdonald thought that it was not so high, and Reynaud that it was much about the same elevation as our own peak.

This mountain was distant a couple of miles or so, and was separated from us by a tremendous abyss, the bottom of which we could not see. On the other side rose this mighty wall-sided peak, too steep for snow, black as night, with sharp ridges and pointed summit. We were in complete ignorance of its whereabouts, for none of us had been on the other side. We imagined that La Bérarde was in the abyss at our feet, while it was in reality beyond the other mountain.[1]

We left the summit at last, and descended to the rocks, where I boiled some water, obtained by melting snow. After we had fed, and smoked our cigars (lighted without difficulty from a common match), we found it was ten minutes past three, and high time to be off. We dashed, waded, and tumbled for twenty-five minutes through the snow, and then began the long descent of the cliffs. It was then nearly four o'clock, and, as it would be dark at eight, it was evident that there was no time to be lost, and we pushed on to the utmost. Nothing remarkable occurred going down. We kept rather closer to the glacier, and crossed at the same point as in the morning. Getting *off* it was like getting *on* it—rather awkward. Old Sémiond had got over—so had Reynaud ; Macdonald came

[1] This mountain is the culminating point of the group, and is named on the French map Pointe des Ecrins. It is seen from the Val Christophe, and from that direction its ridges completely conceal Mont Pelvoux. But on the other side—that is, from the direction of La Bessée or the Vallouise—the reverse is the case : the Pelvoux completely conceals it.

Unaware that this name was going to be applied to it, we gave the name Pic des Arcines, or des Ecrins, to our summit, in accordance with the traditions of the natives.

next, but as he made a long stretch to get on to a higher mass, he slipped, and would have been in the bowels of a crevasse in a moment had he not been tied.

It was nearly dark by the time we had crossed, but I still hoped that we should be able to pass the night at our rock. Macdonald was not so sanguine, and he was right; for at last we found ourselves quite at fault, and wandered helplessly up and down for an hour, while Reynaud and the porter indulged in a little mutual abuse. The dreary fact that, as we could not get down, we must stay where we were, was now quite apparent.

We were at least 10,500 feet high, and if it commenced to rain or snow, as the gathering clouds and rising wind seemed to threaten, we might be in a sore plight. We were hungry, having eaten little since 3 a.m., and a torrent we heard close at hand, but could not discover, aggravated our thirst. Sémiond endeavoured to get some water from it; and, although he succeeded in doing so, he was wholly unable to return, and we had to solace him by shouting at intervals through the night.

It would be difficult to select a more detestable locality for a night out of doors. There was not shelter of any kind, and it was too steep to promenade. Loose rubbly stones covered the ground, and had to be removed before we could sit with any comfort. This was an advantage, although we hardly thought so at the time, as it gave us some employment; and, after an hour's active exercise of that interesting kind, I obtained a small strip about nine feet long, on which it was possible to walk. Reynaud was furious at first, and soundly abused the porter, whose opinion as to the route had been followed rather than that of our friend, and at last settled down to a deep dramatic despair, and wrung his hands with frantic gesture, as he exclaimed, "Oh, malheur, malheur! Oh misérables!"

Thunder commenced to growl, and lightning to play among the peaks above, and the wind, which had brought the temperature down to nearly freezing-point, began to chill us to the bones. We examined our resources. They were six and a half cigars, two boxes of vesuvians, one-third of a pint of brandy-and-water, and half-a-pint of spirits of wine. The spirit-lamp was lighted, and the remaining spirits of wine, the brandy and some snow were heated by it. It made a strong liquor, but we only wished for more of it. When that was over, Macdonald endeavoured to dry his socks by the lamp, and then the three lay down under my plaid to pretend to sleep. Reynaud's woes were aggravated by toothache ; Macdonald somehow managed to close his eyes.

The longest night must end, and ours did at last. We got down to our rock in an hour and a quarter, and found the lad not a little surprised at our absence. We feasted at the cave, and performed some very necessary ablutions. The persons of the natives are infested by certain agile creatures, rapid of motion, numerous and voracious. It is dangerous to approach too near, and one has to study the wind, so as to get on their weather-side. In spite of all such precautions my unfortunate companion and myself were being rapidly devoured alive. We only expected a temporary lull of our tortures, for the interiors of the inns are like the exteriors of the natives, swarming with this species of animated creation.

It is said that once, when these tormentors were filled with a unanimous desire, an unsuspecting traveller was dragged bodily from his bed ! This needs confirmation. One word more, and I have done with this vile subject. We returned from our ablutions, and found the Frenchmen engaged in conversation. " Ah ! " said old Sémiond, " as to fleas, I don't pretend to be different from anyone else,—*I have them.*" This time he certainly spoke the truth.

We got down to La Ville in good time, and luxuriated there for several days ; played many games of bowls with the natives, and were invariably beaten by them. At last it was necessary to part, and I walked southwards towards Monte Viso, while Macdonald went to Briançon.

While I have not attempted to conceal that the ascent of

Mont Pelvoux is of a rather monotonous character, the view from its summit may be confidently recommended. A glance at the map will show that, with the single exception of Monte Viso, it is better situated than any other mountain of considerable height for viewing the Western Alps.

Our discovery that the peak which is now called the Pointe des Ecrins was a separate and distinct mountain from Mont Pelvoux—and not its highest point—gave us satisfaction, although it was also rather of the nature of a disappointment.

On our return to La Bessée we wrongly identified it with the peak which is seen from that place on the left of Mont Pelvoux. The two mountains bear a considerable resemblance to each other, so the mistake is not, perhaps, unpardonable. The latter mountain is considerably higher than the Wetterhorn or Monte Viso, and it had no name. We called it the Pic Sans Nom, and this name has been adopted.

It has been observed that it is improbable the French surveyors would have remained for several days upon the Pic de la Pyramide without visiting the loftier and true summit of Mont Pelvoux. If they did, it is strange that they did not leave some memorial of their visit. The natives who accompanied them asserted that they did not pass from one to the other, and we therefore claimed to have made the ascent of the loftiest point for the first time. The claim, however, cannot be sustained, on account of the ascent of M. Puiseux. It is a matter of little moment; the excursion had for us all the interest of a first ascent; and I look back upon this, my first serious mountain scramble, with more satisfaction, and with as much pleasure as upon any that is recorded in this volume.

After parting from my agreeable companions, I walked by the gorge of the Guil to Abriès, and made the acquaintance at that place of an ex-harbour-master of Marseilles,—a genial man, who spoke English well. Besides the ex-harbour-master and some fine trout in the neighbouring streams, there was little to invite a stay at Abriès. The inn—l'Etoile, chez Richard—was a place to be avoided. Richard, it may be observed, possessed the instincts of a robber. At a later date, when forced to seek shelter in his house, he desired to see my passport, and, catching sight of the words John Russell, he entered that name instead of my own in a report to the gendarmerie, uttering an exclamation of joyful surprise at the same time. I foolishly allowed the mistake to pass, and had to pay dearly for it ; for he made out a lordly bill, against which all protest was unavailing.

His innocent and not very extraordinary mistake was eclipsed by a gendarme of Bourg d'Oisans, who took the passport, gravely held it *upside down* for several minutes, pretended to read it, and handed it back, saying it was all right.

Round about Abriès the patois of the district is more or less Italian in character, and the pronunciation of the natives reminds one of a cockney who attempts to speak French for the first time. Here bread is pronounced pane, and cheese, fromargee. There are a considerable number of dialects in use in this corner of France ; and sometimes in the space of only a few miles one can find several, which are almost as unintelligible to the natives of the surrounding districts as they are to the traveller. In some districts the spelling of the patois is the same, but the pronunciation is different—in this resembling Chinese. It is not easy for the stranger to understand these dialects, either written or spoken ; and this will be readily perceived from the samples given below, which are different versions of the parable of the Prodigal Son.[1]

[1] " Un Sarten homme aïe dous garçous ; lou pus jouve dissec à soun païre :— ' Moun païre, beila me la pourtiou d'ou ben que me reven.' Et lou païre fec en chascu sa part. Et paou de tens après, lou cadet, quant aguec fachs sa pacoutilla, se mettec en routo et s'en anec dinc un païs eiloigna, ounte mangec tout ce qu'aïé enbe les fumelles. Et quant aguec tout fricassa l'y aguec dinc aqueou païs-acqui une grande famine, et coumensec à aver famp."

The above is a specimen of the patois of the neighbourhood of Gap ; the following is that of Monêtier :—

" Un home avas dou bos. Lou plus giouve de isou disse à son pere :—

I quitted the abominations of Abriès to seek a quiet bundle of hay at La Chalp—a village some miles nearer to Monte Viso. On approaching the place the odour of sanctity [1] became distinctly perceptible ; and on turning a corner the cause was manifested—there was the priest of the village, surrounded by some of his flock. I advanced humbly, hat in hand, but almost before a word could be said, he broke out with, " Who are you ? " " What are you ? " " What do you want ? " I endeavoured to explain. " You are a deserter ; I know you are a deserter ; go away, you can't stay here ; go to La Monta, down there ; I won't have you here," and he literally drove me away. The explanation of his strange behaviour was, that Piedmontese soldiers who were tired of the service had not unfrequently crossed the Col de la Traversette into the valley, and trouble had arisen from harbouring them. However, I did not know this at the time, and was not a little indignant that I, who was marching to the attack, should be taken for a deserter.

So I walked away, and shortly afterwards, as it was getting dark, encamped in a lovely hole—a cavity or kind of basin in the earth, with a stream on one side, a rock to windward, and some broken branches close at hand. Nothing could be more perfect : rock, hole, wood, and water. After making a roaring fire, I nestled in my blanket bag (an ordinary blanket sewn up double round the legs, with a piece of elastic riband round the open end), and slept, but not for long. I was troubled with dreams of the Inquisition ; the tortures were being applied— priests were forcing fleas down my nostrils and into my eyes—

' Moun pere, moun pere, douna-me soque me duou reveni de vatre be.' Et lou pere lour faze ou partage de soun be. Paouc de giours apres, lou plus giouve deiquelou dou bos, apres aveira amassa tout so que aou lavie, sen ane diens un païs etrangie ben leigu, aount aous dissipe tout soun be diens la grande deipensa et en deibaucha. Apres qu'aou lague tout deipensa, larribe una grand famina diens iquaou païs ilai, et aou cheique diens lou besoign."— Ladoucette's *Histoire des Hautes-Alpes*, pp. 613, 618.

[1] See p. 23.

and with red-hot pincers were taking out bits of flesh, and then cutting off my ears and tickling the soles of my feet. This was too much ; I yelled a great yell and awoke, to find myself covered with innumerable crawling bodies. They were ants. I had camped by an ant-hill, and, after making its inhabitants mad with the fire, had coolly lain down in their midst.

THE BLANKET BAG.

The night was fine, and as I settled down in a neighbouring hole, a brilliant meteor sailed across full sixty degrees of the cloudless sky, leaving a trail of light behind which lasted for several seconds. It was the herald of a splendid spectacle. Stars fell by hundreds ; and not dimmed by intervening vapours, they sparkled with greater brightness than Sirius in our damp climate.

The next morning, after walking up the valley to examine Monte Viso, I returned to Abriès, and engaged a man from a neighbouring hamlet, for whom the ex-harbour-master had sent ; an inveterate smoker, and thirsty in proportion, whose pipe never left his mouth except to allow him to drink. We returned up the valley together, and slept in a hut of a shepherd, whose yearly wage was almost as small as that of the herdsman spoken of in " Hyperion " by Longfellow ; and the next morning, in his company, proceeded to the summit of the pass which I had crossed in 1860.   We were baffled in our attempt to get closer to the mountain.   A deep notch [1] with precipitous cliffs cut us off from it.   The snow-slope, too, which existed in the preceding year on the Piedmontese side of the pass, was now wanting, and we were unable to descend the rocks which lay beneath.   A fortnight afterwards the mountain was, however, ascended for the first time by Messrs. Mathews and Jacomb, with the two Croz of Chamonix.   Their attempt was made from the *southern* side, and the ascent, which was formerly considered a thing totally impossible, has become one of the most common and favourite excursions of the district.

We returned crestfallen to Abriès.   The shepherd, whose boots were very much out of repair, slipped upon the steep snow-slopes, and performed wonderful and alarming gyrations, which took him to the bottom of the valley more quickly than he could otherwise have descended.   He was not much hurt, and was made happy by a few needles and a little thread to repair his abraded garments.   The other man, however, considered it wilful waste to give him brandy to rub in his cuts, when it could be disposed of in a more ordinary and pleasant manner.

The night of the 14th of August found me at St. Véran, a village made famous by Neff, but in no other respect remarkable, saving that it is supposed to be the highest in Europe.[2]   The Protestants *now* form only a miserable minority ;   in 1861 there

---

[1] There are three cols or passes close to Monte Viso on its northern side, which lead from the valley of the Po into that of the Guil.   The deep notch spoken of above is the nearest to the mountain, and although it is by far the lowest gap in that part of the chain, and would seem to be the true Col Viso, it does not appear to be used as a pass.   The second, which I crossed in 1860, has the name Col del Color del Porco given to it upon the Sardinian map !   The third is the Col de la Traversette ; and this, although higher than at least one of those mentioned above, is that which is used by the natives who pass from one valley to the other.

[2] Its height is about 6,600 feet above the sea.

were said to be 120 to 780 Catholics. The poor inn was kept by one of the former, and it gave the impression of great poverty. There was no meat, no bread, no butter or cheese, and almost the only things that could be obtained were eggs. The bill for supper, bed, and breakfast, amounted to one and sevenpence.

In this neighbourhood, and indeed all round about Monte Viso, chamois still remain in considerable numbers. They said at St. Véran that six had been seen from the village on the day I was there, and the innkeeper declared that he had seen fifty together in the previous week ! I myself saw in this and in the previous season several small companies round about the Viso. It is perhaps as favourable a district as any in the Alps for a sportsman who wishes to hunt chamois, as the ground over which they wander is by no means of excessive difficulty.

The next day I descended the valley to Ville Vieille, and passed near the village of Molines, on the opposite side of the valley, a remarkable natural pillar, in form not unlike a champagne bottle, about seventy feet high, which had been produced by the action of the weather, and, in all probability, chiefly by rain. In this case a " block of euphotide or diallage rock protects a friable limestone." [1] The contrast of this dark cap with the white base, and the singularity of the form, made it a striking object. These natural pillars are among the most remarkable examples of the potent effects which can be produced by long-continued action of quiet-working forces. They are found in several other places in the Alps,[2] as well as elsewhere.

The village of Ville Vieille boasts of an inn with the sign of the Elephant ; which, in the opinion of local amateurs, is a

[1] J. D. Forbes.
[2] In the gorge of the Dard, near Aosta ; near Euseigne, in the Val d'Hérens ; near Stalden, in the Visptal ; near Ferden, in the Lötschental ; and, on a grander scale, near Bozen, in Tyrol, and in America on the Colorado river of the west.

proof that Hannibal passed through the gorge of the Guil. I remember the place, because its bread, being only a month old, was unusually soft ; and, for the first time during ten days, it was possible to eat some, without first of all chopping

NATURAL PILLAR NEAR MOLINES (WEATHER ACTION).

it into small pieces and soaking it in hot water, which produced a slimy paste on the outside, but left a hard untouched kernel.

The same day I crossed the Col d'Izouard to Briançon. It was the 15th of August, and all the world was *en fête* ; sounds of revelry proceeded from the houses of Servières as I passed over the bridge upon which the pyrrhic dance is annually performed,[1]

---

[1] See Ladoucette's *Hautes-Alpes*, p. 596.

and natives in all degrees of inebriation staggered about the paths. It was late before the lights of the great fortress came into sight ; but unchallenged I passed through its gates, and once more sought shelter under the roof of the Hôtel de l'Ours.

CHAPTER III

MY FIRST SCRAMBLE ON THE MATTERHORN

" What power must have been required to shatter and to sweep away the missing parts of this pyramid ; for we do not see it surrounded by heaps of fragments ; one only sees other peaks—themselves rooted to the ground—whose sides, equally rent, indicate an immense mass of débris, of which we do not see any trace in the neighbourhood. Doubtless this is that débris which, in the form of pebbles, boulders, and sand, fills our valleys and our plains."

SAUSSURE.

Two summits amongst those in the Alps which yet remained virgin had excited my admiration. One of these had been attacked numerous times by good mountaineers without success ; the other, surrounded by traditional inaccessibility, was almost untouched. These mountains were the Weisshorn and the Matterhorn.

After visiting the great tunnel of the Alps in 1861, I wandered for ten days in the neighbouring valleys, intending, presently, to attempt the ascent of these two peaks. Rumours were floating about that the former had been conquered, and that the latter was shortly to be assailed, and they were confirmed upon arrival at Châtillon, at the entrance of the Val Tournanche. My interest in the Weisshorn abated, but it was raised to the highest pitch on hearing that Professor Tyndall was at Breuil, and intending to try to crown his first victory by another and still greater one.

Up to this time my experience with guides had not been fortunate, and I was inclined, improperly, to rate them at a low value. They represented to me pointers out of paths, and

48

large consumers of meat and drink, but little more ; and, with
the recollection of Mont Pelvoux, I should have greatly preferred
the company of a couple of my countrymen to any number
of guides. In answer to inquiries at Châtillon, a series of men
came forward whose faces expressed malice, pride, envy, hatred,
and roguery of every description, but who seemed to be destitute of all good qualities. The arrival of two gentlemen with
a guide, who they represented was the embodiment of every
virtue, and exactly the man for the Matterhorn, rendered it
unnecessary to engage any of the others. He was a man of
large proportions ; and, although in acquiring him I did not
obtain exactly what was wanted, his late employers did exactly
what *they* wanted, for I incurred the responsibility, without
being aware of it, of paying his back fare, which must have
been a relief at once to their minds and to their purses.

When walking up towards Breuil we inquired for another
man of all the knowing ones, and they, with one voice, proclaimed that Jean-Antoine Carrel, of the village of Valtournanche, was the cock of his valley. We sought, of course, for
Carrel ; and found him a well-made, resolute-looking fellow,
with a certain defiant air which was rather taking. Yes, he
would go. Twenty francs a day, whatever was the result, was
his price. I assented. But I must take his comrade. " Why
so ? " Oh, it was impossible to get along without another
man. As he said this an evil countenance came forth out of
the darkness and proclaimed itself the comrade. I demurred,
the negotiations broke off, and we went up to Breuil. This
place will be frequently mentioned in subsequent chapters, and
was in full view of the extraordinary peak, the ascent of which
we were about to attempt.

It is unnecessary to enter into a minute description of the
Matterhorn, after all that has been written about that famous
mountain. Those by whom this book is likely to be read will
know that the summit of the peak is nearly 15,000 feet above the

level of the sea, and that it rises abruptly, by a series of cliffs which may properly be termed precipices, a clear 5,000 feet above the glaciers which surround its base. They will know too that it was the last great Alpine peak which remained unscaled,—less on account of the difficulty of doing so, than from the terror inspired by its invincible appearance. There seemed to be a *cordon* drawn around it, up to which one might go, but no farther. Within that invisible line djinns and effreets were supposed to exist—the Wandering Jew and the spirits of the damned. The superstitious natives in the surrounding valleys (many of whom firmly believed it to be not only the highest mountain in the Alps, but in the world) spoke of a ruined city on its summit wherein the spirits dwelt ; and if you laughed, they gravely shook their heads ; told you to look yourself to see the castles and the walls, and warned one against a rash approach, lest the infuriate demons from their impregnable heights might hurl down vengeance for one's derision. Such were the traditions of the natives. Stronger minds felt the influence of the wonderful form, and men who ordinarily spoke or wrote like rational beings, when they came under its power seemed to quit their senses, and ranted, and rhapsodized, losing for a time all common forms of speech. Even the sober Saussure was moved to enthusiasm when he saw the mountain, and— inspired by the spectacle—he anticipated the speculations of later geologists, in the striking sentences which are placed at the head of this chapter.

The Matterhorn looks equally imposing from whatever side it is seen. It never seems commonplace ; and in this respect, and in regard to the impression it makes upon spectators, it stands almost alone amongst mountains. It has no rivals in the Alps, and but few in the world.

The seven or eight thousand feet which compose the actual peak have several well-marked ridges and numerous others.[1] The most continuous is that which leads towards the north-

[1] See the Map of the Matterhorn and its Glaciers.

east ; the summit is at its higher, and the little peak, called Hörnli, is at its lower end. Another one that is well pronounced descends from the summit to the ridge called the Furggengrat. The slope of the mountain that is between these two ridges will be referred to as the eastern face. A third, somewhat less continuous than the others, descends in a south-westerly direction, and the portion of the mountain that is seen from Breuil is confined to that which is comprised between this and the second ridge. This section is not composed, like that between the first and second ridge, of one grand face ; but it is broken up into a series of huge precipices, spotted with snow-slopes, and streaked with snow-gullies. The other half of the mountain, facing the Z'Mutt Glacier, is not capable of equally simple definition. There are precipices, apparent, but not actual ; there are precipices absolutely perpendicular ; there are precipices overhanging ; there are glaciers, and there are hanging glaciers ; there are glaciers which tumble great *séracs* over greater cliffs, whose débris, subsequently consolidated, becomes glacier again ; there are ridges split by the frost, and washed by the rain and melted snow into towers and spires : while, everywhere, there are ceaseless sounds of action, telling that the causes are still in operation which have been at work since the world began ; reducing the mighty mass to atoms, and effecting its degradation.

Most tourists obtain their first view of the mountain either from the valley of Zermatt or from that of Tournanche. From the former direction the base of the mountain is seen at its narrowest, and its ridges and faces seem to be of prodigious steepness. The tourist toils up the valley, looking frequently for the great sight which is to reward his pains, without seeing it (for the mountain is first perceived in that direction about a mile to the north of Zermatt), when, all at once, as he turns a rocky corner of the path, it comes into view ; not, however, where it is expected ; the face has to be raised up to look at it— it seems overhead. Although this is the *impression*, the fact is that the summit of the Matterhorn from this point makes an angle with the eye of less than 16°, while the Dom, from the same place, makes a larger angle, but is passed by unobserved. So little can dependence be placed on unaided vision.

The view of the mountain from Breuil, in the Val Tournanche, is scarcely less striking than that on the other side ; but, usually, it makes less impression, because the spectator has grown accustomed to the sight while coming up the valley. From this direction the mountain is seen to be broken up into a series of pyramidal wedge-shaped masses.   On the other side it is remarkable for the large, unbroken extent of cliffs that it presents, and for the simplicity of its outline.   It was natural to suppose that a way would more readily be found to the summit on a side thus broken up than in any other direction.   The eastern face, fronting Zermatt, seemed one smooth, inaccessible cliff, from summit to base.   The ghastly precipices which face the Z'Mutt Glacier forbade any attempt in *that* direction.   There remained only the side of Val Tournanche ; and it will be found that nearly all the earliest attempts to ascend the mountain were made upon that side.

The first efforts to ascend the Matterhorn of which I have heard, were made by the guides, or rather by the chasseurs, of Val Tournanche.[1]   These attempts were made in the years 1858-9, from the direction of Breuil, and the highest point that was attained was about as far as the place which is now called the " Chimney " (cheminée), a height of about 12,650 feet.   Those who were concerned in these expeditions were Jean-Antoine Carrel, Jean Jacques Carrel, Victor Carrel, the Abbé Gorret, and Gabriel Maquignaz.   I have been unable to obtain any further details respecting them.

The next attempt was a remarkable one ; and of it, too, there is no published account.   It was made by the Messrs. Alfred, Charles, and Sandbach Parker, of Liverpool, in July 1860. These gentlemen, *without guides*, endeavoured to storm the

[1] There were no guides, properly speaking, in this valley at that time, with the exception of one or two Pessions and Pelissiers.

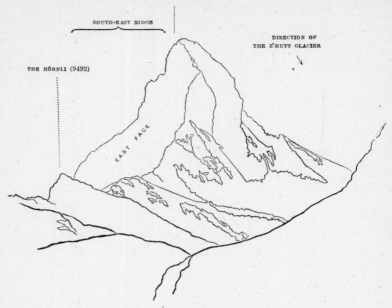

SUMMIT (14782)

SOUTH-EAST RIDGE

DIRECTION OF
THE Z'MUTT GLACIER

THE HÖRNLI (9492)

EAST FACE

THE MATTERHORN, FROM NORTH-EAST.

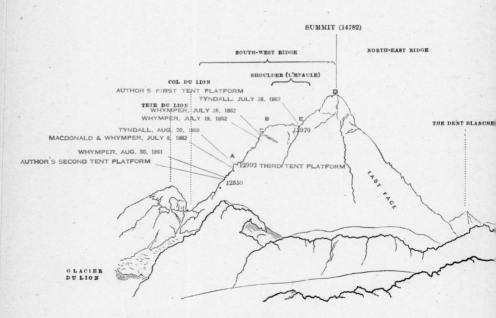

SUMMIT (14782)

SOUTH-WEST RIDGE

NORTH-EAST RIDGE

SHOULDER (L'ÉPAULE)

COL DU LION

AUTHOR'S FIRST TENT PLATFORM

TYNDALL, JULY 28, 1862

TÊTE DU LION
WHYMPER, JULY 26, 1862
WHYMPER, JULY 19, 1862

THE DENT BLANCHE

B

E

TYNDALL, AUG. 20, 1860

C

13970

MACDONALD & WHYMPER, JULY 8, 1862

D

WHYMPER, AUG. 30, 1861

A

AUTHOR'S SECOND TENT PLATFORM

12992 THIRD TENT PLATFORM

EAST FACE

12550

GLACIER
DU LION

THE MATTERHORN, FROM THE SUMMIT OF THE THEODULE PASS.
(10,899 FEET)

[53]

citadel by attacking its eastern face [1]—that to which reference was just now made as a smooth, impracticable cliff. Mr. Sandbach Parker informs me that he and his brothers went along the ridge between the Hörnli and the peak until they came to the point where the ascending angle is considerably increased. This place is marked on Dufour's map of Switzerland 3,298 metres (10,820 feet). They were then obliged to bear a little to the left to get on to the face of the mountain, and, afterwards, they turned to the right, and ascended about 700 feet farther, keeping as nearly as was practicable to the crest of the ridge, but, occasionally, bearing a little to the left— that is, more on to the face of the mountain. The brothers started from Zermatt, and did not sleep out. Clouds, a high wind, and want of time, were the causes which prevented these daring gentlemen from going farther. Thus, their highest point was under 12,000 feet.

The third attempt to ascend the mountain was made towards the end of August 1860, by Mr. Vaughan Hawkins,[2] from the side of the Val Tournanche. A vivid account of his expedition has been published by him in *Vacation Tourists* ; [3] and it has been referred to several times by Professor Tyndall in the numerous papers he has contributed to Alpine literature. I will dismiss it, therefore, as briefly as possible.

Mr. Hawkins had inspected the Matterhorn in 1859, with the guide J. J. Bennen, and had formed the opinion that the south-west ridge [4] would lead to the summit. He engaged

[1] This face is on the right hand of the large engraving facing this page. It is represented, more prominently, in the plate of the Matterhorn from the Riffelberg.

[2] Mr. Hawkins was unaware that any attempts had been made before his own, and spoke of it as the first.

[3] *Macmillan*, 1861.

[4] This ridge is seen on the left of the large engraving accompanying this chapter ; and if the reader consults this view, the explanatory outlines, and the maps, he will be able to form a fair idea of the points which were attained on this and upon the subsequent attempts.

J. Jacques Carrel, who was concerned in the first attempts, and, accompanied by Bennen (and by Professor Tyndall, whom he had invited to take part in the expedition), he started for the gap between the little and the great peak.[1]

Bennen was a guide who was beginning to be talked about. During the chief part of his brief career he was in the service of Wellig, then landlord of the inn on the Eggishorn, and was

J. J. BENNEN (1862).

hired out by him to tourists. Although his experience was limited, he had acquired a good reputation ; and his book of certificates, which is lying before me,[2] shows that he was highly esteemed by his employers. A good-looking man, with courteous, gentlemanly manners, skilful and bold, he might have taken a front place amongst guides if he had only been

[1] Since this time the small peak has received the name Tête du Lion. The gap is now called the Col du Lion ; the glacier at its base, the Glacier du Lion ; and the gully which connects the col with the glacier, the Couloir du Lion.
[2] By the kindness of its owner, Mr. F. F. Tuckett.

COL DU LION   THE "SHOULDER"   EAST FACE   DENT BLANCHE

THE MATTERHORN, FROM NEAR THE SUMMIT OF THE THEODULE PASS.

endowed with more prudence. He perished miserably, in the spring of 1864, not far from his home, on a mountain called the Haut de Cry, in the Valais.[1]

Mr. Hawkins' party, led by Bennen, climbed the rocks abutting against the Couloir du Lion, on its south side, and attained the Col du Lion, although not without difficulty. They then followed the south-west ridge, passed the place at which the earliest explorers had turned back (the Chimney),[2] and ascended about 300 feet more. Mr. Hawkins and J. J. Carrel then stopped, but Bennen and Professor Tyndall mounted a few feet higher. They retreated, however, in less than half an hour, finding that there was too little time ; and, descending to the col by the same route as they had followed on the ascent, proceeded thence to Breuil, down the couloir instead of by the rocks. The point at which Mr. Hawkins stopped is easily identified from his description. Its height is 12,992 feet above the sea. I think that Bennen and Tyndall could not have ascended more than 50 or 60 feet beyond this in the few minutes they were absent from the others, as they were upon one of the most difficult parts of the mountain. This party therefore accomplished an advance of about 350 or 400 feet.

Mr. Hawkins did not, so far as I know, make another attempt ; and the next was made by the Messrs. Parker, in July 1861. They again started from Zermatt, followed the route they had struck out on the previous year, and got a little higher than before ; but they were defeated by want of time, shortly afterwards left Zermatt on account of bad weather, and did not again renew their attempts. Mr. Parker says—" In neither case did we go as high as we could. At the point where we turned we saw our way for a few hundred feet farther ; but, beyond that, the difficulties seemed to increase." I am informed that both attempts should be considered as excursions undertaken with the view of ascertaining whether there was any encour-

[1] See Appendix A.
[2] A view of this place faces p. 85.

agement to make a more deliberate attack on the north-east side.

My guide and I arrived at Breuil on the 28th of August 1861, and we found that Professor Tyndall *had* been there a day or two before, but had done nothing. I had seen the mountain from nearly every direction, and an ascent of it seemed, even to a novice like myself, far too much for 24 hours. I intended to sleep out upon it, as high as possible, and to attempt to reach the summit on the following day. We endeavoured to induce another man to accompany us, but without success. Matthias zum Taugwald and other well-known guides were there at the time, but they declined to go on any account. A sturdy old fellow—Peter Taugwalder by name—said he would go ! His price ? " Two hundred francs." " What, whether we ascend or not ? " " Yes—nothing less." The end of the matter was, that all the men who were more or less capable showed a strong disinclination, or positively refused to go (their disinclination being very much in proportion to their capacity), or else asked a prohibitive price. This, it may be said once for all, was the reason why so many futile attempts were made upon the Matterhorn. One first-rate guide after another was brought up to the mountain, and patted on the back, but all declined the business. The men who went had no heart in the matter, and took the first opportunity to turn back.[1] For they were, with the exception of one man, to whom reference will be made presently, universally impressed with the belief that the summit was entirely inaccessible.

We resolved to go alone, and anticipating a cold bivouac, begged the loan of a couple of blankets from the innkeeper. He refused them ; giving the curious reason, that we had bought a bottle of brandy at Valtournanche, and had not bought any from him ! No brandy, no blankets, appeared to be his rule. We did not require them that night, as it was passed in the

[1] The guide Bennen must be excepted.

highest cow-shed in the valley, which is about an hour nearer
to the mountain than is the hotel. The cowherds, good fellows,
seldom troubled by tourists, hailed our company with delight,
and did their best to make us comfortable ; brought out their
little stores of simple food, and, as we sat with them round
the great copper pot which hung over the fire, bade us in husky
voice, though with honest intent, to beware of the perils of the
haunted cliffs. When night was coming on, we saw, stealing

JEAN-ANTOINE CARREL (1869).

up the hill-side, the forms of Jean-Antoine Carrel and the
comrade. " Oh ho ! " I said, " you have repented ? " " Not
at all ; you deceive yourself." " Why then have you come
here ? " " Because we ourselves are going on the mountain
to-morrow." " Oh, then it is *not* necessary to have more than
three." " Not for *us*." I admired their pluck, and had a strong
inclination to engage the pair ; but, finally, decided against it.
The comrade turned out to be the J. J. Carrel who had been
with Mr. Hawkins, and was nearly related to the other man.
Both were bold mountaineers ; but Jean-Antoine was incom-

parably the better man of the two, and was the finest rock-climber I have ever seen. He was the only man who persistently refused to accept defeat, and who continued to believe, in spite of all discouragements, that the great mountain was not inaccessible, and that it could be ascended from the side of his native valley.

The night wore away without any excitement, except from some fleas, a party of whom executed a spirited fandango on my cheek, to the sound of music produced on the drum of my ear, by one of their fellows beating with a wisp of hay. The two Carrels crept noiselessly out before daybreak, and went off. We did not leave until nearly seven o'clock, and followed them leisurely, leaving all our properties in the cow-shed ; sauntered over the gentian-studded slopes which intervene between the shed and the Glacier du Lion, left cows and their pastures behind, traversed the stony wastes, and arrived at the ice. Old beds of hard snow lay on its right bank (our left hand), and we mounted over them on to the lower portion of the glacier with ease. But, as we ascended, crevasses became numerous, and we were at last brought to a halt by some which were of very large dimensions ; and, as our cutting powers were limited, we sought an easier route, and turned, naturally, to the lower rocks of the Tête du Lion, which overlook the glacier on its west. Some good scrambling took us in a short time on to the crest of the ridge which descends towards the south ; and thence, up to the level of the Col du Lion, there was a long natural staircase, on which it was seldom necessary to use the hands. I dubbed the place " The Great Staircase." Then the cliffs of the Tête du Lion, which rise above the couloir, had to be skirted. This part varies considerably in different seasons, and in 1861 we found it difficult ; for the fine weather of that year had reduced the snow-beds abutting against it to a lower level than usual, and the rocks which were left exposed at the junction of the snow with the cliffs had few ledges or cracks to which we could hold. But by half-past ten o'clock we stood on the col, and looked down upon the magnificent basin out of which the Z'Mutt Glacier flows. We decided to pass the night upon the col, for we were charmed with the capabilities

THE COL DU LION : LOOKING TOWARDS THE TETE DU LION.

of the place, although it was one where liberties could not be taken. On one side a sheer wall overhung the Tiefenmatten Glacier. On the other, steep, glassy slopes of hard snow descended to the Glacier du Lion, furrowed by water and by falling stones. On the north there was the great peak of the Matterhorn,[1] and on the south the cliffs of the Tête du Lion. Throw a bottle down to the Tiefenmatten—no sound returns for more than a dozen seconds.

> . . . " how fearful
> And dizzy 'tis, to cast one's eyes so low ! "

But no harm could come from that side. Neither could it from the other. Nor was it likely that it would from the Tête du Lion, for some jutting ledges conveniently overhung our proposed resting-place. We waited for a while, basked in the sunshine, and watched or listened to the Carrels, who were sometimes seen or heard, high above us, upon the ridge leading towards the summit ; and, leaving at midday, we descended to the cow-shed, packed up the tent and other properties, and returned to the col, although heavily laden, before six o'clock. This tent was constructed on a pattern suggested by Mr. Francis Galton, and it was not a success. It looked very pretty when set up in London, but it proved thoroughly useless in the Alps. It was made of light canvas, and opened like a book ; had one end closed permanently and the other with flaps ; it was supported by two alpenstocks, and had the canvas sides prolonged so as to turn in underneath. Numerous cords were sewn to the lower edges, to which stones were to be attached ; but the main fastenings were by a cord which passed underneath the ridge and through iron rings screwed into the tops of the alpenstocks, and were secured by pegs. The wind, which playfully careered about the surrounding cliffs, was driven through our gap as through a blow-pipe ; the flaps of the tent would not keep down, the pegs would not stay in, and it exhibited so marked a desire to go to the top of the Dent Blanche, that we thought it prudent to take it down and sit upon it. When night came on we wrapped ourselves in it, and made our camp

[1] The engraving is made after a sketch taken from the rocks of the Matterhorn, just above the col.

as comfortable as the circumstances would allow. The silence was impressive. No living thing was near our solitary bivouac ; the Carrels had turned back and were out of hearing ; the stones had ceased to fall, and the trickling water to murmur—

> " The music of whose liquid lip
> Had been to us companionship,
> And, in our lonely life, had grown
> To have an almost human tone." [1]

It was bitterly cold. Water froze hard in a bottle under my head. Not surprising, as we were actually on snow, and in a position where the slightest wind was at once felt. For a time we dozed, but about midnight there came from high aloft a tremendous explosion, followed by a second of dead quiet. A great mass of rock had split off, and was descending towards us. My guide started up, wrung his hands, and exclaimed, " O my God, we are lost ! " We heard it coming, mass after mass pouring over the precipices, bounding and rebounding from cliff to cliff, and the great rocks in advance smiting one another. They seemed to be close, although they were probably distant, but some small fragments, which dropped upon us at the same time from the ledges just above, added to the alarm, and my demoralized companion passed the remainder of the night in a state of shudder, ejaculating " terrible," and other adjectives.

We put ourselves in motion at daybreak, and commenced the ascent of the south-west ridge. There was no more sauntering with hands in the pockets,—each step had to be earned by downright climbing. But it was the most pleasant kind of climbing. The rocks were fast and unencumbered with débris ; the cracks were good, although not numerous ; and there was nothing to fear except from one's self. So we thought, at least, and shouted to awake echoes from the cliff. Ah ! there is no response. Not yet ; wait a while, everything here is upon a superlative scale. Count a dozen, and then the echoes will return from the walls of the Dent d'Hérens, miles away,

[1] J. G. Whittier.

in waves of pure and undefiled sound ; soft, musical, and sweet. Halt a moment to regard the view ! We overlook the Tête du Lion, and nothing except the Dent d'Hérens, whose summit is still a thousand feet above us, stands in the way ; the ranges of the Graian Alps—an ocean of mountains—are seen at a glance, governed by their three great peaks, the Grivola, Grand Paradis, and Tour du Grand St. Pierre. How soft, and yet how sharp, they look in the early morning ! The midday mists have not begun to rise ; nothing is obscured ; even the pointed Viso, all but a hundred miles away, is perfectly defined.

Turn to the east, and watch the sun's slanting rays coming across the Monte Rosa snow-fields. Look at the shadowed parts, and see how even they—radiant with reflected light—are more brilliant than man knows how to depict. See how— even there—the gentle undulations give shadows within shadows ; and how—yet again—where falling stones or ice have left a track, there are shadows upon shadows, each with a light and a dark side, with infinite gradations of matchless tenderness. Then, note the sunlight as it steals noiselessly along, and reveals countless unsuspected forms ;—the delicate ripple-lines which mark the concealed crevasse, and the waves of drifted snow ; producing each minute more lights and fresh shadows ; sparkling on the edges and glittering on the ends of the icicles ; shining on the heights and illuminating the depths, until all is aglow, and the dazzled eye returns for relief to the sombre crags.

Hardly an hour had passed since we left the col before we arrived at the Chimney. It proved to be the counterpart of the place to which reference has been made at p. 7 ; a smooth, straight slab of rock was fixed, at a considerable angle, between two others equally smooth.[1] My companion essayed to go up, and, after crumpling his long body into many ridiculous positions, he said that he would not, for he could not, manage it. With some little trouble I got up unassisted, and then my guide tied

[1] Mr. Hawkins referred to this place as one of excessive difficulty. He, however, found it coated with ice ; we found it free from ice.

R. L. G. Irvi

MATTERHORN, FROM DENT D'HERENS.

himself on to the end of our rope, and I endeavoured to pull him up. But he was so awkward that he did little for himself, and so heavy that he proved too much for *me*, and after several attempts he untied himself, and quietly observed that he should go down. I told him he was a coward, and *he* mentioned his opinion of *me*. I requested him to go to Breuil, and to say that he had left his " monsieur " on the mountain, and he turned to go ; whereupon I had to eat humble pie and ask him to come back ; for, although it was not very difficult to go up, and not at all dangerous with a man standing below, it was quite another thing to come down, as the lower edge overhung in a provoking manner.

The day was perfect ; the sun was pouring down grateful warmth ; the wind had fallen ; the way seemed clear, no insuperable obstacle was in sight ; but what could one do alone ? I stood on the top, chafing under this unexpected contretemps, and remained for some time irresolute ; but as it became apparent that the Chimney was swept more frequently than was necessary (it was a natural channel for falling stones), I turned at last, descended with the assistance of my companion, and returned with him to Breuil, where we arrived about midday.

The Carrels did not show themselves. We were told that they had not got to any great height,[1] and that the " comrade," who for convenience had taken off his shoes and tied them round his waist, had managed to let one of them slip, and had come down with a piece of cord fastened round his naked foot. Notwithstanding this, they had boldly glissaded down the Couloir du Lion, J. J. Carrel having his shoeless foot tied up in a pocket handkerchief.

The Matterhorn was not assailed again in 1861. I left Breuil

[1] I learned afterwards from Jean-Antoine Carrel that they got considerably higher than upon their previous attempts, and about 250 or 300 feet higher than Professor Tyndall in 1860. In 1862, I saw the initials of J.-A. Carrel cut on the rocks at the place where he and his comrade had turned back.

with the conviction that it was little use for a single person to organize an attack upon it, so great was its influence on the moral of the guides ; and persuaded that it was desirable at least two should go, to back each other when required : and departed with my guide [1] over the Col Théodule, longing, more than before, to make the ascent, and determined to return, if possible, with a companion, to lay siege to the mountain until one or the other was vanquished.

[1] This man proved to be both willing and useful on lower ground, and voluntarily accompanied me a considerable distance out of his way, without fee or reward.

CHAPTER IV

RENEWED ATTEMPTS TO ASCEND THE MATTERHORN

" 'Tis a lesson you should heed,
Try, try, try again.
If at first you don't succeed,
Try, try, try again.
Then your courage should appear,
For if you will persevere
You will conquer, never fear.
Try, try, try again."

HICKSON.

THE year 1862 was still young, and the Matterhorn, clad in its wintry garb, bore but little resemblance to the Matterhorn of the summer, when a new force came to do battle with the mountain, from another direction. Mr. T. S. Kennedy of Leeds conceived the extraordinary idea that the peak might prove less impracticable in January than in June, and arrived at Zermatt in the former month to put his conception to the test. With stout Peter Perren and sturdy Peter Taugwalder he slept in the little chapel at the Schwarzsee, and on the next morning, like the Messrs. Parker, followed the ridge between the peak called Hörnli and the great mountain. But they found that snow in winter obeyed the ordinary laws, and that wind and frost were not less unkind than in summer. " The wind whirled up the snow and spiculæ of ice into our faces like needles, and flat pieces of ice a foot in diameter, carried up from the glacier below, went flying past. Still no one seemed to like to be the

65

first to give in, till a gust fiercer than usual forced us to shelter for a time behind a rock. Immediately it was tacitly understood that our expedition must now end ; but we determined to leave some memento of our visit, and, after descending a considerable distance, we found a suitable place with loose stones of which to build a cairn. In half an hour a tower six feet high was erected ; a bottle, with the date, was placed inside, and we retreated as rapidly as possible." [1]   This cairn was placed at the spot marked upon Dufour's Map of Switzerland 10,820 feet (3,298 mètres), and the highest point attained by Mr. Kennedy was not, I imagine, more than two or three hundred feet above it.

Shortly after this Professor Tyndall gave, in his little tract *Mountaineering in 1861*, an account of the reason why he had left Breuil, in August 1861, without doing anything.[2]   It seems that he sent his guide Bennen to reconnoitre, and that the latter made the following report to his employer :—" Herr, I have examined the mountain carefully, and find it more difficult and dangerous than I had imagined. There is no place upon it where we could well pass the night. We might do so on yonder col upon the snow, but there we should be almost frozen to death, and totally unfit for the work of the next day. On the rocks there is no ledge or cranny which could give us proper harbourage ; and starting from Breuil it is certainly impossible to reach the summit in a single day." " I was entirely taken aback," says Tyndall, " by this report. I felt like a man whose grip had given way, and who was dropping through the air. . . . Bennen was evidently dead against any attempt upon the mountain. ' We can, at all events, reach the lower of the two summits,' I remarked. ' Even that is difficult,' he replied ; ' but when you have reached it, what then ? The peak has neither name nor fame.' " [3]

---

[1] *Alpine Journal*, 1863, p. 82.   [2] See p. 56.

[3] *Mountaineering in 1861*, pp. 86–7. Tyndall and Bennen were mistaken in supposing that the mountain has two summits ; it has only one. They seem to have been deceived by the appearance of that part of the south-west ridge which

I was more surprised than discouraged by this report by Bennen. One half of his assertions I knew to be wrong. The col to which he referred was the Col du Lion, upon which we had passed a night less than a week after he had spoken so authoritatively ; and I had seen a place not far below the Chimney,—a place about 500 feet above the col—where it seemed possible to construct a sleeping-place. Bennen's opinions seem to have undergone a complete change. In 1860 he is described as having been enthusiastic to make an attempt ; in 1861 he was dead against one. Nothing dismayed by this, my friend Mr. Reginald Macdonald, our companion on Mont Pelvoux, to whom so much of our success had been due, agreed to join me in a renewed assault from the south ; and, although we failed to secure Melchior Anderegg and some other notable guides, we obtained two men of repute, namely, Johann zum Taugwald and Johann Kronig, of Zermatt. We met at that place early in July, but stormy weather prevented us for some days even from passing to the other side of the chain ; and when we crossed the Col Théodule on the 5th the weather was thoroughly unsettled—it was raining in the valleys, and snowing upon the mountains. Shortly before the summit was gained we were made extremely uncomfortable by hearing mysterious, rushing sounds, which sometimes seemed as if a sudden gust of wind was sweeping along the snow, and, at others, almost like the swishing of a long whip : yet the snow exhibited no signs of motion, and the air was perfectly calm. The dense, black storm-clouds made us expect that our bodies might be used as lightning-conductors, and we were well satisfied to get under shelter of the inn at Breuil, without having submitted to any such experience.[1]

is called " the shoulder " (l'épaule), as seen from Breuil. Viewed from that place, its southern end has certainly, through foreshortening, the semblance of a peak ; but when one regards it from the Col Théodule, or from any place in the same direction, the delusion is at once apparent.

[1] The late Principal Forbes was similarly situated while crossing the same pass in 1842. He described the sounds as rustling, fizzing, and hissing. See his

We had need of a porter, and, by the advice of our landlord, descended to the chalets of Breuil in search of one Luc Meynet. We found his house a mean abode, encumbered with cheese-making apparatus, and tenanted only by some bright-eyed children ; but as they said that uncle Luc would soon be home, we waited at the door of the little chalet and watched for him. At last a speck was seen coming round the corner of the patch of pines below Breuil, and then the children clapped their hands, dropped their toys, and ran eagerly forward to meet him. We saw an ungainly, wobbling figure stoop down and catch up the little ones, kiss them on each cheek, and put them into the empty panniers on each side of the mule, and then heard it come on carolling, as if this was not a world of woe : and yet the face of little Luc Meynet, the hunchback of Breuil, bore traces of trouble and sorrow, and there was more than a touch of sadness in his voice when he said that he must look after his brother's children.   All his difficulties were, however, at length overcome, and he agreed to join us to carry the tent.

In the past winter I had turned my attention to tents, and that which we had brought with us was the result of experiments to devise one which should be sufficiently portable to be taken over the most difficult ground, whilst combining lightness with stability.   Its base was just under six feet square, and a cross-section perpendicular to its length was an equilateral triangle, the sides of which were six feet long.   It was intended to accommodate four persons.   It was supported by four ash-poles, six feet and a half long, and one inch and a quarter thick,

Travels in the Alps of Savoy, second ed., p. 323.   Dr. R. Spence Watson experienced the same upon the upper part of the Aletsch Glacier in July 1863, and he spoke of the sounds as singing or hissing.   See the Athenæum, Sept. 12, 1863.   The respective parties seem to have been highly electrified on each occasion.   Forbes says that his fingers " yielded a fizzing sound " ; and Watson says that his " hair stood on end in an uncomfortable but very amusing manner," and that " the veil on the wide-awake of one of the party stood upright in the air ! "

tapering to the top to an inch and an eighth ; these were shod
with iron points. The order of proceeding in the construction
of the tent was as follows. Holes were drilled through the
poles about five inches from their tops, for the insertion of two
wrought-iron bolts, three inches long and one quarter of an
inch thick. The bolts were then inserted, and the two pairs of
poles were set out (and fixed up by a cord), to the proper
dimensions. The roof was then put on. This was made of
the rough, unbleached calico called forfar, which can be obtained
in six-feet widths, and it was continued round for about two
feet, on each side, on to the floor. The width of the material
was the length of the tent, and seams were thus avoided in the
roof. The forfar was sewn round each pole ; particular care
being taken to avoid wrinkles, and to get the whole perfectly
taut. The flooring was next put in and sewn down to the
forfar. This was of the ordinary plaid mackintosh, about nine
feet square ; the surplus three feet being continued up the
sides to prevent draughts. It is as well to have two feet of this
surplus on one side, and only one foot on the other ; the latter
amount being sufficient for the side occupied by the feet. One
end was then permanently closed by a triangular piece of forfar
which was sewn down to that which was already fixed. The
other end was left open, and had two triangular flaps that over-
lapped each other, and which were fastened up when we were
inside by pieces of tape. Lastly, the forfar was nailed down
to the poles to prevent the tent getting out of shape. The
cord which was used for climbing served for the tent. It was
passed over the crossed poles and underneath the ridge of the
roof, and the two ends—one fore and the other aft—were
easily secured to pieces of rock. Such a tent cost about four
guineas, and its weight is about twenty-three pounds ; or, if
the lightest kind of forfar is used, it need not exceed twenty
pounds. When it was fastened up for transport it presented
the appearance shown in the portrait of Meynet at p. 254, and
it could be unrolled and set up by two persons in three

minutes,—a point of no small importance during extreme weather.

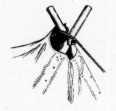

This tent is intended and is adapted for camping out at high altitudes, or in cold climates. It is not pretended that it is perfectly waterproof, but it can be made so by the addition of mackintosh to the roof; and this increases the weight by only two and a half pounds. It is then fit for general use.[1] It may be observed that the pattern of this tent is identical in all essential points with that arrived at (after

ALPINE TENT.

[1] I have described this tent at length, as applications have often been made to me for information on the subject. I would strongly recommend any person who wishes to have one for long-continued use, to have it made under his own eye, and to be particularly careful to test the poles. My experience goes to

great experience) by Sir Leopold M'Clintock for Arctic work, and frequent use by many persons, under varied conditions, has shown that the pattern is both practical and substantial.[1]

[From Whymper's diary :
A most picturesque procession, as we defiled over the little stone bridge below the inn. Myself carrying knapsack and axe, enveloped in a plaid. Carrel carried his knapsack, axe, a coil of ropes, and his bag at his side in a condition of repletion. Meynet carried a large bag of provisions of a most stuffy appearance. What a scarecrow is Meynet ! I made an accurate valuation of his clothes (by weight as old rags) and found they were worth about 1s. 5d. His hat is a real curiosity, and so is his face ; the latter has somewhat of the appearance of a chimney-sweep, who thinks he has washed himself and leaves all the dirt in the furrows. Cæsar Carrel carried the ladder and a coil of ropes. He had also a short axe.]

Sunday, the 6th of July, was showery, and snow fell on the Matterhorn, but we started on the following morning with our three men, and pursued my route of the previous year. I was requested to direct the way, as none save myself had been on the mountain before. I did not distinguish myself on this occasion, and led my companions nearly to the top of the Tête du Lion before the mistake was discovered. The party becoming rebellious, a little exploration was made towards our right, and we found that we were upon the top of the cliff overlooking the Col du Lion. The upper part of the small peak is very different in character from the lower part ; the rocks are not so

show that poles which (when supported upon their extremities) will bear a dead weight of 100 lb. suspended from their centres, will stand any wind to which they are likely to be submitted.

[1] It has been used, amongst others, by Messrs. Freshfield, Moore, and Tucker, in the Caucasus ; by the Rev. W. H. Hawker in Corsica ; by Sir J. D. Hooker and Mr. John Ball in Morocco ; by Mr. Conway in the Himalaya ; and by myself in Greenland and on the Great Andes of the Equator.

firm, and they are usually covered, or intermixed, with snow, and glazed with ice : the angle too is more severe. While descending a small snow-slope, to get on to the right track, Kronig slipped on a streak of ice, and went down at a fearful pace. Fortunately he kept on his legs, and, by a great effort, succeeded in stopping just before he arrived at some rocks that jutted through the snow, which would infallibly have knocked him over. When we rejoined him a few minutes later, we found that he was incapable of standing, much less of moving, with a face corpse-like in hue, and trembling violently. He remained in this condition for more than an hour, and the day was consequently far advanced before we arrived at our camping-place on the col. Profiting by the experience of last year, we did not pitch the tent actually on the snow, but collected a quantity of débris from the neighbouring ledges, and after constructing a rough platform of the larger pieces, levelled the whole with the dirt and mud.

Meynet had proved invaluable as a tent-bearer ; for—although his legs were more picturesque than symmetrical, and although he seemed to be built on principle with no two parts alike—his very deformities proved of service ; and we quickly found he had spirit of no common order, and that few peasants are more agreeable companions, or better climbers, than little Luc Meynet, the hunchback of Breuil. He now showed himself not less serviceable as a scavenger, and humbly asked for gristly pieces of meat, rejected by the others, or for suspicious eggs ; and seemed to consider it a peculiar favour, if not a treat, to be permitted to drink the coffee-grounds. With the greatest contentment he took the worst place at the door of the tent, and did all the dirty work which was put upon him by the guides, as gratefully as a dog—who has been well beaten—will receive a stroke.

A strong wind sprang up from the east during the night, and in the morning it was blowing almost a hurricane. The tent behaved nobly, and we remained under its shelter for several hours after the sun had risen, uncertain what it was best to do.

A lull tempted us to move, but we had scarcely ascended a hundred feet before the storm burst upon us with increased fury. Advance or return was alike impossible ; the ridge was denuded of its débris ; and we clutched our hardest when we saw stones as big as a man's fist blown away horizontally into space. We dared not attempt to stand upright, and remained stationary, on all fours, glued, as it were, to the rocks. It was intensely cold, for the blast had swept along the main chain of the Pennine Alps, and across the great snow-fields around Monte Rosa. Our warmth and courage rapidly evaporated, and at the next lull we retreated to the tent, having to halt several times even in that short distance. Taugwald and Kronig then declared that they had had enough, and refused to have anything more to do with the mountain. Meynet also informed us that he would be required down below for important cheese-making operations on the following day. It was therefore needful to return to Breuil, and we arrived there at 2.30 p.m., extremely chagrined at our complete defeat.

Jean-Antoine Carrel, attracted by rumours, had come up to the inn during our absence, and after some negotiations agreed to accompany us, with one of his friends named Pession, on the first fine day. We thought ourselves fortunate ; for Carrel clearly considered the mountain a kind of *preserve*, and regarded our late attempt as an act of *poaching*. The wind blew itself out during the night, and we started again, with these two men and a porter, at 8 a.m. on the 9th, with unexceptionable weather. Carrel pleased us by suggesting that we should camp even higher than before ; and we accordingly proceeded, without resting at the col, until we overtopped the Tête du Lion. Near the foot of the Chimney, a little below the crest of the ridge, and on its eastern side, we found a protected place ; and by building up from ledge to ledge (under the direction of our leader, who at that time was a working mason), we at length constructed a platform of sufficient size and of considerable solidity. Its height was about 12,550 feet above the sea ; and it exists, I believe, at the present time.[1] We then pushed on, as the day was very fine, and, after a short hour's scramble, got to the foot of the Great Tower upon the ridge (that is to say, to Mr. Hawkins' farthest point), and afterwards returned to our bivouac. We turned out again at 4 a.m., and at 5.15 started upwards once more, with fine weather and the thermometer at 28°. Carrel scrambled up the Chimney, and Macdonald and I after him. Pession's turn came, but when he arrived at the top he looked very ill, declared himself to be thoroughly incapable, and said that he must go back. We waited some time, but he did not get better, neither could we learn the nature of his illness. Carrel flatly refused to go on with us alone. We were helpless. Macdonald, ever the coolest of the cool, suggested that we should try what we could do without them ; but our better judgment prevailed, and, finally, we returned together to Breuil. On the next day my friend started for London.

Three times I had essayed the ascent of this mountain, and on each occasion had failed ignominiously. I had not advanced a yard beyond my predecessors. Up to the height of nearly 13,000 feet there were no extraordinary difficulties ; the way so far might even become "a matter of amusement." Only 1,800 feet remained ; but they were as yet untrodden, and might present the most formidable obstacles. No man could expect to climb them by himself. A morsel of rock only seven feet high might at any time defeat him, if it were perpendicular. Such a place might be possible to two, or a bagatelle to three men. It was evident that a party should consist of three men at least. But where could the other two men be obtained ?

---

[1] The heights given on the outlines of the Matterhorn accompanying Chap. III., and quoted throughout the book, are after the barometric (mercurial) measurements of Signor F. Giordano in 1866 and 1868. I have ventured to differ from him only in regard to the height of the second tent-platform, and have assigned to it a somewhat lower elevation than his estimate.

Carrel was the only man who exhibited any enthusiasm in the matter ; and he, in 1861, had absolutely refused to go unless the party consisted of at least *four* persons. Want of men made the difficulty, not the mountain.

The weather became bad again, so I went to Zermatt on the chance of picking up a man, and remained there during a week of storms.[1] Not one of the better men, however, could be induced to come, and I returned to Breuil on the 17th, hoping to combine the skill of Carrel with the willingness of Meynet on a new attempt, by the same route as before ; for the upper part of the north-eastern ridge, which I had inspected in the meantime, seemed to be entirely impracticable. Both men were inclined to go, but their ordinary occupations prevented them from starting at once.[2]

My tent had been left rolled up at the second platform, and whilst waiting for the men it occurred to me that it might have been blown away during the late stormy weather ; so I started off on the 18th to see if this were so or not. The way was by this time familiar, and I mounted rapidly, astonishing the friendly herdsmen—who nodded recognition as I flitted past them and the cows—for I was alone, because no man was available. But more deliberation was necessary when the pastures were passed, and climbing began, as it was needful to mark each step, in case of mist, or surprise by night. It is one of the few things which can be said in favour of mountaineering alone (a practice which has little besides to commend it), that it awakens a man's faculties, and makes him observe. When one has no arms to help, and no head to guide him except his own, he must needs take note even of small things, for he cannot afford to throw away a chance ; and so it came to pass, upon my solitary scramble, when above the snow-line, and beyond the ordinary limits of flowering plants, when peering about, noting angles and landmarks, that my eyes fell upon the tiny straggling plants

---

[1] During this time making the ascent of Monte Rosa.
[2] They were not guides by profession.

—oftentimes a single flower on a single stalk—pioneers of vegetation, atoms of life in a world of desolation, which had found their way up—who can tell how ?—from far below, and were obtaining bare sustenance from the scanty soil in protected nooks ; and it gave a new interest to the well-known rocks to see what a gallant fight the survivors made (for many must have perished in the attempt) to ascend the great mountain. The Gentian, as one might have expected, was there, but it was run close by Saxifrages, and by *Linaria alpina*, and was beaten by *Thlaspi rotundifolium*, which latter plant was the highest I was able to secure, although it too was overtopped by a little white flower that I knew not, and was unable to reach.[1]

---

[1] Those which I collected were as follow :—*Myosotis alpestris*, Gm. ; *Veronica alpina*, L. ; *Linaria alpina*, Desf. ; *Gentiana Bavarica*, L. ; *Thlaspi rotundifolium*, Gaud. ; *Silene acaulis*, L. (?) ; *Potentilla* sp. ; *Saxifraga* sp. ; *Saxifraga muscoides*, Wulf. I am indebted for these names to Mr. William Carruthers of the British Museum. The plants ranged from about 10,500 to a little below 13,000 feet, and are the highest which I have seen anywhere in the Alps. Several times this number of species might be collected, I have no doubt, within these limits. Very few lichens are seen on the higher parts of this mountain ; their rarity is due, doubtless, to the constant disintegration of the rocks, and the consequent exposure of fresh surfaces. *Silene acaulis* was the highest plant found by Saussure on his travels in the Alps. He mentions (§ 2018) that he found a tuft " near the place where I slept on my return (from the ascent of Mont Blanc), about 1,780 toises (11,388 feet) above the level of the sea."

Mr. William Mathews and Mr. Charles Packe, who have botanised respectively for many years in the Alps and Pyrenees, have favoured me with the names of the highest plants that they have obtained upon their excursions. Their lists, although not extensive, are interesting as showing the extreme limits attained by some of the hardiest of Alpine plants. Those mentioned by Mr. Mathews are—*Campanula cenisia*, L. (Grivola, 12,047 feet) ; *Saxifraga bryoides*, L. and *Androsace glacialis*, Steud. (summits of Mont Emilius, 11,677, and the Ruitor, 11,480) ; *Ranunculus glacialis*, L., *Armeria alpina*, Willd. and *Pyrethrum alpinum*, Willd. (Monte Viso, from 10,000 to 10,500 feet) ; *Thlaspi rotundifolium*, Gaud. and *Saxifraga biflora*, All. (Monte Viso, 9,500 feet) ; and *Campanula rotundifolia*, L. (?), *Artemisia spicata*, Jacq., *Aronicum Doronicum*, Rehb. and *Petrocallis Pyrenaica*, R. Br. (Col de Seylières, 9,247).

Mr. Packe obtained, on or close to the summit of the Pic de Mulhahacen,

The tent was safe, although snowed up ; and I turned to contemplate the view, which, when seen alone and undisturbed, had all the strength and charm of complete novelty. The highest peaks of the Pennine chain were in front—the Breithorn (13,685 feet), the Lyskamm (14,889), and Monte Rosa (15,217) ; then, turning to the right, the entire block of mountains which separated the Val Tournanche from the Val d'Ayas was seen at a glance, with its culminating point the Grand Tournalin (11,086). Behind were the ranges dividing the Val d'Ayas from the valley of Gressoney, backed by higher summits. More still to the right, the eye wandered down the entire length of the Val Tournanche, and then rested upon the Graian Alps with their innumerable peaks, and upon the isolated pyramid of Monte Viso (12,609) in the extreme distance. Next, still turning to the right, came the mountains intervening between the Val Tournanche and the Val St. Barthélemy. Mont Rouss (a

Sierra Nevada of Granada (11,600 to 11,700 feet), *Papaver alpinum*, L. (var. *Pyrenaicum*), *Artemisia Nevadensis* (used for giving the flavour to the Manzanilla sherry), *Viola Nevadensis*, Boiss., *Galium Pyrenaicum*, Gouan, *Trisetum glaciale*, Boiss., *Festuca Clementei*, Boiss., *Saxifraga Grænlandica*, L. (var. *Mista*), *Erigeron alpinum*, L. (var. *glaciale*), and *Arenaria tetraquetra*, L. On the Picacho de Veleta (11,440 feet), and the Alcazaba (11,350), the same plants were obtained, with the exception of the first named. At 11,150 feet on these mountains he collected *Ptilotrichum purpureum*, *Lepidium stylatum*, and *Biscutella saxatilis* ; and, at 10,000 feet, *Alyssum spicatum* and *Sideritis scordiodes*. Mr. Packe says the following plants occur at 9,000 to 10,000 feet in the Pyrenees :— *Cerastium latifolium*, *Draba Wahlenbergii*, *Hutchinsia alpina*, *Linaria alpina*, *Oxyria reniformis*, *Ranunculus glacialis*, *Saxifraga nervosa*, *S. oppositifolia*, *S. Grænlandica*, *Statice Armeria*, *Veronica alpina*.

Information on the botany of the Val Tournanche is contained in the little pamphlet by the late Canon G. Carrel, entitled *La Vallée de Valtornenche en 1867* ; and a list of the plants which have hitherto been collected on the glacier-surrounded ridge (Furggengrat) connecting the Matterhorn with the Col Théodule, will be found in Dollfus-Ausset's *Matériaux pour l'étude des Glaciers*, vol. viii., part first, 1868.

In the section of *Illustrated Europe* upon Zermatt (published at Zürich by Orell Füssli & Co.), Herr F. O. Wolf states that he found several plants in flower on the *northern* side of the Matterhorn nearly as high as " the shoulder."

round-topped snowy summit, which seems so important from Breuil, but which is in reality only a buttress of the higher mountain, the Château des Dames) had long ago sunk, and the eye passed over it, scarcely heeding its existence, to the Punta di Cian—a miniature Matterhorn—and to other, and more important heights. Then the grand mass of the Dent d'Hérens (13,715) stopped the way ; a noble mountain, encrusted on its northern slopes with enormous hanging glaciers, which broke away at midday in immense slices, and thundered down on to the Tiefenmatten Glacier ; and lastly, most splendid of all, came the Dent Blanche (14,318), soaring above the basin of the great Z'Mutt Glacier. Such a view is hardly to be matched in the Alps, and *this* view is very rarely seen, as I saw it, perfectly unclouded.[1]

[1] I have already had occasion to mention the rapid changes which occur in the weather at considerable elevations in the Alps, and shall have to do so again in subsequent chapters. No one can regret more than myself the variable weather which afflicts that otherwise delightful chain of mountains, or the necessity of speaking about it. Its summits appear to enjoy more than their fair share of wind and tempests. Meteorological disturbances, it would seem, are by no means necessary accompaniments of high regions. There are some happy places which are said to be favoured with almost perpetual calm. Take the case of the Sierra Nevada of California, for example, which includes numerous summits from 13,000 to 15,000 feet. Mr. Whitney, of San Francisco, says (in his *Guide-book to the Yosemite Valley, and the adjacent region*), " At high altitudes, all through the mountains, the weather during the summer is almost always the finest possible for travelling. There are occasional storms in the high mountains ; but, in ordinary seasons, these are quite rare, and one of the greatest drawbacks to the pleasure of travelling in the Alps, the uncertainty of the weather, is here almost entirely wanting." It is probable that a more thorough acquaintance with that region will modify this opinion ; for it must be admitted that it is very difficult to judge of the state of the atmosphere at great heights from the valleys, and it often occurs that a terrific storm is raging above when there is a dead calm below, at a distance perhaps of not more than three or four miles. A case of this kind is described in Chapter VI, and another may be mentioned here. At the very time that I was regarding the Dent Blanche from a height of 12,550 feet on the Matterhorn, Mr. T. S. Kennedy was engaged in attempting the first ascent of the

Time sped away unregarded, and the little birds which had built their nests on the neighbouring cliffs had begun to chirp their evening hymn before I thought of returning. Half mechanically I turned to the tent, unrolled it, and set it up. It contained food enough for several days, and I resolved to stay over the night. I had started from Breuil without provisions, or telling Favre—the innkeeper, who was accustomed to my erratic ways—where I was going. I returned to the view. The sun was setting, and its rosy rays, blending with the snowy blue, had thrown a pale, pure violet far as the eye could see ; the valleys were drowned in purple gloom, whilst the summits shone with unnatural brightness : and as I sat in the door of the tent, and watched the twilight change to darkness, the earth seemed to become less earthy and almost sublime ; the world seemed dead, and I, its sole inhabitant. By and by, the moon as it rose brought the hills again into sight, and by a judicious repression of detail rendered the view yet more magnificent. Something in the south hung like a great glow-worm in the air ; it was too large for a star, and too steady for a meteor ; and it was long before I could realize the scarcely credible fact that it was the moonlight glittering on the great snow-slope on the north side of Monte Viso, at a distance, as the crow flies,

former mountain. He described his ascent in a very picturesque paper in the *Alpine Journal* (1863)', and I learn from it that he experienced severe weather. " The wind roared over our ridge, making fearfully wild music among the desolate crags. . . . It rendered an ordinary voice inaudible," and " nothing at a distance greater than fifty yards could be seen at all. . . . Thick mists and driving clouds of snow swept over and past us ; " the thermometer fell to 20° F., and his companion's hair became a mass of white icicles. Now, at this time, Mr. Kennedy was distant from me only four and a half miles. With me, and in my immediate neighbourhood, the air was perfectly calm, and the temperature was agreeably warm ; even during the night it fell only two or three degrees below freezing-point. During most of the day the Dent Blanche was perfectly unclouded, though, for a time, light fleecy clouds were hovering about its upper 2,000 feet. Still no one would have supposed from appearances that my friend was experiencing a storm such as he has described.

of 98 miles.   Shivering, at last I entered the tent and made my coffee.   The night was passed comfortably, and the next morning, tempted by the brilliancy of the weather, I proceeded yet higher in search of another place for a platform.

Solitary scrambling over a pretty wide area had shown me that a single individual is subjected to many difficulties which do not trouble a party of two or three men, and that the disadvantages of being alone are more felt while descending than during the ascent.   In order to neutralize these inconveniences, I devised two little appliances, which were now brought into use for the first time. One was a claw—a kind of grapnel—about five inches long, made of shear steel, one-fifth of an inch thick.   This was of use in difficult places where there was no hold within arm's length, but where there were cracks or ledges some distance higher.   The claw could be stuck on the end of the alpenstock and dropped into such places, or, on extreme occasions, flung up until it attached itself to something.   The edges that laid hold of the rocks were serrated, which tended to make them catch more readily, and the other end had a ring to which a rope was fastened.   It must not be understood that this was employed for hauling oneself up for any great distance, but that it was used in ascending, at the most, for only a few yards at a time.   In descending, however, it could be prudently used for a greater distance at a time, as the claws could be planted firmly ; but it was necessary to keep the rope taut, and the pull constantly in the direction of the length of the implement, otherwise it had a tendency to slip away.   The second device was merely a modification of a dodge practised by all climbers.   It is often necessary for a solitary climber (or for the last man of a party during a descent) to make a loop in the end of his rope, to pass it over some rocks, and to come down holding the free end. The loop is then jerked off, and the process may be repeated. But as it sometimes happens that there are no rocks at hand which will allow a loose loop to be used, a slip-knot has to be resorted to, and the rope is drawn in tightly. Consequently, it will occur that it is not possible to jerk the loop off, and the rope has to be cut and left behind. To prevent this, I had a wrought-iron ring (two and a quarter inches in diameter and three-eighths of an inch thick) attached to one end of my rope. A loop could be made in a moment by passing the other end of the rope through this ring, which of course slipped up and held tightly as I descended holding the free end. A strong piece of cord was also attached to the ring, and, on arriving at the bottom, this was pulled ; the ring slid back again, and the loop was whipped off readily. By means of these two simple appliances I was able to ascend and descend rocks, which otherwise would have been completely impassable. The combined weight of these two things amounted to less than half-a-pound.

It has been mentioned (p. 61) that the rocks of the south-west ridge are by no means difficult for some distance above the Col du Lion.[1] This is true of them up to the level of the Chimney,

[1] CHANGES ON THE SOUTHERN SIDE OF THE MATTERHORN.—In August 1895, I ascended the south-west ridge as far as the base of the Great Tower, to photograph places in which I was interested. More than thirty years had elapsed since my last visit, and I found that great changes had taken place in the interval. The summit of the Col du Lion was lower than it was formerly, from diminution of the snow ; and the passage across it was shorter than it used to be. For the next 150 feet or so of ascent there was little alteration, but thence upwards the ridge had tumbled to pieces, and many familiar places were unrecognizable. No spot on this ridge is more firmly fixed in my

but they steepen when that is passed, and remaining smooth and with but few fractures, and still continuing to dip outwards, present some steps of a very uncertain kind, particularly when they are glazed with ice.   At this point (just above the Chimney) the climber is obliged to follow the southern (or Breuil) side of the ridge, but, in a few feet more, one must turn over to the northern (or Z'Mutt) side, where, in most years, nature kindly provides a snow-slope.   When this is surmounted, one can again return to the crest of the ridge, and follow it, by easy rocks, to the foot of the Great Tower.   This was the highest point attained by Mr. Hawkins in 1860, and it was also our highest on the 9th of July.

This Great Tower is one of the most striking features of the ridge.   It stands out like a turret at the angle of a castle.   Behind -it a battlemented wall leads upwards to the citadel.[1]   Seen from the Théodule pass it looks only an insignificant pinnacle, but as one approaches it (on the ridge) so it seems to rise, and, when one is at its base, it completely conceals the upper parts of the

recollection than the Chimney. [See Illustration facing p. 85.] Only a remnant of it was left—more than half the Chimney had disappeared ; and from that point upwards everything was altered.   Difficult places had become easy, and easy places had become difficult.   The angle in which a thick knotted rope is now dangling, which is one of the steepest bits of the ascent, did not exist in 1864.

The first Refuge on the southern side of the Matterhorn was made on the ledge called the " cravate " [p. 347].   Later on, a *cabane* was built close to the base of the Great Tower.   Its life seeming precarious, a third refuge, another *cabane*, was erected in 1893 about 160 feet lower down, and came into use in 1894.   This latter hut occupies very nearly the position of my third tent-platform.   A view of it is given in Chap. II of my *Guide to Zermatt and the Matterhorn*, after photographs taken in 1895.

I have characterized the Great Tower as " one of the most striking features on the ridge:"   In 1864 there were no signs of decay about the base of this huge pinnacle.   In 1895 it seemed to me that it would not be long before it would collapse.   Woe betide those who may be beneath the Great Tower when it falls.

[1] See the engraving " Crags of the Matterhorn," facing p. 130.

mountain. I found here a suitable place for the tent ; which, although not so well protected as the second platform, possessed the advantage of being 300 feet higher up ; and fascinated by the wildness of the cliffs, and enticed by the perfection of the weather, I went on to see what was behind.

The first step was a difficult one. The ridge became diminished to the least possible width—it was hard to keep one's balance— and just where it was narrowest, a more than perpendicular mass barred the way. Nothing fairly within arm's reach could be laid hold of ; it was necessary to spring up, and then to haul oneself over the sharp edge by sheer strength. Progression directly upwards was then impossible. Enormous and appalling precipices plunged down to the Tiefenmatten Glacier on the left, but round the right-hand side it was just possible to go. One hindrance then succeeded another, and much time was consumed in seeking a way. I have a vivid recollection of a gully of more than usual perplexity at the side of the Great Tower, with minute ledges and steep walls ; of the ledges dwindling away and at last ceasing ; and of finding myself, with arms and legs divergent, fixed as if crucified, pressing against the rock, and feeling each rise and fall of my chest as I breathed ; of screwing my head round to look for hold, and not seeing any, and of jumping sideways on to the other side. 'Tis vain to attempt to describe such places. Whether they are sketched with a light hand, or wrought out in laborious detail, one stands an equal chance of being misunderstood. Their enchantment to the climber arises from their calls on his faculties, in their demands on his strength, and on overcoming the impediments which they oppose to his skill. The non-mountaineering reader cannot feel this, and his interest in descriptions of such places is usually small, unless he supposes that the situations are perilous. They are not necessarily perilous, but I think it is impossible to avoid giving such an impression if the difficulties are particularly insisted upon.

There was a change in the quality of the rock, and there was a change in the appearance of the ridge. The rocks (talcose gneiss) below this spot were singularly firm ; it was rarely necessary to test one's hold ; the way led over the living rock, and not up rent-off fragments. But here, all was decay and ruin. The crest of the ridge was shattered and cleft, and the feet sank in the chips which had drifted down ; while above, huge blocks, hacked and carved by the hand of time, nodded to the sky, looking like the grave-stones of giants. Out of curiosity I wandered to a notch in the ridge, between two tottering piles of immense masses, which seemed to need but a few pounds on one or the other side to make them fall ; so nicely poised that they would literally have rocked in the wind, for they were put in motion by a touch ; and based on support so frail that I wondered they did not collapse before my eyes. In the whole range of my Alpine experience I have seen nothing more striking than this desolate, ruined, and shattered ridge at the back of the Great Tower. I have seen stranger shapes,— rocks which mimic the human form, with monstrous leering faces—and isolated pinnacles, sharper and greater than any here ; but I have never seen exhibited so impressively the tremendous effects which may be produced by frost, and by the long-continued action of forces whose individual effects are imperceptible.

It is needless to say that it is impossible to climb by the crest of the ridge at this part ; still one is compelled to keep near to it, for there is no other way. Generally speaking, the angles on the Matterhorn are too steep to allow the formation of considerable beds of snow, but here there is a corner which permits it to accumulate, and it is turned to gratefully, for, by its assistance, one can ascend four times as rapidly as upon the rocks.

The Tower was now almost out of sight, and I looked over the central Pennine Alps to the Grand Combin, and to the chain of Mont Blanc. My neighbour, the Dent d'Hérens, still rose above me, although but slightly, and the height which had been attained could be measured by its help. So far, I had no doubts

"THE CHIMNEY"

(ON THE SOUTH-WEST RIDGE OF THE MATTERHORN).

about my capacity to descend that which had been ascended ; but, in a short time, on looking ahead, I saw that the cliffs steepened, and I turned back (without pushing on to them, and getting into inextricable difficulties), exulting in the thought that they would be passed when we returned together, and that I had, without assistance, got nearly to the height of the Dent d'Hérens, and considerably higher than anyone had been before.[1] My exultation was a little premature.

About 5 p.m. I left the tent again, and thought myself as good as at Breuil. The friendly rope and claw had done good service, and had smoothened all the difficulties. I lowered myself through the Chimney, however, by making a fixture of the rope, which I then cut off, and left behind, as there was enough and to spare. My axe had proved a great nuisance in coming down, and I left it in the tent. It was not attached to the bâton, but was a separate affair,—an old navy boarding-axe. While cutting up the different snow-beds on the ascent, the bâton trailed behind fastened to the rope ; and, when climbing, the axe was carried behind, run through the rope tied round my waist, and was sufficiently out of the way ; but in descending, when coming down face outwards (as is always best where it is possible), the head or the handle of the weapon caught frequently against the rocks, and several times nearly upset me. So, out of laziness if you will, it was left in the tent. I paid dearly for the imprudence.

The Col du Lion was passed, and fifty yards more would have placed me on the Great Staircase, down which one can run. But on arriving at an angle of the cliffs of the Tête du Lion, while skirting the upper edge of the snow which abuts against them, I found that the heat of the two past days had nearly obliterated the steps which had been cut when coming up.

---

[1] A remarkable streak of snow (marked **C** in the outline of the Matterhorn, as seen from the Théodule) runs across the cliff at this part of the mountain. My highest point was somewhat higher than the lowest part of this snow, and was consequently nearly 13,500 feet above the sea.

The rocks happened to be impracticable just at this corner, and it was necessary to make the steps afresh. The snow was too hard to beat or tread down, and at the angle it was all but ice ; half-a-dozen steps only were required, and then the ledges could be followed again. So I held to the rock with my right hand, and prodded at the snow with the point of my stick until a good step was made, and then, leaning round the angle, did the same for the other side. So far well, but in attempting to pass the corner (to the present moment I cannot tell how it happened), I slipped and fell.

The slope was steep on which this took place, and was at the top of a gully that led down through two subordinate buttresses towards the Glacier du Lion—which was just seen, a thousand feet below. The gully narrowed and narrowed, until there was a mere thread of snow lying between two walls of rock, which came to an abrupt termination at the top of a precipice that intervened between it and the glacier. Imagine a funnel cut in half through its length, placed at an angle of 45 degrees, with its point below and its concave side uppermost, and you will have a fair idea of the place.

The knapsack brought my head down first, and I pitched into some rocks about a dozen feet below ; they caught something and tumbled me off the edge, head over heels, into the gully ; the bâton was dashed from my hands, and I whirled downwards in a series of bounds, each longer than the last ; now over ice, now into rocks ; striking my head four or five times, each time with increased force. The last bound sent me spinning through the air, in a leap of fifty or sixty feet, from one side of the gully to the other, and I struck the rocks, luckily, with the whole of my left side. They caught my clothes for a moment, and I fell back on to the snow with motion arrested. My head fortunately came the right side up, and a few frantic catches brought me to a halt, in the neck of the gully, and on the verge of the precipice. Bâton, hat, and veil skimmed by and disappeared, and the crash of the rocks—which I had started—as they fell on to the glacier,

"IN ATTEMPTING TO PASS THE CORNER I SLIPPED AND FELL."

told how narrow had been the escape from utter destruction. As it was, I fell nearly 200 feet in seven or eight bounds. Ten feet more would have taken me in one gigantic leap of 800 feet on to the glacier below.

The situation was sufficiently serious. The rocks could not be let go for a moment, and the blood was spirting out of more than twenty cuts. The most serious ones were in the head, and I vainly tried to close them with one hand, whilst holding on with the other. It was useless ; the blood jerked out in blinding jets at each pulsation. At last, in a moment of inspiration, I kicked out a big lump of snow, and stuck it as a plaster on my head. The idea was a happy one, and the flow of blood diminished. Then, scrambling up, I got, not a moment too soon, to a place of safety, and fainted away. The sun was setting when consciousness returned, and it was pitch dark before the Great Staircase was descended ; but, by a combination of luck and care, the whole 4,900 feet of descent to Breuil was accomplished without a slip, or once missing the way. I slunk past the cabin of the cowherds, who were talking and laughing inside, utterly ashamed of the state to which I had been brought by my imbecility, and entered the inn stealthily, wishing to escape to my room unnoticed. But Favre met me in the passage, demanded " Who is it ? " screamed with fright when he got a light, and aroused the household. Two dozen heads then held solemn council over mine, with more talk than action. The natives were unanimous in recommending that hot wine mixed with salt should be rubbed into the cuts. I protested, but they insisted. It was all the doctoring they received. Whether their rapid healing was to be attributed to that simple remedy, or to a good state of health, is a question. They closed up remarkably quickly, and in a few days I was able to move again.

It was sufficiently dull during this time. I was chiefly occupied in meditating on the vanity of human wishes, and in watching my clothes being washed in the tub which was turned by the stream in the front of the house ; and I vowed that if an Englishman should at any time fall sick in the Val Tournanche, he should not feel so solitary as I did at this dreary time.[1]

The news of this accident brought Jean-Antoine Carrel up to Breuil, and along with the haughty chasseur came one of his

AT BREUIL (GIOMEIN).

[1] As it seldom happens that one survives such a fall, it may be interesting to record what my sensations were during its occurrence. I was perfectly conscious of what was happening, and felt each blow ; but, like a patient under chloroform, experienced no pain. Each blow was, naturally, more severe than that which preceded it, and I distinctly remember thinking, " Well, if the next is harder still, that will be the end ! " Like persons who have been rescued from drowning, I remember that the recollection of a multitude of things rushed through my head, many of them trivialities or absurdities, which had been forgotten long before ; and, more remarkable, this bounding through space did not feel disagreeable. But I think that in no very great distance more, consciousness as well as sensation would have been lost, and upon that I base my belief, improbable as it seems, that death by a fall from a great height is as painless an end as can be experienced.

The battering was very rough, yet no bones were broken. The most severe cuts were one of four inches long on the top of the head, and another of three inches on the right temple : this latter bled frightfully. There was a formidable-looking cut, of about the same size as the last, on the palm of the left hand, and every limb was grazed, or cut, more or less seriously. The tips of the ears were taken off, and a sharp rock cut a circular bit out of the side of the left boot, sock, and ankle, at one stroke. The loss of blood, although so great, did not seem to be permanently injurious. The only relatives, a strong and able young fellow named Cæsar. With these two men and Meynet I made another start on the 23rd of July. We got to the tent without any trouble, and on the following day had ascended beyond the Tower, and were picking our way cautiously over the loose rocks behind (where my traces of the week before were well apparent) in lovely weather, when one of those abominable and almost instantaneous changes occurred, to which the Matterhorn is so liable on its southern side. Mists were created out of invisible vapours, and in a few minutes snow fell heavily. We stopped, as this part was exceedingly difficult, and, unwilling to retreat, remained on the spot several hours, in hopes that another change would occur ; but, as it did not, we at length went down to the base of the Great Tower, and commenced to make a third platform, at the height of 12,992 feet above the sea. It still continued to snow, and we took refuge in the tent. Carrel argued that the weather had broken up, and that the mountain would become so glazed with ice as to render any attempt futile ; and I, that the change was only temporary, and that the rocks were too hot to allow ice to form upon them. I wished to stay until the weather improved, but my leader would not endure contradiction, grew more positive, and insisted that we must go down. We went down, and when we got below the col his opinion was found to be wrong ; the cloud was confined to the upper 3,000 feet, and outside it there was brilliant weather.

Carrel was not an easy man to manage. He was perfectly aware that he was the cock of the Val Tournanche, and he commanded the other men as by right. He was equally conscious that he was indispensable to me, and took no pains to conceal his knowledge of the fact. If he had been commanded, or if he had been entreated to stop, it would have been all the same.

serious effect has been the reduction of a naturally retentive memory to a very commonplace one ; and although my recollections of more distant occurrences remain unshaken, the events of that particular day would be clean gone but for the few notes which were written down before the accident.

But, let me repeat, he was the only first-rate climber I could find who believed that the mountain was not inaccessible. With him I had hopes, but without him none ; so he was allowed to do as he would. His will on this occasion was almost incomprehensible. He certainly could not be charged with cowardice, for a bolder man could hardly be found ; nor was he turning away on account of difficulty, for nothing to which we had yet come seemed to be difficult to *him* ; and his strong personal desire to make the ascent was evident. There was no occasion to come down on account of food, for we had taken, to guard against this very casualty, enough to last for a week ; and there was no danger, and little or no discomfort, in stopping in the tent. It seemed to me that he was spinning out the ascent for his own purposes, and that although he wished very much to be the first man on the top, and did not object to be accompanied by anyone else who had the same wish, he had no intention of letting one succeed too soon,—perhaps to give a greater appearance of *éclat* when the thing was accomplished. As he feared no rival, he may have supposed that the more difficulties he made the more valuable he would be estimated ; though, to do him justice, he never showed any great hunger for money. His demands were fair, not excessive ; but he always stipulated for so much per day, and so, under any circumstances, he did not do badly.

Vexed at having my time thus frittered away, I was still well pleased when he volunteered to start again on the morrow, if it was fine. We were to advance the tent to the foot of the Tower, to fix ropes in the most difficult parts beyond, and to make a push for the summit on the following day.

The next morning (Friday the 25th) when I arose, good little Meynet was ready and waiting, and he said that the two Carrels had gone off some time before, and had left word that they intended marmot-hunting, as the day was favourable for that sport.[1]

[1] An incident like this goes far to make one look favourably upon the *réglements* of Chamonix and other places. This could not have occurred at Chamonix, nor here, if there had been a *bureau des guides*.

My holiday had nearly expired, and these men clearly could not be relied upon ; so, as a last resort, I proposed to the hunchback to accompany me alone, to see if we could not get higher than before, though of reaching the summit there was little or no hope. He did not hesitate, and in a few hours we stood—for the third time together—upon the Col du Lion. It was the first time Meynet had seen the view unclouded. The poor little deformed peasant gazed upon it silently and reverently for a time, and then, unconsciously, fell on one knee in an attitude of adoration, and clasped his hands, exclaiming in ecstasy, " Oh, beautiful mountains ! " His actions were as appropriate as his words were natural, and tears bore witness to the reality of his emotion.

Our power was too limited to advance the tent, so we slept at the old station, and starting very early the next morning, passed the place where we had turned back on the 24th, and, subsequently, my highest point on the 19th. We found the crest of the ridge so treacherous that we took to the cliffs on the right, although most unwillingly. Little by little we fought our way up, but at length we were both spread-eagled on the all but perpendicular face, unable to advance, and barely able to descend. We returned to the ridge. It was almost equally difficult, and infinitely more unstable ; and at length, after having pushed our attempts as far as was prudent, I determined to return to Breuil, and to have a light ladder made to assist us to overcome some of the steepest parts.[1] I expected, too, that by this time Carrel would have had enough marmot-hunting, and would deign to accompany us again.

[1] This appeared to be the most difficult part of the mountain. One was driven to keep to the edge of the ridge, or very near to it ; and at the point where we turned back (which was almost as high as the *highest* part of the " cravate," and perhaps 100 feet higher than my scramble on the 19th) there were smooth walls seven or eight feet high in every direction, which were impassable to a single man, and which could only be surmounted by the assistance of ladders, or by using one's comrades as ladders.

We came down at a great pace, for we were now so familiar with the mountain, and with each other's wants, that we knew immediately when to give a helping hand, and when to let alone. The rocks also were in a better state than I had ever seen them, being almost entirely free from glaze of ice. Meynet was always merriest on the difficult parts, and, upon the most difficult, kept on enunciating the sentiment, " We can only die once," a thought which seemed to afford him infinite satisfaction. We arrived at the inn early in the evening, and I found my projects summarily and unexpectedly knocked on the head.

Professor Tyndall had arrived while we were absent, and had engaged both Cæsar and Jean-Antoine Carrel. Bennen was also with him, together with a powerful and active friend, a Valaisan guide, named Anton Walter. They had a ladder already pre-pared, provisions were being collected, and they intended to start on the following morning (Sunday). This new arrival took me by surprise. Bennen, it will be remembered, refused point-blank to take Professor Tyndall on the Matterhorn in 1861. " He was dead against any attempt on the mountain," says Tyndall. He was now eager to set out. Professor Tyndall has not explained in what way this revolution came about in his guide. I was equally astonished at the faithlessness of Carrel, and attributed it to pique at our having presumed to do without him. It was useless to compete with the Professor and his four men, who were ready to start in a few hours, so I waited to see what would come of their attempt.

Everything seemed to favour it, and they set out on a fine morning in high spirits, leaving me tormented with envy and all uncharitableness. If they succeeded, they carried off the prize for which I had been so long struggling ; and if they failed, there was no time to make another attempt, for I was due in a few days more in London. When this came home clearly to me, I resolved to leave Breuil at once, but, when packing up, found that some necessaries had been left behind in the tent. So I went off about midday to recover them ;

A CANNONADE ON THE MATTERHORN (1862).

caught the army of the Professor before it reached the col, as they were going very slowly ; left them there (stopping to take food), and went on to the tent. I was near to it when all at once I heard a noise aloft, and, on looking up, perceived a stone of at least a foot cube flying straight at my head. I ducked, and scrambled under the lee side of a friendly rock, while the missile went by with a loud buzz. It was the advance guard of a perfect storm of stones, which descended with infernal clatter down the very edge of the ridge, leaving a trail of dust behind, with a strong smell of sulphur, that told who had sent them. The men below were on the look-out, but the stones did not come near them, and breaking away on one side descended to the glacier.[1]

I waited at the tent to welcome the Professor, and when he arrived went down to Breuil. Early next morning someone ran to me saying that a flag was seen on the summit of the Matterhorn. It was not so, however, although I saw that they had passed the place where we had turned back on the 26th. I had now no doubt of their final success, for they had got beyond the point which Carrel, not less than myself, had always considered to be the most questionable place on the whole mountain. Up to it there was no choice of route. I suppose that at no one point between it and the col was it possible to diverge a dozen paces to the right or left ; but beyond it it was otherwise, and we had always agreed, in our debates, that if it could be passed success was certain. The accompanying

[1] Professor Tyndall describes this incident in the following words :—" We had gathered up our traps, and bent to the work before us, when suddenly an explosion occurred overhead. We looked aloft and saw in mid-air a solid shot from the Matterhorn describing its proper parabola, and finally splitting into fragments as it smote one of the rocky towers in front. Down the shattered fragments came like a kind of spray, slightly wide of us, but still near enough to compel a sharp look-out. Two or three such explosions occurred, but we chose the back fin of the mountain for our track, and from this the falling stones were speedily deflected right or left."—*Saturday Review*, Aug. 8, 1863. Reprinted in *Macmillan's Magazine*, April 1869.

outline from a sketch taken from the door of the inn at Breuil will help to explain. The letter **A** indicates the position of the Great Tower ; **C** the " cravate " (the strongly-marked streak of snow referred to on p. 91 which we just failed to arrive at on the 26th) ; **B** the place where we now saw something that looked like a flag. Behind the point **B** a nearly level ridge

leads up to the foot of the final peak. This will be understood by a reference to the outline facing p. 53, where the same letters indicate the same places. It was just now said, we considered that if the point **C** could be passed, success was certain. Tyndall was at **B** very early in the morning, and I did not doubt that he would reach the summit, although it yet remained problematical whether he would be able to stand on the very highest point. The summit was evidently formed of a long ridge, on which there were two points nearly equally elevated—so equally that one could not say which was the highest—and between the two there seemed to be a deep notch, marked **D** on the outlines, which might defeat one at the very last moment.

My knapsack was packed, and I had drunk a parting glass of wine with Favre, who was jubilant at the success which was to make the fortune of his inn ; but I could not bring myself to leave until the result was heard, and lingered about, as a foolish lover hovers round the object of his affections, even after he has been contemptuously rejected. The sun had set before the men were descried coming over the pastures. There was no spring in their steps—they, too, were defeated. The Carrels hid their heads, and the others said, as men will do when they have been beaten, that the mountain was horrible, impossible, and so forth. Professor Tyndall told me they had arrived *within a stone's throw of the summit,* and admonished me to have nothing more to do with the mountain. I understood him to say that he should not try again, and ran down to the village of Val-tournanche, almost inclined to believe that the mountain was inaccessible ; leaving the tent, ropes, and other matters in the hands of Favre, to be placed at the disposal of any person who wished to ascend it, more, I am afraid, out of irony than for generosity. There may have been those who believed that the Matterhorn could be ascended, but, anyhow, their faith did not bring forth works. No one tried again in 1862.

Business took me into Dauphiné before returning to London, and a week after Tyndall's defeat I lay one night, after a sultry day, half-asleep, tossing about in one of the abominations which served for beds in the inn kept by the Deputy-Mayor of La Ville de Vallouise ; looking at a strange ruddiness on the ceiling, which I thought might be some effect of electricity produced by the irritation of the myriads of fleas ; when the great bell of the church, close at hand, pealed out with loud and hurried clangour. I jumped up, for the voices and movements of the people in the house made me think of fire. It was fire ; and from my window I saw, on the other side of the river, great forked flames shooting high into the sky, black dots with long shadows hurrying towards the place, and the crests of the ridges catching the light and standing out like spectres. All the world was in motion, for the neighbouring villages—now aroused—rang out the alarm. I pulled on my shirt, and tore over the bridge. Three large chalets on fire were surrounded by a mass of people, who were bringing all their pots and pans, and anything that would hold water. They formed themselves into several chains, each two deep, leading towards the nearest stream, and passed the water up one side, and the empty utensils down the other. My old friend the mayor was there, in full force striking the ground with his stick, and vociferating, " Work ! work ! " but the men, with much presence of mind, chiefly ranged themselves on the sides of the empty buckets, and left the real work to their better halves. Their efforts were useless, and the chalets burnt themselves out.

The next morning I visited the still-smouldering ruins, and saw the homeless families sitting in a dismal row in front of their charred property. The people said that one of the houses had been well insured, and that its owner had endeavoured to forestall luck. He had arranged the place for a bonfire, set the lower rooms on fire in several places, and had then gone out of the way, leaving his wife and children in the upper rooms, to be roasted or not as the case might be. His plans only partially succeeded, and it was satisfactory to see the scoundrel brought back in the custody of two stalwart gendarmes. Three days afterwards I was in London.

BUT WHAT IS THIS ?

CHAPTER V

THE VAL TOURNANCHE—DIRECT PASS FROM BREUIL TO ZERMATT (BREUILJOCH)—ZERMATT —FIRST ASCENT OF THE GRAND TOURNALIN

" How like a winter hath my absence been
From thee, the pleasure of a fleeting year ! "
W. SHAKESPEARE.

I CROSSED the Channel on the 29th of July 1863, embarrassed by the possession of two ladders, each twelve feet long, which joined together like those used by firemen, and shut up like parallel rulers. My luggage was highly suggestive of house-breaking, for, besides these, there were several coils of rope, and numerous tools of suspicious appearance, and it was re-luctantly admitted into France, but it passed through the custom-house with less trouble than I anticipated, after a timely expendi-ture of a few francs.

I am not in love with the douane. It is the purgatory of travellers, where uncongenial spirits mingle together for a time, before they are separated into rich and poor. The douaniers look upon tourists as their natural enemies ; see how eagerly they pounce upon the portmanteaux ! One of them has dis-

97

covered something ! He has never seen its like before, and he holds it aloft in the face of its owner, with inquisitorial insolence. " But *what is* this ? " The explanation is only half-satisfactory. " But what is *this* ? " says he, laying hold of a little box. " Powder." " But that it is forbidden to carry of powder on the railway." " Bah ! " says another and older hand, " pass the effects of Monsieur " ; and our countryman—whose cheeks had begun to redden under the stares of his fellow-travellers— is allowed to depart with his half-worn tooth-brush, while the discomfited douanier gives a mighty shrug at the strange habits of those " whose insular position excludes them from the march of continental ideas."

My real troubles commenced at Susa. The officials there, more honest and more obtuse than the Frenchmen, declined at one and the same time to be bribed, or to pass my baggage until a satisfactory account of it was rendered ; and, as they refused to believe the true explanation, I was puzzled what to say, but was presently relieved from the dilemma by one of the men, who was cleverer than his fellows, suggesting that I was going to Turin to exhibit in the streets ; that I mounted the ladder and balanced myself on the end of it, then lighted my pipe and put the point of the bâton in its bowl, and caused the bâton to gyrate around my head. The rope was to keep back the spectators, and an Englishman in my company was the agent. " Monsieur is acrobat then ? " " Yes, certainly." " Pass the effects of Monsieur the acrobat ! "

These ladders were the source of endless trouble. Let us pass over the doubts of the guardians of the Hôtel d'Europe (Trombetta), whether a person in the possession of such ques- tionable articles should be admitted to their very respectable house, and get to Châtillon, at the entrance of the Val Tour- nanche. A mule was chartered to carry them, and, as they were too long to sling across its back, they were arranged lengthways, and one end projected over the animal's head, while the other extended beyond its tail. A mule when going up or down hill

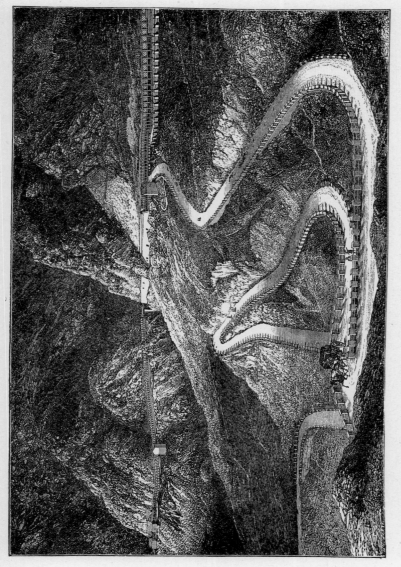

THE MONT CENIS ROAD AND THE FELL RAILWAY, NEAR THE SUMMIT OF THE PASS, ON THE ITALIAN SIDE.

always moves with a jerky action, and in consequence of this the ladders hit my mule severe blows between its ears and on its flanks. The beast, not knowing what strange creature it had on its back, naturally tossed its head and threw out its legs, and this, of course, only made the blows that it received more severe. At last it ran away, and would have perished by rolling down a precipice, if the men had not caught hold of its tail. The end of the matter was that a man had to follow the mule, holding

CROSSING MONT CENIS (1861).

the end of the ladders, which obliged him to move his arms up and down incessantly, and to bow to the hind-quarters of the animal in a way that afforded more amusement to his comrades than it did to him.

I was once more *en route* for the Matterhorn, for I had heard in the spring of 1863 the cause of the failure of Professor Tyndall, and learnt that the case was not so hopeless as it appeared to be at one time. I found that he arrived as far only as the northern end of " the shoulder." The point at which he says,[1] they

[1] *Saturday Review*, August 8, 1863.

" sat down with broken hopes, the summit within a stone's-throw of us, but still defying us," was not the notch or cleft at **D** (which is literally within a stone's-throw of the summit), but another and more formidable cleft that intervenes between the northern end of " the shoulder " and the commencement of the final peak. It is marked **E** on the outline which faces p. 53. Carrel and all the men who had been with me knew of the existence of this cleft, and of the pinnacle which rose between it and the final peak ; and we had frequently talked about the best manner of passing the place. On this we disagreed, but we were both of opinion that when we got to " the shoulder," it would be necessary to bear down gradually to the right or to the left, to avoid coming to the top of the notch. Tyndall's party, after arriving at " the shoulder," was led by his guides along the crest of the ridge, and, consequently, when they got to its northern end, they came to the top of the notch, instead of the bottom—to the dismay of all but the Carrels. Dr. Tyndall's words are, " The ridge was here split by a deep cleft which separated it from the final precipice, and the case became more hopeless as we came more near." The Professor adds, " The mountain is 14,800 feet high, and 14,600 feet had been accomplished." He greatly deceived himself ; by the barometric measurements of Signor Giordano the notch is no less than 800 feet below the summit. The guide Walter (Dr. Tyndall says) said it was impossible to proceed, and the Carrels, appealed to for their opinion (this is their own account), gave as an answer, " We are porters, ask your guides." Bennen, thus left to himself, " was finally forced to accept defeat." Tyndall had nevertheless accomplished an advance of about 400 feet over one of the most difficult parts of the mountain.

There are material discrepancies between the published narratives of Professor Tyndall [1] and the verbal accounts of the Carrels. The former says the men had to be " urged on," that " they pronounced flatly against the final precipice," " they

[1] *Saturday Review*, 1863, and *Macmillan's Magazine*, 1869.

yielded so utterly," and that Bennen said, in answer to a final appeal made to him, " ' What could I do, sir ? not one of them would accompany me.' It was the accurate truth." Jean-Antoine Carrel says that. when Professor Tyndall gave the order to turn *he* would have advanced to examine the route, as he did not think that further progress was impossible, but he was stopped by the Professor, and was naturally obliged to follow the others.[1] These disagreements may well be left to be settled by those who are concerned. Tyndall, Walter, and Bennen now disappear from this history.[2]

The Val Tournanche is one of the most charming valleys in the Italian Alps ; it is a paradise to an artist, and if the space at my command were greater, I would willingly linger over its groves of chestnuts, its bright trickling rills and its roaring torrents, its upland unsuspected valleys and its noble cliffs. The path rises steeply from Châtillon, but it is well shaded, and the heat of the summer sun is tempered by cool air and spray which

---

[1] I have entered into this matter because much surprise has been expressed that Carrel was able to pass the place without any great difficulty in 1865, which turned back so strong a party in 1862. The cause of Professor Tyndall's defeat was simply that his second guide (Walter) did not give aid to Bennen when it was required, and that the Carrels *would not act as guides after having been hired as porters.* J.-A. Carrel not only knew of the existence of this place before they came to it, but always believed in the possibility of passing it, and of ascending the mountain ; and had he been leader to the party I do not doubt that he might have taken Tyndall to the top. But when appealed to to assist Bennen (a Swiss, and the recognized leader of the party), was it likely that he (an Italian, a porter), who intended to be the first man up the mountain by a route which he regarded peculiarly his own, would render any aid ?

It is not so easy to understand how Dr. Tyndall and Bennen overlooked the existence of this cleft, for it is seen over several points of the compass, and particularly well from the southern side of the Théodule pass. Still more difficult is it to explain how the Professor came to consider that he was only " a stone's-throw " from the summit ; for, when he got to the end of " the shoulder," he must have been perfectly aware that the *whole height of the final peak was still above him.*

[2] Dr. Tyndall ascended the Matterhorn in 1868.

comes off the ice-cold streams. One sees from the path, at several places on the right bank of the valley, groups of arches which have been built high up against the faces of the cliffs. Guide-books repeat—on whose authority I know not—that they are the remains of a Roman aqueduct. They have the Roman boldness of conception, but the work has not the usual Roman solidity. The arches have always seemed to me to be the remains of an *unfinished* work, and I learn from Jean-Antoine Carrel that there are other groups of arches, which are not seen from the path, all having the same appearance. It may be questioned whether those seen near the village of Antey are Roman. Some of them are semicircular, whilst others are distinctly pointed. Here is one of the latter, which might pass for fourteenth-century work, or later ;—a two-centred arch, with mean voussoirs, and the masonry in rough courses. These arches are well worth the attention of an archæologist, but some

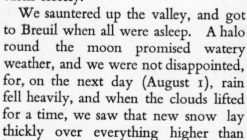

difficulty will be found in approaching them closely.

We sauntered up the valley, and got to Breuil when all were asleep. A halo round the moon promised watery weather, and we were not disappointed, for, on the next day (August 1), rain fell heavily, and when the clouds lifted for a time, we saw that new snow lay thickly over everything higher than 9,000 feet. J.-A. Carrel was ready and waiting (as I had determined to give the bold cragsman another chance) ; and he did not need to say that the Matterhorn would be impracticable for several days after all this new snow, even if the weather were to arrange itself at once. Our first day together was accordingly spent upon a neighbouring summit, the Cimes Blanches ; a degraded mountain, well known for its fine panoramic view. It was little that we saw ; for, in every direction except to the south, writhing masses of heavy clouds obscured everything ; and to the south our view was intercepted by a peak higher than the Cimes Blanches, named the Grand Tournalin. But we got some innocent pleasure out of watching the gambolings of a number of goats, who became fast friends after we had given them some salt ; in fact, too fast, and caused us no little annoyance when we were descending. " Carrel," I said, as a number of stones whizzed by which they had dislodged, " this must be put a stop to." " Diable ! " he grunted, " it is very well to talk, but how will you do it ? " I said that I would try ; and sitting down, poured a little brandy into the hollow of my hand, and allured the nearest goat with deceitful gestures. It was one who had gobbled up the paper in which the salt had been carried— an animal of enterprising character—and it advanced fearlessly and licked up the brandy. I shall not easily forget its surprise. It stopped short, and coughed, and looked at me as much as to say, " Oh, you cheat ! " and spat and ran away ; stopping now and then to cough and spit again. We were not troubled any more by those goats.

More snow fell during the night, and our attempt on the Matterhorn was postponed indefinitely. As there was nothing to be done at Breuil, I determined to make the tour of the mountain, and commenced by inventing a pass from Breuil to Zermatt,[1] in place of the hackneyed Théodule. Anyone who looks at the map will see that the latter pass makes a considerable détour to the east, and, apparently, goes out of the way. I thought that it was possible to strike out a shorter route, both in distance and in time, and we set out on the 3rd of August, to carry out the idea. We followed the Théodule path for some time, but quitted it when it bore away to the east, and kept straight on until we struck the moraine of the Mont Cervin Glacier. Our track still continued in a straight line up the centre of the glacier to the foot of a tooth of rock, which juts prominently out of the ridge (Furggengrat) connecting the Matterhorn with the Theodulhorn. The head of the glacier

[1] See the Map of the Matterhorn and its Glaciers.

was connected with this little peak by a steep bank of snow ; but we were able to go straight up, and struck the col at its lowest point, a little to the right (that is to say, to the east) of the above-mentioned peak. On the north there was a snow-slope corresponding to that on the other side. Half an hour took us to its base. We then bore away over the nearly level plateau of the Furggen Glacier, making a straight track to the Hörnli, whence we descended to Zermatt by one of the well-known paths. This pass has been dubbed the Breuiljoch by the Swiss surveyors. It is a few feet higher than the Théodule, and it may be recommended to those who are familiar with that pass, as it gives equally fine views, and is accessible at all times. But it will never be frequented like the Théodule, as the snow-slope at its summit, at certain times, will require the use of the axe. It took us six hours and a quarter to go from one place to the other.

It is stated in one of the MS. note-books of the late Principal J. D. Forbes, that this depression, now called the Breuiljoch, was formerly *the* pass between the Val Tournanche and Zermatt, and that it was abandoned for the Théodule in consequence of changes in the glaciers. The authority for the statement was not given. I presume it was from local tradition, but I readily credit it ; for, before the time that the glaciers had shrunk to so great an extent, the steep snow-slopes above mentioned, in all probability, did not exist ; and, very likely, the glaciers led by gentle gradients up to the summit ; in which case this route would have formed the natural highway between the two places.[1] It is far from impossible, if the glaciers continue to diminish, that the Théodule

---

[1] A few days before we crossed the Breuiljoch in 1863, Mr. F. Morshead made a parallel pass to it (which is now called the Furggenjoch). He crossed the ridge on the *western* side of the little peak, and followed a somewhat more difficult route than ours. In 1865 I wanted to use Mr. Morshead's pass (see Chap. XIV) but found that it was not possible to descend the Zermatt side, for, during the two years which had elapsed, the glacier had shrunk so much that it was completely severed from the summit of the pass, and we could not get down the rocks that were exposed.

itself, the easiest and the most frequented of all the higher Alpine passes, may become somewhat difficult ; and, if this should be the case, the prosperity of Zermatt may possibly suffer.[1]

Carrel and I wandered out again in the afternoon, and went, first of all, to a favourite spot with tourists near the end of the Gorner Glacier (or, properly speaking, the Boden Glacier), to a little verdant flat—studded with *Euphrasia officinalis*—the delight of swarms of bees, who gather there the honey which afterwards appears at the *table d'hôte*.

On our right the glacier-torrent thundered down the valley

[1] The summit of the Théodule pass is 10,899 feet above the sea. It is estimated that of late about a thousand tourists have crossed it per annum. In the winter, when the crevasses are bridged over and partially filled up, and the weather is favourable, cows and sheep can still pass over it from Zermatt to Valtournanche, and *vice versa*.

In the *middle of August* 1792, Saussure appears to have taken mules from Breuil, over the Valtournanche Glacier to the summit of the Théodule ; and on a previous journey he did the same, also in the middle of August. He distinctly mentions (§ 2220) that the glacier was completely covered with snow, and that *no* crevasses were open. Of late years, the glacier has usually been very bare of snow in the month of August, and has had many open crevasses.

Since 1855, or thereabouts, Zermatt has become one of the most popular Alpine resorts, and it is still growing in favour. Fifty years ago, the Théodule pass, the Weisstor, and the Col d'Hérens were, I believe, the only routes taken from this place across the Pennine Alps. At the present time there are more than two dozen ways by which a tourist may arrive or depart. The summits of some of the cols are more than 14,000 feet above the sea.

Down to the middle of the century, the only inn at Zermatt was kept by the village doctor (Lauber). In 1852 M. Clemenz opened the Mont Cervin hotel, and in 1855 M. Alexandre Seiler acquired and extended the original village inn (Monte Rosa hotel). In 1867 he took over the Mont Cervin hotel, and afterwards gradually made himself monarch of the place by his enterprise and geniality. The three principal hotels of Zermatt, as well as the hotel on the Riffelberg (now termed the Riffelhaus), the larger establishment called the Riffelalp hotel, and the hotel at the Lac Noir (Schwarzsee), are all under the control of his family.

The opening of the railway from Visp to Zermatt has again caused a large accession of visitors, and in the height of the season the place is overcrowded.

through a gorge with precipitous sides, not easily approached ; [1] for the turf at the top was slippery, and the rocks had everywhere been rounded by the glacier,—which formerly extended lower down. This gorge seems to have been made chiefly by the torrent, and to have been excavated subsequently to the

WATER-WORN ROCKS IN THE GORGE BELOW THE GORNER GLACIER.

retreat of the glacier. It seems so because not merely upon its walls are there the marks of running water, but even upon the rounded rocks at the top of its walls, at a height of 70 or 80 feet above the present level of the torrent, there are some of those queer concavities which rapid streams alone are known to produce on rocks.

A little bridge, apparently frail, spans the torrent just above

[1] It is now a regular show-place.

the entrance to this gorge, and from it one perceives, being fashioned in the rocks below, concavities similar to those to which reference has just been made. The torrent is seen hurrying forwards. Not everywhere. In some places the water strikes projecting angles, and, thrown back by them, remains almost stationary, eddying round and round : in others, obstructions fling it up in fountains, which play perpetually on the *under* surfaces of overhanging masses ; and sometimes do so in such a way that the water not only works upon the under surfaces, but round the corner ; that is to say, upon the surfaces which are *not* opposed to the general direction of the current. In all cases *concavities* are being produced. Projecting angles are rounded, it is true, and are more or less convex, but they are overlooked on account of the prevalence of concave forms.

Cause and effect help each other here. The inequalities of the torrent's bed and walls cause its eddyings, and the eddies fashion the concavities. The more profound the latter become, the more disturbance is caused in the water. The destruction of the rocks proceeds at an ever-increasing rate ; for the larger the amount of surface that is exposed, the greater are the opportunities for the assaults of heat and cold.

When water is in the form of glacier it has not the power of making concavities, such as these, in rocks, and of working upon surfaces which are not opposed to the direction of the current. Its nature is changed ; it operates in a different way, and it leaves marks which are readily distinguished from those produced by torrent-action.

The prevailing forms which result from glacier-action are more or less *convex*. Ultimately, all angles and almost all curves are obliterated, and large areas of flat surfaces are produced. This perfection of abrasion is rarely found, except in such localities as have sustained a grinding much more severe than that which has occurred in the Alps ; and, generally speaking, the dictum of the veteran geologist Studer, quoted below, is undoubtedly true.[1] Not merely can the operations of extinct glaciers be traced in detail by means of the bosses of rock popularly termed *roches moutonnées*, but their effects in the aggregate,

STRIATIONS PRODUCED BY GLACIER-ACTION (AT GRINDELWALD).

on a range of mountains or large district, can be recognized sometimes at a distance of fifteen or twenty miles from the incessant repetition of these convex forms.

[1] " Un des faits les mieux constatés est que l'érosion des glaciers se distingue de celle des eaux en ce que la première produit des roches convexes ou moutonnées, tandis que la seconde donne lieu à des concavités."—Prof. B. Studer, *Origine des Lacs Suisses.*

We finished up the 3rd of August with a walk over the Findelen Glacier, and returned to Zermatt at a later hour than we intended, both very sleepy. This is noteworthy only on account of that which followed. We intended to cross the Col de Valpelline on the next day, and an early start was desirable. Monsieur Seiler, excellent man, knowing this, called us himself, and when he came to my door, I answered, ". All right, Seiler, I will get up," and immediately turned over to the other side, saying to myself, " First of all, ten minutes more sleep." But Seiler waited and listened, and, suspecting the case, knocked again. " Herr Whymper, have you got a light ? " Without thinking what the consequences might be, I answered, " No," and then the worthy man actually forced the lock off his own door to give me one. By similar and equally friendly and disinterested acts, Monsieur Seiler acquired his enviable reputation.

At 4 a.m. we left his Monte Rosa hotel, and were soon pushing our way through the thickets of grey alder that skirt the path up the picturesque little valley which leads to the Z'Mutt Glacier.[1]

Nothing can seem or be more inaccessible than the Matterhorn upon this side, and even in cold blood one holds the breath when looking at its stupendous cliffs. There are few equal to them in size in the Alps, and there are none which can more truly be termed *precipices*. Greatest of them all is the immense north cliff, —that which bends over towards the Z'Mutt Glacier. Stones which drop from the top of that amazing wall fall for about 1,500 feet before they touch anything ; and those which roll down from above, and bound over it, fall to a much greater depth, and leap wellnigh 1,000 feet beyond its base. This side of the mountain has always seemed sombre—sad—terrible. It is painfully suggestive of decay, ruin, and death ; and it is now, alas ! more than terrible by its associations.

[1] The path on the right bank (southern side) of the valley is much more picturesque than that on the other side. For our route, see the maps of the valley of Zermatt and the valley of Valpelline.

"There is no aspect of destruction about the Matterhorn cliffs," says Professor Ruskin. Granted,—when they are seen from afar. But approach, and sit down by the side of the Z'Mutt Glacier, and you will hear that their piecemeal destruction is proceeding ceaselessly—incessantly. You will *hear*, but, probably, you will not *see* ; for even when the descending masses thunder as loudly as heavy guns, and the echoes roll back from the Ebihorn opposite, they will still be as pin-points against the grand old face, so vast is its scale !

If you would see the " aspects of destruction," you must come still closer, and climb its cliffs and ridges, or mount to the plateau of the Matterhorn Glacier, which is cut up and ploughed up by these missiles, and strewn on the surface with their smaller fragments. The larger masses, falling with tremendous velocity, plunge into the snow and are lost to sight.

The Matterhorn Glacier, too, sends down *its* avalanches, as if in rivalry with the rocks behind. Round the whole of its northern side it does not terminate in the usual manner by gentle slopes, but comes to a sudden end at the top of the steep rocks which lie betwixt it and the Z'Mutt Glacier ; and seldom does an hour pass without a huge slice breaking away, and falling with wild uproar on to the slopes below, where it is re-compacted.

The desolate pines on the outskirts of the Z'Mutt forests, stripped of their bark, and blanched by the weather, are a fit foreground to a scene that can hardly be surpassed in solemn grandeur. It is a subject worthy of the pencil of a great painter, and one which would tax the powers of the very greatest.

Higher up the glacier the mountain is less savage in appearance, though scarcely less impracticable ; and, three hours later, when we arrived at the island of rock called the Stockje (which marks the end of the Z'Mutt Glacier proper, and separates its higher feeder, the Stock Glacier, from its lower and greater one, the Tiefenmatten), Carrel himself, one of the least demonstrative of men, could not refrain from expressing wonder at the steepness of its faces, and at the audacity that had prompted us to camp upon the south-west ridge ; the profile of which is seen very well from the Stockje.[1] Carrel then saw the north and north-west sides of the mountain for the first time, and was more firmly persuaded than ever that an ascent was possible *only* from the direction of Breuil.

Three years afterwards I was traversing the same spot with the guide Franz Biener, when all at once a puff of wind brought to us a very bad smell ; and, on looking about, we discovered a dead chamois half-way up the southern cliffs of the Stockje. We clambered up, and found that it had been killed by a most uncommon and extraordinary accident. It had slipped on the upper rocks, had rolled over and over down a slope of débris, without being able to regain its feet, had fallen over a little patch of rocks that projected through the débris, and had caught the points of both horns on a tiny ledge, not an inch broad. It had just been able to touch the débris, where it led away down from the rocks, and had pawed and scratched until it could no longer touch. It had evidently been starved to death, and we found the poor beast almost swinging in the air, with its head thrown back and tongue protruding, looking to the sky as if imploring help.

We had no such excitement as this in 1863, and crossed this easy pass to the chalets of Prarayé in a very leisurely fashion. From the summit to Prarayé let us descend in one step. The way has been described before ; and those who wish for information about it should consult the description of Mr. Jacomb, the

---

[1] Professor Ruskin's view of " the Cervin from the north-west " (*Modern Painters*, vol. iv) is taken from the Stockje. The Col du Lion is the little depression on the ridge, close to the margin of the engraving, on the right-hand side ; the third tent-platform was formed at the foot of the perpendicular cliff, on the ridge, exactly one-third way between the Col du Lion and the summit. The battlemented portion of the ridge, a little higher up, is called the " *crête du coq* " ; and the nearly horizontal portion of the ridge above it is " the shoulder."

discoverer of the pass.[1]   Nor need we stop at Prarayé, except to remark that the owner of the chalets (who has sometimes been taken for a common herdsman) must not be judged by appearances.   He is a man of substance, with many flocks and herds ; and although, when approached politely, he is courteous, he can (and probably will) act as the *master* of Prarayé if his position is *not* recognized, and with all the importance of a man who pays taxes to the extent of 500 francs per annum to his government.

The hill-tops were clouded when we rose from our hay on the 5th of August.   We decided not to continue the tour of our mountain immediately, and returned over our track of the preceding day to the highest chalet on the left bank of the valley, with the intention of attacking the Dent d'Hérens on the next morning.   We were interested in this summit, more on account of the excellent view which it commanded of the south-west ridge and the terminal peak of the Matterhorn, than from any other reason.

The Dent d'Hérens had not been ascended at this time, and we had diverged from our route on the 4th, and had scrambled some distance up the base of Mont Brulé, to see how far its south-western slopes were assailable.   We were divided in

---

[1] *Peaks, Passes, and Glaciers*, second series, vol. i., pp. 313-38.

The summit of the Col de Valpelline is 11,687 feet above the sea.   The pass is the easiest one in the Alps of this height, and (if the best route is followed) it may be crossed during fine weather, under favourable circumstances, without cutting a single step.   If one does not take the best route, the pass, however, may become a difficult one.   Much time and trouble will be saved by strictly adhering to the left bank (eastern side) of the Za de Zan (Zardesan) glacier.   Mr. Jacomb followed the right bank.

There is a very fine view from a point that is situated about two-thirds of a mile S. by E. of the summit of the col.   This is marked 3,813 metres (= 12,510 feet) on the Map of the valley of Zermatt.   It is connected with the col by snow-covered glacier at a very moderate angle, and from it one looks well over the Tête Blanche, which is 200 feet less in elevation.   I ascended it in 1866, presumably for the first time.   On recently published maps of the Swiss Survey, it is called " Tête de Valpelline."

opinion as to the best way of approaching the peak. Carrel, true to his habit of sticking to rocks in preference to ice, counselled ascending by the long buttress of the Tête de Bellazà (which descends towards the west, and forms the southern boundary of the last glacier that falls into the Glacier de Za de Zan), and thence traversing the heads of all the tributaries of the Za de Zan to the western and rocky ridge of the Dent. I, on the other hand, proposed to follow the Glacier de Za de Zan itself throughout its entire length, and from the plateau at its head (where my proposed route would cross Carrel's) to make directly towards the summit, up the snow-covered glacier slope, instead of by the western ridge. The hunchback, who was accompanying us on these excursions, declared in favour of Carrel's route, and it was accordingly adopted.

The first part of the programme was successfully executed ; and at 10.30 a.m. on the 6th of August, we were sitting astride the western ridge, at a height of about 12,500 feet, looking down upon the Tiefenmatten Glacier. To all appearance another hour would place us on the summit ; but in another hour we found that we were not destined to succeed. The ridge (like all of the principal rocky ridges of the great peaks upon which I have stood) had been completely shattered by frost, and was nothing more than a heap of piled-up fragments. It was always narrow, and where it was narrowest it was also the most unstable and the most difficult. On neither side could we ascend it by keeping a little below its crest,—on the side of the Tiefenmatten because it was too steep, and on both sides because the dislodgment of a single block would have disturbed the equilibrium of all those which were above. Forced, therefore, to keep to the very crest of the ridge, and unable to deviate a single step either to the right or to the left, we were compelled to trust ourselves upon unsteady masses, which trembled under our tread, which sometimes settled down, grating in a hollow and ominous manner, and which seemed as if a little shake would send the whole roaring down in one great avalanche.

I followed my leader, who said not a word, and did not rebel until we came to a place where a block had to be surmounted which lay poised across the ridge. Carrel could not climb it without assistance, or advance beyond it until I joined him above ; and as he stepped off my back on to it, I felt it quiver and bear down upon me. I doubted the possibility of another man standing upon it without bringing it down. Then I rebelled. There was no honour to be gained by persevering, or dishonour in turning from a place which was dangerous on account of its excessive difficulty. So we returned to Prarayé, for there was too little time to allow us to re-ascend by the other route, which was subsequently shown to be the right way up the mountain.

Four days afterwards a party of Englishmen (including my friends, W. E. Hall, Craufurd Grove, and Reginald Macdonald), arrived in the Valpelline, and (unaware of our attempt) on the 12th, under the skilful guidance of Melchior Anderegg, made the first ascent of the Dent d'Hérens by the route which I had proposed. This is the only mountain in the Alps which I have essayed to ascend, that has not, sooner or later, fallen to me. Our failure was mortifying, but I am satisfied that we did wisely in returning, and that if we had persevered, by Carrel's route, another Alpine accident would have been recorded.[1]

[1] On p. 11 it is stated that there was not a pass from Prarayé to Breuil in 1860, and this is correct. On July 8, 1868, my enterprising guide, Jean-Antoine Carrel, started from Breuil at 2 a.m. with a trusty comrade—J. Baptiste Bich, of Valtournanche—to endeavour to make one. They went towards the glacier which descends from the Dent d'Hérens to the south-east, and on arriving at its base, ascended at first by some snow between it and the cliffs on its south, and afterwards took to the cliffs themselves. This glacier they called the glacier of Montabel, after the local name of the peak which on Mr. Reilly's map of the Valpelline is called " Les Jumeaux." On Mr. Reilly's map the glacier is called " Glacier d'Erin." They ascended the rocks to a considerable height, and then struck across the glacier, towards the north, to a small " rognon " (isolated patch of rocks) that is nearly in the centre of the glacier. They passed above this, and between it and the great séracs. Afterwards their route led them towards the Dent d'Hérens, and they arrived at the base of its final peak by mounting a couloir (gully filled with snow),

On the 7th of August we crossed the Valcournera pass, and
had a good look at the mountain named the Grand Tournalin as
we descended the Val de Cignana. This mountain was seen
from so many points, and was so much higher than any peak
in its immediate neighbourhood, that it was bound to give a
very fine view ; and (as the weather continued unfavourable for
the Matterhorn) I arranged with Carrel to ascend it the next
day, and despatched him direct to the village of Valtournanche
to make the necessary preparations, whilst I, with Meynet, made
a short cut to Breuil, at the back of Mont Panquero, by a little
pass locally known as the Col de Fenêtre. I rejoined Carrel
the same evening at Valtournanche

[*From Whymper's diary* : I visited Carrel's house. With all
respects to him, it was a dirty den, filled with a most miscel-
laneous collection : marmot-skins, chamois-horns, and old bits
of rope being prominent. Of course there was a large portrait
of the Chanoine Carrel.]

and we started from that place at a little before 5 a.m. on the
8th, to attack the Tournalin.

Meynet was left behind for that day, and most unwillingly did
the hunchback part from us, and begged hard to be allowed to
come. " Pay me nothing, only let me go with you " ; " I shall

and the rocks at the head of the glacier. They gained the summit of their
pass at 1 p.m., and descending by the glacier of Za de Zan, arrived at Prarayé
at 6.30 p.m.

As their route joins that taken by Messrs. Hall, Grove, and Macdonald, on
their ascent of the Dent d'Hérens in 1863, it is evident that that mountain can
be ascended from Breuil. Carrel considers that the route taken by himself
and his comrade Bich can be improved upon ; and, if so, it is possible that
the ascent of the Dent d'Hérens can be made from Breuil in less time than
from Prarayé. Breuil is very much to be preferred as a starting-point. On
July 17–18, 1873, Mr. A. G. Puller, with J.-J., J.-P., and E. Maquignaz, and
Louis Carrel, ascended the Dent d'Hérens by this route, and descended to
Prarayé.

want but a little bread and cheese, and I won't eat much " ;
" I would much rather go with you than carry things down
the valley." Such were his arguments, and I was really sorry
that the rapidity of our movements obliged us to desert the good
little man.

Carrel led over the meadows on the south and east of the bluff
upon which the village of Valtournanche is built, and then by
a zigzag path through a long and steep forest, making many
short cuts, which showed he had a thorough knowledge of the
ground.

[*From Whymper's diary* : We stumped away in silence from
Valtournanche up a Riffel-like path for an hour without a
halt, a very stiff pull, and then he suddenly turned round and
asked how long we had been. " An hour, Carrel." " I usually
take two," was the reply, and off we stumped again.]

After we came again into daylight, our route took us up one of
those little, concealed, lateral valleys which are so numerous on
the slopes bounding the Valtournanche.

This valley, the Combe de Ceneil, has a general easterly trend,
and contains but one small cluster of houses (Ceneil). The
Tournalin is situated at the head of the Combe, and nearly due
east of the village of Valtournanche, but from that place no
part of the mountain is visible. After Ceneil is passed it comes
into view, rising above a cirque of cliffs (streaked by several
fine waterfalls), at the end of the Combe. To avoid these cliffs
the path bends somewhat to the south, keeping throughout to
the left bank of the valley, and at about 3,500 feet above Valtournanche, and 1,500 feet above Ceneil and a mile or so to
its east, arrives at the base of some moraines, which are remarkably
large considering the dimensions of the glaciers which formed
them. The ranges upon the western side of the Val Tournanche
are seen to great advantage from this spot ; but here the path
ends and the way steepens.

When we arrived at these moraines, we had a choice of two routes. One, continuing to the east, over the moraines themselves, the débris above them, and a large snow-bed still higher up, to a kind of col or depression to the *south* of the peak, whence an easy ridge led towards the summit. The other, over a shrunken glacier on our north-east (now, perhaps, not in existence), which led to a well-marked col on the *north* of the peak, whence a less easy ridge rose directly to the highest point. We followed the first named of these routes, and in a little more than half an hour stood upon the col, which commanded a most glorious view of the southern side of Monte Rosa, and of the ranges to its east, and to the east of the Val d'Ayas.

Whilst we were resting at this point a large party of vagrant chamois arrived on the summit of the mountain from the northern side, some of whom—by their statuesque position—seemed to appreciate the grand panorama by which they were surrounded, while others amused themselves, like two-legged tourists, in rolling stones over the cliffs. The clatter of these falling fragments made us look up. The chamois were so numerous that we could not count them, and were clustered around the summit, totally unaware of our presence. They scattered in a panic, as if a shell had burst amongst them, when saluted by the cries of my excited comrade ; and plunged wildly down in several directions, with unfaltering and unerring bounds, with such speed and with such grace that we were filled with admiration and respect for their mountaineering abilities.

The ridge that led from the col towards the summit was singularly easy, although well broken up by frost, and Carrel thought that it would not be difficult to arrange a path for mules out of the shattered blocks ; but when we arrived on the summit we found ourselves separated from the very highest point by a cleft which had been concealed up to that time. Its southern side was nearly perpendicular, but it was only fourteen or fifteen feet deep. Carrel lowered me down, and afterwards descended on to the head of my axe, and subsequently on to my shoulders, with a cleverness which was almost as far removed from my awkwardness as his own efforts were from those of the chamois.

A few easy steps then placed us on the highest point. It had not been ascended before, and we commemorated the event by building a huge cairn, which was seen for many a mile, and would have lasted for many a year, had it not been thrown down by the orders of the late Canon Carrel, on account of its interrupting the sweep of a camera which he took to the lower summit in 1868, in order to photograph the panorama. According to the Italian Survey, the summit of the Grand Tournalin is 6,086 feet above the village of Valtournanche, and 11,086 feet above the sea. Its ascent (including halts) occupied us only four hours.

I recommend the ascent of the Tournalin to any person who has a day to spare in the Val Tournanche. It should be remembered, however

"CARREL LOWERED ME DOWN." (if its ascent is made for the sake of the view), that these southern Pennine Alps seldom remain unclouded after midday, and, indeed, frequently not later than 10 or 11 a.m. Towards sunset the equilibrium of the atmosphere is restored, and the clouds very commonly disappear.

I advise the ascent of this mountain not on account of its height, or from its accessibility or inaccessibility, but simply for the wide and splendid view which may be seen from its summit. Its position is superb, and the list of the peaks which can be seen from it includes almost the whole of the principal mountains of the Cottian, Dauphiné, Graian, Pennine, and Oberland groups. The view has, in the highest perfection, those elements of picturesqueness which are wanting in the purely panoramic views seen from higher summits. There are three principal sections, each with a central or dominating point, to which the eye is naturally drawn. All three alike are pictures in themselves ; yet all are dissimilar. In the south, softened by the vapours of the Val d'Aosta, extends the long line of the Graians, with mountain after mountain 12,000 feet and upwards in height. It is not upon these, noble as some of them are, that the eye will rest, but upon the Viso, far off in the background. In the west and towards the north the range of Mont Blanc, and some of the greatest of the Central Pennine Alps (including the Grand Combin and the Dent Blanche), form the background, but they are overpowered by the grandeur of the ridges which culminate in the Matterhorn. Nor in the east and north, where pleasant grassy slopes lead downwards to the Val d'Ayas, nor upon the glaciers and snow-fields above them, nor upon the Oberland in the background, will the eye long linger, when immediately in front, several miles away, but seeming close at hand, thrown out by the pure azure sky, there are the glittering crests of Monte Rosa.

Those who would, but cannot, stand upon the highest Alps, may console themselves with the knowledge that they do not usually yield the views that make the strongest and most permanent impressions. Marvellous some of the panoramas seen from the greatest peaks undoubtedly are ; but they are necessarily without those isolated and central points which are so valuable pictorially. The eye roams over a multitude of objects (each, perhaps, grand individually), and, distracted by an embarrassment of riches, wanders from one to another, erasing by the contemplation of the next the effect that was produced by the last ; and when those happy moments are over, which always fly with too great rapidity, the summit is left with an impression that is seldom durable, because it is usually vague.

No views create such lasting impressions as those which are seen but for a moment, when a veil of mist is rent in twain, and a single spire or dome is disclosed. The peaks which are seen at these moments are not, perhaps, the greatest or the noblest, but the recollection of them outlives the memory of any panoramic view, because the picture, photographed by the eye, has time to dry, instead of being blurred, while yet wet, by contact with other impressions. The reverse is the case with the bird's-eye panoramic views from the great peaks, which sometimes embrace a hundred miles in nearly every direction. The eye is confounded by the crowd of details, and is unable to distinguish the relative importance of the objects which are seen. It is almost as difficult to form a just estimate (with the eye) of the respective heights of a number of peaks from a very high summit, as it is from the bottom of a valley. I think that the grandest and the most satisfactory standpoints for viewing mountain scenery are those which are sufficiently elevated to give a feeling of depth, as well as of height, which are lofty enough to exhibit wide and varied views, but not so high as to sink everything to the level of the spectator. The view from the Grand Tournalin is a favourable example of this class of panoramic views.

We descended from the summit by the northern route, and found it tolerably stiff clambering as far as the col. Thence, down the glacier, the way was straightforward, and we joined the route taken on the ascent at the foot of the ridge leading towards the east. In the evening we returned to Breuil.

There is an abrupt rise in the valley about two miles to the north of the village of Valtournanche, and at this step the torrent has eaten its way into its bed and formed an extraordinary chasm, which has long been known by the name Gouffre des Busserailles. We lingered about this spot to listen to the thunder of the concealed water, and to watch its tumultuous boiling as it issued from the gloomy cleft, but our efforts to peer into the mysteries of the place were baffled. In November 1865,

the intrepid Carrel induced two trusty comrades—the Maquignaz of Valtournanche—to lower him by a rope into the
chasm and over the cataract. The feat required iron nerves,
and muscles and sinews of no ordinary kind ; and its per
formance alone stamped Carrel as a man of dauntless courage
One of the Maquignaz subsequently descended in the sam.
way, and these two men were so astonished at what they saw
that they forthwith set to work with hammer and chisel to make
a way into this romantic gulf. In a few days they constructed
a rough but convenient plank gallery into the centre of the
gouffre, along its walls ; and, on payment of a franc, anyone can
now enter the Gouffre des Busserailles.

I cannot, without a couple of sections and a plan, give an
exact idea to the reader of this remarkable place. It corresponds
in some of its features to the gorge figured upon page 106, but
it exhibits in a much more notable manner the characteristic
action and extraordinary power of running water. The length
of the chasm or *gouffre* is about 320 feet, and from the top of
its walls to the surface of the water is about 110 feet. At no
part can the entire length or depth be seen at a glance ; for,
although the width at some places is 15 feet or more, the view
is limited by the sinuosities of the walls. These are everywhere
polished to a smooth, vitreous-in-appearance surface. In some
places the torrent has wormed into the rock, and has left natural
bridges. The most extraordinary features of the Gouffre des
Busserailles, however, are the caverns (or *marmites* as they are
termed), which the water has hollowed out of the heart of the
rock. Carrel's plank path leads into one of the greatest,—a
grotto that is about 28 feet across at its largest diameter, and
15 or 16 feet high ; roofed above by the living rock, and with
the torrent roaring 50 feet or thereabouts below, at the bottom
of a fissure. This cavern is lighted by candles, and talking in it
can only be managed by signs.

I visited the interior of the *gouffre* in 1869, and my wonder
at its caverns was increased by observing the hardness of the

hornblende out of which they have been hollowed. Carrel chiselled off a large piece, which is now lying before me. It has a highly polished, glassy surface, and might be mistaken, for a moment, for ice-polished rock. But the water has found out the atoms which were least hard, and it is dotted all over by minute depressions, much as the face of one is who has suffered from smallpox. The edges of these little hollows are *rounded*, and the whole surfaces of the depressions are polished nearly, or quite, as highly as the general surface of the fragment.[1] The water has eaten more deeply into some veins of steatite than in other places, and the presence of the steatite may possibly have had something to do with the formation of the *gouffre*.

I arrived at Breuil again after an absence of six days, well satisfied with my tour of the Matterhorn, which had been rendered very pleasant by the willingness of my guides, and by the kindliness of the natives. But it must be admitted that the inhabitants of the Val Tournanche are behind the times. Their paths are as bad as, perhaps worse than, they were in the time of Saussure, and their inns are much inferior to those on the Swiss side. If it were otherwise there would be nothing to prevent the valley becoming one of the most popular and frequented of all the valleys in the Alps. As it is, tourists who enter it seem to think only about how soon they can get out of it, and hence it is much less known than it deserves to be on account of its natural attractions.

I believe that the great hindrance to the improvement of the paths in the Italian valleys generally is the widespread impression that the innkeepers would alone directly benefit by any amelioration of their condition. To a certain extent this view is correct ; but inasmuch as the prosperity of the natives is connected with that of the innkeepers, the interests of both are pretty nearly identical. Until their paths are rendered less rough and swampy, I think the Italians must submit to see the golden harvest prin-

[1] The depressions in glaciated rocks (which are not water-worn) are more or less angular.

cipally reaped in Switzerland and Savoy.   At the same time, let the innkeepers look to the commissariat.   Their supplies are not unfrequently deficient in quantity, and, according to my experience, very often deplorable in quality.

I will not venture to criticize in detail the dishes which are brought to table, since I am profoundly ignorant of their constitution.   It is commonly said amongst Alpine tourists that goat-flesh represents mutton, and mule does service for beef and chamois.   I reserve my own opinion upon this point until it has been shown what becomes of all the dead mules.   But I may say, I hope, without wounding the susceptibilities of my acquaintances among the Italian innkeepers, that it would tend to smoothen their intercourse with their guests if requests for solid food were less frequently regarded as criminal.   The deprecating airs with which inquiries for really substantial food are sometimes received remind me of a Dauphiné innkeeper, who remarked that he had heard a good many tourists travel in Switzerland.   " Yes," I answered, " there are a good many." " How many ? "   " Well," I said, " I have seen a hundred or more sit down at a table d'hôte."   He lifted up his hands— " Why," said he, " they would want meat every day ! "   " Yes, that is not improbable."   " In that case," he replied, " *I think we are better without them.*"

CHAPTER VI

OUR SIXTH ATTEMPT TO ASCEND THE MATTERHORN [1]

> " *But mighty Jove cuts short, with just disdain,*
> *The long, long views of poor, designing man.*"
>
> HOMER.

CARREL had *carte blanche* in the matter of guides, and his choice fell upon his relative Cæsar, Luc Meynet, and two others whose names I do not know. These men were now brought together, and our preparations were completed, as the weather was clearing up.

We rested on Sunday, August 9, eagerly watching the lessening of the mists around the great peak, and started just before dawn upon the 10th, on a still and cloudless morning, which seemed to promise a happy termination to our enterprise.

By going always, though gently, we arrived upon the Col du Lion before nine o'clock. Changes were apparent. Familiar ledges had vanished ; the platform, whereupon my tent had stood, looked very forlorn, its stones had been scattered by wind and frost, and had half disappeared ; and the summit of the col itself, which in 1862 had always been respectably broad, and covered by snow, was now sharper than the ridge of any church roof, and was hard ice. Already we had found that the bad weather of the past week had done its work. The rocks for several hundred feet below the col were varnished with ice. Loose, incoherent snow covered the older and harder beds

---

[1] A brief account of this excursion was published in the *Athenæum*, August 29, 1863.

below, and we nearly lost our leader through its treacherousness. He stepped on some snow which seemed firm, and raised his axe to deliver a swinging blow, but, just as it was highest, the crust of the slope upon which he stood broke away, and poured down in serpentine streams, leaving long, bare strips, which glittered in the sun, for they were glassy ice. Carrel, with admirable readiness, flung himself back on to the rock off which he had stepped, and was at once secured. He simply remarked, " It is time we were tied up," and, after we had been tied up, he went to work again as if nothing had happened.[1]

We had abundant illustrations during the next two hours of the value of a rope to climbers. We were tied up rather widely apart, and advanced, generally, in pairs. Carrel, who led, was followed closely by another man, who lent him a shoulder or placed an axe-head under his feet, when there was need ; and when this couple were well placed the second pair advanced, in similar fashion,—the rope being drawn in by those above, and paid out gradually by those below. The leading men again advanced, or the third pair, and so on. This manner of progression was slow, but sure. One man only moved at a time, and if he slipped (and we frequently did slip) he could slide scarcely a foot without being checked by the others. The certainty and safety of the method gave confidence to the one who was moving, and not only nerved him to put out his powers to the utmost, but sustained nerve in really difficult situations. For these rocks (which, it has been already said, were easy enough under ordinary circumstances) were now difficult in a high degree. The snow-water which had trickled

[1] This incident occurred close to the place represented in the engraving facing p. 86. The new, dry snow was very troublesome, and poured down like flour into the steps which were cut across the slopes. The front man accordingly moved ahead as far as possible, and anchored himself to rocks. An extra rope was sent across to him, was fixed at each end, and was held as a rail by the others as they crossed. We did not trust to this rope alone, but were tied in the usual manner. The second rope was employed as an additional security against slips.

down for many days past in little streams, had taken, naturally, the very route by which we wished to ascend ; and, refrozen in the night, had glazed the slabs over which we had to pass,— sometimes with a fine film of ice as thin as a sheet of paper, and sometimes so thickly that we could almost cut footsteps in it. The weather was superb, the men made light of the toil, and shouted to rouse the echoes from the Dent d'Hérens.

We went on gaily, passed the second tent platform, the Chimney, and the other well-remembered points, and reckoned, confidently, on sleeping that night upon the top of " the shoulder " ; but, before we had well arrived at the foot of the Great Tower, a sudden rush of cold air warned us to look out. It was difficult to say where this air came from. It did not blow as a wind, but descended rather as the water in a shower-bath ! All was tranquil again ; the atmosphere *showed* no signs of disturbance ; there was a dead calm, and not a speck of cloud to be seen anywhere. But we did not remain very long in this state. The cold air came again, and this time it was difficult to say where it did *not* come from. We jammed down our hats as it beat against the ridge, and screamed amongst the crags. Before we had got to the foot of the Tower, mists had been formed above and below. They appeared at first in small, isolated patches (in several places at the same time), which danced and jerked and were torn into shreds by the wind, but grew larger under the process. They were united together, and rent again,—showing us the blue sky for a moment, and blotting it out the next ; and augmented incessantly, until the whole heavens were filled with whirling, boiling clouds. Before we could take off our packs, and get under any kind of shelter, a hurricane of snow burst upon us from the east. It fell very heavily, and in a few minutes the ridge was covered by it. " What shall we do ? " I shouted to Carrel. " Monsieur," said he, " the wind is bad ; the weather has changed ; we are heavily laden. Here is a fine *gîte* ; let us stop ! If we go on we shall be half-frozen. That is *my* opinion." No one differed from him ; so we fell to work to make a place for the tent, and in a couple of hours completed the platform which we had commenced in 1862. The clouds had blackened during that time, and we had hardly finished our task before a thunderstorm broke upon us with appalling fury. Forked lightning shot out at the turrets above, and at the crags below. It was so close that we quailed at its darts. It seemed to scorch us,—we were in the very focus of the storm. The thunder was simultaneous with the flashes ; short and sharp, and more like the noise of a door that is violently slammed, multiplied a thousand-fold, than any noise to which I can compare it.

When I say that the thunder was *simultaneous* with the lightning, I speak as an inexact person. My meaning is that the time which elapsed between seeing the flash and hearing the report was inappreciable to me. I wish to speak with all possible precision, and there are two points in regard to this storm upon which I can speak with some accuracy. The first is in regard to the distance of the lightning from our party. We *might* have been 1,100 feet from it if a second of time had elapsed between seeing the flashes and hearing the reports ; and a second of time is not appreciated by inexact persons. It was certain that we were sometimes less than that distance from the lightning, because I saw it pass in front of well-known points on the ridge, both above and below us, which were less (sometimes considerably less) than a thousand feet distant.

Secondly, in regard to the difficulty of distinguishing sounds which are merely echoes from true thunder, or the noise which occurs simultaneously with lightning. Arago entered into this subject at some length in his *Meteorological Essays*, and seemed to doubt if it would ever be possible to determine whether echoes are *always* the cause of the rolling sounds commonly called thunder.[1] I shall not attempt to show whether the rolling

[1] " There is, therefore, little hope of thus arriving at anything decisive as to the exact part which echoes take in the production of the rolling sound of thunder." P. 165, English ed., translated by Col. Sabine : Longmans, 1855.

sounds should ever, or never, be regarded as true thunder, but only that during this storm upon the Matterhorn it was possible to distinguish the sound of the thunder itself from the sounds (rolling and otherwise) which were merely the echoes of the first, original sound.

At the place where we were camped a remarkable echo could be heard (one so remarkable that if it could be heard in this country it would draw crowds for its own sake) ; I believe it came from the cliffs of the Dent d'Hérens. It was a favourite amusement with us to shout to rouse this echo, which repeated any sharp cry, in a very distinct manner, several times, after the lapse of something like a dozen seconds. The thunderstorm lasted nearly two hours, and raged at times with great fury ; and the prolonged rollings from the surrounding mountains, after one flash, had not usually ceased before another set of echoes took up the discourse, and maintained the reverberations without a break. Occasionally there was a pause, interrupted presently by a single clap, the accompaniment of a single discharge, and after such times I could recognize the echoes from the Dent d'Hérens by their peculiar repetitions, and by the length of time which had passed since the reports had occurred of which they were the echoes.

If I had been unaware of the existence of this echo, I should have supposed that the resounds were original reports of explosions which had been unnoticed, since in intensity they were scarcely distinguishable from the true thunder, which, during this storm, seemed to me upon every occasion to consist of a single, harsh, instantaneous sound.[1]

Or if, instead of being placed at a distance of less than a

---

[1] The same has seemed to me to be the case at all times when I have been close to the points of explosion. There has been always a distinct interval between the first explosion and the rolling sounds and secondary explosions which I have *believed* to be merely echoes ; but it has never been possible (except in the above-mentioned case) to *identify* them as such.

Others have observed the same. " The geologist, Professor Theobald, of

thousand feet from the points of explosion (and consequently hearing the report almost in the same moment as we saw the flash, and the rollings after a considerable interval of time), we had been placed so that the original report had fallen on our ears nearly at the same moment as the echoes, we should probably have considered that the successive reports and rollings of the echoes were reports of successive explosions occurring nearly at the same moment, and that they were not *echoes* at all.

This is the only time (out of many storms witnessed in the Alps) I have obtained evidence that the rollings of thunder are actually echoes ; and that they are not, necessarily, the reports of a number of discharges over a long line, occurring at varying distances from the spectator, and consequently unable to arrive at his ear at the same moment, although they follow each other so swiftly as to produce a sound more or less continuous.[1]

The wind during all this time seemed to blow tolerably consistently from the east. It smote the tent so vehemently (notwithstanding it was partly protected by rocks) that we had grave fears our refuge might be blown away bodily, with ourselves inside ; so, during some of the lulls, we issued out and built a wall to windward. At half-past three the wind changed to the north-west, and the clouds vanished. We immediately took the opportunity to send down one of the porters (under protection of some of the others, a little beyond the Col du Lion), as the

Chur, who was in the Solferino storm, between the Tschiertscher and Urden Alp, in the electric clouds, says that the peals were short, like cannon shots, but of a clearer, more cracking tone, and that the rolling of the thunder was only heard farther on." Berlepsch's *Alps*, English ed., p. 133.

[1] Mr. J. Glaisher has frequently pointed out that all sounds in balloons at some distance from the earth are notable for their brevity. " It is one sound only ; *there is no reverberation, no reflection* ; and this is characteristic of all sounds in the balloon, one clear sound, continuing during its own vibrations, then gone in a moment."—*Good Words*, 1863, p. 224.

I learn from Mr. Glaisher that the thunder-claps which have been heard by him during his " travels in the air " have been no exception to the general rule, and the absence of rolling has fortified his belief that the rolling sounds which accompany thunder are echoes, and echoes *only*.

tent could not accommodate more than five persons. From this time to sunset the weather was variable. It was sometimes blowing and snowing hard, and sometimes a dead calm. The bad weather was evidently confined to the Matterhorn, for when the clouds lifted we could see everything that could be seen from our gîte. Monte Viso, a hundred miles off, was clear, and the sun set gorgeously behind the range of Mont Blanc. We passed the night comfortably—even luxuriously—in our blanket-bags, but there was little chance of sleeping, between the noise of the wind, of the thunder, and of the falling rocks. I forgave the thunder for the sake of the lightning. A more splendid spectacle than its illumination of the Matterhorn crags I do not expect to see.

The greatest rock-falls always seemed to occur in the night, between midnight and daybreak. This was noticeable on each of the seven nights which I passed upon the south-west ridge, at heights varying from 11,800 to 13,000 feet.

I may be wrong in supposing that the falls in the night are greater than those in the daytime, since sound is much more startling during darkness than when the cause of its production is seen. Even a sigh may be terrible in the stillness of the night. In the daytime one's attention is probably divided between the sound and the motion of rocks which fall ; or it may be concentrated on other matters. But it is certain that the greatest of the falls which happened during the night took place after midnight, and this I connect with the fact that the maximum of cold during any twenty-four hours very commonly occurs between midnight and dawn.

We turned out at 3.30 a.m. on the 11th, and were dismayed to find that it still continued to snow. At 9 a.m. it ceased to fall, and the sun showed itself feebly, so we packed up our baggage, and set out to try to get upon " the shoulder." We struggled upwards until eleven o'clock, and then it commenced to snow again. We held a council ; the opinions expressed at it were unanimous against advancing, and I decided to retreat.

—TENT.

THE CRAGS OF THE MATTERHORN, DURING THE STORM, MIDNIGHT,
AUG. 10, 1863.

For we had risen less than 300 feet in the past two hours, and had not even arrived at the rope which Tyndall's party left behind, attached to the rocks, in 1862. At the same rate of progression it would have taken us from four to five hours to get upon "the shoulder." Not one of us cared to attempt to do so under the existing circumstances ; for besides having to move our own weight, which was sufficiently troublesome at this part of the ridge, we had to transport much heavy baggage, tent, blankets, and provisions, ladder, and 450 feet of rope, besides many other smaller matters. These, however, were not the most serious considerations. Supposing that we got upon "the shoulder," we might find ourselves detained there several days, unable either to go up or down.[1] I could not risk any such detention, being under obligations to appear in London at the end of the week.

MONSIEUR FAVRE.

We returned to Breuil in the course of the afternoon. It was quite fine there, and the tenants of the inn received our statements with evident scepticism. They were astonished to learn that we had been exposed to a snow-storm of twenty-six hours' duration. "Why," said Favre, the innkeeper, "*we* have had no snow ; it has been fine all the time you have been absent, and there has been only that small cloud upon the mountain." Ah ! that small cloud ! None except those who have had experience of it can tell what a formidable obstacle it is.

Why is it that the Matterhorn is subject to these abominable variations of weather ? The ready answer is, "Oh, the mountain is so isolated ; it attracts the clouds." This is not a sufficient

[1] Since then several persons have found themselves in this predicament for five or six consecutive days !

answer. Although the mountain *is* isolated, it is not so much more isolated than the neighbouring peaks that it should gather clouds when none of the others do so. It will not at all account for the cloud to which I refer, which is not formed by an aggregation of smaller, stray clouds drawn together from a distance (as scum collects round a log in the water), but is created against the mountain itself, and springs into existence where no clouds were seen before. It is formed and hangs chiefly against the southern sides, and particularly against the south-eastern side. It frequently does not envelop the summit, and rarely extends down to the Glacier du Lion, and to the Glacier du Mont Cervin below. It forms in the finest weather ; on cloudless and windless days.

I conceive that we should look to differences of temperature rather than to the height or isolation of the mountain for an explanation. I am inclined to attribute the disturbances which occur in the atmosphere of the southern sides of the Matterhorn on fine days,[1] principally to the fact that the mountain is a *rock* mountain. It absorbs a great amount of heat, and is not only warmer itself, but is surrounded by an atmosphere of a higher temperature than such peaks as the Weisshorn and the Lyskamm, which are eminently *snow* mountains.

In certain states of the atmosphere its temperature may be tolerably uniform over wide areas and to great elevations. I have known the thermometer to show 70° in the shade at the top of an Alpine peak 13,000 feet high, and but a very few degrees more at stations 6,000 or 7,000 feet lower. At other times, there will be a difference of forty or fifty degrees F. between two stations, the higher not more than 6,000 or 7,000 feet above the lower.

Provided that the temperature was uniform, or nearly so, on all sides of the Matterhorn, and to a considerable distance above its summit, no clouds would be likely to form upon it. But if the atmosphere immediately surrounding it is warmer than the contiguous strata, a local " courant ascendant " must neces-

[1] I am speaking exclusively of the disturbances which occur in the daytime during fine weather.

sarily be generated ; and portions of the cooler superincumbent (or circumjacent) air will naturally be attracted towards the mountain, where they will speedily condense the moisture of the warm air in contact with it. I cannot explain the down-rushes of cold air which occur on it, when all the rest of the neighbourhood appears to be tranquil, in any other way. The clouds are produced by the contact of two strata of air (of widely different temperatures) charged with invisible moisture, as surely as certain colourless fluids produce a white, turbid liquid, when mixed together. The order has been—wind of a low temperature—mist—rain—snow or hail.[1]

This opinion is borne out to some extent by the behaviour of the neighbouring mountains. The Dom (14,942 feet) and the Dent Blanche (14,318) have both of them large cliffs of bare rock upon their southern sides, and against those cliffs clouds commonly form (during fine, still weather) at the same time as the cloud on the Matterhorn ; whilst the Weisshorn (14,804) and the Lyskamm (14,889), (mountains of about the same altitude, and which are in corresponding situations to the former pair) usually remain perfectly clear.

I arrived at Châtillon at midnight on the 11th, defeated and disconsolate ; but, like a gambler who loses each throw, only the more eager to have another try, to see if the luck would change ; and returned to London ready to devise fresh combinations, and to form new plans.

[1] The mists are extremely deceptive to those who are on the mountain itself. Sometimes they *seem* to be created at a *considerable distance*, as if the whole of the atmosphere of the neighbourhood was undergoing a change, when in reality they are being formed in immediate proximity to the mountain.

CROSSING THE CHANNEL.

CHAPTER VII

FROM ST. MICHEL ON THE MONT CENIS ROAD, BY THE COL DES AIGUILLES D'ARVES, COL DE MARTIGNARE, AND THE BRECHE DE LA MEIJE, TO LA BERARDE.[1]

" The more to help the greater deed is done."
HOMER.

WHEN we arrived upon the highest summit of Mont Pelvoux, in Dauphiné, in 1861, we saw, to our surprise and disappointment, that it was not the culminating point of the district ; and that another mountain—distant about a couple of miles, and separated from us by an impassable gulf—claimed that distinction. I was troubled in spirit about this mountain, and my thoughts often reverted to the great wall-sided peak, second in apparent inaccessibility only to the Matterhorn.

The year 1862 passed away without a chance of getting to it, and my holiday was too brief in 1863 even to think about it ; but in the following year it was possible, and I resolved to set my mind at rest by completing the task which had been left unfinished in 1861.

In the meantime others had turned their attention to Dauphiné. First of all (in 1862) came Mr. F. F. Tuckett—that mighty mountaineer, whose name is known throughout the length and breadth of the Alps—with the guides Michel Croz, Peter Perren, and Bartolommeo Peyrotte, and great success attended his arms.

[1] For routes described in this chapter, see the General Map and the plan in the text at p. 138.

But Mr. Tuckett halted before the Pointe des Ecrins, and, dismayed by its appearance, withdrew his forces to gather less dangerous laurels elsewhere.

His expedition, however, threw some light upon the Ecrins. He pointed out the direction from which an attack was most likely to be successful, and Mr. William Mathews and the Rev.

MICHEL-AUGUSTE CROZ (1865).

T. G. Bonney (to whom he communicated the result of his labours) attempted to execute the ascent, with the brothers Michel and J. B. Croz, by following his indications. But they too were defeated, as I shall relate more particularly presently.

The guide Michel Croz had thus been engaged in both of these expeditions in Dauphiné, and I naturally looked to him for assistance. Mr. Mathews (to whom I applied for information) gave him a high character, and concluded his reply to me by saying that Croz " was only happy when upwards of 10,000 feet high."

I know what my friend meant. Croz was happiest when he was employing his powers to the utmost. Places where you and I would " toil and sweat, and yet be freezing cold," were bagatelles to him, and it was only when he got above the range of ordinary mortals, and was required to employ his magnificent strength, and to draw upon his unsurpassed knowledge of ice and snow, that he could be said to be really and truly happy.

Of all the guides with whom I travelled, Michel Croz was the man who was most after my own heart. He did not work like a blunt razor, and take to his toil unkindly. He did not need urging, or to be told a second time to do anything. You had only to say *what* was to be done, and *how* it was to be done, and the work *was* done, if it was possible. Such men are not common, and when they are known they are valued. Michel was not widely known, but those who did know him came again and again. The inscription that is placed upon his tomb truthfully records that he was " beloved by his comrades and esteemed by travellers."

At the time that I was planning my journey, my friends Messrs. A. W. Moore and Horace Walker were also drawing up their programme ; and, as we found that our wishes were very similar, we agreed to unite our respective parties. The excursions which are described in this and the two following chapters are mutual ideas which were jointly executed.

Our united programme was framed so as to avoid sleeping in inns, and so that we should see from the highest point attained on one day, a considerable portion of the route which was intended to be followed on the next. This latter matter was an important one to us, as all of our projected excursions were new ones, and led over ground about which there was very little information in print.

My friends had happily secured Christian Almer of Grindel-wald as their guide. The combination of Croz and Almer was a perfect one. Both men were in the prime of life [1] ; both were endued with strength and activity far beyond the average ; and the courage and the knowledge of each was alike undoubted. The temper of Almer it was impossible to ruffle ; he was ever obliging and enduring,—a bold but a safe man. That which he lacked in fire—in dash—was supplied by Croz, who, in his turn, was kept in place by Almer. It is pleasant to remember how they worked together, and how each one confided to you that he liked the other *so* much because he worked *so* well ; but it is sad, very sad, to those who have known the men, to know that they can never work together again.

We met at St. Michel on the Mont Cenis road, at midday on June 20, 1864, and proceeded in the afternoon over the Col de Valloire to the village of the same name. The summit of this pretty little pass is about 3,500 feet above St. Michel, and from it we had a fair view of the Aiguilles d'Arves, a group of three peaks of singular form, which it was our especial object to investigate.[2] They had been seen by ourselves and others from numerous distant points, and always looked very high and very inaccessible ; and we had been unable to obtain any information about them, except the few words in Joanne's *Itinéraire du Dauphiné*. Having made out from the summit of the Col de Valloire that they could be approached from the valley of Valloire, we hastened down to find a place where we could pass the night, as near as possible to the entrance of the little valley leading up to them.

By nightfall we arrived at the entrance to this little valley

[1] Croz was born at the village of Le Tour, in the valley of Chamonix, on April 22, 1830 ; Almer was a year or two older.

[2] The Pointe des Ecrins is also seen from the top of the Col de Valloire, rising above the Col du Galibier. This is the lowest elevation from which I have seen the actual summit of the Ecrins.

(Vallon des Aiguilles d'Arves), and found some buildings placed just where they were wanted. The proprietress received us with civility, and placed a large barn at our disposal, on the conditions that no lights were struck or pipes smoked therein ; and when her terms were agreed to, she took us into her own chalet,

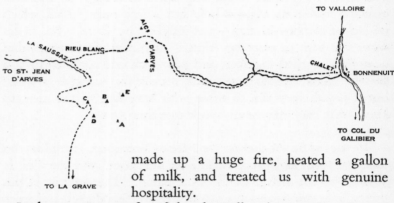

made up a huge fire, heated a gallon of milk, and treated us with genuine hospitality.

In the morning we found that the Vallon des Aiguilles d'Arves led away nearly due west from the valley of Valloire, and that the village of Bonnenuit was placed (in the latter valley) almost exactly opposite to the junction of the two.

At 3.55 a.m. on the 21st we set out up the Vallon, passed for a time over pasture-land, and then over a stony waste, deeply channelled by watercourses. At 5.30 the two principal Aiguilles were well seen, and as by this time it was evident that the authors of the Sardinian official map had romanced as extensively in this neighbourhood as elsewhere, it was necessary to hold a council.

Three questions were submitted to it :—Firstly, Which is the highest of these Aiguilles ? Secondly, Which shall we go up ? Thirdly, How is it to be done ?

The French engineers, it was said, had determined that the two highest of them were respectively 11,513 and 11,529 feet in height ; but we were without information as to which two they had measured.[1] Joanne indeed said (but without specifying whether he meant all three), that the Aiguilles had been several times ascended, and particularly mentioned that the one of 11,513 feet was " relatively easy."

We therefore said, " We will go up the peak of 11,529 feet." But that determination did not settle the second question. Joanne's " relatively easy " peak, according to his description, was evidently the most northern of the three. *Our* peak then was to be one of the other two ;—but which of them ? We were inclined to favour the central one, though we had doubts, for they looked very equal in height. When, however, the council came to study the third question—" How is it to be done ? " it was unanimously voted that upon the eastern and southern sides it was certainly relatively difficult, and that a move should be made round to the northern side.

The movement was duly executed, and after wading up some snow-slopes of considerable steepness (going occasionally beyond 40°), we found ourselves in a gap or nick, between the central and northernmost Aiguille, at 8.45 a.m. We then studied the northern face of our intended peak, and finally arrived at the conclusion that it was relatively impracticable. Croz shrugged his big shoulders, and said, " My faith ! I think you will do well to leave it to others." Almer was more explicit, and volunteered the information that a thousand francs would not tempt him to *try* it. We then turned to the northernmost peak, and found its southern faces even more hopeless than the northern faces of the central one. We enjoyed accordingly the unwonted luxury of a three hours' rest on the top of our pass ; for pass we were determined it should be.

We might have done worse. We were 10,300 or 10,400 feet

---

[1] It should be observed that these mountains were included in the territory recently ceded to France. The Sardinian map above referred to was the old official map. The French survey alluded to afterwards is the survey in continuation of the great French official map. The sheet including the Aiguilles d'Arves was not then published.

THE AIGUILLES D'ARVES FROM ABOVE THE
CHALETS OF RIEUBLANC.

above the level of the sea, and commanded a most picturesque view of the mountains of the Tarentaise ; while, somewhat east of south, we saw the monarch of the Dauphiné *massif*, whose closer acquaintance it was our intention to make. Three sunny hours passed away, and then we turned to the descent. We saw the distant pastures of a valley (which we supposed was the Vallon or Ravine de la Saussaz), and a long snow-slope leading down to them. But from that slope we were cut off by precipitous rocks, and our first impression was that we should have to return in our track. Some running about, however, discovered two little gullies, filled with threads of snow, and down the most northern of these we decided to go. It was a steep way but a safe one, for the cleft was so narrow that we could press the shoulders against one side whilst the feet were against the other, and the last remnant of the winter's snow, well hardened, clung to the rift with great tenacity, and gave us a path when the rocks refused one. In half an hour we got to the top of the great snow-slope. Walker said—" Let us glissade " ; the guides—" No, it is too steep." Our friend, however, started off at a standing glissade, and advanced for a time very skilfully ; but after a while he lost his balance, and progressed downwards and backwards with great rapidity, in a way that seemed to us very much like tumbling head over heels. He let go his axe, and left it behind, but it overtook him and batted him heartily. He and it travelled in this fashion for some hundreds of feet, and at last subsided into the rocks at the bottom. In a few moments we were reassured as to his safety, by hearing him ironically request us not to keep him waiting down there.

We others followed the track shown by the dotted line upon the engraving (making zigzags to avoid the little groups of rocks jutting through the snow, by which Walker had been upset), descended by a *sitting* glissade, and rejoined our friend at the bottom. We then turned sharply to the left, and tramped down the summit ridge of an old moraine of great size. Its mud was excessively hard, and where some large erratic blocks lay perched upon its crest, we were obliged to cut steps (in the mud) with our ice-axes.

Guided by the sound of a distant " moo," we speedily found the highest chalets in the valley, named Rieublanc. They were tenanted by three old women (who seemed to belong to one of the missing links sought by naturalists), destitute of all ideas except in regard to cows, and who spoke a barbarous patois, well-nigh unintelligible to the Savoyard Croz. They would not believe that we had passed between the Aiguilles,—" It is impossible, the *cows* never go there." " Could we get to La Grave over yonder ridge ? " " Oh yes ! the *cows* often crossed ! " Could they show us the way ? No ; but we could follow the *cow*-tracks.

We stayed a while near these chalets, to examine the western sides of the Aiguilles d'Arves, and, according to our united opinion, the central one appeared as inaccessible from this direction as from the east, north, or south. On the following day we saw them again, when at a height of about 11,000 feet, from a south-westerly direction, and our opinion remained unchanged.

We saw (on June 20–22) the central Aiguille from all sides, and very nearly completely round the southernmost one. The northern one we also saw on all sides excepting from the north. (It is, however, precisely from this direction M. Joanne says that its ascent is relatively easy.) We do not, therefore, venture to express any opinion respecting its ascent, except as regards its actual summit. This is formed of two curious prongs, or pinnacles of rock, and we do not understand in what way they (or either of them) can be ascended ; nor shall we be surprised if this ascent is discovered to have been made in spirit rather than body ; in fact, in the same manner as the celebrated ascent of Mont Blanc, " not quite to the summit, but as far as the Montenvers ! "

All three of the Aiguilles *may* be accessible, but they look as inaccessible as anything I have seen. They are the highest summits between the valleys of the Romanche and the Arc ; they are placed slightly to the north of the watershed between those two valleys, and a line drawn through them runs, pretty nearly, north and south.[1]

We descended by a rough path from Rieublanc to the chalets

[1] These three Aiguilles have now been climbed, on several occasions. See the *Alpine Journal*, vol. viii., pp. 57–79, 1876 ; and vol. ix., pp. 95, 96, 1878.

of La Saussaz, which give the name to the Vallon or Ravine de la Saussaz, in which they are situated. This is one of the numerous branches of the valley that descends to St. Jean d'Arves, and subsequently to St. Jean de Maurienne.

Two passes, more or less known, lead from this valley to the village of La Grave (on the Lautaret road) in the valley of the Romanche, namely, the Col de l'Infernet and the Col de Martignare. The former pass was crossed in 1841 by Prof. J. D. Forbes, and was mentioned by him at pp. 292–4 of his *Norway and its Glaciers*. The latter one lies to the north of the former, and is seldom traversed by tourists, but it was convenient for us, and we set out to cross it on the morning of the 22nd, after having passed a comfortable, though not luxurious, night in the hay at La Saussaz, where, however, the simplicity of the accommodation was more than counterbalanced by the civility and hospitality of the people in charge.[1]

' Our object now was to cross to La Grave (on the high road from Grenoble to Briançon), and to ascend, *en route*, some point sufficiently high to give us a good view of the Dauphiné Alps in general, and of the grand chain of the Meije in particular. Before leaving England a careful study of " Joanne " had elicited the fact that the shortest route from La Saussaz to La Grave

---

[1] Whilst stopping in the hospice on the Col de Lautaret, in 1869, I was accosted by a middle-aged peasant, who asked if I would ride (for a consideration) in his cart towards Briançon. He was inquisitive as to my knowledge of his district, and at last asked, " Have you been at La Saussaz ? " " Yes." " Well, then, I tell you, *you saw there some of the first people in the world.*" " Yes," I said, " they were primitive, certainly." But he was serious, and went on—" Yes, real brave people " ; and, slapping his knee to give emphasis, " *but that they are first-rate for minding the cows !* "

After this he became communicative. " You thought, probably," said he, " when I offered to take you down, that I was some poor——, not worth a *sou* ; but I will tell you, that was my mountain ! *my* mountain ! that you saw at La Saussaz ; they were *my* cows ! a hundred of them altogether." " Why, you are rich." " Passably rich. I have another mountain on the Col du Galibier, and another at Villeneuve." He (although a common peasant in outward appearance) confessed to being worth four thousand pounds.

was by the Col de Martignare ; and also that from the aforesaid col it was possible to ascend a lofty summit, called by
him the Bec du Grenier, also called Aiguille du Goléon. On
referring, however, to the Sardinian survey, we found there
depicted, to the east of the Col de Martignare, not *one* peak
bearing the above *two* names, but *two distinct summits* ; one—
just above the col—the Bec du Grenier (the height of which
was not stated) ; the other, still farther to the east, and somewhat to the south of the watershed—the Aiguille du Goléon
(11,251 English feet in height), with a very considerable glacier—
the Glacier Lombard—between the two. On the French map,[1]
on the other hand, neither of the above names was to be found,
but a peak called Aiguille de la Saussaz (10,876 feet) was placed
in the position assigned to the Bec du Grenier in the Sardinian
map ; while farther to the east was a second and nameless peak
(10,841), not at all in the position given to the Aiguille du
Goléon, of which and of the Glacier Lombard there was not
a sign. All this was very puzzling and unsatisfactory ; but
as we had no doubt of being able to climb one of the points
to the east of the Col de Martignare (which overhung the
Ravine de la Saussaz), we determined to make that col the
basis of our operations.' [2]

We left the chalets at 4.15 a.m., " under a shower of good
wishes from our hostesses," proceeded at first towards the
upper end of the ravine, then doubled back up a long buttress
which projects in an unusual way, and went towards the Col
de Martignare ; but before arriving at its summit we again
doubled, and resumed the original course. At 6 a.m. we stood
on the watershed, and followed it towards the east ; keeping
for some distance strictly to the ridge, and afterwards diverging
a little to the south to avoid a considerable secondary aiguille,

---

[1] We had seen a tracing from the unpublished sheets of the French Government Survey.

[2] The paragraphs in single inverted commas in Chaps. VII, VIII and IX
are extracted from the Journal of Mr. A. W. Moore.

which prevented a straight track being made to the summit at which we were aiming. At 9.15 we stood on its top, and saw at once the lay of the land.

We found that our peak was one of four which enclosed a plateau that was filled by a glacier. Let us call these summits **A, B, C, D** (see plan on p. 138). We stood upon **C**, which was almost exactly the same elevation as **B**, but was higher than **D**, and lower than **A**. Peak **A** was the highest of the four, and was about 200 feet higher than **B** and **C** ; we identified it as the Aiguille du Goléon (French survey, 11,251 feet). Peak **D** we considered was the Bec du Grenier ; and, in default of other names, we called **B** and **C** the Aiguilles de la Saussaz. The glacier flowed in a south-easterly direction, and was the Glacier Lombard.

Peaks **B** and **C** overhung the Ravine de la Saussaz, and were connected with another aiguille—**E**—which did the same. A continuation of the ridge out of which these three aiguilles rose joined the Aiguilles d'Arves. The head of the Ravine de la Saussaz was therefore encircled by six peaks ; three of which it was convenient to term the Aiguilles de la Saussaz, and the others were the Aiguilles d'Arves.[1]

We were fortunate in the selection of our summit. Not to speak of other things, it gave a grand view of the ridge which culminates in the peak called La Meije (13,081 feet), which used to be mentioned by travellers under the name Aiguille du Midi de la Grave. The view of this mountain from the village of La Grave can hardly be spoken of too highly,—it is one of the very finest road-views in the Alps. The Ortler from the Stelvio is, in fact, its only worthy competitor ; and the opinions generally of those who have seen the two views are in favour of the former. But from La Grave one can no more appreciate the

---

[1] It would be unprofitable to enter into a discussion of the confusion of these names at greater length. It is sufficient to say that they were confounded in a most perplexing manner by all the authorities we were able to consult, and also by the natives on the spot.

noble proportions and the towering height of the Meije, than understand the symmetry of the dome of St. Paul's by gazing upon it from the churchyard. To see it fairly, one must be placed at a greater distance and at a greater height.

I shall not try to describe the Meije. The same words, and the same phrases, have to do duty for one and another mountain ; their repetition becomes wearisome ; and 'tis a discouraging fact that any description, however true or however elaborated, seldom or never gives an idea of the reality.

Yet the Meije deserves more than a passing notice. It was the last great Alpine peak to be trodden by the foot of man, and one can hardly speak in exaggerated terms of its jagged ridges, torrential glaciers, and tremendous precipices.[1] But were I to discourse upon these things without the aid of pictures, or to endeavour to convey in *words* a sense of the loveliness of *curves*, of the beauty of *colour*, or of the harmonies of *sound*, I should try to accomplish that which is impossible ; and, at the best, should succeed in but giving an impression that the things spoken of may have been pleasant to hear or to behold, although they are perfectly incomprehensible to read about. Let me therefore avoid these things, not because I have no love for or thought of them, but because they cannot be translated into language ; and presently, when topographical details must, of necessity, be returned to again, I will endeavour to relieve the poverty of the pen by a free use of the pencil.

Whilst we sat upon the Aiguille de la Saussaz, our attention

[1] The ridge called La Meije runs from E.S.E. to W.N.W., and is crowned by numerous aiguilles of tolerably equal elevation. Two of the highest are towards the eastern and western ends of the ridge, and are rather more than a mile apart. To the former the French surveyors assign a height of 12,832, and to the latter 13,081 feet.

In 1869 I carefully examined the eastern end of the ridge from the top of the Col de Lautaret, and saw that the summit at that end could be ascended by following a long glacier which descends from it towards the N.E. into the valley of Arsine. I thought that the *highest* summit might present difficulties, but was possibly accessible.

was concentrated on a point which was immediately opposite—
on a gap or cleft between the Meije and the mountain called
the Râteau. It was, indeed, in order to have a good view of
this place that we made the ascent of the Aiguille. It (that is
the gap itself) looked, as my companions remarked, obtrusively
and offensively a pass. It had not been crossed, but it ought to
have been ; and this seemed to have been recognized by the
natives, who called it, very appropriately, the Brèche de la
Meije.

I had seen this gap in 1860, and again in 1861, but had not
then thought about getting through it. Our information in
respect to it was chiefly derived from a photographic reproduction of the then unpublished sheet 189 of the great map of
France, which Mr. Tuckett had placed at our disposal. It was
evident from this map that if we could succeed in passing the
Brèche, we should make the most direct route possible between
the villages of La Grave and La Bérarde, and that the distance
between these two places, by this route, would be less than one-
third that of the ordinary way *via* the villages of Le Freney
and Vénosc. It may occur to some of my readers, why had
not this been done before ? For the very sound reason that the
valley on the southern side (Vallon des Etançons) is uninhabited,
and La Bérarde itself is a miserable village, without interest, without commerce, and almost without population. Why then did
we wish to cross it ? Because we were bound for the Pointe
des Ecrins, to which La Bérarde was the nearest inhabited place.

When we sat upon the Aiguille de la Saussaz, we were rather
despondent about our prospects of crossing the Brèche, which
seemed to present a combination of all that was formidable.
There was, evidently, but one way by which it could be approached. We saw that at the top of the pass there was a steep
wall of snow or ice (so steep that it was most likely ice) protected
at its base by a big schrund or moat, which severed it from the
snow-fields below. Then (tracking our course downwards) we
saw undulating snow-fields leading down to a great glacier.

The snow-fields would be easy work, but the glacier was riven and broken in every direction ; huge crevasses seemed to extend entirely across it in some places, and everywhere it had that strange twisted look, which tells of the unequal motion of the ice. Where could we get on to it ? At its base it came to a violent end, being cut short by a cliff, over which it poured periodical avalanches, as we saw by a great triangular bed of débris below. We could not venture there,—the glacier must be taken in flank. On which side ? Not on the west,— no one could climb those cliffs. It must, if anywhere, be by the rocks on the east ; and *they* looked as if they were *roches moutonnées.* So we hurried down to La Grave, to hear what Melchior Anderegg (who had just passed through the village with the family of our friend Walker) had to say on the matter. Who is Melchior

MELCHIOR ANDEREGG IN 1864.

Anderegg ? Those who ask the question cannot have been in Alpine Switzerland, where the name of Melchior is as well known as the name of Napoleon. Melchior, too, is an Emperor in his way—a very Prince among guides. His empire is amongst the " eternal snows,"—his sceptre is an ice-axe.

Melchior Anderegg, more familiarly, and perhaps more generally known simply as Melchior, was born at Zaun, near Meiringen, on April 6, 1828. He was first brought into public notice in Hinchliff's *Summer Months in the Alps*, and was known to very few persons at the time that little work was published. In 1855 he was " Boots " at the Grimsel hotel, and in those days, when he went out on expeditions, it was for the benefit of his master, the proprietor ; Melchior himself only got the *Trinkgeld*. In 1856 he migrated to the Schwarenbach inn on the Gemmi, where he employed his time in carving objects for sale. In 1858 he made several expeditions with Messrs. Hinchliff and Stephen, and proved to his employers that he possessed first-rate skill, indomitable courage, and an admirable character. His position has never been doubtful since that year, and for a long time there has been no guide whose services have been more in request. He is usually engaged a year in advance.

It would be almost an easier task to say what he has not done than to catalogue his achievements. Invariable success attends his arms. He leads his followers to victory, but not to death. I believe that no accident has ever befallen travellers in his charge. Like his friend Almer, he can be called a *safe* man. It is the highest praise that can be given to a first-rate guide.

Early in the afternoon we found ourselves in the little inn at La Grave, on the great Lautaret road ; a rickety, tumble-down sort of place, with nothing stable about it, as Moore wittily remarked, except the smell.[1] Melchior had gone, and had left behind a note which said, " I think the passage of the Brèche is possible, but that it will be very difficult." His opinion coincided with ours, and we went to sleep, expecting to be afoot about eighteen or twenty hours on the morrow.

At 2.40 the next morning we left La Grave, in a few minutes crossed the Romanche, and at 4 a.m. got to the moraine of the

---

[1] The justness of the observation will be felt by those who knew La Grave in or before 1864. At that time the horses of the couriers who were passing from Grenoble to Briançon, and *vice versa*, were lodged immediately underneath the *salle-à-manger* and bedrooms, and a pungent, steamy odour rose from them through the cracks in the floor, and constantly pervaded the whole house.

eastern branch of the glacier that descends from the Brèche.[1]
The rocks by which we intended to ascend were placed between

SCALE, THREE MILES TO
AN INCH.

the two branches of this glacier, and
still looked smooth and unbroken. By
five o'clock we were upon them, and
saw that we had been deluded by them.
No carpenter could have planned a more
convenient staircase. They were *not*
moutonnées, their smooth look from a
distance was only owing to their singular firmness. 'It was really quite a
pleasure to scale such delightful rocks.
We felt the stone held the boot so well,
that, without making a positive effort to
do so, it would be almost impossible to
slip.' In an hour we had risen above
the most crevassed portion of the glacier,
and began to look for a way on to it.
Just at the right place there was a patch
of old snow at the side, and, instead of
gaining the ice by desperate acrobatic
feats, we passed from the rocks on to it
as easily as one walks across a gangway.
At half-past six we were on the centre of
the glacier, and the inhabitants of La
Grave turned out *en masse* into the
road, and watched us with amazement as they witnessed the
falsification of their confident predictions. Well might they
stare, for our little caravan, looking to them like a train of flies
on a wall, crept up and up, without hesitation and without a
halt—lost to their sight one minute as it dived into a crevasse,
then seen again clambering up the other side. The higher we
rose, the easier became the work. The angles lessened, and our

[1] Our route from La Grave to La Bérarde will be seen on the accompanying
map

pace increased. The snow remained shadowed, and we walked as easily as on a high road ; and when (at 7.45) the summit of the Brèche was seen, we rushed at it as furiously as if it had been a breach in the wall of a fortress, carried the moat by a dash, with a push behind and a pull before, stormed the steep slope above, and at 8.50 stood in the little gap, 10,827 feet above the level of the sea. The Brèche was won. Well might they stare ; five hours and a quarter had sufficed for 6,500 feet of ascent.[1] We screamed triumphantly as they turned in to breakfast.

All mountaineers know how valuable it is to study beforehand an intended route over new ground from a height at some distance. None but blunderers fail to do so, if it is possible ; and one cannot do so too thoroughly. As a rule, the closer one approaches underneath a summit, the more difficult it is to pick out a path with judgment. Inferior peaks seem unduly important, subordinate ridges are exalted, and slopes conceal points beyond ; and if one blindly undertakes an ascent, without having acquired a tolerable notion of the relative importance of the parts, and of their positions to one another, it will be miraculous if great difficulties are not encountered.

But although the examination of an intended route from a height at a distance will tell one (who knows the meaning of the things he is looking at) a good deal, and will enable him to steer clear of many difficulties against which he might otherwise blindly run, it will seldom allow one to pronounce positively upon the practicability or impracticability of the whole of the route. No living man, for example, can pronounce positively from a distance in regard to rocks. There is an illustration of this in the case which has just been mentioned. Three of the ablest and most experienced guides concurred in thinking that the rocks we should have to pass would be found very difficult, and they presented no difficulty whatever. In truth, the sounder

---

[1] Taking one kind of work with another, a thousand feet of height per hour is about as much as is usually accomplished on great Alpine ascents.

and less broken up are rocks, the more impracticable do they
usually look from a distance ; while soft and easily rent rocks,
which are often amongst the most difficult and perilous to
climb, very frequently look from afar as if they might be
traversed by a child.

It is possible to decide with greater certainty in regard to the
practicability of glaciers. When one is seen to have few open
crevasses (and this may be told from a great distance), then we
know that it is *possible* to traverse it ; but to what extent it, or
a glacier that is much broken up by crevasses, will be troublesome, will depend upon the width and length of the crevasses,
and upon the angles of the surface of the glacier itself. A
glacier may be greatly crevassed, but the fissures may be so
narrow that there is no occasion to deviate from a straight line
when passing across them ; or a glacier may have few open
crevasses, and yet may be practically impassable on account of
the steepness of the angles of its surface. Nominally, a man
with an axe can go anywhere upon a glacier, but in practice
it is found that to move freely upon ice one must have to deal
only with small angles. It is thus necessary to know approximately the angles of the surfaces of a glacier before it is possible
to determine whether it will afford easy travelling, or will be
so difficult as to be (for all practical purposes) impassable. This
cannot be told by looking at glaciers in full face from a distance ;
they must be seen in profile ; and it is often desirable to examine
them both from the front and in profile,—to do the first to study
the direction of the crevasses, to note where they are most and
least numerous ; and the second to see whether its angles are
moderate or great. Should they be very steep, it may be better
to avoid them altogether, and to mount even by difficult rocks ;
but upon glaciers of *gentle* inclination, and with few open
crevasses, better progress can always be made than upon the
easiest rocks.

We did not trouble ourselves much with these matters when
we sat on the top of the Brèche. Our day's work was as good

as over (for we knew from Messrs. Mathews and Bonney that there was no difficulty upon the other side), and we abandoned ourselves to ease and luxury ; wondering, alternately, as we gazed upon the Râteau and the Ecrins, how the one mountain could possibly hold itself together, and whether the other would hold out against *us*. The former looked ' so rotten that it seemed as if a puff of wind or a clap of thunder might dash the whole fabric to pieces ' ; while the latter asserted itself the monarch of the group, and towered head and shoulders above all the rest of the peaks which form the great horse-shoe of Dauphiné. At length a cruel rush of cold air made us shiver, and shift our quarters to a little grassy plot, 3,000 feet below— an oasis in a desert—where we lay nearly four hours admiring the splendid wall which protects the summit of the Meije from assault upon this side.[1] Then we tramped down the Vallon des Etançons ; a howling wilderness, the abomination of desola- tion ; destitute alike of animal or vegetable life ; pathless, of course ; suggestive of chaos, but of little else ; covered almost throughout its entire length with débris from the size of a walnut up to that of a house ; in a word, it looked as if half a dozen first-class moraines had been carted and shot into it. Our tempers were soured by constant pitfalls ; ' it was impossible to take the eyes from the feet, and if an unlucky individual so much as blew his nose, without standing still to perform the operation, the result was either an instantaneous tumble, or a barked shin, or a half-twisted ankle. There was no end to it, and we became more savage at every step, unanimously agree- ing that no power on earth would ever induce us to walk up or down this particular valley again.' It was not just to the valley, which was enclosed by noble mountains,—unknown, it is true, but worthy of a great reputation, and which, if placed

[1] This wall may be described as an exaggerated Gemmi, as seen from Leukerbad. From the highest summit of La Meije right down to the Glacier des Etançons (a depth of about 3,200 feet), the cliff is all but perpendicular, and appeared to us to be completely unassailable.

in other districts, would be sought after, and cited as types of daring form and graceful outline.

Not so very long ago, perhaps, the Vallon des Etançons wore a more cheerful aspect. It is well known that many of the French Alpine valleys have rapidly deteriorated in quite modern

THE VALLON DES ETANÇONS (LOOKING TOWARDS LA BERARDE).[1]

times. Blanqui pointed out, a few years ago, some of the causes which have brought this about, in an address to the Academy of Sciences ; and, although his remarks are not entirely applicable to this very valley, the chapter may be properly closed with some of his vigorous sentences. He said, " The abuse of the right of pasturage, and the felling of the woods, have stripped the soil of all its grass and all its trees, and the scorching sun bakes it to the consistence of porphyry. When moistened by

[1] The drawing was inadvertently made the right way on the wood, and the view is now *reversed* in consequence.

the rain, as it has neither support nor cohesion, it rolls down into the valleys, sometimes in floods resembling black, yellow, or reddish lava, and sometimes in streams of pebbles, and even huge blocks of stone, which pour down with a frightful roar. . . . Vast deposits of flinty pebbles, many feet in thickness, which have rolled down and spread far over the plain, surround large trees, bury even their tops, and rise above them. . . . The gorges, under the influence of the sun which cracks and shivers to fragments the very rocks, and of the rain which sweeps them down, penetrate deeper and deeper into the heart of the mountain, while the beds of the torrents issuing from them are sometimes raised several feet in a single year by the débris. . . . An indirect proof of the increase of the evil is to be found in the depopulation of the country. . . . Unless prompt and energetic measures are taken, it is easy to fix the epoch when the French Alps will be but a desert. . . . Every year will aggravate the evil, and in half a century France will count more ruins, and a department the less." [1]

[1] Quoted from Marsh's *Man and Nature.*

CHAPTER VIII

THE FIRST ASCENT OF THE POINTE DES ECRINS

" Filled with high mountains, rearing their heads as if to reach to heaven, crowned with glaciers, and fissured with immense chasms, where lie the eternal snows guarded by bare and rugged cliffs ; offering the most varied sights, and enjoying all temperatures ; and containing everything that is most curious and interesting, the most simple and the most sublime, the most smiling and the most severe, the most beautiful and the most awful ; such is the department of the High Alps."

LADOUCETTE.

BEFORE five o'clock on the afternoon of June 23, we were trotting down the steep path that leads into La Bérarde. We put up, of course, with the chasseur-guide Rodier (who, as usual, was smooth and smiling), and, after congratulations were over, we returned to the exterior to watch for the arrival of one Alexandre Pic, who had been sent overnight with our baggage *via* Le Freney and Vénosc. But when night fell, and no Pic appeared, we saw that our plans must be modified ; for he was necessary to our very existence—he carried our food, our tobacco, our all. So, after some discussion, it was agreed that a portion of our programme should be abandoned, that the night of the 24th should be passed at the head of the Glacier de Bonnepierre, and that, on the 25th, a push should be made for the summit of the Ecrins. We then went to straw.[1]

[1] In 1887, a little inn was opened at La Bérarde, under the auspices of the Société des Touristes du Dauphiné.

Our porter Pic strolled in next morning with a very jaunty air, and we seized upon our tooth-brushes ; but, upon looking for the cigars, we found starvation staring us in the face. " Hullo ! Monsieur Pic, where are the cigars ? " " Gentlemen," he began, " I am desolated ! " and then, quite pat, he told a long rigmarole about a fit on the road, of brigands, thieves, of their ransacking the knapsacks when he was insensible, and of finding them gone when he revived ! " Ah ! Monsieur Pic, we see

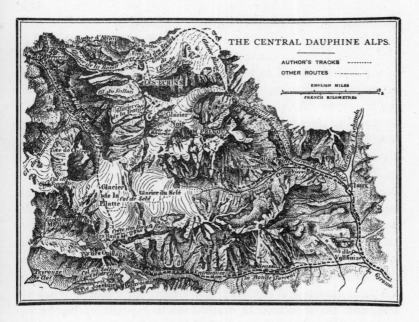

what it is, you have smoked them yourself ! " " Gentlemen, I never smoke, *never* ! " Whereupon we inquired secretly if he was known to smoke, and found that he was. However, he said that he had never spoken truer words, and perhaps he had not, for he was reported to be the greatest liar in Dauphiné !

We were now able to start, and set out at 1.15 p.m. to bivouac upon the Glacier de Bonnepierre, accompanied by Rodier, who staggered under a load of blankets. Many slopes had to be mounted, and many torrents to be crossed, all of which has been described by Mr. Tuckett.[1] We, however, avoided the difficulties he experienced with the torrents by crossing them high up, where they were subdivided. But when we got on to the moraine on the right bank of the glacier (or, properly speaking, on to one of the moraines, for there are several), mists descended, to our great hindrance ; and it was 5.30 before we arrived on the spot at which it was intended to camp.

Each one selected his nook, and we then joined round a grand fire made by our men. Fortnum and Mason's portable soup was sliced up and brewed, and was excellent ; but it should be said that before it *was* excellent, three times the quantity named in the directions had to be used. Art is required in drinking as in making this soup, and one point is this—always let your friends drink first ; not only because it is more polite, but because the soup has a tendency to burn the mouth if taken too hot, and one drink of the bottom is worth two of the top, as all the goodness settles.

' While engaged in these operations, the mist that enveloped the glacier and surrounding peaks was becoming thinner ; little bits of blue sky appeared here and there, until suddenly, when we were looking towards the head of the glacier, far, far above us, at an almost inconceivable height, in a tiny patch of blue, appeared a wonderful rocky pinnacle, bathed in the beams of the fast-sinking sun. We were so electrified by the glory of the sight that it was some seconds before we realized what we saw, and understood that that astounding point, removed apparently miles from the earth, was one of the highest summits of Les Ecrins ; and that we hoped, before another sun had set, to have stood upon an even loftier pinnacle. The mists rose and fell, presenting us with a series of dissolving views of ravishing grandeur, and finally died away, leaving the glacier and its mighty bounding precipices under an exquisite pale blue sky, free from a single speck of cloud.'

[1] *Alpine Journal,* December 1863.

The night passed over without anything worth mention, but we had occasion to observe in the morning an instance of the curious evaporation that is frequently noticeable in the High Alps. On the previous night we had hung up on a knob of rock our mackintosh bag containing five bottles of Rodier's bad wine. In the morning, although the stopper appeared to have been in all night, about four-fifths had evaporated. It was strange ; my friends had not taken any, neither had I, and the guides each declared that they had not seen anyone touch the bag. In fact, it was clear that there was no explanation of the phenomenon, but in the dryness of the air. Still it is remarkable that the dryness of the air (or the evaporation of wine) is always greatest when a stranger is in one's party. The dryness caused by the presence of even a single Chamonix porter is sometimes so great that not four-fifths but the entire quantity disappears. For a time I found difficulty in combating this phenomenon, but at last discovered that if I used the wine-flask as a pillow during the night, the evaporation was completely stopped.

At 4 a.m. we moved off across the glacier in single file towards the foot of a great gully, which led from the upper slopes of the Glacier de Bonnepierre, to the lowest point in the ridge that connects the Ecrins with the mountain called Roche Faurio,— cheered by Rodier, who now returned with his wraps to La Bérarde. This gully (or *couloir*) was discovered and descended by Mr. Tuckett, and we will now return for a minute to the explorations of that accomplished mountaineer.

In the year 1862 he had the good fortune to obtain from the *Dépôt de la Guerre* at Paris, a MS. copy of the then unpublished sheet 189 of the map of France, and, with it in hand, he swept backwards and forwards across the central Dauphiné Alps, untroubled by the doubts as to the identity of peaks, which had perplexed Mr. Macdonald and myself in 1861 ; and, enlightened by it, he was able to point out (which he did in the fairest manner) that we had confounded the Ecrins with another mountain—the Pic Sans Nom. We made this blunder through imperfect knowledge of the district and inaccurate reports of the natives, but it was not an extraordinary one, considering the difficulty that there is in obtaining from any except the very highest summits a complete view of this intricate group.

The situations of the principal summits can be perceived at a glance on the map upon page 157, which is a reproduction of a portion of sheet 189. The main ridge of the chain runs, at this part, nearly north and south. Roche Faurio, at the northern extreme, is 3,716 metres, or 12,192 feet, above the level of the sea. The lowest point between that mountain and the Ecrins (the Col des Ecrins) is 11,000 feet. The ridge again rises, and passes 13,000 feet in the neighbourhood of the Ecrins. The highest summit of that mountain (13,462 feet) is, however, placed a little to the east of and off the main ridge. It then again falls, and in the vicinity of the Col de la Temple it is, perhaps, below 11,000 feet; but immediately to the south of the summit of that pass, there is upon the ridge a point which has been determined by the French surveyors to be 12,323 feet. This peak is without a name.[1] The ridge continues to gain height as we come to the south, and culminates in the mountain which the French surveyors have called Sommet de l'Ailefroide. On the spot it is called, very commonly, the Aléfroide.[2]

Mont Pelvoux is to the east of the Ailefroide and off the main ridge, and the Pic Sans Nom (12,845 feet) is placed between these two mountains. The latter is one of the grandest of the Dauphiné peaks, but it is so shut in by the other mountains that it is seldom seen except from a distance, and then is usually confounded with the neighbouring summits. Its name has been accidentally omitted on the map, but its situation is represented by the large patch of rocks, nearly surrounded by glaciers, that is seen between the words Ailefroide and Mt. Pelvoux.

[1] Now called Pic Coolidge.

[2] It is shown in the engraving facing p. 36. It has several points nearly equally elevated, all of which seem to be accessible. One of them was ascended in 1870.

The lowest depression on the main ridge to the south of the Ailefroide is the Col du Sélé, and the height of this pass, according to Mr. Tuckett, is 10,834 feet.   The ridge soon rises again, and, a littler farther to the south, joins another ridge running nearly east and west.   To a mountain at the junction of these two ridges the Frenchmen have given the singular name Crête des Bœufs Rouges !   The highest point hereabouts is 11,333 feet ; and a little to the west there is another peak (Les Bans) of 11,979 feet.   The main ridge runs from this last-named point, in a north-westerly direction, to the Cols du Says and du Chardon, both of which exceed 10,000 feet.

It will thus be seen that the general elevation of this main ridge is almost equal to that of the range of Mont Blanc, or of the central Pennine Alps ; and if we were to follow it out more completely, or to follow the other ridges surrounding it or radiating from it, we should find that there is a remarkable absence, throughout the entire district, of low gaps and depressions, and that there are an extraordinary number of peaks of medium elevation.[1]   The difficulty which the early explorers of Dauphiné experienced in identifying peaks very much arose from the elevation of the ridges in general being more uniform than is commonly the case in the Alps, and the consequent facile concealment of one point by another.   The difficulty was enhanced by the narrowness and erratic courses of the valleys.

The possession of the " advance copy " of sheet 189 of the French map enabled Mr. Tuckett to grasp most of what I have just said, and much more ; and he added, in 1862, three interesting passes across this part of the chain to those already known. The first, from Ville Vallouise to La Bérarde, via the village of Claux, and the Glaciers du Sélé and de la Pilatte,—this he called the Col du Sélé ; the second, between Ville Vallouise and Villard d'Arène (on the Lautaret road), via Claux and the Glaciers

[1] There are more than twenty peaks exceeding 12,000 feet, and thirty others exceeding 11,000 feet, within the district bounded by the rivers Romanche, Drac, and Durance.

Blanc and d'Arsine,—the Col du Glacier Blanc ; and the third, from Vallouise to La Bérarde, *via* the Glacier Blanc, the Glacier de l'Encula, and the Glacier de Bonnepierre,—the Col des Ecrins.

This last pass was discovered accidentally. Mr. Tuckett set out intending to endeavour to ascend the Pointe des Ecrins, but circumstances were against him, as he relates in the following words :—" Arrived on the plateau " (of the Glacier de l'Encula), " a most striking view of the Ecrins burst upon us, and a hasty inspection encouraged us to hope that its ascent would be practicable. On the sides of La Bérarde and the Glacier Noir it presents, as has been already stated, the most precipitous and inaccessible faces that can well be conceived ; but in the direction of the Glacier de l'Encula, as the upper plateau of the Glacier Blanc is named on the French map, the slopes are less rapid, and immense masses of *névé* and *séracs* cover it nearly to the summit."

" The snow was in very bad order, and as we sank at each step above the knee, it soon became evident that our prospects of success were extremely doubtful. A nearer approach, too, disclosed traces of fresh avalanches, and after much deliberation and a careful examination through the telescope, it was decided that the chances in our favour were too small to render it desirable to waste time in the attempt. . . . I examined the map, from which I perceived that the glacier seen through the gap " (in the ridge running from Roche Faurio to the Ecrins) " to the west, at a great depth below, must be that of Bonnepierre ; and if a descent to its head was practicable, a passage might probably be effected to La Bérarde. On suggesting to Croz and Perren that, though baffled by the state of the snow on the Ecrins, we might still achieve something of interest and impor- tance by discovering a new col, they both heartily assented, and in a few minutes Perren was over the edge, and cutting his way down the rather formidable couloir," etc. etc.[1]

[1] *Alpine Journal*, vol. i., pp. 166–67, Dec. 1863.

This was the couloir at the foot of which we found ourselves at daybreak on the 25th of June 1864 ; but before commencing the relation of our doings upon that eventful day, I must recount the experiences of Messrs. Mathews and Bonney in 1862.

These gentlemen, with the two Croz's, attempted the ascent of the Ecrins a few weeks after Mr. Tuckett had inspected the mountain. On August 26, says Mr. Bonney, " we pushed on, and our hopes each moment rose higher and higher ; even the cautious Michel committed himself so far as to cry, ' Ah, malheureux Ecrins, vous serez bientôt morts,' as we addressed ourselves to the last slope leading up to the foot of the final cone. The old proverb about ' many a slip' was, however, to prove true on this occasion. Arrived at the top of this slope, we found that we were cut off from the peak by a formidable bergschrund, crossed by the rottenest of snow-bridges. We looked to the right and to the left, to see whether it would be possible to get on either arête at its extremity ; but instead of rising directly from the snow, as they appeared to do from below, they were terminated by a wall of rock some forty feet high. There was but one place where the bergschrund was narrow enough to admit of crossing, and there a cliff of ice had to be climbed, and then a path to be cut up a steep slope of snow, before the arête could be reached. At last, after searching in vain for some time, Michel bade us wait a little, and started off to explore the gap separating the highest peak from the snow-dome on the right, and see if it were possible to ascend the rocky wall. Presently he appeared, evidently climbing with difficulty, and at last stood on the arête itself. Again we thought the victory was won, and started off to follow him. Suddenly he called to us to halt, and turned to descend. In a few minutes he stopped. After a long pause he shouted to his brother, saying that he was not able to return by the way he had ascended. Jean was evidently uneasy about him, and for some time we watched him with much anxiety. At length he began to hew out steps in the snow along the face of the peak towards us.

Jean now left us, and, making for the ice-cliff mentioned above, chopped away until, after about a quarter of an hour's labour, he contrived, somehow or other, to worm himself up it, and began to cut steps to meet his brother. Almost every step appeared to be cut right through the snowy crust into the hard ice below, and an incipient stream of snow came hissing down the sides of the peak as they dug it away with their axes. Michel could not have been much more than 100 yards from us, and yet it was full three-quarters of an hour before the brothers met. This done, they descended carefully, burying their axe-heads deep in the snow at every step.

"Michel's account was that he had reached the arête with great difficulty, and saw that it was practicable for some distance, in fact, as far as he could see ; but that the snow was in a most dangerous condition, being very incoherent and resting on hard ice ; that when he began to descend in order to tell us this, he found the rocks so smooth and slippery that return was impossible ; and that for some little time he feared that he should not be able to extricate himself, and was in considerable danger. Of course the arête could have been reached by the way our guides had descended, but it was so evident that their judgment was against proceeding, that we did not feel justified in urging them on. We had seen so much of them that we felt sure they would never hang back unless there was real danger, and so we gave the word for retreating." [1]

On both of these expeditions there was fine weather and plenty of time. On each occasion the parties slept out at, and started from, a considerable elevation, and arrived at the base of the final peak of the Ecrins early in the day, and with plenty of superfluous energy. Guides and travellers alike, on each occasion, were exceptional men, experienced mountaineers, who had proved their skill and courage on numerous antecedent occasions, and who were not accustomed to turn away from a thing merely because it was difficult. On each occasion the

[1] *Alpine Journal*, vol. i., pp. 72–73, June 1863.

attempts were abandoned because the state of the snow on and below the final peak was such that avalanches were anticipated ; and, according to the judgment of those who were concerned, there was such an amount of *positive danger* from this condition of things, that it was unjustifiable to persevere.

We learnt privately, from Messrs. Mathews, Bonney, and Tuckett, that unless the snow was in a good state upon the final peak (that is to say, coherent and stable), we should probably be of the same opinion as themselves ; and that although the face of the mountain fronting the Glacier de l'Encula was much less steep than its other faces, and was apparently the *only* side upon which an attempt was at all likely to be successful, it was nevertheless so steep, that for several days, at least, after a fall of snow upon it, the chances in favour of avalanches would be considerable.

The reader need scarcely be told, after all that has been said about the variableness of weather in the High Alps, the chance was small indeed that we should find upon the 25th of June, or any other set day, the precise condition of affairs that was deemed indispensable for success. We had such confidence in the judgment of our friends, that it was understood amongst us the ascent should be abandoned, unless the conditions were manifestly favourable.

By five minutes to six we were at the top of the gully (a first-rate couloir, about 1,000 feet high), and within sight of our work. Hard, thin, and wedge-like as the Ecrins had looked from afar, it had never looked so hard and so thin as it did when we emerged from the top of the couloir through the gap in the ridge. No tender shadows spoke of broad and rounded ridges, but sharp and shadowless its serrated edges stood out against the clear sky. It had been said that the route must be taken by one of the ridges of the final peak, but both were alike repellent, hacked and notched in numberless places. They reminded me of my failure on the Dent d'Hérens in 1863, and of a place on a similar ridge, from which advance or retreat was alike difficult.

But, presuming one or other of these ridges or arêtes was practicable, there remained the task of getting to them, for completely round the base of the final peak swept an enormous bergschrund, almost separating it from the slopes which lay beneath. It was evident thus early that the ascent would not be accomplished without exertion, and that it would demand

THE POINTE DES ECRINS, FROM THE COL DU GALIBIER.

all our faculties and all our time. In more than one respect we were favoured. The mists were gone, the day was bright and perfectly calm ; there had been a long stretch of fine weather beforehand, and the snow was in excellent order ; and, most important of all, the last new snow which had fallen on the final peak, unable to support itself, had broken away and rolled in a mighty avalanche, over schrund, névé, séracs, over hills and valleys in the glacier (levelling one and filling the other), completely down to the col, where it lay in huge jammed masses, powerless to harm us ; and had made a broad track, almost a road, over which, for part of the way at least, we might advance with rapidity.

We took in all this in a few minutes, and seeing there was no time to be lost, despatched a hasty meal, left knapsacks, provisions, and all incumbrances by the col, started again at half-past six, and made direct for the left side of the schrund, for it was there alone that a passage was practicable. We crossed it at 8.10. Our route can now be followed upon the annexed outline. The arrow marked **D** points out the direction of the Glacier de Bonnepierre. The ridge in front, that extends right across, is the ridge that is partially shown on the top of the map at page 157, leading from Roche Faurio towards the W.N.W.

We arrived upon the plateau of the Glacier de l'Encula, behind this ridge, from the direction of **D**, and then made a nearly straight track to the left hand of the bergschrund at **A**.

Thus far there was no trouble, but the nature of the work changed immediately. If we regard the upper 700 feet alone of the final peak of the Ecrins, it may be described as a three-sided pyramid. One face is towards the Glacier Noir, and forms one of the sheerest precipices in the Alps. Another is towards the Glacier du Vallon, and is less steep, and less uniform in angle than the first. The third is towards the Glacier de l'Encula, and it was by this one we approached the summit. Imagine a triangular plane, 700 or 800 feet high, set at an angle exceeding 50° ; let it be smooth, glassy ; let the uppermost edges be cut into spikes and teeth, and let them be bent, some one way, some another. Let the glassy face be covered with minute fragments of rock, scarcely attached, but varnished with ice ; imagine this, and then you will have a very faint idea of the face of the Ecrins on which we stood. It was not possible to avoid detaching stones, which, as they fell, caused words unmentionable to rise. The greatest friends would have reviled each other in such a situation. We gained the eastern arête, and endeavoured for half an hour to work upwards towards the summit ; but it was useless (each yard of progress cost an incredible time) ; and having no desire to form the acquaintance of the Glacier Noir in a precipitate manner, we beat a retreat, and returned to the schrund. We again held a council, and it was unanimously decided that we should be beaten if we could not cut along the upper edge of the schrund, and, when nearly beneath the summit, work up to it. So Croz took off his coat and went to work ;— on ice,—not that black ice so often mentioned and so seldom seen, though on ice as hard as ice could be. Weary work for the guides. Croz cut for more than half an hour, and we did not seem to have advanced at all. Someone behind, seeing how great the labour was, and how slow the progress, suggested that after all we might do better on the arête. Croz's blood was up, and indignant at this slight on his powers, he ceased working, turned in his steps, and rushed towards me with a haste that made me shudder : " By all means let us go there, the sooner the better." No slight was intended, and he resumed his work, after a time being relieved by Almer. Half-past ten came ; an hour had passed ; they were still cutting. Dreary work for us, for no capering about could be done here. Hand as well as foot holes were necessary ; the fingers and toes got very cold ; the ice, as it boomed in bounding down the bergschrund, was very suggestive ; conversation was very restricted, separated as we were by our tether of 20 feet apiece. Another hour passed. We were now almost immediately below the summit, and we stopped to look up. We were nearly as far off it (vertically) as we had been more than three hours before. The day seemed going against us. The only rocks near at hand were scattered ; no bigger than tea-cups, and most of these, we found afterwards,

POINTE DES ECRINS, FROM THE COL EMILE PIC.

were glazed with ice. Time forbade cutting right up to the summit, even had it been possible, which it was not. We decided to go up to the ridge again by means of the rocks ; but had we not had a certain confidence in each other, it unquestionably would not have been done ; for this, it must be understood, was a situation where not only *might* a slip have been fatal to everyone, but it would have been so beyond doubt : nothing, moreover, was easier than to make one. It was a place where all had to work in unison, where there must be no slackening of the rope, and no undue tension. For another hour we were in this trying situation, and at 12.30 we gained the arête again, at a much higher point (**B**), close to the summit. Our men were, I am afraid, well-nigh worn out. Cutting up a couloir 1,000 feet high was not the right sort of preparation for work of this kind. Be it so or not, we were all glad to rest for a short time, for we had not sat down a minute since leaving the col six hours before. Almer, however, was restless, knowing that midday was past, and that much remained to be accomplished, and untied himself, and commenced working towards the summit. Connecting the teeth of rock were beds of snow, and Almer, only a few feet from me, was crossing the top of one of these, when suddenly, without a moment's warning, it broke away under him, and plunged down on to the glacier. As he staggered for a second, one foot in the act of stepping, and the other on the falling mass, I thought him lost ; but he happily fell on to the right side and stopped himself. Had he taken the step with his right instead of the left foot, he would, in all probability, have fallen several hundred feet without touching anything, and would not have been arrested before reaching the glacier, a vertical distance of at least 3,000 feet.

Small, ridiculously small, as the distance was to the summit, we were occupied nearly another hour before it was gained. Almer was a few feet in front, and he, with characteristic modesty, hesitated to step on the highest point, and drew back to allow us to pass. A cry was raised for Croz, who had done the chief part of the work, but he declined the honour, and we marched on to the top simultaneously ; that is to say, clustered round it, a yard or two below, for it was much too small to get upon.

According to my custom, I bagged a piece from off the highest rock [1] (chlorite slate), and I found afterwards that it had a striking similarity to the final peak of the Ecrins. I have noticed the same thing on other occasions,[2] and it is worthy of remark that not only do fragments of such rock as limestone often present the charac-

FRAGMENT FROM THE SUMMIT OF THE
POINTE DES ECRINS.

teristic forms of the cliffs from which they have been broken, but that morsels of mica slate will represent, in a wonderful manner, the identical shape of the peaks of which they have formed part. Why should it not be so, if the mountain's mass is more or less homogeneous ? The same causes which produce the small forms fashion the large ones ; the same influences are at work ; the same frost and rain give shape to the mass as well as to its parts.

Did space permit me, I could give a very poor idea of the view, but it will be readily imagined that a panorama extending over as much ground as the whole of England is one worth taking some trouble to see, and one which is not often to be seen even in the Alps. No clouds obscured it, and a list of the summits that we saw would include nearly all the highest peaks of the chain. I saw the Pelvoux now—as I had seen the Ecrins

[1] This piece of rock is now in the possession of the Alpine Club.

[2] The most remarkable example which has come under my notice is referred to in Chapter XX.

from it three years before—across the basin of the Glacier Noir. It is a splendid mountain, although in height it is equalled, if not surpassed, by its neighbour the Ailefroide.

We could stay on the summit only a short time, and at a quarter to two prepared for the descent. Now, as we looked down, and thought of what we had passed over in coming up, we one and all hesitated about returning the same way. Moore said, no. Walker said the same, and I too ; the guides were both of the same mind : this, be it remarked, although we had considered that there was no chance whatever of getting up any other way. But those " last rocks " were not to be forgotten. Had they only protruded to a moderate extent, or had they been merely glazed, we should doubtless still have tried. But they were not reasonable rocks,—they would neither allow us to hold, nor would do it themselves. So we turned to the western arête, trusting to luck that we should find a way down to the schrund, and some means of getting over it afterwards. Our faces were a tolerable index to our thoughts, and apparently the thoughts of the party were not happy ones. Had anyone then said to me, " You are a great fool for coming here," I should have answered with humility, " It is too true." And had my monitor gone on to say, " Swear you will never ascend another mountain if you get down safely," I am inclined to think I should have taken the oath. In fact, the game here was not worth the risk. The guides felt it as well as ourselves and, as Almer led off, he remarked, with more piety than logic, " The good God has brought us up, and he will take us down in safety," which showed pretty well what he was thinking about.

The ridge down which we now endeavoured to make our way was not inferior in difficulty to the other. Both were serrated to an extent that made it impossible to keep strictly to them, and obliged us to descend occasionally for some distance on the northern face and then mount again. Both were so rotten that the most experienced of our party, as well as the least, continually upset blocks large and small. Both arêtes were so narrow, so thin, that it was often a matter for speculation on which side an unstable block would fall.

At one point it seemed that we should be obliged to return to the summit and try the other way down. We were on the very edge of the arête. On one side was the enormous precipice facing the Pelvoux, which is not far from perpendicular ; on the other a slope exceeding 50°. A deep notch brought us to an abrupt halt. Almer, who was leading, advanced cautiously to the edge on hands and knees, and peered over ; his care was by no means unnecessary, for the rocks had broken away from under us unexpectedly several times. In this position he gazed down for some moments, and then, without a word, turned his head and looked at us. His face *may* have expressed apprehension or alarm, but it certainly did not show hope or joy. We learned that there was no means of getting down, and that we must, if we wanted to pass the notch, jump across on to an unstable block on the other side. It was decided that it should be done, and Almer, with a larger extent of rope than usual, jumped. The rock swayed as he came down upon it, but he clutched a large mass with both arms and brought himself to anchor. That which was both difficult and dangerous for the first man was easy enough for the others, and we got across with less trouble than I expected ; stimulated by Croz' perfectly just observation, that if we couldn't get across there we were not likely to get down the other way.

We had now arrived at **C**, and could no longer continue on the arête, so we commenced descending the face again. Before long we were close to the schrund, but unable to see what it was like at this part, as the upper edge bent over. Two hours had already passed since leaving the summit, and it began to be highly probable that we should have to spend a night on the Glacier Blanc. Almer, who yet led, cut steps right down to the edge, but still he could not see below. Therefore, warning us to hold tight, he made his whole body rigid, and (standing in the large step which he had cut for the purpose), had the

DESCENDING THE WESTERN ARETE OF THE POINTE DES ECRINS.

upper part of his person lowered out until he saw what he wanted. He shouted that our work was finished, made me come close to the edge and untie myself, advanced the others until he had rope enough, and then with a loud *jodel* jumped down on to soft snow. Partly by skill and partly by luck he had hit the crevasse at its easiest point, and we had only to make a downward jump of eight or ten feet.

We had been more than eight hours and a half accomplishing the ascent of the final peak, which, according to an observation by Mr. Bonney in 1862, is only 525 feet high.[1] During this period we had not stopped for more than half an hour, and our nerves and muscles had been kept at the highest degree of tension the whole time. It may be imagined that we accepted the ordinary conditions of glacier travelling as an agreeable relief, and that that which at another time might have seemed formidable we treated as the veriest bagatelle. Late in the day as it was, and soft as was the snow, we put on such pace that we reached the Col des Ecrins in less than forty minutes. We lost no time in arranging our baggage, for we had still to traverse a long glacier, and to get clear of two ice-falls before it was dark ; so, at 5.35 we resumed the march, adjourning eating and drinking, and put on a spurt which took us clear of the Glacier Blanc by 7.45 p.m.[2] We got off the moraine of the Glacier Noir at 8.45, just as the last remnant of daylight vanished. Croz and myself were a trifle in advance of the others, and fortunately so for us ; for as they were about to commence the descent of the snout of the glacier, the whole of the moraine that rested on its face peeled off, and came down with a tremendous roar.

We had now the pleasure of walking over a plain that is known by the name of the Pré de Madame Carle, covered with

[1] See vol. i., p. 73, of *Alpine Journal*. We considered the height assigned to the final peak by Mr. Bonney was too small, and thought it should have been about 200 feet more.

[2] The Glacier Blanc is in the direction indicated by the arrow below the letter **E** on the outline on p. 167.

pebbles of all sizes, and intersected by numerous small streams or torrents. Every hole looked like a stone, every stone like a hole, and we tumbled about from side to side until our limbs and our tempers became thoroughly jaded. My companions, being both short-sighted, found the travelling especially disagreeable ; so there was little wonder that when we came upon a huge mass of rock as big as a house, which had fallen from the flanks of Pelvoux, a regular cube that offered no shelter whatever, Moore cried out in ecstasy, " Oh, how delightful ! the very thing I have been longing for. Let us have a perfectly extemporaneous bivouac." This, it should be said, was when the night threatened thunder and lightning, rain, and all other delights.

The pleasures of a perfectly extemporaneous bivouac under these circumstances not being novelties to Croz and myself, we thought we would try for the miseries of a roof ; but Walker and Almer, with their usual good-nature, declared it was the very thing that they, too, were longing for ; so the trio resolved to stop. We generously left them all the provisions (a dozen cubic inches or thereabouts of bacon fat, and half a candle), and pushed on for the chalets of Ailefroide, or at least we thought we did, but could not be certain. In the course of half an hour we got uncommonly close to the main torrent, and Croz all at once disappeared. I stepped cautiously forward to peer down into the place where I thought he was, and quietly tumbled head over heels into a big bush. Extricating myself with some trouble, I fell backwards over some rocks, and got wedged in a cleft so close to the torrent that it splashed all over me.

The colloquy which then ensued amid the thundering of the stream was as follows :—

" Hullo, Croz ! " " Eh, Monsieur." " Where are you ? " " Here, Monsieur." " Where *is* here ? " " I don't know ; where are you ? " " Here, Croz ; " and so on.

The fact was, from the intense darkness, and the noise of the torrent, we had no idea of each other's situation. In the course of ten minutes, however, we joined together again, agreed we had had quite enough of that kind of thing, and adjourned to a most eligible rock at 10.15.

How well I remember the night at that rock, and the jolly way in which Croz came out ! We were both very wet about

A NIGHT WITH CROZ.

the legs, and both uncommonly hungry, but the time passed pleasantly enough round our fire of juniper, and until long past midnight we sat up recounting, over our pipes, wonderful stories of the most incredible description, in which, I must admit, my companion beat me hollow. Then, throwing ourselves on our beds of rhododendron, we slept an untroubled sleep, and rose on a bright Sunday morning as fresh as might be, intending to enjoy a day's rest and luxury with our friends at La Ville de Vallouise.

I have failed to give the impression I wish if it has not been made evident that the ascent of the Pointe des Ecrins was not an ordinary piece of work. There is an increasing disposition nowadays amongst those who write on the Alps, to underrate the difficulties and dangers which are met with, and this disposition is, I think, not less mischievous than the old-fashioned style of making everything terrible. Difficult as we found the peak, I believe we took it at the best, perhaps the only possible, time of the year. The great slope on which we spent so much time was, from being denuded by the avalanche of which I have spoken, deprived of its greatest danger. Had it had the snow still resting upon it, and had we persevered with the expedition, we should almost without doubt have ended with calamity instead of success. The ice of that slope is always below, its angle is severe, and the rocks do not protrude sufficiently to afford the support that snow requires, to be stable, when at a great angle. So far am I from desiring to tempt anyone to repeat the expedition, that I put it on record as my belief, however sad and however miserable a man may have been, if he is found on the summit of the Pointe des Ecrins after a fall of new snow, he is likely to experience misery far deeper than anything with which he has hitherto been acquainted.[1]

[1] The second ascent of the Pointe des Ecrins was made by a French gentleman, named Vincent, with the Chamonix guides Jean Carrier and Alexandre Tournier. They followed our route, but reversed it ; that is to say, ascended by the western and descended by the eastern arête.

CHAPTER IX

ON THE FIRST PASSAGE OF THE COL DE LA PILATTE

" How pleasant it is for him who is saved to remember his danger."
EURIPIDES.

FROM Ailefroide to Claux, but for the path, travel would be scarcely more easy than over the Pré de Madame Carle.[1] The valley is strewn with immense masses of gneiss, from the size of a large house downwards, and it is only occasionally that rock *in situ* is seen, so covered up is it by the débris, which seems to have been derived almost entirely from the neighbouring cliffs.[2]

It was Sunday, a " day most calm and bright." Golden sunlight had dispersed the clouds, and was glorifying the heights, and we forgot hunger through the brilliancy of the morning and beauty of the mountains.

We meant the 26th to be a day of rest, but it was little that we found in the *cabaret* of Claude Giraud, and we fled before the babel of sound which rose in intensity as men descended to a depth which is unattainable by the beasts of the field, and found at the chalets of Entraigues [3] the peace that had been denied to us at Vallouise.

[1] For route, see map on p. 157.

[2] About half a mile above Claux there is a precipitous fall in the valley, and there (where the bed rock is too steep to allow débris to accumulate) *roches moutonnées* can be seen. At the same place the torrent of Ailefroide falls by some steep rapids through a wall-sided gorge, and the former eddyings of the water can be traced high up upon the cliffs.

[3] The path from La Ville de Vallouise to Entraigues is good, and well shaded by luxuriant foliage. The valley (d'Entraigues) is narrow ; bordered

177

Again we were received with the most cordial hospitality. Everything that was eatable or drinkable was brought out and pressed upon us ; every little curiosity was exhibited ; every information that could be afforded was given ; and when we retired to our clean straw we again congratulated each other that we had escaped from a foul den, and had cast in our lot with those who dwell in chalets. Very luxurious that straw seemed after two nights upon quartz pebbles and glacier mud, and I felt quite aggrieved (expecting it was the summons for departure) when, about midnight, the heavy wooden door creaked on its hinges, and a man hem'd and ha'd to attract attention ; but when he whispered, " Monsieur Edvard," I perceived my mistake,—it was our Pelvoux companion, Monsieur Jean Reynaud, the excellent *agent-voyer* of La Bessée.

Monsieur Reynaud had been invited to accompany us on the excursion that is described in this chapter, but had arrived at Vallouise after we had left, and had energetically pursued us during the night. Our idea was that a pass might be made over the high ridge called (on the French map) Crête des Bœufs Rouges,[1] near to the peak named Les Bans, and that it might be the shortest route in time (as it certainly would be in distance) from Vallouise, across the Central Dauphiné Alps. We had seen the northern (or Pilatte) side from the Brèche de la Meije, and it seemed to be practicable at one place near Les Bans.

by fine cliffs ; and closed at its western end by a noble block of mountains, which looks much higher than it is. The highest point (the Pic Bonvoisin) is 11,680 feet. Potatoes, peas, and other vegetables, are grown at Entraigues (5,282 feet), although the situation of the chalets is bleak, and cut off from the sun.

The Combe (or Vallon) de la Selle joins the main valley at Entraigues, and one can pass from the former by the little-known Col du Loup (immediately to the south of the Pic Bonvoisin) into the Valgaudemar. Two other passes, both of considerable height, lead from the head of the Vallon de la Selle into the valleys of Champoléon and Argentière.

[1] This, like many other names given to mountains and glaciers on sheet 189, is not a local name, or, at least, is not one that is in common use.

More than that could not be told at a distance of eleven miles. We intended to try to hit a point on the ridge immediately above the part where it seemed to be easiest.

We left Entraigues at 3.30 on the morning of June 27, and proceeded, over very gently-inclined ground, towards the foot of the Pic Bonvoisin (following in fact the route of the Col du Sellar, which leads from the Vallouise into the Valgaudemar) ; [1] and at 5 a.m., finding that there was no chance of obtaining a view from the bottom of the valley of the ridge over which our route was to be taken, sent Almer up the lower slopes of the Bonvoisin to reconnoitre. He telegraphed that we might proceed ; and at 5.45 we quitted the snow-beds at the bottom of the valley for the slopes which rose towards the north.

The course was N.N.W., and was prodigiously steep. *In less than two miles' difference of latitude we rose one mile of absolute height.* But the route was so far from being an exceptionally difficult one, that at 10.45 we stood on the summit of the pass, having made an ascent of more than 5,000 feet in five hours, inclusive of halts.

Upon sheet 189 of the French map a glacier is laid down on the south of the Crête des Bœufs Rouges, extending along the entire length of the ridge, at its foot, from east to west. In 1864 this glacier did not exist as *one* glacier, but in the place where it should have been there were several small ones, all of which were, I believe, separated from each other.[2]

We commenced the ascent from the Val d'Entraigues, to the west of the most western of these small glaciers, and quitted the

[1] The height of Col du Sellar (or de Celar) is 10,063 feet (Forbes). I was told by peasants at Entraigues that sheep and goats can be easily taken across it.

[2] See map on p. 157. It is perhaps just possible, although improbable, that these little glaciers were united together at the time that the survey was made. Since then the glaciers of Dauphiné (as throughout the Alps generally) have shrunk very considerably. A notable diminution took place in their size in 1869, which was attributed by the natives to the very heavy rains of that year.

valley by the first great gap in its cliffs after that glacier was passed. We did not take to the ice until it afforded an easier route than the rocks; then (8.30) Croz went to the front, and led with admirable skill through a maze of crevasses up to the foot of a great snow couloir, that rose from the head of the glacier to the summit of the ridge over which we had to pass.

We had settled beforehand in London, without knowing anything whatever about the place, that such a couloir as this should be in this angle; but when we got into the Val d'Entraigues, and found that it was not possible to see into the corner, our faith in its existence became less and

A SNOW COULOIR.

less, until the telegraphing of Almer, who was sent up the opposite slopes to search for it, assured us that we were true prophets.

Snow couloirs are nothing more or less than gullies partly filled by snow. They are most useful institutions, and may be considered as natural highways placed, by a kind Providence, in convenient situations for getting over places which would otherwise be inaccessible. They are a joy to the mountaineer, and, from afar, assure him of a path when all beside is uncertain ; but they are grief to novices, who, when upon steep snow, are usually seized with two notions—first, that the snow will slip, and secondly, that those who are upon it must slip too.

Nothing, perhaps, could look much more unpromising to those who do not know the virtues of couloirs than such a place as the engraving represents,[1] and if persons inexperienced in mountain craft had occasion to cross a ridge or to climb rocks, in which there were such couloirs, they would instinctively avoid them. But practised mountaineers would naturally look to them for a path, and would follow them almost as a matter of course, unless they turned out to be filled with ice, or too much swept by falling stones, or the rock at the sides proved to be of such an exceptional character as to afford an easier path than the snow.

Couloirs look prodigiously steep when seen from the front, and, so viewed, it is impossible to be certain of their inclination within many degrees. Snow, however, does actually lie at steeper angles in couloirs than in any other situations ;—45 to 50 degrees is not an uncommon inclination. Even at such angles, two men with proper axes can mount on snow at the rate of 700 to 800 feet per hour. The same amount can only be accomplished in the same time on steep rocks when they are of the very easiest character, and four or five hours may be readily

[1] This drawing was made to illustrate the remarks which follow. It does not represent any particular couloir, but it would serve, tolerably well, as a portrait of the one which we ascended when crossing the Col de la Pilatte.

spent upon an equal height of difficult rocks. Snow couloirs
are therefore to be commended because they economize time.
Of course, in all gullies, one is liable to be encountered by
falling stones. Most of those which fall from the rocks of a
couloir, sooner or later spin down the snow which fills the
trough ; and, as their course and pace are more clearly apparent
when falling over snow than when jumping from ledge to ledge,
persons with lively imaginations are readily impressed by them.
The grooves which are usually seen wandering down the length
of snow couloirs are deepened (and, perhaps, occasionally originated) by falling stones, and they are sometimes pointed out by
cautious men as reasons why couloirs should not be followed.
I think they are very frequently only gutters, caused by water
trickling off the rocks. Whether this is so or not, one should
always consider the possibility of being struck by falling stones,
and, in order to lessen the risk as far as possible, should mount
upon the sides of the snow, and not up its centre. Stones that
come off the rocks then fly over one's head, or bound down
the middle of the trough at a safe distance.

At 9.30 a.m. we commenced the ascent of the couloir leading
from the nameless glacier to a point in the ridge, just to the east
of Les Bans. So far the route had been nothing more than a
steep grind in an angle where little could be seen, but now views
opened out in several directions, and the way began to be interesting. It was more so, perhaps, to us than to our companion
M. Reynaud, who had no rest in the last night. He was, moreover, heavily laden. Science was to be regarded—his pockets
were stuffed with books ; heights and angles were to be observed
—his knapsack was filled with instruments ; hunger was to be
guarded against—his shoulders were ornamented with a huge
nimbus of bread, and a leg of mutton swung behind from his
knapsack, looking like an overgrown tail. Like a good-hearted
fellow, he had brought this food, thinking we might be in need
of it. As it happened, we were well provided for, and having
our own packs to carry, could not relieve him of his superfluous

burdens, which, naturally, he did not like to throw away. As the angles steepened, the strain on his strength became more and more apparent. At last he began to groan. At first a most gentle and mellow groan ; but as we rose so did his groans, till at last the cliffs were groaning in echo, and we were moved to laughter.

Croz cut the way with unflagging energy throughout the whole of the ascent, and at 10.45 we stood on the summit of our pass, intending to refresh ourselves with a good halt ; but just at that moment a mist, which had been playing about the ridge, swooped down and blotted out the whole of the view on the northern side. Croz was the only one who caught a glimpse of the descent, and it was deemed advisable to push on immediately, while its recollection was fresh in his memory. We are consequently unable to tell anything about the summit of the pass, except that it lies immediately to the east of Les Bans, and is elevated about 11,300 feet above the level of the sea. It is one of the highest passes in Dauphiné. We called it the Col de la Pilatte.

We commenced to descend towards the Glacier de la Pilatte by a slope of smooth ice, the face of which, according to the measurement of Mr. Moore, had an inclination of 54° ! Croz still led, and the others followed at intervals of about 15 feet, all being tied together, and Almer occupying the responsible position of last man : the two guides were therefore about 70 feet apart. They were quite invisible to each other from the mist, and looked spectral even to us. But the strong man could be heard by all hewing out the steps below, while every now and then the voice of the steady man pierced the cloud,—" Slip not, dear sirs ; place well your feet ; stir not until you are certain."

For three-quarters of an hour we progressed in this fashion. The axe of Croz all at once stopped. " What is the matter, Croz ? " " Bergschrund, gentlemen." " Can we get over ? " " Upon my word, I don't know ; I think we must jump."

The clouds rolled away right and left as he spoke. The effect was dramatic ! It was a *coup de théâtre*, preparatory to the " great sensation leap " which was about to be executed by the entire company.

Some unseen cause, some cliff or obstruction in the rocks underneath, had caused our wall of ice to split into two portions, and the huge fissure which had thus been formed extended, on each hand, as far as could be seen. We, on the slope above, were separated from the slope below by a mighty crevasse. No running up and down to look for an easier place to cross could be done on an ice-slope of 54°; the chasm had to be passed then and there.

A downward jump of 15 or 16 feet, and a forward leap of 7 or 8 feet had to be made at the same time. That is not much, you will say. It was not much. It was not the quantity, but it was the quality of the jump which gave to it its particular flavour. You had to hit a narrow ridge of ice. If that was passed, it seemed as if you might roll down for ever and ever. If it was not attained, you dropped into the crevasse below, which, although partly choked by icicles and snow that had fallen from above, was still gaping in many places, ready to receive an erratic body.

Croz untied Walker in order to get rope enough, and warning us to hold fast, sprang over the chasm. He alighted cleverly on his feet; untied himself and sent up the rope to Walker, who followed his example. It was then my turn, and I advanced to the edge of the ice. The second which followed was what is called a supreme moment. That is to say, I felt supremely ridiculous. The world seemed to revolve at a frightful pace, and my stomach to fly away. The next moment I found myself sprawling in the snow, and then, of course, vowed that it was nothing, and prepared to encourage my friend Reynaud.

He came to the edge and made declarations. I do not believe that he was a whit more reluctant to pass the place than we others, but he was infinitely more demonstrative,—in a word,

"WE SAW A TOE—IT SEEMED TO BELONG TO MOORE—WE SAW
REYNAUD A FLYING BODY."

he was French. He wrung his hands, " Oh ! what a *diable* of a place ! " " It is nothing, Reynaud," I said, " it is nothing." " Jump," cried the others, " jump." But he turned round, as far as one can do such a thing in an ice-step, and covered his face with his hands, ejaculating, " Upon my word, it is not possible. No ! no ! ! no ! ! ! it is not possible."

How he came over I scarcely know. We saw a toe—it seemed to belong to Moore ; we saw Reynaud a flying body, coming down as if taking a header into water ; with arms and legs all abroad, his leg of mutton flying in the air, his bâton escaped from his grasp ; and then we heard a thud as if a bundle of carpets had been pitched out of a window. When set upon his feet he was a sorry spectacle ; his head was a great snowball ; brandy was trickling out of one side of the knapsack, chartreuse out of the other—we bemoaned its loss, but we roared with laughter.

I cannot close this chapter without paying tribute to the ability with which Croz led us, through a dense mist, down the remainder of the Glacier de la Pilatte. As an exhibition of strength and skill, it has seldom been surpassed in the Alps or elsewhere. On this almost unknown and very steep glacier, he was perfectly at home, even in the mists. Never able to see 50 feet ahead, he still went on with the utmost certainty, and without having to retrace a single step ; and displayed from first to last consummate knowledge of the materials with which he was dealing. Now he cut steps down one side of a *sérac*, went with a dash at the other side, and hauled us up after him ; then cut away along a ridge until a point was gained from which we could jump on to another ridge ; then, doubling back, found a snow-bridge, over which he crawled on hands and knees, towed us across by the legs, ridiculing our apprehensions, mimicking our awkwardness, declining all help, bidding us only to follow him.

About 1 p.m. we emerged from the mist and found ourselves

just arrived upon the level portion of the glacier, having, as Reynaud properly remarked, come down as quickly as if there had not been any mist at all. Then we attacked the leg of mutton which my friend had so thoughtfully brought with him, and afterwards raced down, with renewed energy, to La Bérarde.

Reynaud and I walked together to St. Christophe, where we parted. Since then we have talked over the doings of this momentous day ; and I know that he would not, for a good deal, have missed the passage of the Col de la Pilatte, although we failed to make it an easier or a shorter route than the Col du Sélé. I rejoined Moore and Walker, the same evening, at Vénosc, and on the next day went with them over the Lautaret road to the hospice on its summit, where we slept.

So our little campaign in Dauphiné came to an end. It was remarkable for the absence of failures, and for the precision with which all our plans were carried out. This was due very much to the spirit of my companions ; but it was also owing to the fine weather which we were fortunate enough to enjoy, and to our making a very early start every morning. By beginning our work at or before the break of day, on the longest days in the year, we were not only able to avoid hurrying when deliberation was desirable, but could afford to spend several hours in delightful ease whenever the fancy seized us.

I cannot too strongly recommend to tourists in search of amusement to avoid the inns of Dauphiné. Sleep in the chalets. Get what food you can from the inns, but by no means attempt to pass a night in them. *Sleep* in them you cannot.[1] M. Joanne said that the inventor of the insecticide powder was a native of Dauphiné. I can well believe it. He must have often felt the necessity of such an invention in his infancy and childhood.

On June 29 I crossed the Col du Galibier to St. Michel ; on the 30th, the Col des Encombres to Moûtiers ; on July 1, the

---

[1] This passage, written in 1864, is perhaps, now, somewhat too sweeping ; though, from recent experience in Dauphiné, it does not appear to stand in need of much qualification.

Col du Bonhomme to Contamines ; and on the 2nd, by the Pavillon Bellevue to Chamonix, where I joined Mr. Adams-Reilly to take part in some expeditions which had been planned long before.

CHAPTER X

IN THE MONT BLANC RANGE—PASSAGE OF THE
COL DE TRIOLET, AND FIRST ASCENTS OF
MONT DOLENT, AIGUILLE DE TRELATETE, AND
AIGUILLE D'ARGENTIERE

" Nothing binds men so closely together as agreement in plans and desires."
CICERO.

IN the year 1864, very few persons knew from personal know-ledge with what extreme inaccuracy the chain of Mont Blanc was delineated. During the previous half-century thousands had made the tour of the chain, and in that time at least *one* thousand individuals had stood upon its highest summit ; but out of all this number there was not one at the same time capable, willing, and able, to map the mountain which, until recently, was regarded the highest in Europe.

Many persons knew that great blunders had been perpetrated, and it was notorious that even Mont Blanc itself was represented in a ludicrously incorrect manner on all sides excepting the north ; but there was not, perhaps, a single individual who knew, at the time to which I refer, that errors of no less than a thousand feet had been committed in the determination of heights at each end of the chain ; that some glaciers were represented of double their real dimensions ; and that ridges and mountains were laid down which actually had no existence.

One portion alone of the entire chain had been surveyed at the time of which I speak with anything like accuracy. It was not done (as one would have expected) by a Government, but by a private individual,—by the British Saussure,—the late J. D. Forbes. In the year 1842, he " made a special survey of the

Mer de Glace of Chamonix and its tributaries, which, in some of the following years, he extended by further observations, so as to include the Glacier des Bossons." The map produced from this survey was worthy of its author ; and subsequent explorers of the region he investigated have been able to detect only trivial inaccuracies in his work.

The district surveyed by Forbes remained a solitary bright spot in a region where all besides was darkness until the year 1861. Praiseworthy attempts were made by different hands to throw light upon the gloom, but the efforts were ineffectual, and showed how labour may be thrown away by a number of observers working independently, without the direction of a single head.

In 1861, Sheet XXII of Dufour's great Map of Switzerland appeared. It included the section of the chain of Mont Blanc that belonged to Switzerland, and this portion of the sheet was executed with the admirable fidelity and thoroughness which characterize the whole of Dufour's unique map. The remainder of the chain (amounting to about four-fifths of the whole) was laid down after the work of previous topographers, and its wretchedness was made more apparent by contrast with the finished work of the Swiss surveyors.

Strong hands were needed to complete the survey, and it was not long before the right men appeared.

In 1863, Mr. Adams-Reilly, who had been travelling in the Alps during several years, resolved to attempt a survey of the unsurveyed portions of the chain of Mont Blanc. He provided himself with a good theodolite, and starting from a base-line measured by Forbes in the valley of Chamonix, determined the positions of no less than two hundred points. The accuracy of his work may be judged from the fact that, after having turned many corners and carried his observations over a distance of fifty miles, his Col Ferret " fell within two hundred yards of the position assigned to it by General Dufour ! "

In the winter of 1863 and the spring of 1864, Mr. Reilly constructed an entirely original map from his newly acquired data. The spaces between his trigonometrically determined points he filled in after photographs, and a series of panoramic sketches which he made from his different stations. The map so produced was a distinct advance upon those which were already in existence, and it was the first which exhibited the great peaks in their proper positions.

This extraordinary piece of work revealed Mr. Reilly to me as a man of wonderful determination and perseverance. With very small hope that my proposal would be accepted, I invited him to take part in renewed attacks on the Matterhorn. He entered heartily into my plans, and met me with a counter-proposition, namely, that I should accompany him on some expeditions which he had projected in the chain of Mont Blanc. The unwritten contract took this form :—I will help you to carry out your desires, and you shall assist me to carry out mine. I eagerly closed with an arrangement in which all the advantages were upon my side.

At the time that Mr. Reilly was carrying on his survey, Captain Mieulet was executing another in continuation of the great map of France ; for about one-half of the chain of Mont Blanc (including the whole of the valley of Chamonix) had recently become French once more. Captain Mieulet was at first directed to survey up to the frontier only, and the sheet which was destined to include his work was to be engraved upon the scale of the rest of the map, namely, $\frac{1}{80000}$ of nature. Representations were, however, made at head-quarters that it would be of great advantage to extend the survey as far as Courmayeur, and Captain Mieulet was subsequently directed to continue his observations into the south (or Italian) side of the chain. A special sheet on the scale of $\frac{1}{40000}$ was promptly engraved from the materials he accumulated, and was published in 1865, by order of the late Minister of War, Marshal Randon.[1] This sheet was admirably

[1] Under the title of *Massif du Mont Blanc, extrait des minutes de la Carte de France, levé par M. Mieulet, Capitaine d'Etat Major.*

executed, but it included the central portion of the chain only, and a complete map was still wanting.

Mr. Reilly presented his MS. map to the English Alpine Club. It was resolved that it should be published ; but before it passed into the engraver's hands its author undertook to revise it carefully. To this end he planned a number of expeditions to high points which up to that time had been regarded inaccessible, and it was upon some of these ascents he invited me to accompany him.[1] Before I pass on to these expeditions (which will be described very briefly), it will be convenient to devote a few paragraphs to the topography of the chain of Mont Blanc.[2]

At the present time the chain is divided betwixt France, Switzerland, and Italy. France has the lion's share, Switzerland the most fertile portion, and Italy the steepest side. It has acquired a reputation which is not extraordinary, though not entirely merited. It has neither the beauty of the Oberland, nor the sublimity of Dauphiné. It attracts the vulgar by the possession of the highest summit in the Alps. If that is removed, the elevation of the chain is in nowise remarkable. In fact, excluding Mont Blanc itself, the mountains of which the chain is made up are *less* important than those of the Oberland and the Central Pennine groups.

The frontier-line follows the main ridge. Very little of it can be seen from the valley of Chamonix, and from the village itself two small strips only are visible (amounting to scarcely three miles in length), viz. from the summit of Mont Blanc to the Dôme du Goûter, and in the neighbourhood of the Col de Balme.

[1] Mr. Reilly's map was published on a scale of $\frac{1}{80000}$ in 1865, at the cost of the Alpine Club, under the title *The Chain of Mont Blanc*.

[2] See the Map of the chain of Mont Blanc at the end of the volume. This map has been drawn after the surveys of Mieulet, Dufour, and Reilly. To assist in its production, the Dépôt de la Guerre at Paris furnished me with special copies of Captain Mieulet's map. The nomenclature of these authorities has been strictly followed. It may be remarked, however, that Captain Mieulet has departed, in many instances, from the spelling in common use.

All the rest is concealed by outlying ridges and by mountains of secondary importance.

Mont Blanc itself is bounded by the two glaciers of Miage, the Glaciers de la Brenva and du Géant, the Val Veni and the valley of Chamonix. A long ridge runs out towards the N.N.E. from the summit, through Mont Maudit, to the Aiguille du Midi. Another ridge proceeds towards the N.W., through the Bosses du Dromadaire to the Dôme du Goûter ; this then divides into two, of which one continues N.W. to the Aiguille du Goûter, and the other (which is a part of the main ridge of the chain) towards the W. to the Aiguille de Bionnassay. The two routes which are commonly followed for the ascent of Mont Blanc lie between these two principal ridges—one leading from Chamonix, *viâ* the Grands Mulets, the other from the village of Bionnassay, *viâ* the Aiguille and Dôme du Goûter.[1]

The ascent of Mont Blanc has been made from several directions besides these, and perhaps there is no single point of the compass from which the mountain cannot be ascended. But there is not the least probability that any one will discover easier ways to the summit than those already known.

I believe it is correct to say that the Aiguille du Midi and the Dôme de Miage were the only two summits in the chain of Mont Blanc which had been ascended at the beginning of 1864.[2] The latter of these two is an insignificant point ; and the former is only a portion of one of the ridges just now mentioned, and can hardly be regarded as a mountain separate and distinct from Mont Blanc. The really great peaks of the chain were considered inaccessible, and, I think, with the exception of the Aiguille Verte, had never been assailed.

The finest, as well as the highest peak in the chain (after Mont Blanc itself), is the Grandes Jorasses. The next, without a doubt, is the Aiguille Verte. The Aiguille de Bionnassay, which in actual height follows the Verte, should be considered as a part

[1] These routes are laid down on the Map.
[2] Besides Mont Blanc itself.

of Mont Blanc ; and in the same way the summit called Les Droites is only a part of the ridge which culminates in the Verte. The Aiguille de Trélatête is the next on the list that is entitled to be considered a separate mountain, and it is by far the most important peak (as well as the highest) at the south-west end of the chain. Then comes the Aiguille d'Argentière, which occupies the same rank at the north-east end as the last-mentioned mountain does in the south-west. The rest of the aiguilles are comparatively insignificant ; and although some of them (such as Mont Dolent) look well from low elevations, and seem to possess a certain importance, they sink into their proper places directly one arrives at a considerable altitude.

The summit of the Aiguille Verte would have been one of the best stations out of all these mountains for the purposes of my friend. Its great height, and its isolated and commanding position, make it a most admirable point for viewing the intricacies of the chain ; but he exercised a wise discretion in passing it by, and in selecting as our first excursion the passage of the Col de Triolet.[1]

We slept under some big rocks on the Couvercle on the night of July 7, with the thermometer at 26·5 F., and at 4.30 a m. on the 8th made a straight track to the north of the Jardin, and thence went in zigzags, to break the ascent, over the upper slopes of the Glacier de Talèfre towards the foot of the Aiguille de Triolet. Croz was still my guide, Reilly was accompanied by one of the Michel Payots of Chamonix, and Henri Charlet, of the same place, was our porter.

The way was over an undulating plain of glacier of moderate inclination until the corner leading to the col, whence a steep secondary glacier led down into the basin of the Talèfre. We experienced no difficulty in making the ascent of this secondary

---

[1] Previous to this we made an attempt to ascend the Aiguille d'Argentière, and were defeated by a violent wind when within a hundred feet of the summit. It is more convenient to refer to this expedition at the end of the chapter.

glacier with such ice-men as Croz and Payot, and at 7.50 a.m.
arrived on the top of the so-called pass, at a height of 12,110
feet, and 4,530 above our camp on the Couvercle.

The descent was commenced by very steep, but firm, rocks, and
then by a branch of the Glacier de Triolet.   Schrunds [1] were
abundant ;   there were no less than five extending completely
across the glacier, all of which had to be jumped.   Not one was
equal in dimensions to the extraordinary chasm on the Col de la
Pilatte, although in the aggregate they far surpassed it.   " Our
lives," so Reilly expressed it, " were made a burden to us with
schrunds."

Several spurs run out towards the south-east from the ridge at
the head of the Glacier de Triolet, and divide it into a number of
bays.   We descended the most northern of these, and when we
emerged from it on to the open glacier, just at the junction of our
bay with the next one, there we came across a most beautiful ice-
arch, festooned with icicles, the decaying remnant of an old sérac,
which stood, isolated, full 30 feet above the surface of the glacier !
It was an accident, and I have not seen its like elsewhere.   When
I passed the spot in 1865 no vestige of it remained.

We flattered ourselves that we should arrive at the chalets of
Pré de Bar very early in the day ; but, owing to much time being
lost on the slopes of Mont Rouge, it was nearly 4 p.m. before
we got to them.   There were no bridges across the torrent nearer
than Gruetta, and, rather than descend so far, we preferred to
round the base of Mont Rouge, and to cross the snout of the
Glacier du Mont Dolent.[2]

[1] Great crevasses.   A bergschrund is a schrund, and something more.   (See
Chap. XIII.)

[2] The passage of the Col de Triolet from the Couvercle to Pré de Bar occupied 8½ hours of actual walking.   If the pass had been taken in the contrary
direction it would have consumed a much longer time.   It gave a route
shorter than any known at the time between Chamonix and the St. Bernard.
As a pass I cannot conscientiously recommend it to anyone (see Chap. XVIII),
nor am I desirous to go again over the moraine on the left bank of the Glacier
de Triolet, or the rocks of Mont Rouge.

MONT DOLENT, FROM THE COL D'ARGENTIERE.

We occupied the 9th with a scramble up Mont Dolent. This was a miniature ascent. It contained a little of everything. First we went up to the Petit Col Ferret, and had a little grind over shaly banks ; then there was a little walk over grass ; then a little tramp over a moraine (which, strange to say, gave a pleasant path) ; then a little zigzagging over the snow-covered glacier of Mont Dolent. Then there was a little bergschrund ; then a little wall of snow,—which we mounted by the side of a little buttress ; and when we struck the ridge descending S.E. from the summit, we found a little arête of snow leading to the highest point. The summit itself was little,—very small indeed ; it was the loveliest little cone of snow that was ever piled up on mountain-top ; so soft, so pure ; it seemed a crime to defile it ; it was a miniature Jungfrau, a toy summit, you could cover it with the hand.[1]

But there was nothing little about the *view* from the Mont Dolent. " Situated at the junction of three mountain ridges, it rises in a positive steeple far above anything in its immediate neighbourhood ; and certain gaps in the surrounding ridges, which seem contrived for that especial purpose, extend the view in almost every direction. The precipices which descend to the Glacier d'Argentière I can only compare to those of the Jungfrau, and the ridges on both sides of that glacier, especially the steep rocks of Les Droites and Les Courtes, surmounted by the sharp snow-peak of the Aiguille Verte, have almost the effect of the Grandes Jorasses. Then, framed, as it were, between the massive tower of the Aiguille de Triolet and the more distant Jorasses, lies, without exception, the most delicately beautiful picture I have ever seen—the whole *massif* of Mont Blanc, raising its great head of snow far above the tangled series of flying buttresses which uphold the Monts Maudits, supported on the left by Mont Peuteret and by the mass of ragged aiguilles which overhang the Brenva. This aspect of Mont Blanc is not new, but from this

---

[1] The ascent of Mont Dolent and return to Pré de Bar (halts included) occupied less than eleven hours.

point its *pose* is unrivalled, and it has all the superiority of a picture grouped by the hand of a master . . . The view is as extensive, and far more lovely than that from Mont Blanc itself." [1]

We went down to Courmayeur, and on the afternoon of July 10 started from that place to camp on Mont Suc, for the ascent of the Aiguille

de Trélatête ; hopeful that the mists which were hanging about would clear away. They did not, so we deposited ourselves, and a great load of straw, on the moraine of the Miage Glacier, just above the Lac de Combal, in a charm-ing little hole which some solitary shepherd had excavated beneath

a great slab of rock. We spent the night there, and the whole of the next day, unwilling to run away, and equally so to get into difficulties by venturing into the mist. It was a dull time, and I grew restless. Reilly read to me a lecture on the excellence of patience, and composed himself in an easy attitude, to pore over the pages of a yellow-covered book. " Patience," I said to him viciously, " comes readily to fellows who have shilling novels ; but I have not got one ; I have picked

all the mud out of the nails of my boots, and have skinned my face ; what shall I do ? " " Go and study the moraine of the Miage," said he. I went, and came back after an hour. "What news ? " cried Reilly, raising himself on his elbow. " Very little ; it's a big moraine, bigger than I thought, with ridge outside

[1] From the notes of Mr. Reilly.

ridge, like a fortified camp ; and there are walls upon it which have been built and loop-holed, as if for defence." "Try again," he said, as he threw himself on his back. But I went to Croz, who was asleep, and tickled his nose with a straw until he awoke ; and then, as that amusement was played out, watched Reilly, who was getting numbed, and shifted uneasily from side to side, and threw himself on his stomach, and rested his head on his elbows, and lighted his pipe and puffed at it

OUR CAMP ON MONT SUC.[1]

savagely. When I looked again, how was Reilly ? An indistinguishable heap ; arms, legs, head, stones, and straw, all mixed together, his hat flung on one side, his novel tossed far away ! Then I went to him, and read him a lecture upon the excellence of patience.

Bah ! it was a dull time. Our mountain, like a beautiful

[1] From a sketch by Mr. Adams-Reilly. This camp was immediately at the foot of the snow seen upon the map to the N.W. of the words Mont Suc.

coquette, sometimes unveiled herself for a moment, and looked charming above, although very mysterious below. It was not until eventide she allowed us to approach her ; then, as darkness came on, the curtains were withdrawn, the light drapery was lifted, and we stole up on tiptoe through the grand portal formed by Mont Suc. But night advanced rapidly, and we found ourselves left out in the cold, without a hole to creep into or shelter from overhanging rock. We might have fared badly, except for our good plaids. When they were sewn together down their long edges, one end tossed over our rope (which was passed round some rocks), and the other secured by stones, there was sufficient protection ; and we slept on this exposed ridge, 9,700 feet above the level of the sea, more soundly, perhaps, than if we had been lying on feather beds.

We left our bivouac at 4.45 a.m., and at 9.40 arrived upon the highest of the three summits of the Trélatête, by passing over the lowest one. It was well above everything at this end of the chain, and the view from it was of the grandest character. The whole of the western face of Mont Blanc was spread out before us ; we were the first by whom it had been ever seen. I cede the description of this view to my comrade, to whom it rightfully belongs.

" [1] For four years I had felt great interest in the geography of the chain ; the year before I had mapped, more or less successfully, all but this spot, and this spot had always eluded my grasp. The praises, undeserved as they were, which my map had received, were as gall and wormwood to me when I thought of that great slope which I had been obliged to leave a blank, speckled over with unmeaning dots of rock, gathered from previous maps—for I had consulted them all without meeting an intelligible representation of it. From the surface of the Miage Glacier I had gained nothing, for I could only see the feet of magnificent ice-streams ; but now, from the top of the dead wall of rock which had so long closed my view, I saw those

[1] From the notes of Mr. Reilly.

fine glaciers from top to bottom, pouring down their streams, nearly as large as the Bossons, from Mont Blanc, from the Bosse, and from the Dôme.

The head of Mont Blanc is supported on this side by two buttresses, between which vast glaciers descend. Of these the most southern [1] takes its rise at the foot of the precipices which fall steeply down from the Calotte,[2] and its stream, as it joins that of the Miage, is cut in two by an enormous *rognon* of rock. Next, to the left, comes the largest of the buttresses of which I have spoken, almost forming an aiguille in itself. The next glacier [3] descends from a large basin which receives the snows of the summit-ridge between the Bosse and the Dôme, and it is divided from the third and last glacier [4] by another buttress, which joins the summit-ridge at a point between the Dôme and the Aiguille de Bionnassay."

[*From Whymper's diary : Tuesday, July* 12, 1864.
Ascent of the highest and southern peaks of Aiguille de Trélatête.

The morning was lovely but horribly cold ; we warmed ourselves with hot wine and a spirited discussion whether our luggage should go up. I voted yes, having a prospective col in view as well as a prospective peak. We started at 4.45 and walked up the arête of Mont Suc, but as this was broad we saw little on either side ; at last some rocks rose out of it and stopped our progress in front. To the right, if we went, we knew we should stand on the precipices overlooking the Miage Glacier ; so we went through a gap on the left, through the rocks, and then looked down on the north branch of the Allée Blanche Glacier. The view of this and of Peak No. 114 on the Trélatête at the other side of it was magnificent, and we saw that the Graians would

---

[1] This glacier is named on the map Glacier du Mont Blanc.
[2] The Calotte is the name given to the dome of snow at the summit of Mont Blanc.
[3] Glacier du Dôme.   [4] Glacier de Bionnassay.

have been so too, only they were clouded. We had another
lively discussion about the route. Croz wanted to descend on
to the glacier, go down and across it, and see if the peak could
be g)t up from the other side, at the back. I on the contrary
saw no reason, as we were so far up the glacier, why we should
not go up to the top, get on the arête again and see if *that* side
was not practicable. If it was not, we had still plenty of time
to come down to look at *his* route, and so it was settled, and
fortunately for us, for it turned out the right route, and we saw
afterwards that the other would have been a *bêtise*. But Croz
was riled and without waiting to rope stamped off in the direction
I indicated. We only went down 100 feet or so, and then curved
round the left bank of the glacier ; snow excessively deep and
soft. We mutually pulled and floundered in the trail of Croz.
A depression in the arête in front of us seemed as if it must
command a view, and we accordingly diverged somewhat from
his track. A view it did command—one which no eyes save
our own had ever seen. From the summit of Mont Blanc an
enormous glacier streamed, which was one mass of séracs from its
commencement to its termination in the Miage, which we could
just see at the bottom of the trough. From the Dôme du
Goûter another descended in like manner, nearly parallel with
the first. Both of these were of the very first order, and as
the fall from the summit to the Miage is somewhere about
7,500 feet—all of which we commanded at one view—the
grandeur of the spectacle must needs be evident. Croz had
halted a couple of hundred feet higher, and we went up to him
and halted to feed, with the Trélatête at last before our eyes, and
a seemingly practicable route leading up to it. Avalanches fell
frequently from the couloirs around and beneath us on to the
Miage ; one of them was quite regular in its discharges, every
eight minutes a bang and a roar woke us up and we saw the
masses of snow and ice trickling as it were down its long length
and then shoot out at the bottom in a cloud of white dust. The
way to the highest summit, although not difficult in appearance,

was sufficiently awkward, for it seemed and we afterwards found it absolutely necessary to arrive at it by passing over one of the lower and nearer peaks. What the other side of this was, we could not tell, so remained until we had climbed it in a state of pleasing uncertainty. At five minutes to 8 we started again, followed the very edge of the arête until it became too steep, and then diverged on to the right flank of the near peak. We passed close under what may be described as "faults" in the snow-bed, rather than crevasses or séracs, and then did some ticklish snow-bridge dodging, occasionally where the slopes were severe coming on to hard ice. The snow, owing to the warmth of the previous night, was very incohesive, and we all came croppers in turn. The slopes close to the summit were steep, 40° to 48° perhaps, but near the summit the snow was better, and we arrived there in a good state of temper which lasted exactly one second. As our heads topped it, they were severally saluted with a freezing blast, which carried it away in the direction of Mont Blanc, and we were glad to cower under the leeside. Croz hadn't yet recovered himself and stamped off in the direction of the highest summit. We followed, all tied, for a slip was a thing to shudder at. However, we didn't slip, and by cautious behaviour, i.e. descending to hands and feet and frequently crawling like caterpillars (anything but in the manner brilliant mountaineers are supposed to go !), we got to the bottom of the depression and by the arête on the other side to the top of the middle and highest peak. The wind swept up from the side of the Allée Blanche Glacier, and writhed around the summit ; gusts seemed every now and then to make a rush at one particular man, and there was really danger of our blowing away. On the Allée Blanche Glacier side a chaotic mass of clouds filled the space, and the other side of my would-be pass was in consequence hidden. Still, every now and then, as the clouds blew aside, we saw that the rocks below were climbable for a considerable distance, and I believe it was to be done. The others declined to try. We plant our flag, back to other summit, and down straightway. On gaining the second col, we found the snow on arête was in the nastiest condition possible, and every minute one or the other slipped sideways from the steps breaking away, and sheets and showers of the nasty stuff went hissing down over the harder substratum. At the crystal gap violent wind blew hats and food away ; it was amusing but painful to see the sausage chasing the prunes, which latter being the lightest had the advantage. Down again same way, through the gully, round the base of Mont Suc, across Allée Blanche Glacier, and stopped to milk at chalet.]

We descended in our track to the Lac de Combal, and thence went over the Col de la Seigne to Mottets, where we slept ; on July 13, crossed the Col du Mont Tondu to Contamines (in a sharp thunderstorm), and the Col de Voza to Chamonix. Two days only remained for excursions in their neighbourhood, and we resolved to employ them in another attempt to ascend the Aiguille d'Argentière, upon which mountain we had been cruelly defeated eight days before.

It happened in this way.—Reilly had a notion that the ascent of the Aiguille could be accomplished by following the ridge leading to its summit from the Col du Chardonnet. At half-past six, on the morning of the 6th, we found ourselves accordingly on the top of that pass.[1] The party consisted of our friend Moore and his guide Almer, Reilly and his guide François Couttet, myself and Michel Croz. So far the weather had been calm, and the way easy ; but immediately we arrived on the summit of the pass, we got into a furious wind. Five minutes earlier we were warm,—now we were frozen. Fine snow, whirled up into the air, penetrated every crack in our harness, and assailed our skins as painfully as if it had been red hot instead of freezing cold. The teeth chattered involuntarily—talking was laborious ; the breath froze instantaneously ; eating was disagreeable ; sitting was impossible !

[1] The Col du Chardonnet is 10,909 feet above the level of the sea.

We looked towards our mountain. Its aspect was not encouraging. The ridge that led upwards had a spiked arête, palisaded with miniature aiguilles, banked up at their bases by heavy snow-beds, which led down, at considerable angles, on one side towards the Glacier de Saleinaz, on the other towards the Glacier du Chardonnet. Under any circumstances, it would have been a stiff piece of work to clamber up that way. Prudence and comfort counselled " Give it up." Discretion overruled valour. Moore and Almer crossed the Col du Chardonnet to go to Orsières, and we others returned towards Chamonix.

But when we got some distance down we were tempted to stop, and to look back at the Aiguille d'Argentière. The sky was cloudless ; no wind could be felt, nor sign of it perceived ; it was only eight o'clock in the morning ; and there, right before us, we saw another branch of the glacier leading high up into the mountain—far above the Col du Chardonnet—and a little couloir rising from its head almost to the top of the peak. This was clearly the right route to take. We turned back, and went at it.

The glacier was steep, and the snow gully rising out of it was steeper. Seven hundred steps were cut. Then the couloir became *too* steep. We took to the rocks on its left, and at last gained the ridge, at a point about 1,500 feet above the col. We faced about to the right, and went along the ridge ; keeping on some snow a little below its crest, on the Saleinaz side. Then we got the wind again ; but no one thought of turning, as we were within 250 feet of the summit.

The axes of Croz and Couttet went to work once more, for the slope was about as steep as snow could be. Its surface was covered with a loose, granular crust ; dry and utterly incoherent ; which slipped away in streaks directly it was meddled with. The men had to cut through this into the old beds underneath, and to pause incessantly to rake away the powdery stuff, which poured down in hissing streams over the hard substratum. Ugh ! How

cold it was ! How the wind blew ! Couttet's hat was torn
from its fastenings, and went on a tour of Switzerland. The
flour-like snow, swept off the ridge above, was tossed
spirally upwards, eddying in *tourmentes* ; then, dropt in lulls,
or caught by other gusts, was flung far and wide to feed the
Saleinaz.

" My feet are getting suspiciously numbed," cried Reilly :
" how about frost-bites ? "   " Kick hard, sir," shouted the men ;
" it's the only way." *Their* fingers were kept alive by their
work ; but it was cold for the feet, and they kicked and hewed
simultaneously. I followed their example too violently, and
made a hole clean through my footing. A clatter followed as
if crockery had been thrown down a well.

I went down a step or two, and discovered in a second that all
were standing over a cavern (not a crevasse, speaking properly)
that was bridged over by a thin vault of ice, from which great
icicles hung in groves. Almost in the same minute Reilly
pushed one of his hands right through the roof. The whole
party might have tumbled through at any moment. " Go ahead,
Croz, we are over a chasm ! "   " We know it," he answered,
" and we can't find a firm place."

In the blandest manner, my comrade inquired if to persevere
would not be to do that which is called " tempting Providence."
My reply being in the affirmative, he further observed, " Suppose
we go down ? "   " Very willingly."   " Ask the guides." They
had not the least objection ; so we went down, and slept that
night at the Montenvers.

Off the ridge we were out of the wind. In fact, a hundred feet
down *to windward*, on the slope fronting the Glacier du Chardonnet, we were broiling hot ; there was not a suspicion of a
breeze. Upon that side there was nothing to tell that a hurricane
was raging a hundred feet higher. The cloudless sky looked
tranquillity itself, whilst to leeward the only. sign of a disturbed
atmosphere was the friskiness of the snow upon the crests of the
ridges.

We set out on the 14th, with Croz, Payot, and Charlet, to finish off the work which had been cut short so abruptly, and slept, as before, at the Chalets de Lognan. On the 15th, about midday, we arrived upon the summit of the aiguille, and found that we had actually been within one hundred feet of it when we turned back upon the first attempt.

It was a triumph to Reilly. In this neighbourhood he had performed the feat (in 1863) of joining together "two mountains, each about 13,000 feet high, standing on the map about a mile and a half apart." Long before we made the ascent he had procured evidence which could not be impugned, that the Pointe des Plines, a fictitious summit which had figured on other maps as a distinct mountain, could be no other than the Aiguille d'Argentière, and he had accordingly obliterated it from the preliminary draft of his map. We saw that it was right to do so. The Pointe des Plines did not exist. We had ocular demonstration of the accuracy of his previous observations.

I do not know which to admire most, the fidelity of Mr. Reilly's map, or the indefatigable industry by which the materials were accumulated from which it was constructed. To men who are sound in limb it may be amusing to arrive on a summit (as we did upon the top of Mont Dolent), sitting astride a ridge too narrow to stand upon ; or to do battle with a ferocious wind (as we did on the top of the Aiguille de Trélatête) ; or to feel half-frozen in midsummer (as we did on the Aiguille d'Argentière). But there is extremely little amusement in making sketches and notes under such conditions. Yet upon all these expeditions, under the most adverse circumstances, and in the most trying situations, Mr. Reilly's brain and fingers were always at work. Throughout all he was ever alike ; the same genial, equable-tempered companion, whether victorious or whether defeated ; always ready to sacrifice his own desires to suit our comfort and convenience. By a happy union of audacity and prudence, combined with untiring perseverance, he eventually completed his self-imposed task—a work which would have been intolerable except as a labour of love—and which, for a single individual, may well-nigh be termed Herculean.[1]

We separated upon the level part of the Glacier d'Argentière, Reilly going with Payot and Charlet *viâ* the chalets of Lognan and de la Pendant, whilst I, with Croz, followed the right bank of the glacier to the village of Argentière. At 7 p.m. we entered the humble inn, and ten minutes afterwards heard the echoes of the cannon which were fired upon the arrival of our comrades at Chamonix.[2]

[1] To the deep regret of his many friends, Mr. Anthony Adams-Reilly died suddenly in Dublin on April 15, 1885, aged 49. See the *Alpine Journal*, vol. xii., pp. 256–9.

[2] The lower Chalet de Lognan is 2½ hours' walking from Chamonix. From thence to the summit of the Aiguille d'Argentière, and down to the village of the same name, occupied 12½ hours.

CHAPTER XI

THE FIRST PASSAGE OF THE MOMING PASS— ZERMATT

" A daring leader is a dangerous thing."

EURÍPIDES.

ON July 10, Croz and I went to Sierre, in the Valais, *viâ* the Col de Balme, the Col de la Forclaz, and Martigny. The Swiss side of the Forclaz is not creditable to Switzerland. The path from Martigny to the summit has undergone successive improvements in these latter years, but mendicants permanently disfigure it.

We passed many tired pedestrians toiling up this oven, persecuted by trains of parasitic children. These children swarm there like maggots in a rotten cheese. They carry baskets of fruit with which to plague the weary tourist. They flit around him like flies ; they thrust the fruit in his face ; they pester him with their pertinacity. Beware of them !—taste, touch not their fruit. In the eyes of these children, each peach, each grape, is worth a prince's ransom. It is to no purpose to be angry ; it is like flapping wasps—they only buzz the more. Whatever you do, or whatever you say, the end will be the same. " Give me something," is the alpha and omega of all their addresses. They learn the phrase, it is said, before they are taught the alphabet. It is in all their mouths. From the tiny toddler up to the maiden of sixteen, there is nothing heard but one universal chorus of —" Give me something ; will you have the goodness to give me something ? "

From Sierre we went up the Val d'Anniviers to Zinal, to join our former companions, Moore [1] and Almer. Moore was ambitious to discover a shorter way from Zinal to Zermatt than the two passes which were known.[2]   He had shown to me, upon Dufour's map, that a direct line, connecting the two places, passed exactly over the depression between the Zinal Rothorn and the Schallihorn.   He was confident that a passage could be effected over this depression, and was sanguine that it would (in consequence of its directness) prove to be a quicker route than the circuitous ones over the Triftjoch and the Col Durand.

He was awaiting us, and we immediately proceeded up the valley, and across the foot of the Zinal Glacier to the Arpitetta Alp, where a chalet was supposed to exist in which we might pass the night. We found it at length,[3] but it was not equal to our expectations.   It was not one of those fine timbered chalets, with huge overhanging eaves, covered with pious sentences carved in unintelligible characters.   It was a hovel, growing, as it were, out of the hill-side ; roofed with rough slabs of slaty stone ; without a door or window ; surrounded by quagmires of ordure, and dirt of every description.

A foul native invited us to enter.   The interior was dark ; but, when our eyes became accustomed to the gloom, we saw that our palace was in plan about 15 by 20 feet.   On one side it was scarcely five feet high, and on the other was nearly seven. Upon this side there was a raised platform, about six feet wide, littered with dirty straw and still dirtier sheepskins.   This was the bedroom.   The remainder of the width of the apartment was the parlour.   The rest was the factory.   Cheese was the

---

[1] Mr. Adolphus W. Moore, C.B., died at Monte Carlo, on Feb. 2, 1887, aged 46, having only just before been appointed Political and Secret Secretary at the India Office.   See the *Alpine Journal*, vol. xiii., pp. 258–61.

[2] The Triftjoch, between the Trifthorn and the Ober Gabelhorn ; and the Col Durand between the last-mentioned mountain and the Dent Blanche. For our route from Zinal to Zermatt, see the Map of the valley of Zermatt.

[3] High above the Glacier de Moming at the foot of the Tête de Millon.

article which was being fabricated, and the foul native was engaged in its manufacture. He was garnished behind with a regular cowherd's one-legged stool, which gave him a queer, uncanny look when it was elevated in the air as he bent over into his tub ; for the making of his cheese required him to blow into a tub about ten minutes at a time. He then·squatted on his stool to gain breath, and took a few whiffs at a short pipe ; after which he blew away more vigorously than before. We were told that this procedure was necessary. It appeared to us to be nasty. It accounts, perhaps, for the flavour possessed by certain Swiss cheeses.

Big, black, and leaden-coloured clouds rolled up from Zinal, and met in combat on the Moming Glacier with others which descended from the Rothorn. Down came the rain in torrents, and crash went the thunder. The herd-boys hurried under shelter, for the frightened cattle needed no driving, and tore spontaneously down the alp as if running a steeple-chase. Men, cows, pigs, sheep, and goats forgot their mutual animosities, and rushed to the only refuge on the mountain. The spell was broken which had bound the elements for some weeks past, and the *cirque* from the Weisshorn to Lo Besso was the theatre in which they spent their fury.

A sullen morning succeeded an angry night.

[*From Whymper's diary : Sunday, July 17th,* 1864. *Arpitetta Alp.*

. . . The herdboys, who have a particular objection to being washed, even by rain, now flocked in, and at last, besides ourselves, we had four or five men and as many boys assembled together. The wood with which we tried to make a great fire, had become damp, and smoked and hissed but would not burn ; the wind blew it down the hole that served for a chimney, and it soon filled the room, adding to the wildness of the scene if not to its comfort. We ate, and were then invited to select our sheepskins. This, I for one declined, as I desired repose and not torture. But Moore, gallantly braving the encounter, threw himself on them and in some mysterious manner fell asleep. I chose the corner farthest from the door, and raked away all the upper stratum until I came to the damp earth below. I arranged my plaid and lay down, rather priding myself on my selection of a place. Before long, a large drop fell on my nose and woke me from a doze. I turned over and hit my head against a projecting bit of rubble in the wall, and again dozed off. Before long I found a stream of water trickling down my neck, coming from the bank against which the wall was built, through a hole in the wall. Raising myself up to arrange differently, I disturbed a pool of water that had collected in a fold of the plaid, and caused it to flow down my flannels. This was not agreeable, so I got up and went to the fire, dried myself partially and tried again. The wind was howling, and every now and then a sharp peal of thunder burst out, crashing most grandly. The animals—cows, sheep, goats and pigs—frightened by the tempest, came crowding round the hut and made a babel of sound. Several women too, caught on the Alp, came in and sat round the fire, and whether they talked scandal I know not ; but judging by interest taken in them, their conversation seemed to be of a peculiarly piquant character. Sleep was now out of the question, but I lay on my back and tried to smoke. I say tried, for the streams now poured through the roof so numerously that even this was difficult. The animals, too, cold and wet, huddled themselves on the roof, and fighting who should be closest to the chimney-hole, disturbed the slabs of the roof, which caused one to move uneasily. So the night wore away sometime. I went to the door ; snow mingled with the rain was falling fast, and rendered it impossible to stay outside.]

[*From Moore's Journal : Monday, 18th July.*

. . . About 1.0 a.m. there was a movement amongst the guides to see what was the aspect of the weather, and, as I had expected from the ominous pattering on the roof of our refuge, the report was unfavourable ; a thick fog enveloped everything in its clammy folds, and heavy rain was falling, so that it was obviously impossible to start. Whymper had throughout abjured the sheepskins, but I quickly composed myself afresh, and was rewarded by a good, long sleep, which lasted unbroken till 4.30, when I awoke to the consciousness of a dull miserable day. In spite of their unprepossessing appearance, I must do the sheepskins the justice to admit that they really made a not uncomfortable couch, and, so far as my experience goes, were not infested with fleas to the extent that might have been expected. When I went to the door of our sty, the appearance of things was not encouraging ; the rain had certainly ceased, and the fog in our immediate neighbourhood had lifted, the col being clear, but the sky was encumbered with heavy masses of clouds, which concealed every high peak, and completely shut out the Durand Glacier from view. It was certainly not a day on which to try a new and difficult pass, but the idea of vegetating twenty-four hours in the foul den in which we were, was too fearful to be seriously entertained. . . .]

We were undecided in our council whether to advance or to return down the valley. Good seemed likely to overpower bad ; so, at 5.40, we left the chalet *en route* for our pass " amidst the most encouraging assurances from all the people on the alp that we need not distress ourselves about the weather, as it was not possible to get to the point at which we were aiming."[1]

Our course led us at first over ordinary mountain slopes, and then over a flat expanse of glacier. Before this was quitted, it was needful to determine the exact line which was to be taken. We were divided betwixt two opinions. I advocated that a course should be steered due south, and that the upper plateau of the Moming Glacier should be attained by making a great detour to our right. This was negatived without a division. Almer declared in favour of making for some rocks to the south-west of the Schallihorn, and attaining the upper plateau of the

[1] Moore's Journal.

glacier by mounting them. Croz advised a middle course, up some very steep and broken glacier. Croz's route seemed likely to turn out to be impracticable, because much step-cutting would be required upon it. Almer's rocks did not look good ; they were, possibly, unassailable. I thought both routes were bad, and declined to vote for either of them. Moore hesitated, Almer gave way, and Croz's route was adopted.

He did not go very far, however, before he found that he had undertaken too much, and after " glancing occasionally round at us, to see what we thought about it, suggested that it might, after all, be wiser to take to the rocks of the Schallihorn." That is to say, he suggested the abandonment of his own and the adoption of Almer's route. No one opposed the change of plan, and, in the absence of instructions to the contrary, he proceeded to cut steps across an ice-slope towards the rocks.

Let the reader now cast his eye upon the map of the valley of Zermatt, and he will see that when we quitted the slopes of the Arpitetta Alp, we took a south-easterly course over the Moming Glacier. We halted to settle the plan of attack shortly after we got upon the ice. The rocks of the Schallihorn, whose ascent Almer recommended, were then to our south-east. Croz's proposed route was to the south-west of the rocks, and led up the southern side of very steep and broken glacier.[1] The part he intended to traverse was, in a sense, undoubtedly practicable. He gave it up because it would have involved too much step-cutting. But the part of this glacier which intervened between his route and Almer's rocks was, in the most complete sense of the word, impracticable. It passed over a continuation of the rocks, and was broken in half by them. The upper portion was separated from the lower portion by a long slope of ice that had been built up from the débris of the glacier which had fallen from above. The foot of this slope was surrounded by immense quantities of the larger avalanche blocks. These we cautiously skirted, and when Croz halted they had been left far

[1] Through what is technically called an " ice fall."

E. Gyger, Adelboden.

MOMING PASS (LEFT) AND ROTHORN, ZINAL SIDE.

below, and we were half-way up the side of the great slope which led to the base of the ice-wall above.

Across this ice-slope Croz now proceeded to cut. It was executing a flank movement in the face of an enemy by whom we might be attacked at any moment. The peril was obvious. It was a monstrous folly. It was foolhardiness. A retreat should have been sounded.[1]

" I am not ashamed to confess," wrote Moore in his Journal, " that during the whole time we were crossing this slope my heart was in my mouth, and I never felt relieved from such a load of care as when, after, I suppose, a passage of about twenty minutes, we got on to the rocks and were in safety. . . . I have never heard a positive oath come from Almer's mouth, but the language in which he kept up a running commentary, more to himself than to me, as we went along, was stronger than I should have given him credit for using. His prominent feeling seemed to be one of *indignation* that we should be in such a position, and self-reproach at being a party to the proceeding ; while the emphatic way in which, at intervals, he exclaimed, ' Quick ; be quick,' sufficiently betokened his alarm."

It was not necessary to admonish Croz to be quick. He was fully as alive to the risk as any of the others. He told me afterwards, that this place was the most dangerous he had ever crossed, and that no consideration whatever would tempt him to cross it again. Manfully did he exert himself to escape from the impending destruction. His head, bent down to his work, never turned to the right or to the left. One, two, three, went his axe, and then he stepped on to the spot where he had been cutting. How painfully insecure should we have considered those steps at any other time ! But now, we thought only of the rocks in front, and of the hideous séracs, lurching over above us, apparently in the act of falling.

We got to the rocks in safety, and if they had been doubly

[1] The responsibility did not rest with Croz. His part was to advise, but not to direct.

as difficult as they were, we should still have been well content. We sat down and refreshed the inner man ; keeping our eyes on the towering pinnacles of ice under which we had passed, but which, now, were almost beneath us. Without a preliminary warning sound, one of the largest—as high as the Monument at London Bridge—fell upon the slope below. The stately mass heeled over as if upon a hinge (holding together until it bent 30 degrees forwards), then it crushed out its base, and, rent into a thousand fragments, plunged vertically down upon the

ICE-AVALANCHE ON THE MOMING PASS.

slope that we had crossed ! Every atom of our track, that was in its course, was obliterated ; all the new snow was swept away, and a broad sheet of smooth, glassy ice, showed the resistless force with which it had fallen.

It was inexcusable to follow such a perilous path, but it is easy to understand why it was taken. To have retreated from the place where Croz suggested a change of plan, to have descended below the reach of danger, and to have mounted again by the route which Almer suggested, would have been equivalent to abandoning the excursion ; for no one would have passed another night in the chalet on the Arpitetta Alp. " Many," says Thucydides, " though seeing well the perils ahead, are forced along by fear of dishonour—as the world calls it—so that, vanquished by a mere word, they fall into irremediable calamities." Such was nearly the case here. No one could say a word in justification of the course which was adopted ; all were alive to the danger that was being encountered ; yet a grave risk was deliberately—although unwillingly—incurred, in preference to admitting, by withdrawal from an untenable position, that an error of judgment had been committed.

After a laborious trudge over many species of snow, and through many varieties of vapour—from the quality of a Scotch mist to that of a London fog—we at length stood on the depression between the Rothorn and the Schallihorn.[1] A steep wall of snow was upon the Zinal side of the summit ; but what the descent was like on the other side we could not tell, for a billow of snow tossed over its crest by the western winds, suspended o'er Zermatt with motion arrested, resembling an ocean-wave frozen in the act of breaking, cut off the view.[2]

Croz—held hard in by the others, who kept down the Zinal side—opened his shoulders, flogged down the foam, and cut

[1] The summit of the pass has been marked on Dufour's map, 3,793 metres, or 12,445 feet.

[2] These snow-cornices are common on the crests of high mountain ridges, and it is always prudent, just before arriving upon the summit of a mountain or ridge, to *sound* with the alpenstock, that is to say, drive it in, to discover whether there is one or not. Men have often narrowly escaped losing their lives from neglecting this precaution.

These cornices are frequently rolled round in a volute, and sometimes take extravagant forms. See page 35.

away the cornice to its junction with the summit ; then boldly leaped down, and called on us to follow him.

It was well for us now that we had such a man as leader. An inferior or less daring guide would have hesitated to enter upon the descent in a dense mist ; and Croz himself would have done right to pause had he been less magnificent in physique. He acted, rather than said, " Where snow lies fast, there man can go ; where ice exists, a way may be cut ; it is a question of power ; I have the power,—all you have to do is to follow me." Truly, he did not spare himself, and could he have performed the feats upon the boards of a theatre that he did upon this occasion, he would have brought down the house with thunders of applause. Here is what Moore wrote in *his* Journal.

" The descent bore a strong resemblance to the Col de la Pilatte, but was very much steeper and altogether more difficult, which is saying a good deal. Croz was in his element, and selected his way with marvellous sagacity, while Almer had an equally honourable and, perhaps, more responsible post in the rear, which he kept with his usual steadiness. . . . One particular passage has impressed itself on my mind as one of the most nervous I have ever made. We had to pass along a crest of ice, a mere knife-edge,—on our left a broad crevasse, whose bottom was lost in blue haze, and on our right, at an angle of 70°, or more, a slope falling to a similar gulf below. Croz, as he went along the edge, chipped small notches in the ice, in which we placed our feet, with the toes well turned out, doing all we knew to preserve our balance. While stepping from one of these precarious footholds to another, I staggered for a moment. I had not really lost my footing ; but the agonized tone in which Almer, who was behind me, on seeing me waver, exclaimed, " Slip not, sir ! " gave us an even livelier impression than we already had of the insecurity of the position. . . . One huge chasm, whose upper edge was far above the lower one, could neither be leaped nor turned, and threatened to prove an insuper-

THE SUMMIT OF THE MOMING PASS IN 1864.

able barrier. But Croz showed himself equal to the emergency. Held up by the rest of the party, he cut a series of holes for the hands and feet, down and along the almost perpendicular wall of ice forming the upper side of the schrund. Down this slippery staircase we crept, with our faces to the wall, until a point was reached where the width of the chasm was not too great for us to drop across. Before we had done, we got quite accustomed to taking flying leaps over the schrunds. . . . To make a long story short ; after a most desperate and exciting struggle, and as bad a piece of ice-work as it is possible to imagine, we emerged on to the upper plateau of the Hohlicht Glacier."

The glimpses which had been caught of the lower part of the Hohlicht Glacier were discouraging, so it was now determined to cross over the ridge between it and the Rothorn Glacier. This was not done without a good deal of trouble. Again we rose to a height exceeding 12,000 feet. Eventually we took to the track of the despised Triftjoch, and descended by the well-known, but rough, path which leads to that pass ; arriving at the Monte Rosa hotel at Zermatt at 7.20 p.m. We occupied nearly twelve hours of actual walking in coming from the chalet on the Arpitetta Alp (which was 2½ hours above Zinal), and we consequently found that the Moming Pass was not the shortest route from Zinal to Zermatt, although it was the most direct.

Two dozen guides—good, bad, and indifferent ; French, Swiss, and Italian—can commonly be seen sitting on the wall on the front of the Monte Rosa hotel ; waiting on their employers, and looking for employers ; watching new arrivals, and speculating on the number of francs which may be extracted from their pockets. The *Messieurs*—sometimes strangely and wonderfully dressed—stand about in groups, or lean back in chairs, or lounge on the benches which are placed by the door. They wear extraordinary boots, and still more remarkable head-dresses. Their peeled, blistered, and swollen faces are worth studying. Some, by the exercise of watchfulness and unremitting care, have been fortunate enough to acquire a fine raw sienna complexion. But most of them have not been so happy. They' have been scorched on rocks, and roasted on glaciers. Their cheeks—first puffed, then cracked—have exuded a turpentine-like matter, which has coursed down their faces, and has dried in patches like the resin on the trunks of pines. They have removed it, and at the same time have pulled off large flakes of their skin. They have gone from bad to worse—their case has become hopeless—knives and scissors have been called into play ; tenderly, and daintily, they have endeavoured to reduce their cheeks to one, uniform hue. It is not to be done. But they have gone on, fascinated, and at last have brought their unhappy countenances to a state of helpless and complete ruin. Their lips are cracked ; their cheeks are swollen ; their eyes are blood-shot ; their noses are peeled and indescribable.

Such are the pleasures of the mountaineer ! Scornfully and derisively the last-comer compares the sight with his own flaccid face and dainty hands ; unconscious that he too, perhaps, will be numbered with those whom he now ridicules.

There is a frankness of manner about these strangely apparelled and queer-faced men, which does not remind one of drawing-room, or city life ; and it is good to see—in this club-room of Zermatt—those cold bodies, our too-frigid countrymen, regele together when brought into contact ; and it is pleasant to witness the hearty welcome given to the new-comers by the host and his excellent wife.[1]

I left this agreeable society to seek letters at the post. They yielded disastrous intelligence, and my holiday was brought to

---

[1] The opportunity is taken here to introduce to the reader some of the mountaineers who might have been seen at Zermatt in 1860–5, and a few of the guides who are mentioned in the course of my story. A key to this plate is given.

The description is left unaltered, though it is, now, a picture of the past. Our good friend and host—the " cordial and courteous " Seiler—died on July 10, 1891, aged 72.

KEY TO THE CLUB-ROOM OF ZERMATT (SEE PAGE 218).

1. Mr. F. CRAUFURD GROVE, President of the Alpine Club, 1884–1886. 2. Mr. GEORGE E. FOSTER. 3. Rev. J. ROBERTSON. 4. Mr. FRANK WALKER. 5. Mr. LESLIE STEPHEN, President of the Alpine Club, 1866–1868. 6. Mr. A. W. MOORE. 7. Mr. REGINALD S. MACDONALD. 8. Mr. JOHN BALL, Original Member, and first President of the Alpine Club. 9. Mr. WILLIAM MATHEWS, Original Member, and President of the Alpine Club, 1869–1871. 10. Mr. E. S. KENNEDY, Original Member, and President of the Alpine Club, 1861–1863. 11. Prof. T. G. BONNEY, President of the Alpine Club, 1881–1883. 12. ULRICH LAUENER. 13. Prof. JOHN TYNDALL. 14. Mr. (Justice) ALFRED WILLS, Original Member, and President of the Alpine Club, 1864–1865. 15. J. JOSEPH MAQUIGNAZ. 16. FRANZ ANDERMATTEN. 17. PETER TAUGWALDER fils. 18. PETER PERREN.

THE CLUB-ROOM OF ZERMATT IN 1864.

an abrupt termination. I awaited the arrival of Reilly (who was convoying stores for the attack on the Matterhorn) only to inform him that our arrangements were upset ; and then travelled home, day and night, as fast as express trains would carry me.

[*From Whymper's diary* : Tuesday July 19. Reilly did not arrive until too late in the day to get the afternoon diligence from Visp. Told him that I could not wait and advised him to try the Matterhorn himself. Offered him Croz, but he declined.]

[On January 18, 1864, Whymper wrote to Adams Reilly : " I think I must have another go at the Matterhorn. I have got a most original idea which I should like to try. Something totally different from any idea I have had before. I should, however, require Melchior, Almer, Croz, and two subordinates, and I fear this is likely to prove fatal to the scheme."]

[*Letter from Alexander Albrecht to Adams Reilly* (*in possession of the Alpine Club*).

Visp, May the 6 : 1864.

My Dear Sir !

I have been since six weeks at Sion, prevented by military service ; where your letter was sent to me. At first I received a letter from Mr. Strutt. He will come to Switzerland during the May, and he will stay there about to the middle of the month of June.

After that I got a letter from Mr. Walker. He want me from the 24th June untille to the end of July, and so I would bee free for you from that time as long as you please.

But I would not like to try the Matterhorn before to the end of July or before beginning of August. For I find out, it one of the wisest thing to try such high and steep mountains, like Matterhorn, only when all the snow is felled down.

Do you remember, Sir, at the Aiguille Verte ? And even

that, we have tryed to early in the year. I have allready many latin books, which I don't want more, but if you have Ovid's vers : liber tristis that is all what I wish.

I should like much more if you woud bring me a good english Kautschoug, or Makintosh.

But in all case I hop to have a letter from you very soon, for to hear where I have to meet you.

I remain whith kind regards,

your most sincerely,

Albrecht,

guide.]

CHAPTER XII

THE FIRST ASCENT OF THE GRAND CORNIER

> " *Ye crags and peaks, I'm with you once again !*
> *. . . Methinks I hear*
> *A spirit in your echoes answer me,*
> *And bid your tenant welcome to his home*
> *Again ! . . .*"
>
> S. KNOWLES.

OUR career in 1864 had been one of unbroken success, but the great ascent upon which I had set my heart was not attempted, and, until it was accomplished, I was unsatisfied. Other things, too, influenced me to visit the Alps once more. I wished to travel elsewhere, in places where the responsibility of direction would rest with myself alone. It was well to know how far my judgment in the choice of routes could be relied upon.

The journey of 1865 was chiefly undertaken, then, to find out to what extent I was capable to select a way over mountainous country. The programme which was drawn up for this journey was rather ambitious, since it included almost all of the great peaks which had not then been ascended ; but it was neither lightly undertaken nor hastily executed. All pains were taken to secure success. Information was sought from those who could give it, and the defeats of others were studied, that their errors might be avoided. The results which followed came not so much, perhaps, from luck, as from forethought and careful calculation.

For success does not, as a rule, come by chance, and when one fails there is a reason for it. But when any notable, or so-called brilliant thing is done, we are too apt to look upon the success alone, without considering how it was attained. Whilst, when men fail, we inquire why they have not succeeded. So failures are frequently more instructive than successes, and the disappointments of some become profitable to others.

Up to a certain point, the programme was completely and happily carried out. Nothing but success attended our efforts so long as the excursions were executed as they had been planned. Most of them were made upon the very days which had been fixed for them months beforehand ; and all were accomplished, comparatively speaking, so easily, that their descriptions must be, in the absence of difficulty and danger, less interesting to the general reader than they would have been if our course had been marked by blunders and want of judgment. Before proceeding to speak of these excursions, it will not be entirely useless to explain the reasons which influenced the selection of the routes which were adopted upon them.

In the course of the past five seasons my early practices were revolutionized. My antipathy to snow was overcome, and my predilection for rocks was modified. Like all those who are not mountaineers born, I was, at the first, extremely nervous upon steep snow. The snow seemed bound to slip, and all those who were upon it to go along with it. Snow of a certain quality is undoubtedly liable to slip when it is at a certain inclination.[1] The exact states which are dangerous, or safe, it is not possible to describe in writing. That is only learnt by experience, and confidence upon snow is not really felt until one has gained experience. Confidence gradually came to me, and as it came so did my partiality for rocks diminish. For it was evident, to use a common expression, that it paid better to travel upon snow than over rocks. This applies to snow-beds pure and simple, or to snow which is lying over glacier ; and in the selection of routes it has, latterly, always been my practice to look for the places where snow-slopes, or snow-covered glaciers, extend highest upon mountains.[2]

[1] See pp. 125 and 203.   [2] See pp. 151, 152.

E. Gyger, Adelboden.

ALPINE CORNICES.

It is comparatively seldom, however, that an ascent of a great mountain can be executed exclusively over snow and glacier. Ridges peep through which have to be surmounted. In my earlier scramblings I usually took to, or was taken upon, the summits (or arêtes) of the ridges, and a good many mountaineers habitually take to them on principle, as the natural and proper way. According to my experience, it is seldom well to do so when any other course is open. As I have already said, and presently shall repeat more particularly, the crests of all the main ridges of the great peaks of the Alps are shattered and cleft by frost ; and it not unfrequently happens that a notch in a ridge, which appears perfectly insignificant from a distance, is found to be an insuperable barrier to further progress ; and a great détour, or a long descent, has to be made to avoid the obstacle. When committed to an arête one is tied, almost always, to a particular course, from which it is difficult to deviate. Much loss of time generally results if any serious obstruction occurs upon it.

But it rarely happens that a great Alpine peak is seen that is cut off abruptly, in all directions, from the surrounding snows and glaciers. In its gullies snow will cling, although its faces may be too steep for the formation of permanent snow-beds. The merits of these snow-gullies (or *couloirs*) have been already pointed out,[1] and it is hardly necessary to observe, after that which was just now said about snow, that ascents of snow-gullies (with proper precautions) are very much to be preferred to ascents of rocky arêtes.

By following the glaciers, the snow-slopes above, and the couloirs rising from them, it is usually possible to get very close to the summits of the great peaks in the Alps. The final climb will, perhaps, necessarily be by a rocky arête. The less of it the better.

It occasionally occurs that considerable mountain slopes, or faces, are destitute of snow-gullies. In that case it will, very

[1] See pp. 180, 181.

likely, be best to adhere to the faces (or to the gullies or minor ridges upon them) rather than to take to the *great* ridges. Upon a face one can move to the right or to the left with more facility than upon the crest of a ridge ; and when a difficulty is arrived at, it is, consequently, less troublesome to circumvent.

In selecting the routes which were taken in 1865, I looked, first, for places where glaciers and snow extended highest up into the mountains which were to be ascended, or the ridges which were to be crossed. Next, for gullies filled with snow leading still higher ; and finally, from the heads of the gullies we completed the ascents, whenever it was practicable, by faces instead of by arêtes. The ascent of the Grand Cornier (13,022), of the Dent Blanche (14,318), Grandes Jorasses (13,797), Aiguille Verte (13,541), Ruinette (12,727), and the Matterhorn (14,782), were all accomplished in this way ; besides the other excursions which will be referred to by and by. The route selected, before the start was made, was in every case strictly followed out.

We inspected all of these mountains from neighbouring heights before entering upon their ascents. I explained to the guides the routes I proposed to be taken, and (when the courses were at all complicated) sketched them out on paper to prevent misunderstanding. In some few cases they suggested variations, and in every case the route was well discussed. The *execution* of the work was done by the guides, and I seldom interfered with, or attempted to assist in it.

The 13th of June 1865 I spent in the valley of Lauterbrunnen with the Rev. W. H. Hawker and the guides Christian and Ulrich Lauener ; and on the 14th crossed the Petersgrat with Christian Almer and Johann Tannler to Turtmann in the Valais. Tannler was then paid off, as Michel Croz and Franz Biener were awaiting me.

[From Whymper's diary : June 13th, 1865.

Attempt to make a new pass by the Ebnefluh to the Eggishorn. Started at 2.30 a.m. (an hour late) with Christian Almer and

Johann Tannler as my guides, and the two Laueners for Hawker. Got to chalets at Steinberg at 3.45, having lost 10 minutes by halts. Left again after hot milk at 4.45. The Laueners led up straight away through a very rotten forest, most beastly scrambling. Then over a very rough path passing some higher chalets near the Schmadribach falls, then bearing to the left over rough débris-slopes, and after these to a long buttress sinking down from the Mittaghorn, and separating the Schmadri and Mittaghorn Glaciers. On this we halted (near the top of it) at 6.50, having a most splendid view over the Tschingel Glacier and the precipices opposite to us, and also of the Blümlisalp, Tschingelhorn, Breithorn, Jungfrau and Silberhorn. We looked right down the valley of Lauterbrunnen, the great precipices on either side looking very insignificant. Left again after feeding at 7.45, took almost immediately to the glacier, going right up the middle of its left branch, and then went right across its head. Some very curious sérac-work was done by Almer, but the small crevasses being snowed up we walked right over. We struck the ridge separating the Mittaghorn Glacier from the Breitlauenen Glacier at an easy point at 9.50. Ate again, and started at 10.40. Went up the snow arête of the ridge, and over the névé to the schrund separating us from the last slopes of ice, snow and rocks, leading right up to the col. The snow was granular up above, and a good deal of ice mixed with it. The Laueners sung out when Almer was just getting across the schrund that it would still take 5 or 6 hours to the top, and that we must necessarily be surprised by the night. This so frightened Hawker, who had been calling continued halts much to my annoyance, that he resolved to go back. As he would of course carry off the Laueners, and leave me with only two men and a lot of luggage, I saw it was imprudent to go on, although Almer said he would go on with me if I wished it. We turned at 12.5, and got back to Steinberg chalets at 4.10, having lost, I should say, 45 minutes by halts. The Laueners I consider did not behave well, throwing all the work on Almer or at least leaving it to him, went a route of which I, with reason, disapproved, and took every opportunity of losing time ; coming, moreover, one hour late in the morning, which decidedly helped to lose the expedition. Day was very cloudy at times and gave us much trouble. Ulrich Lauener's patronizing way of calling Christian " Christi " was very amusing ; both are about 6 ft. 5 in. high. . . . Tyndall's Lauitor Almer said was not nearly so steep as the place we tried.]

It was not possible to find two leading guides who worked together more harmoniously than Croz and Almer. Biener's part was subordinate to theirs, and he was added as a convenience rather than as a necessity. Croz spoke French alone ; Almer little else than German. Biener spoke both languages, and was useful on that account ; but he seldom went to the front, excepting during the early part of the day, when the work was easy, and he acted throughout more as a porter than as a guide.

The importance of having a reserve of power on mountain expeditions cannot be too strongly insisted upon. We always had some in hand, and were never pressed, or overworked, so long as we were together. Come what might, we were ready for it. But by a series of chances, which I shall never cease to regret, I was first obliged to part with Croz, and then to dismiss the others ; and so, deviating from the course that I had deliberately adopted, which was successful in practice because it was sound in principle, became fortuitously a member of an expedition that ended with the catastrophe which brings this book, and brought my scrambles amongst the Alps, to a close.[1]

---

[1] I engaged Croz for 1865 before I parted from him in 1864 ; but upon writing to him in the month of April to fix the dates of his engagement, I found that he had supposed he was free (in consequence of not having heard from me earlier), and had engaged himself to a Mr. B—— from the 27th of June. I endeavoured to hold him to his promise, but he considered himself

On June 15 we went from Turtmann to Z'Meiden, and thence over the Forcletta pass to Zinal. We diverged from the summit of the pass up some neighbouring heights to inspect the Grand Cornier, and I decided to have nothing to do with its northern side.

On the 16th we left Zinal at 2.5 a.m., having been for a moment greatly surprised by an entry in the hotel-book,[1] and

unable to withdraw from his later obligation. His letters were honourable to him. The following extract from the last one he wrote to me is given as an interesting souvenir of a brave and upright man :—

Enfin, Monsieur, je regrette beaucoup d'être engagé avec votre compatriote et de ne pouvoir vous accompagner dans vos conquêtes mais dès qu'on a donné sa parole on doit la tenir et être homme.

Ainsi, prenez patience pour cette campagne et espérons que plus tard nous nous retrouverons.

En attendant recevez les humbles salutations de votre tout dévoué

Croz Michel-Auguste

---

[1] It was an entry describing an ascent of the Grand Cornier (which we supposed had never been ascended) from the very direction which we had just pronounced to be hopeless ! It was especially startling, because Franz Biener was spoken of in the account as having been concerned in the ascent. On examining Biener it was found that he had made the excursion, and had supposed at the time he was upon his summit that it was the Grand Cornier. He saw afterwards that they had only ascended one of the several points upon the ridge running northwards from the Grand Cornier—I believe, the Pigne de l'Allée (11,168 feet) !

An attempt was made in 1878 to climb the northern side of the Grand Cornier, and it was found impracticable. See *Alpine Journal*, vol. ix., p. 106.

ascending by the Durand Glacier, and giving the base of our mountain a wide berth in order that it might the better be examined, passed gradually right round to its south, before a way up it was seen.[1] At 8.30 we arrived upon the plateau of the glacier that descends towards the east, between the Grand

PART OF THE SOUTHERN RIDGE OF THE GRAND CORNIER.

Cornier and the Dent Blanche, and from this place a route was

[1] For route, see the Map of the valley of Zermatt. [*Whymper's diary* records :

Easy snow slopes and easy séracs on the glacier between Grand Cornier and Dent Blanche, the latter quite impossible from this side, being on all its faces covered with hanging glaciers that sent down avalanches and all abominations. We went over immense tracks of avalanche débris. Croz as usual, now that he had got to the front, stamping off directly we talked of tying up, and getting a start of nearly a quarter of a mile.]

readily traced. We steered to the north (as shown upon the map) over the glacier, towards the ridge that descends to the east ; gained it by mounting snow-slopes, and followed it to the summit, which was arrived at before half-past twelve. From first to last the route was almost entirely over snow.

The ridges leading to the north and to the south from the summit of the Grand Cornier exhibited in a most striking manner the extraordinary effects that may be produced by violent alternations of heat and cold. The southern one was hacked and split into the wildest forms ; and the northern one was not less cleft and impracticable, and offered the droll piece of rock-carving which is represented upon this page. Some small blocks actually tottered and fell before our eyes, and, starting others

PART OF THE NORTHERN RIDGE OF THE GRAND CORNIER.

in their downward course, grew into a perfect avalanche, which descended with a solemn roar on to the glaciers beneath.

It is natural that the great ridges should present the wildest forms—not on account of their dimensions, but by reason of their positions. They are exposed to the fiercest heat of the sun, and are seldom in shadow as long as it is above the horizon. They are entirely unprotected, and are attacked by the strongest blasts and by the most intense cold. The most durable rocks are not proof against such assaults. These grand, apparently solid—eternal—mountains, seeming so firm, so immutable, are yet ever changing and crumbling into dust. These shattered ridges are evidence of their sufferings. Let me repeat that every

principal ridge of every great peak in the Alps amongst those
I have seen has been shattered in this way; and that every
summit, amongst the rock-summits upon which I have stood,
has been nothing but a piled-up heap of fragments.

The minor ridges do not usually present such extraordinary
forms as the principal ones. They are less exposed, and they
are less broken up; and it is reasonable to assume that their
annual degradation is less than that of the summit-ridges.

The wear and tear does not cease even in winter, for these
great ridges are never completely covered up by snow,[1] and the
sun has still power. The destruction is incessant, and increases
as time goes on; for the greater the surfaces which are exposed
to the practically inexhaustible powers of sun and frost, the
greater ruin will be effected.

The rock-falls which are continually occurring upon all rock
mountains (such as are referred to upon pp. 33, 61) are, of
course, caused by these powers. No one doubts it; but one
never believes it so thoroughly as when the quarries are seen
from which their materials have been hewn; and when the
germs, so to speak, of these avalanches have been seen actually
starting from above.

These falls of rock take place from two causes. First, from

[1] I wrote in the *Athenæum*, August 29, 1863, to the same effect. "This
action of the frost does not cease in winter, inasmuch as it is impossible for
the Matterhorn to be entirely covered by snow. Less precipitous mountains
may be entirely covered up during winter, and if they do not then actually
gain height, the wear and tear is, at least, suspended. . . . We arrive, therefore, at the conclusion that, although such snow-peaks as Mont Blanc *may*
in the course of ages grow higher, the Matterhorn must decrease in height."
These remarks have received confirmation.

The men who were left by M. Dollfus-Ausset in his observatory upon the
summit of the Col Théodule, during the winter of 1865, remarked that the
snow was partially melted upon the rocks in their vicinity upon 19th, 20th,
21st, 22nd, 23rd, 26th, 27th December of that year, and upon the 22nd of
December they entered in their Journal, "*Nous avons vu au Matterhorn que la
neige se fondait sur roches et qu'il s'en écoulait de l'eau.*"—*Matériaux pour l'étude
des Glaciers*, vol. viii., part i., p. 246, 1868; and vol. viii., part ii., p. 77, 1869.

the heat of the sun detaching small stones or rocks which have been arrested on ledges or slopes and bound together by snow or ice. I have seen such released many times when the sun has risen high ; fall gently at first, gather strength, grow in volume, and at last rush down with a cloud trailing behind, like the dust after an express train. Secondly, from the freezing of the water which trickles, during the day, into the clefts, fissures, and crannies. This agency is naturally most active in the night, and then, or during very cold weather, the greatest falls take place.[1]

When one has continually seen and heard these falls, it is easily understood why the glaciers are laden with moraines. The wonder is, not that they are sometimes so great, but that they are not always greater. Irrespective of lithological considerations, one knows that this débris cannot have been *excavated* by the glaciers. The moraines are *borne* by glaciers, but they are *born* from the ridges. They are generated by the sun, and delivered by the frost. " Fire," it is well said in Plutarch's life of Camillus, " is the most active thing in nature, and all generation is motion, or at least, with motion ; all other parts of matter without warmth lie sluggish and dead, and crave the influence of heat as their life, and when that comes upon them, they immediately acquire some active or passive qualities." [2]

If the Alps were granted a perfectly invariable temperature, if they were no longer subjected, alternately, to freezing blasts and to scorching heat, they might more correctly be termed " eternal." They might still continue to decay, but their abasement would be much less rapid.

[1] In each of the seven nights I passed upon the south-west ridge of the Matterhorn in 1861–3 (at heights varying from 11,844 to 12,992 feet above the level of the sea), the rocks fell incessantly in showers and avalanches.

[2] Tonson's Ed. of 1758. Bacon may have had this passage in mind when he wrote, " It must not be thought that heat generates motion, or motion heat (though in some respects this be true), but that the very essence of heat, or the substantial self of heat, is motion and nothing else."—*Novum Organum*, book ii. Devey's Translation.

When rocks are covered up by a sheet of glacier they do enjoy an almost invariable temperature. The extremes of summer and winter are unknown to rocks which are so covered up,—a range of a very few degrees is the most that is possible underneath the ice.[1] There is, *then*, little or no disintegration from unequal expansion and contraction. Frost, *then*, does not penetrate into the heart of the rock, and cleave off vast masses. The rocks, *then*, sustain grinding instead of cleaving. Atoms, *then*, come away instead of masses. Fissures and overhanging surfaces are bridged, for the ice cannot get at them ; and after many centuries of grinding have been sustained, we still find numberless angular surfaces (in the *lee-sides*) which were fashioned before the ice began to work.

The points of difference which are so evident between the operations of heat, cold, and water, and those of glaciers upon rocks, are as follow. The former take advantage of cracks, fissures, joints, and soft places ; the latter do not. The former can work *underneath* overhanging masses ; the latter cannot. The effects produced by the former continually *increase*, because they continually expose fresh surfaces by forming new cracks, fissures, and holes. The effects which the latter produce constantly *diminish*, because the area of the surfaces operated upon becomes less and less, as they become smoother and flatter.

What can one conclude, then, but that sun, frost, and water have had infinitely more to do than glaciers with the fashioning of mountain-forms and valley-slopes ? Who can refuse to believe that powers which are at work everywhere, which have been at work always, which are so incomparably active, capable, and enduring, must have produced greater effects than a solitary

---

[1] Doubtless, *at the sides* of glacier-beds, the range of temperature is greater. But there is evidence that the winter cold does not penetrate to the innermost recesses of glacier-beds in the fact that streams continue to flow underneath the ice all the year round, winter as well as summer, in the Alps and (I was informed in Greenland) in Greenland. Experimental proof can be readily obtained that even in midsummer the bottom temperature is close to 32° F.

power which is always local in its influence, which has worked, *comparatively*, but for a short time, which is always slow and feeble in its operations, and which constantly diminishes in intensity ?

My reverie was interrupted by Croz observing that it was time to be off. Less than two hours sufficed to take us to the glacier plateau below (where we had left our baggage) ; three-quarters of an hour more placed us upon the depression between the Grand Cornier and the Dent Blanche (Col du Grand Cornier [1]), and at 6 p.m. we arrived at Bricolla. Croz and Biener hankered after milk, and descended to a village lower down the valley ; but Almer and I stayed where we were, and passed a chilly night on some planks in a half-burnt chalet.[2]

---

[1] This was crossed, for the first time, on July 27, 1864, by the Rev. J. J. Hornby and Mr. Philpott, with Christian Lauener and Joseph Viennin. See *Alpine Journal*, vol. i., p. 431.

[2] The following details may interest mountain-climbers. Left Zinal (5,505 feet) 2.5 a.m. Thence to plateau S.E. of summit of Grand Cornier, 5 h. 25 min. From the plateau to the summit of the mountain, 2½ hours. The last 300 feet of the ridge followed were exceedingly sharp and narrow, with a great cornice, from which huge icicles depended. We were obliged to go *underneath* the cornice, and to cut a way through the icicles. Descent from summit to plateau, 1 h. 40 min. Sharp snowstorm, with thunder. Plateau to summit of Col du Grand Cornier (rocks easy), 45 min. From the summit of the col to the end of glacier leading to the west, 55 min. Thence to Bricolla (7,959 feet), 15 min.

CHAPTER XIII

THE ASCENT OF THE DENT BLANCHE

" God help thee, Trav'ller, on thy journey far ;
The wind is bitter keen,—the snow o'erlays
The hidden pits, and dang'rous hollow-ways,
And darkness will involve thee.—No kind star
To-night will guide thee." . . .

H. KIRKE WHITE.

CROZ and Biener did not return until past 5 a.m. on June 17, and we then set out at once for Zermatt, intending to cross the Col d'Hérens.   But we did not proceed far before the attractions of the Dent Blanche were felt to be irresistible, and we turned aside up the steep lateral glacier which descends along its south-western face.

The Dent Blanche is a mountain that is little known except to the climbing fraternity.   It was, and is, reputed to be one of the most difficult mountains in the Alps. Many attempts were made to scale it before its ascent was accomplished. Even Leslie Stephen himself, fleetest of foot of the whole Alpine brotherhood, once upon a time returned discomfited from it.

LESLIE STEPHEN.

It was not climbed until 1862 ; but in that year Mr. T. S. Kennedy, with Mr. Wigram, and the guides Jean B. Croz [1] and Kronig, managed to conquer it.   They had a hard fight, though, before

[1] The brother of my guide Michel Croz.

they gained the victory ; a furious wind and driving snow, added to the natural difficulties, nearly turned the scale against them.[1]

Mr. Kennedy started from Bricolla between 2 and 3 a.m. on July 18, 1862, and ascending the glacier that is mentioned in the opening paragraph, went towards the point marked 3,912 metres upon the map ; [2] then turned to the left (that is, to the north), and completed the ascent by the southern ridge,—that which overhangs the western side of the Schönbühl Glacier.

Mr. Kennedy described his expedition in a very interesting paper in the *Alpine Journal* (vol. i., pp. 33–9). His account bore the impress of truth ; yet unbelievers said that it was impossible to have told (in weather such as was experienced) whether the 'summit had actually been attained, and sometimes roundly asserted that the mountain, as the saying is, still remained virgin.

I did not share these doubts, although they influenced me to make the ascent. I thought it might be possible to find an easier route than that taken by Mr. Kennedy, and that if we succeeded in discovering one we should be able at once to refute his traducers, and to vaunt our superior wisdom. Actuated by these elevated motives, I halted my little army at the foot of the glacier, and inquired, " Which is best for us to do ?—to ascend the Dent Blanche, or to cross to Zermatt ? " They answered, with befitting solemnity, " We think Dent Blanche is best."

From the chalets of Bricolla the south-west face of the Dent Blanche is regarded almost exactly in profile. From thence it is seen that the angle of the face scarcely exceeds thirty degrees, and after observing this I concluded that the face would, in all probability, give an easier path to the summit than the crest of the very jagged ridge which was followed by Mr. Kennedy.

We zigzagged up the glacier along the foot of the face, and looked for a way on to it. We looked for some time in vain, for a mighty bergschrund effectually prevented approach, and, like a fortress' moat, protected the wall from assault. We went

---

[1] See note to pp. 78, 79.   [2] See Map of the valley of Zermatt.

up and up, until, I suppose, we were not more than a thousand feet below the point marked 3,912 metres ; then a bridge was discovered, and we dropped down on hands and knees to cross it.

A bergschrund, it was said on p. 194, is a schrund, and something more than a schrund. A schrund is simply a big crevasse. A bergschrund is frequently, although not always, a big crevasse. The term is applied to the last of the crevasses that one finds, in ascending, before quitting the glacier, and taking to the rocks which bound it. It is the mountain's schrund. Sometimes it is *very* large, but early in the season (that is to say in the month of June or before) bergschrunds are usually snowed up, or well bridged over, and do not give much trouble. Later in the year, say in August, they are frequently very great hindrances, and occasionally are completely impassable.

They are lines of rupture consequent upon unequal motion. The glaciers below move quicker than the snow or ice which clings immediately to the mountains ; hence these fissures result. The slower motion of that which is above can only be attributed to its having to sustain greater friction ; for the rule is that the upper portion is set at a steeper angle than the lower. As that is the case, we should expect that the upper portion would move *quicker* than the lower, and it would do so, doubtless, but for the retardation of the rocks over which, and through which, it passes.[1]

We crossed the bergschrund of the Dent Blanche, I suppose, at a height of about 12,000 feet above the level of the sea. Our work may be said to have commenced at that point. The face, although not steep in its general inclination, was so cut up by little ridges and cliffs, and so seamed with incipient couloirs, that it had all the difficulty of a much more precipitous slope. The

[1] Couloirs are invariably protected at their bases by bergschrunds. An example of a couloir with a double bergschrund is given on p. 180.

THE BERGSCHRUND, ON THE DENT BLANCHE IN 1865.

CENTRAL AND EASTERN PENNINE ALPS, FROM THE WEST.

difficulties were never great, but they were numerous, and made a very respectable total when put together. We passed the bergschrund soon after nine in the morning, and during the next eleven hours halted only five-and-forty minutes. The whole of the remainder of the time was occupied in ascending and descending the 2,400 feet which compose this south-western face ; and inasmuch as 1,000 feet per hour (taking the mean of ascent and descent) is an ordinary rate of progression, it is tolerably certain that the Dent Blanche is a mountain of exceptional difficulty.

The hindrances opposed to us by the mountain itself were, however, as nothing compared with the atmospheric obstructions. It is true there was plenty of, " Are you fast, Almer ? " " Yes." " Go ahead, Biener." Biener, made secure, cried, " Come on, sir," and *Monsieur* endeavoured. " No, no," said Almer, " not there,—*here*,"—pointing with his bâton to the right place to clutch. Then 'twas Croz's turn, and we all drew in the rope as the great man followed. " Forwards " once more—and so on.

Five hundred feet of this kind of work had been accomplished when we were saluted (not entirely unexpectedly) by the first gust of a hurricane which was raging above. The day was a lovely one for dwellers in the valleys, but we had, long ago, noted some light, gossamer clouds, that were hovering round our summit, being drawn out in a suspicious manner into long, silky threads. Croz, indeed, prophesied before we had crossed the schrund, that we should be beaten by the wind, and had advised that we should return. But I had retorted, " No, my good Croz, you said just now ' Dent Blanche is best ' ; we must go up the Dent Blanche."

I have a very lively and disagreeable recollection of this wind. Upon the outskirts of the disturbed region it was only felt occasionally. It then seemed to make rushes at one particular man, and when it had discomfited him, it whisked itself away to some far-off spot, only to return, presently, in greater force than before.

My old enemy—the Matterhorn—seen across the basin of the Z'Mutt Glacier, looked totally unassailable. " Do you think," the men asked, " that you, or anyone else, will ever get up *that* mountain ? " And when, undismayed by their ridicule, I stoutly answered, " Yes, but not upon that side," they burst into derisive chuckles. I must confess that my hopes sank ; for nothing can look more completely inaccessible than the Matterhorn on its northern and north-west sides.

" Forwards " once again. We overtopped the Dent d'Hérens. " Not a thousand feet more ; in three hours we shall be on the summit." " You mean *ten*," echoed Croz, so slow had been the progress. But I was not far wrong in the estimate. At 3.15 we struck the great ridge followed by Mr. Kennedy, close to the top of the mountain. The wind and cold were terrible there. Progress was oftentimes impossible, and we waited, crouching under the lee of rocks, listening to " the shrieking of the mindless wind," while the blasts swept across, tearing off the upper snow and blowing it away in streamers over the Schönbühl Glacier—" nothing seen except an indescribable writhing in the air, like the wind made visible."

Our goal was concealed by mist, although it was only a few yards away, and Croz's prophecy, that we should stay all night upon the summit, seemed likely to come true. The men rose with the occasion, although even *their* fingers had nearly lost sensation. There were no murmurings, nor suggestions of return, and they pressed on for the little white cone which they knew must be near at hand. Stopped again ; a big mass perched loosely on the ridge barred the way ; we could not crawl over, and scarcely dared creep round it. The wine went round for the last time. The liquor was half frozen,—still we would more of it. It was all gone ; the bottle was left behind, and we pushed on, for there was a lull.

The end came almost before it was expected. The clouds opened, and I saw that we were all but upon the highest point, and that, between us and it, about twenty yards off, there was a little artificial pile of stones. Kennedy was a true man,—it was a cairn which he had erected. " What is that, Croz ? " " *Homme des pierres*," he bawled. It was needless to proceed farther ; I jerked the rope from Biener, and motioned that we should go back. He did the same to Almer, and we turned immediately. *They* did not see the stones (they were cutting footsteps), and misinterpreted the reason of the retreat. Voices were inaudible, and explanations impossible.[1]

We commenced the descent of the face. It was hideous work. The men looked like impersonations of Winter, with their hair all frosted, and their beards matted with ice. My hands were numbed—dead. I begged the others to stop. "*We cannot afford to stop ; we must continue to move*," was their reply. They were right ; to stop was to be entirely frozen. So we went down ; gripping rocks varnished with ice, which pulled the skin from the fingers. Gloves were useless ; they became iced too, and the bâtons slid through them as slippery as eels. The iron of the axes stuck to the fingers—it felt red-hot ; but it was useless to shrink, the rocks and the axes had to be firmly grasped—no faltering would do here.

We turned back at 4.12 p.m., and at 8.15 crossed the bergschrund again, not having halted for a minute upon the entire descent. During the last two hours it was windless, but time was of such vital importance that we pressed on incessantly, and did not stop until we were fairly upon the glacier. Then we took stock of what remained of the tips of our fingers. There was not much skin left ; they were perfectly raw, and for weeks afterwards I was reminded of the ascent of the Dent Blanche by the twinges which I felt when I pulled on my boots. The others escaped with some slight frost-bites ; and, altogether, we had reason to congratulate ourselves that we got off so lightly. The men complimented me upon the descent, and I could do the same honestly to them. If they had worked less

[1] The summit of the Dent Blanche is a ridge, perhaps 100 yards in length. The highest point is usually at its north-eastern end.

vigorously, or harmoniously, we should have been benighted upon the face, where there was not a single spot upon which it was possible to sit ; and if that had happened, I do not think that one would have survived to tell the tale.

We made the descent of the glacier in a mist, and of the moraine at its base, and of the slopes below, in total darkness, and regained the chalets of Bricolla at 11.45 p.m. We had been absent eighteen and a half hours, and out of that time had been going not less than seventeen. That night we slept the sleep of those who are thoroughly tired.[1]

[*From Whymper's diary : June 17th, 1865. Dent Blanche.*

. . . We stopped when a little distance up at 9.45 to eat, left again at 10. Soon after this we arrived at the place which Croz all along had said would lick us. It was no use going there, he said, we shall have to come back again. " We are too far off to see," was my invariable answer. Arrived there, Almer who was first and Biener who was second, both said it couldn't be passed. The place was awkward undoubtedly, but easier than many places we have passed before and since, and I was annoyed at the readiness with which they all seemed disposed to turn back. I therefore commenced untying myself, and said I would try it myself before I would say it couldn't be done. " Wait a moment," said Almer, who then commenced climbing and who passed it, not absolutely with facility, but sufficiently easily to show that I was right. We went on till 11.15 at same work, and then came to a large and somewhat overhanging rock.

[1] The ascent of the Dent Blanche is one of the hardest that I have made. There was nothing upon it so difficult as the last 500 feet of the Pointe des Ecrins ; but, on the other hand, there was hardly a step upon it which was positively easy. The whole of the face required actual climbing. There was, probably, very little difference in difficulty between the route we took in 1865, and that followed by Mr. Kennedy in 1862.

The second ascent of the Dent Blanche was made by Mr. John Finlaison, with the guides Christian Lauener and Franz Zurfluh, in September 1864. See the *Alpine Journal*, vol. ii., pp. 292–301, June 1866.

Here Croz proposed we should halt, make a gîte, and go on next day ; but the next day was Sunday, and I didn't relish the idea. " Let us make the gîte coming down," I said. " Mais, ma foi ! " and up went his shoulders as usual. " We shan't get to the top before eight o'clock and we shall have to sleep *there*." Croz was manifestly perverse. We now went on steadily, and although it is absurd to say so, Almer made a splendid burst, going without intermission for 3¾ hours.]

T. S. KENNEDY.

Two days afterwards, when walking into Zermatt, whom should we meet but Mr. Kennedy. " Hullo ! " we said, " we have just seen your cairn on the top of the Dent Blanche." " No, you haven't," he answered, very positively. " What do you mean ? " " Why, that you cannot have seen my cairn, because I didn't make one ! " " Well, but we saw *a* cairn." " No doubt ; it was made by a man who went up the mountain last year with Lauener and Zurfluh." " O-o-h," we said, rather disgusted at hearing news when we expected to communicate some. " O-o-h ! good morning, Kennedy." Before this happened, we managed to lose our way upon the Col d'Hérens ; but an account of that must be reserved for the next chapter.

CHAPTER XIV

LOST ON THE COL D'HERENS—MY SEVENTH ATTEMPT TO ASCEND THE MATTERHORN

" Oh ! ye immortal gods, where in the world are we ? "

CICERO.

WE should have started for Zermatt about 7 a.m. on the 18th, had not Biener asked to be allowed to go to mass at Evolena, a village about two and a half hours from Bricolla. He received permission, on the condition that he returned not later than midday, but he did not come back until 2.30 p.m., and we thereby got into a pretty little mess.

The pass which we were about to traverse to Zermatt—the Col d'Hérens—is one of the few glacier-passes in this district which have been known almost from time immemorial. It is frequently crossed in the summer season, and is a very easy route, notwithstanding that the summit of the pass is 11,418 feet above the level of the sea.[1]

From Bricolla to the summit the way lies chiefly over the flat Glacier de Ferpècle. The walk is of the most straightforward kind. The glacier rises in gentle undulations ; its crevasses are small and easily avoided ; and all you have to do, after once getting upon the ice, is to proceed due south, in the most direct manner possible. If you do so, in two hours you should be upon the summit of the pass.

We tied ourselves in line, of course, when we entered upon the glacier, and placed Biener to lead, as he had frequently

[1] See Map of the valley of Zermatt. The route taken upon June 19 is alone marked.

242

crossed the pass ; supposing that his local knowledge might save us some time upon the other side. We had proceeded, I believe, about half-way up, when a little, thin cloud dropped down upon us from above. It was so light and gauzy, that we did not for a moment suppose it would become embarrassing, and hence I neglected to note at the proper moment the course which we should steer,—that is to say, to observe our precise situation, in regard to the summit of the pass.

For some little time Biener progressed steadily, making a tolerably straight track ; but at length he wavered, and deviated sometimes to the right, and sometimes to the left. Croz rushed forward directly he saw this, and taking the poor young man by his shoulders gave him a good shaking, told him that he was an imbecile, to untie himself at once, and to go to the rear. Biener looked half frightened, and obeyed without a murmur. Croz led off briskly, and made a good straight track for a few minutes. Then, it seemed to me, he began to move steadily round to the left. I looked back, but the mist was now too thick to see our traces, and so we continued to follow our leader. At last the others (who were behind, and in a better position to judge) thought the same as I did, and we pulled up Croz to deliver our opinion.

He took our criticism in good part, but when Biener opened his mouth that was too much for him to stand, and he told the young man again, " *You* are imbecile ; I bet you twenty francs to one that *my* track is better than *yours* ; twenty francs, now then, imbecile ! "

[*From Whymper's diary :* An animated discussion ensued, we all opposed his opinion which made him furious ; with Biener he was particularly loud. " Pour vingt francs, vingt francs," he continually shouted, but Biener had not pluck enough to back his opinion.]

Almer went to the front. He commenced by returning in the

track for a hundred yards or so, and then started off at a tangent
from Croz's curve. We kept this course for half an hour, and
then were certain that we were not on the right route, because
the snow became decidedly steep. We bore away more and
more to the right, to avoid this steep bank, but at last I rebelled,
as we had for some time been going almost south-west, which
was altogether the wrong direction. After a long discussion we
returned some distance in our track, and then steered a little east
of south, but we continually met steep snow-slopes, and to avoid
them went right or left as the case might require.

We were greatly puzzled, and could not in the least tell
whether we were too near the Dent Blanche or too close to the
Tête Blanche. The mists had thickened, and were now as dense
as a moderate London fog. There were no rocks or echoes to
direct us, and the guidance of the compass brought us invariably
against these steep snow-banks. The men were fairly beaten ;
they had all had a try, or more than one, and at last gave it up
as a bad job, and asked what was to be done. It was 7.30 p.m.
and only an hour of daylight was left. We were beginning to
feel used up, for we had wandered about at tip-top speed for
the last three hours and a half, so I said, " This is my advice ;
let us turn in our track, and go back as hard as ever we can, not
quitting the track for an instant." They were well content, but
just as we were starting off, the clouds lifted a little, and we
thought we saw the col. It was then to our right, and we went
at it with a dash. Before we had gone a hundred paces down
came the mist again. We kept on nevertheless for twenty
minutes, and then, as darkness was perceptibly coming on, and
the snow was yet rising in front, we turned back, and by running
down the entire distance managed to get clear of the Ferpècle
Glacier just as it became pitch dark. We arrived at our cheerless
chalet in due course, and went to bed supperless, for our food
was gone ; all very sulky—not to say savage—agreeing in
nothing except in bullying Biener.

At 7 a.m. on the 19th, we set out, for the third time, for the

Col d'Hérens. It was a fine day, and we gradually recovered our tempers as we saw the follies which had been committed on the previous evening. Biener's wavering track was not so bad ; but Croz had swerved from the right route from the first, and had traced a complete semicircle, so that when we stopped him we were facing Bricolla—whence we had started. Almer had commenced with great discretion ; but he kept on too long, and crossed the proper route. When I stopped them (because we were going south-west), we were a long way up the Tête Blanche ! Our last attempt was in the right direction ; we were actually upon the summit of the pass, and in another ten yards we should have commenced to go downhill ! It is needless to point out that if the compass had been looked to at the proper moment—that is, immediately the mist came down— we should have avoided all our troubles. It was little use after- wards, except to tell us when we were going *wrong*.

We arrived at Zermatt in six and a half hours' walking from Bricolla, and Seiler's hospitable reception set us all right again. On the 20th we crossed the Théodule pass, and diverged from its summit up the Theodulhorn (11,392) to examine a route which I suggested for the ascent of the Matterhorn. Before continuing an account of our proceedings, I must stop for a minute to explain why this new route was proposed, in place of that up the south-western ridge.

The Matterhorn may be divided into three sections.[1] The first, facing the Z'Mutt Glacier, which looks, and is, completely unassailable ; the second, facing the east, which seems inacces- sibility itself ; the third facing Breuil, which does not look entirely hopeless. It was from this last direction that all my previous attempts were made. It was by the south-western ridge, it will be remembered, that not only I, but Mr. Hawkins, Professor Tyndall, and the chasseurs of Val Tournanche, essayed to climb the mountain. Why then abandon a route which had been shown to be feasible up to a certain point ?

[1] See Chap. III, pp. 49-51.

I gave it up for four reasons.   1. On account of my growing disinclination for arêtes, and preference for snow and rock-faces (see Chap. XII).   2. Because I was persuaded that meteorological disturbances (by which we had been baffled several times) might be expected to occur again and again [1] (see Chaps. IV and VI).   3. Because I found that the east face was a gross imposition—it looked not far from perpendicular, while its angle was, in fact, scarcely more than 40°.   4. Because I observed for myself that the strata of the mountain dipped to the west-south-west.   It is not necessary to say anything more than has been already said upon the first two of these four points, but upon the latter two a few words are indispensable.   Let us consider, first, why most persons receive such an exaggerated impression of the steepness of the eastern face.

When one looks at the Matterhorn from Zermatt, the mountain is regarded (nearly) from the north-east.   The face that fronts the east is consequently neither seen in profile nor in full front, but almost half-way between the two ; it looks, therefore, more steep than it really is.   The majority of those who visit Zermatt go up to the Riffelberg, or to the Gornergrat, and from these places the mountain naturally looks still more precipitous, because its eastern face (which is almost all that is seen of it) is viewed more directly in front.   From the Riffel hotel the slope seems to be set at an angle of 70°.   If the tourist continues to go southwards, and crosses the Théodule pass, he gets, at one point, immediately in front of the eastern face, which then seems to be absolutely perpendicular.   Comparatively few persons correct the erroneous impressions they receive in these quarters by studying the face in profile, and most go away with a very incorrect and exaggerated idea of the precipitousness of this side of the mountain, because they have considered the question from one point of view alone.

Several years passed away before I shook myself clear of my

[1] Subsequent experiences of others have strengthened this opinion.

CAMP

THE MATTERHORN FROM THE RIFFELBERG.

early and false impressions regarding the steepness of this side of the Matterhorn. First of all, I noticed that there were places on this eastern face where snow remained permanently all the year round. I do not speak of snow in gullies, but of the considerable slopes which are seen upon the accompanying engraving, about half-way up the face. Such beds as these could not continue to remain throughout the summer, unless the snow had been able to accumulate in the winter in large masses ; and snow cannot accumulate and remain in large masses, in a situation such as this, at angles much exceeding 45°.[1] Hence I was bound to conclude that the eastern face was many degrees removed from perpendicularity ; and, to be sure on this point, I went to the slopes between the Z'Mutt Glacier and the Matterhorn Glacier, above the chalets of Staffel, whence the face could be seen in profile. Its appearance from this direction would be amazing to one who had seen it only from the east. It looks so totally different from the apparently sheer and perfectly unclimbable cliff one sees from the Riffelberg, that it is hard to believe the two slopes are one and the same thing. Its angle scarcely exceeds 40°.

A great step was made when this was learnt. This knowledge alone would not, however, have caused me to try an ascent by the eastern face instead of by the south-west ridge. Forty degrees may not seem a formidable inclination to the reader, nor is it for only a small cliff. But it is very unusual to find so steep a gradient maintained continuously as the general angle of a great mountain-slope, and very few instances can be quoted from the High Alps of such an angle being preserved over a rise of 3,000 feet.

I do not think that the steepness or the height of this cliff would have deterred climbers from attempting to ascend it, if it had not, in addition, looked so repulsively smooth. Men despaired of finding anything to grasp. Now, some of the diffi-

[1] I prefer to be on the safe side. My impression is that snow cannot accumulate in large masses *at* 45°.

culties of the south-west ridge came from the smoothness of
the rocks, although that ridge, even from a distance, seemed to
be well broken up. How much greater, then, might not have
been the difficulty of climbing a face which looked smooth and
unbroken close at hand ?

A more serious hindrance to mounting the south-west ridge
is found in the dip of its rocks
to the west-south-west. The great
mass of the Matterhorn, it is now
well ascertained, is composed of
regularly stratified rocks, which
rise towards the east. It has been
mentioned in the text, more than
once, that the rocks on some portions of the ridge leading from
the Col du Lion to the summit dip
outwards, and that fractured edges
overhang.[1] This is shown in the
illustrations facing pages 85 and
93 ; and the annexed diagram,
Fig. 1, exhibits the same thing still more clearly. It will be
readily understood that such an arrangement is not favourable
for climbers, and that the degree of facility with which rocks
can be ascended that are so disposed, must depend very much
upon the frequency or paucity of fissures and joints. The
rocks of the south-west ridge are sufficiently provided with
cracks, but if it were otherwise, their texture and arrangement would render them unassailable.[2]

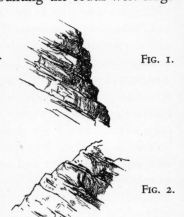

Fig. 1.

Fig. 2.

It is not possible to go a single time upon the rocks of the
south-west ridge, from the Col du Lion to the foot of the Great

---

[1] See pp. 61 and 81.

[2] Weathered granite is admirable rock to climb ; its gritty texture giving
excellent hold to the nails in one's boots. But upon such metamorphic schists
as compose the mass of the great peak of the Matterhorn, the texture of the
rock itself is of little or no value.

Tower, without observing the prevalence of their outward dip, and that their fractured edges have a tendency to overhang ; nor can one fail to notice that it is upon this account that the débris, which is rent off by frost, does not remain *in situ*, but pours down in showers over the surrounding cliffs. Each day's work, so to speak, is cleared away ; the ridge is swept clean ; there is scarcely anything seen but firm rock.[1]

The fact that the mountain is composed of a series of stratified beds was pointed out long ago. Saussure remarked it, and recorded explicitly, in his *Travels* (§ 2243), that they " rose to the north-east at an angle of about 45°." Forbes noticed it also ; and gave it as his opinion that the beds were " less inclined, or nearly horizontal." He added, " Saussure is no doubt correct." [2] The truth, I think, lies between the two.

I was acquainted with both of the above-quoted passages, but did not turn the knowledge to any practical account until I re-observed the same fact for myself. It was not until after my repulse in 1863, that I referred the peculiar difficulties of the south-west ridge to the dip of the strata ; but when once per- suaded that structure and not texture was the real impediment, it was reasonable to infer that the opposite side, that is to say the eastern face, might be comparatively easy. In brief, that an arrangement should be found like Fig. 2, instead of like Fig. 1. This trivial deduction was the key to the ascent of the Matterhorn.

The point was, Did the strata continue with a similar dip throughout the mountain ? If they did, then this great eastern face, instead of being hopelessly impracticable, should be quite the reverse. In fact, it should be a great natural staircase, with

---

[1] I refer here only to that portion of the ridge which is between the Col du Lion and the Great Tower. The remarks would not apply to the rocks higher up (see p. 83) ; higher still the rocks are firm again ; yet higher (upon the " Shoulder ") they are much disintegrated ; and then, upon the final peak, they are again firm.

[2] *Travels through the Alps*, 2nd ed., p. 317.

steps inclining inwards ; and, if it were so, its smooth aspect might be of no account, for the smallest steps, inclined in this fashion, would afford good footing.

They did so, as far as one could judge from a distance. When snow fell in the summer-time, it brought out long terraced lines upon the mountain ; rudely parallel to each other ; and the eastern face, on those occasions, was often whitened almost completely over ; while the other sides, with the exception of the powdered terraces, remained black—for the snow could not rest upon them.

The very outline of the mountain, too, confirmed the con- jecture that its structure would assist an ascent on the eastern face, although it opposed one on all other sides. Look at any photograph of the peak from the north-east, and you will see that upon the right-hand side (that facing the Z'Mutt Glacier) there is a frequent repetition of overhanging cliffs, and of slopes all trending downwards ; in short, that the character of the whole of that side is similar to Fig. 1, p. 248 ; and that upon the left-hand (or south-east) ridge, the forms, as far as they go, are suggestive of the structure of Fig. 2. There is no doubt that the contours of the mountain, seen from this direction, have been largely influenced by the direction of its beds.

It was not, therefore, from a freak, that I invited Mr. Reilly to join in an attack upon the eastern face, but from a gradually acquired conviction that it would afford the easiest way to the summit ; and, if we had not been obliged to part, the mountain would, doubtless, have been ascended in 1864.

My guides readily admitted that they had been greatly deceived as to the steepness of the eastern face, when they were halted to look at it in profile, as we came down the Z'Mutt Glacier, on our way to Zermatt ; but they were far from being satisfied that it would turn out to be easy to climb, and Almer and

J. Gaberell, Thalwil.

MATTERHORN, FROM NORTH-EAST.

Biener expressed themselves decidedly averse to making an attempt upon it. I gave way temporarily before their evident reluctance, and we made the ascent of the Theodulhorn to examine an alternative route, which I expected would commend itself to them in preference to the other, as a great part of it led over snow.

There is an immense gully in the Matterhorn, which leads up from the Glacier du Mont Cervin to a point high up on the south-eastern ridge.[1] I proposed to ascend this to its head, and to cross over the south-east ridge on to the eastern face. This would have brought us on a level with the bottom of the great snow-slope shown upon the centre of the eastern face in the engraving facing p. 246. This snow-slope was to be crossed diagonally, with the view of arriving at the snow upon the north-east ridge, which is shown upon the same engraving, about half an inch from the summit. The remainder of the ascent was to be made by the broken rocks, mixed with snow, upon the north side of the mountain. Croz caught the idea immediately,[2] and thought the plan feasible ; details were settled, and we descended to Breuil. Luc Meynet, the hunchback, was summoned, and expressed himself delighted to resume his old vocation of tent-bearer ;[3] and Favre's kitchen was soon in commotion preparing three days' rations, for I

[1] Its position is shown by the letter **F** on the right of the outline, on p. 94. See also Map of the Matterhorn and its Glaciers.

[2] [*From Whymper's diary* : Croz picked out a couloir up which he thought we could go. The others did not think much or at least slept more, and said little.]

[3] [The following footnote is taken from Cav. Guido Rey's *The Matterhorn*, translated by Mr. J. E. C. Eaton :

Luc Meynet was wont to relate the following anecdote about his adventures with Whymper :

On their return from one of their many adventurous attempts, in the course of which the whole party had all but been swept away by an avalanche of stones, Whymper, Croz and Meynet were resting on the Furggenjoch. Whymper was making barometrical observations, Croz was smoking his

intended to take that amount of time over the affair—to sleep
on the first night upon the rocks at the top of the gully ; to make
a push for the summit, and to return to the tent on the second
day ; and upon the third to come back to Breuil.

We started at 5.45 a.m. on June 21, and followed the route of
the Breuiljoch [1] for three hours. We were then in full view of
our gully, and turned off at right angles for it. The closer we
approached, the more favourable it looked. There was a good
deal of snow in it, which was evidently at a small angle, and it
seemed as if one-third of the ascent, at least, would be a very
simple matter. Some suspicious marks in the snow at its base
suggested that it was not free from falling stones, and, as a
measure of precaution, we turned off on one side, worked up
under cover of the cliffs, and waited to see if anything should
descend. Nothing fell, so we proceeded up its right or northern
side, sometimes cutting steps up the snow and sometimes mount-

pipe ; Luc waited patiently till Croz had finished, and then, taking off his hat,
most respectfully asked him to lend him his pipe because he had left his own
at home.

" You might as well have left your head there too, *drôle de bossu,*" was
Croz's reply. " Do you imagine I am going to lend my pipe to a half-man
like you ? "

The poor man did not answer a word, but Whymper, who had overheard
the dialogue, came up to him with two cigars. " Here," he said, " you smoke
too." And Luc proudly lit a cigar, straightened himself to the best of his
ability, and strutted about in front of Croz, puffing clouds of smoke into
his face.

They started for Breuil, and on the way down the glacier Croz walked
quickly, hoping to make Luc, who was laden with the tent, slip, but Luc
managed the rope in such a way that he saved himself from being pulled down
by the insidious jerks.

It happened that Croz fell into a crevasse and was held up by the strength
and foresight of Luc.

The moral of the story was then pointed by Whymper, who turned to
Croz, and said : " Sachez, Croz, qu'on a souvent besoin d'un plus petit que
soi."]

[1] See p. 104.

ing by the rocks. Shortly before 10 a.m. we arrived at a convenient place for a halt, and stopped to rest upon some rocks, immediately close to the snow, which commanded an excellent view of the gully.

While the men were unpacking the food I went to a little promontory to examine our proposed route more narrowly, and to admire our noble couloir, which led straight up into the heart of the mountain for fully one thousand feet. It then bent towards the north, and ran up to the crest of the south-eastern ridge. My curiosity was piqued to know what was round this corner, and whilst I was gazing up at it, and following with the eye the exquisitely drawn curves which wandered down the snow in the gully, all converging to a large rut in its centre, I saw a few little stones skidding down. I consoled myself with thinking that they would not interfere with us if we adhered to the side. But then a larger one came down, a solitary fellow, rushing at the rate of sixty miles an hour—and another—and another. I was unwilling to alarm the men unnecessarily, and said nothing. They did not hear the stones. Almer was seated on a rock, carving large slices from a leg of mutton, the others were chatting, and the first intimation they had of danger was from a crash—a sudden roar—which reverberated awfully amongst the cliffs, and, looking up, they saw masses of rocks, boulders and stones, big and little, dart round the corner 800 feet or so above us, fly with fearful fury against the opposite cliffs, rebound from them against the walls on our side, and descend ; some ricochetting from side to side in a frantic manner ; some bounding down in leaps of a hundred feet or more over the snow ; and others trailing down in a jumbled, confused mass, mixed with snow and ice, deepening the grooves which, a moment before, had excited my admiration.

The men looked wildly around for protection, and, dropping the food, dashed under cover in all directions. The precious mutton was pitched on one side, the wine-bag was let fall, and its contents gushed out from the unclosed neck, whilst all four cowered under defending rocks, endeavouring to make themselves as small as possible. Let it not be supposed that their fright was unreasonable, or that I was free from it. I took good care to make myself safe, and went and cringed in a cleft until the storm had passed. But their scramble to get under shelter was indescribably ludicrous. Such a panic I have never witnessed, before or since, upon a mountain-side.

This ricochet practice was a novelty to me. It arose, of course, from the couloir being bent, and from the falling rocks having acquired great pace before they passed the angle. In straight gullies it will, probably, never be experienced. The rule is, as I have already remarked (p. 182), that falling stones

MY TENT-BEARER—THE HUNCHBACK.

keep down the centres of gullies, and they are out of harm's way if one follows the sides.

There would have been singularly little amusement, and very great risk, in mounting this gully, and we turned our backs upon it with perfect unanimity. The question then arose, " What is to be done ? " I suggested climbing the rocks above us, but this was voted impossible. I thought the men were right, yet would not give in without being assured of the fact, and clambered up to settle the question. In a few minutes I was brought to a halt. My forces were scattered ; the little hunchback alone was closely following me—with a broad grin upon his face, and the tent upon his shoulder ; Croz, more behind, was still keeping an eye upon his *Monsieur* ; Almer, a hundred feet below, sat on a rock with his face buried in his hands ; Biener was nowhere, out of sight. " Come down, come down," shouted Croz ; " it is useless," and I turned at length, convinced that it was even as he said. Thus my little plan was knocked on the head, and we were thrown back upon the original scheme.

We at once made a straight track for Mr. Morshead's pass [1] (which was the most direct route to take in order to get to the Hörnli, where we intended to sleep, preparatory to attacking the eastern face), and arrived upon its summit at 12.30 p.m. We were then unexpectedly checked. The pass, as one, had vanished ! and we found ourselves cut off from the Furggen Glacier by a precipitous wall of rock ;—the glacier had shrunk so much that descent was impracticable. During the last hour clouds had been coming up from the south ; they now surrounded us and it began to blow hard. The men clustered together, and advocated leaving the mountain alone. Almer asked, with more point than politeness, " Why don't you try to go up a mountain which *can* be ascended ? " " It is impossible," chimed in Biener. " Sir," said Croz, " if we cross to the other side we shall lose three days, and very likely shall not succeed. You want to make ascents in the chain of Mont Blanc, and I believe they can be made. But I shall not be able to make them with you if I spend these days here, for I must be at Chamonix on the 27th." There was force in what he said, and his words made me hesitate. I relied upon his strong arms for some work which it was expected would be unusually difficult. Snow

[1] See note to p. 104.

began to fall ; that settled the matter, and I gave the word to retreat. We went back to Breuil, and on to the village of Valtournanche, where we slept ; and the next day proceeded to Châtillon, and thence up the valley of Aosta to Courmayeur.[1]

I cannot but regret that the counsels of the guides prevailed. If Croz had not uttered his well-intentioned words, he might still have been living. He parted from us at Chamonix at the appointed time, but by a strange chance we met again at Zermatt three weeks later, and two days afterwards he perished before my eyes on the very mountain from which we turned away, at his advice, on the 21st of June.

[*From Whymper's diary : June 21st, 1865.*

Attempt to ascend the Matterhorn (8th).   Started at 5.45 a.m., with Luc Meynet to carry the tent.   He struggled for a camarade, but I wouldn't have it.   Went on route of my direct Zermatt col until glacier was reached ; there we arrived at 7.45 and halted 35 minutes.   We then at first went up middle of glacier, until we got in front of the great couloir up which we proposed to go ; then turned to the left and went straight to it, arrived at foot of it at 9.25 and halted 10 minutes.   We clambered up rocks on the right by its side and stopped again at 9.48 until 10. By this time the sun had got well on to the rocks above, and stones began to fall down the couloir by ones, twos, and showers. This same couloir was very long and ran right up into the heart of the mountain.   On both sides of it were great cliffs, up which it was hopeless to think of climbing, but the rocks at the top of the couloir looked quite practicable.   We argued the matter, and a powerful majority were against going up.   There was therefore only one chance in this direction, viz. by going up

---

[1] [From *Whymper's diary* : Left Aosta at 1.30 and got to Courmayeur at 7. Almer took it into his head to run part of the way, and ran in a very clean style.]

the rocks on the right, commencing right low down. I saw that all of the men, the whole lot, had no heart in the matter ; when it was settled that these rocks should be tried, they did not move off, and their faces showed what they thought plainly enough. I therefore went off in front myself, and soon got on to rocks that took me all I knew to get up ; the hunchback and Croz followed me, but Biener and Almer hung back. We had not been going much more than half an hour before Croz called to me to come down, as it was useless. I thought differently, as there was nothing immediately in front to stop us, and insisted on going on ; they lagged, and I was getting into a fume, disgusted with the whole lot. But I persevered, and went a good bit higher, but finally came to a place where I could neither go up, to the right or left. Croz crowed. I looked down ; the hunchback, with a face a mixture of fright and wonder, was peering up through a gully at me ; Croz just behind him, Almer seated on a bit of rock had buried his face in his hands, Biener was nowhere. We turned at 11.5, and they then asked what was to be done. " Go over to Zermatt, and get on to the Hörnli arête," was my answer. I asked them in my turn which they would do, go over the Théodule or the direct col. They preferred the latter. We therefore went round under cover of the cliffs, to avoid stones, but it was necessary to cross a small couloir ; on arriving here I suggested that we should be tied, as we could go quicker and safer. They objected, all forsook me and fled across. I say all, I should except Meynet, who was behind me and stuck valiantly to me. We got to top of col (Morshead's) at 12.30, when lo ! we could not get down the other side. I then had a small wrangle with Croz, in which he came out bumptious ; when I said I wished to go round by Théodule, they threw obstacles in the way, and when I said we would go to Châtillon at once, were equally sulky. In fact, they didn't behave well. I didn't know what to do, but the matter was at last settled for us. Clouds had been gathering very rapidly, and at last one came down to the col, enveloped us, and it commenced snowing and blowing hard. I sounded a retreat at once, and ordered them to make tracks for Courmayeur.]

THE VILLAGE OF VALTOURNANCHE (1892).

CHAPTER XV

THE VALLEY OF AOSTA, AND ASCENT OF THE GRANDES JORASSES

> . . . " *When we were boys,*
> *Who would believe that there were mountaineers*
> *Dew-lapp'd like bulls, whose throats had hanging at them*
> *Wallets of flesh ?* " . . .
>
> SHAKESPEARE.

THE valley of Aosta is famous for its bouquetins, and infamous for its crétins. The bouquetin, Steinbock, or Ibex, was formerly widely distributed throughout the Alps. It is now confined almost entirely to a small district on the south of the valley of Aosta, and fears have been repeatedly expressed in late years that it will speedily become extinct.

The most sanguine person does not imagine that crétinism will be eradicated for many generations. It is widely spread throughout the Alps ; it is by no means peculiar to the valley of Aosta ; but nowhere does it thrust itself more frequently upon the attention of the traveller, and in no valley where " every prospect pleases " is one so often and so painfully reminded that " only man is vile."

It seems premature to fear that the bouquetin will soon become extinct. It is not easy to take a census of them, for, although they have local habitations, it is extremely difficult to find them at home. Yet there is good reason to believe that there are at least several hundreds still roaming over the mountains in the neighbourhood of the valleys of Grisanche, Rhèmes, Savaranche, and Cogne.

It would be a pity if it were otherwise. They appeal to our sympathies as the remnants of a diminishing race. No mountaineer or athletic person could witness without sorrow the extinction of an animal possessing such noble qualities ;—which a few months after birth can jump over a man's head at a bound, without taking a run ; which passes its whole life in a constant fight for existence ; which has such a keen appreciation of the beauties of nature, and such disregard of pain that it will " stand for hours like a statue, in the midst of the bitterest storm, until the tips of its ears are frozen " ! and which, when its last hour arrives, " climbs to the highest mountain-peaks, hangs on a rock with its horns, twists itself round and round upon them until they are worn off, and then falls down and expires " ! [1] Even Tschudi himself calls this story wonderful.

Forty-five keepers, selected from the most able chasseurs of the district, guard its haunts. Their task is not a light one, although they are, naturally, acquainted with those who are most likely to attempt poaching. If they were withdrawn, it would not be long before the ibex would be an extinct wild animal, so far as the Alps are concerned. The passion for killing something, and the present value of the beast itself, would soon lead to its extermination. For as meat alone the bouquetin is valuable ; the gross weight of one that is full grown ranging from 160 to 200 lb. ; while its skin and horns are worth £10 and upwards, according to condition and dimensions.

In spite of the keepers, and of the severe penalties which may be inflicted for killing a bouquetin, poaching occurs constantly. Knowing that this was the case, I inquired at Aosta, upon one of my last visits, if any skins or horns were for sale, and in ten minutes was taken into a garret where the remains of a splendid beast were concealed,—a magnificent male, presumed to be more than twenty years old, as its massive horns had twenty-two more or less strongly marked knobby rings. The extreme length of the skin, from the tip of the nose to the end of the

[1] Tschudi's *Sketches of Nature in the Alps.*

tail, was 1 metre 69 centimetres (about 5 feet 7 inches), and from the ground to the top of its back had been, apparently, about 77 centimetres. It is rare to meet with a bouquetin of these dimensions, and the owner of this skin might have been

THE BOUQUETIN.

visited with several years' imprisonment if it had been known that it was in his possession.

The chase of the bouquetin is a sport fit for a king, and the Kings of Italy, for whom it is reserved, have been too good sportsmen to slaughter indiscriminately an animal which is an ornament to their dominions. In 1868, His Majesty Victor

Emmanuel presented a fine specimen to the Italian Alpine Club. The members banqueted upon its flesh, and had the skin stuffed, and set up in their rooms at Aosta. From this specimen the accompanying engraving has been made.

It is a full-grown male, about twelve years old, and if it stood upright would measure three feet three and a half inches from the ground to the base of its horns. Its extreme length is four feet seven inches. Its horns have eleven well-marked rings, besides one or two faintly-marked ones, and are (measured round their curvature) 54½ centimetres in length. The horns of the specimen referred to on p. 260 (measured in the same way) had a length of only 53½ centimetres, although they were ornamented with nearly double the number of rings, and were presumably of double the age of the former.[1]

The keepers, and the chasseurs of this district, not only say that the rings upon the horns of the ibex tell its age (each one reckoning as a year), but that the half-developed ones, which sometimes are very feebly marked indeed, show that the animal has suffered from hunger during the winter. Naturalists are sceptical upon this point; but inasmuch as they offer no better reason against the reputed fact than the natives do in its favour (one saying that it is not so, and the other saying that it is so), we may, perhaps, be permitted to consider it an open question. I can only say that if the faintly-marked rings do denote years of famine, the times for the bouquetin are very hard indeed; since, in most of the horns which I have seen, the lesser rings have been numerous, and sometimes more plentiful than the prominent ones.

The Chef of the keepers (who judged by the above-mentioned indications) told me that the ibex not unfrequently arrives at the age of thirty years, and sometimes to forty or forty-five. He

[1] Mr. King, in his *Italian Valleys of the Alps*, says, " In the pair (of horns) I possess, which are *two feet* long, there are eight of these yearly rings." It would seem, therefore (if the rings are annual ones), that the maximum length of horn is attained at a comparatively early age.

said, too, that it is not fond of traversing steep snow, and in descending a couloir that is filled with it, will zigzag down, by springing from one side to the other, in leaps of fifty feet at a time ! Jean Tairraz,[1] the worthy landlord of the Hotel du Mont Blanc at Aosta (who had opportunities of observing the animal closely), assured me that at the age of four or five months it can easily clear a height of nine or ten feet at a bound ! [2] Long life to the bouquetin !

At some very remote period the valley of Aosta was occupied by a vast glacier, which flowed down its entire length from Mont Blanc to the plain of Piedmont, remained stationary, or nearly so, at its mouth for many centuries, and deposited there enormous masses of débris. The length of this glacier exceeded eighty miles, and it drained a basin twenty-five to thirty-five miles across, bounded by the highest mountains in the Alps. It did not fill this basin. Neither the main stream nor its tributaries completely covered up the valleys down which they flowed. The great peaks still rose several thousand feet above the glaciers, and then, as now, shattered by sun and frost, poured down their showers of rocks and stones, in witness of which there are the immense piles of angular fragments that constitute the moraines of Ivrea.[3] The wine which is drunk in that town is produced from soil that was borne by this great glacier from the slopes of Monte Rosa ; and boulders from Mont Blanc are spread over the country between that town and the Po, supplying excellent materials for building purposes, which were known to the Romans, who employed them in some of their erections at Santhia.[4]

[1] Jean Tairraz was the leading guide of the late Albert Smith on his celebrated ascent of Mont Blanc.

[2] In the autumn of 1892, a young bouquetin (supposed to be about three months old) was captured alive near Mont Collon, and was subsequently bought by M. Joseph Seiler, who kept it in the garden of the Mont Cervin hotel, at Zermatt. This little animal roamed about freely, but did not display extraordinary agility.

[3] See General Map.

[4] I was indebted for this fact to the late Professor Gastaldi.

The moraines around Ivrea are of extraordinary dimensions. That which was the lateral moraine of the left bank of the glacier is about *thirteen miles* long, and, in some places, rises to a height of 2,130 feet above the floor of the valley ! Professor Martins termed it " la plus élevée, la plus régulière, et la mieux caractérisée des Alpes." [1] It is locally called *la Serra*. The lateral moraine of the right bank also rises to a height of 1,000 feet, and would be deemed enormous but for the proximity of its greater comrade ; while the terminal moraines cover something like twenty square miles of country.

The erratic nature of the materials of these great rubbish-heaps was distinctly pointed out by Saussure (*Voyages,* §§ 974–978) ; their true origin was subsequently indicated by Messrs. Studer (1844) and Guyot (1847) ; and the excellent account of them which has since been published by Professors Martins and Gastaldi leaves nothing to be desired either in accuracy or completeness. [2] It is not my purpose, therefore, to enter into a description of them, but only to discuss some considerations arising out of the facts which have been already mentioned.

It has been proved beyond doubt that these gigantic mounds around Ivrea are actually the moraines of a glacier (now extinct) which occupied the valley of Aosta ; and it is indisputable that there are boulders from Mont Blanc amongst them. The former facts certify that the glacier was of enormous size, and the latter that it must have existed for a prodigious length of time.

The height of *la Serra* indicates the *depth* of the glacier. It does not fix the depth absolutely, inasmuch as the crest of the moraine must have been degraded during the thousands of years which have elapsed since the retreat of the ice ; and, further, it is possible that some portions of the surface of the glacier may have been considerably elevated above the moraine when the

[1] *Revue des Deux Mondes.*

[2] *Essai sur les terrains superficiels de la Vallée du Po,* extrait du Bulletin de la Société Géologique de France, 1850.

ice was at its maximum thickness. Anyhow, at the mouth of the valley of Aosta, the thickness of the glacier must have been at least 2,000 feet, and its width, at that part, five miles and a quarter.

The boulders from Mont Blanc, upon the plain below Ivrea, assure us that the glacier which transported them existed for a prodigious length of time. Their present distance from the cliffs from which they were derived is about 420,000 feet, and if we assume that they travelled at the rate of 400 feet per annum, their journey must have occupied them no less than 1,055 years ! In all probability they did not travel so fast. But even if they were to be credited with a quicker rate of motion, the length of time which their journey must have taken will be sufficient for my purposes.[1]

The space of 1,055 years, however, by no means represents the duration of the life of the glacier of Aosta. It may have existed for immense periods both anterior and posterior to the journeys

[1] See Forbes' *Occasional Papers on the Theory of Glaciers*, pp. 193-5, and *Travels through the Alps of Savoy*, 2nd ed., pp. 86-7, for information bearing upon the mean annual motion of existing Alpine glaciers. In the former work an account is given of the discovery of the remains of a knapsack ten years after it had been dropped in a crevasse, at a horizontal distance of 4,300 feet from the place at which it had been lost, showing an average annual motion of 430 feet. In the latter work there is a relation of the recovery of the remains of a ladder used by Saussure, which had travelled about 13,000 feet in forty-four years, or 295 feet per annum. Forbes says that the first of these two examples is better ascertained in all its particulars than the other. It should be observed that the knapsack in question made the descent of the well-known " icefall " of the Glacier de Talèfre, and that there was a difference of level between the place at which it was lost and that at which it was found of 1,145 feet ; that is to say, it descended one foot in every four that it advanced. This rapid descent undoubtedly accelerates the motion of the Glacier de Talèfre. The town of Ivrea, on the other hand, is 768 feet (Ball) above the level of the sea, while Entrèves (at the foot of Mont Blanc) is 4,216 feet (Mieulet). So that the glacier which once spread over the sites of these two places (which are about sixty-five miles apart) descended by an average gradient of almost exactly 1 in 100. This moderate rate of inclination would as certainly tend to retard the motion of the glacier.

of the Mont Blanc boulders. The frontal terminal moraines, which stretch from Caluso to Viverone (a distance of more than ten miles), are evidence that the snout of the glacier remained stationary, or nearly so, for a length of time which must at least be estimated by centuries, and probably extended over thousands of years. These moraines constitute important chains of hills whose bases are several miles across, and which attain a height of more than a thousand feet ; and, as they were formed by the gradual and slow spreading out of the medial and lateral moraines, it is evident that they were not built up in a day.

Moreover, when the glacier of Aosta shrank away from Ivrea, its retrogression may have been comparatively rapid, or it may have been conducted with extreme deliberation. But, under any circumstances, the extinction of such a tremendous body of ice must have extended over many years, and for a portion of that time a large part of the mass must have been advancing down the valley, although the snout of the glacier was retreating, and although the entire mass was diminishing in volume. If the time is considered which was consumed during this phase of its life, and the time which elapsed during its prolonged sojourn at Ivrea, and the time which passed before it attained its maximum dimensions, it must be conceded that the period of 1,055 years was, in all probability, only a *small* portion of the epoch during which the valley of Aosta sustained the grinding of this enormous mass of ice.

The town of Ivrea is placed at the mouth of, though not actually within the valley, and several miles of flat, dusty road have to be traversed before it is entered. Upon this portion of the country civilization is doing its best to efface the traces of the glacial period. Cultivation of the soil disturbs all deposits, and the hammers of the masons destroy the erratics. After quitting Ivrea, almost the first object of interest is the castle of Montalto, perched on a commanding crag, nearly in the centre of the valley. Thence, from Settimo Vittone up to the foot of the existing glaciers of the range of Mont Blanc, there are traces

of glacier-action upon each hand. The road need not be quitted to seek for them ;—they are *everywhere*. I refer especially to the rocks *in situ*. The rock-forms called *roches moutonnées* are universally distributed, and it is needless, at the present moment, to point to any in particular. Although of varying degrees of resistancy, they have, upon the whole, stood the weathering remarkably well of the thousands of years which have elapsed since the glacier covered them. The floor of the valley, generally speaking, has not been lowered since that time, by the combined agencies of sun, frost, and water, to any appreciable extent. The forms which the *roches moutonnées* present to-day are the forms which they presented, perhaps, ten thousand years ago. Many of those which are *freely* exposed to the atmosphere retain a high polish and fine striations. If the soil were to be removed that covers the flatter portions of the valley, we should doubtless find *higher* polish, and still *finer* striations. Those which are visible remain so perfect that it is certain weathering has done exceedingly little to alter their contours, and we may argue regarding them as if their icy covering had been but just removed.

Our thoughts were more than usually set upon *roches moutonnées*, and rocks of that *genus*, upon the 23rd of June 1865. My guides and I were reposing upon the top of Mont Saxe, scanning the Grandes Jorasses, with a view to ascending it. Five thousand feet of glacier-covered precipices rose above us, and up all that height we planned a way to our satisfaction. Three thousand feet more of glacier and forest-covered slopes lay beneath, and *there*, there was only one point at which it was doubtful if we should find a path. The glaciers were shrinking, and were surrounded by bastions of rounded rock, far too polished to please the rough mountaineer. We could not trace a way across them. However, at 4 a.m. the next day,[1] under the dexterous leading of Michel Croz, we passed the doubtful spot. Thence it was all plain sailing, and at 1 p.m. we gained the

[1] For route, see map of the chain of Mont Blanc.

summit.[1] The weather was boisterous in the upper regions, and storm-clouds driven before the wind, and wrecked against our heights, enveloped us in misty spray, which danced around and fled away, which cut us off from the material universe, and caused us to be, as it were, suspended betwixt heaven and earth, seeing both occasionally, but seeming to belong to neither.

The mists lasted longer than my patience, and we descended without having attained the object for which the ascent was made. At first we followed the little ridge shown upon the accompanying engraving, leading from our summit towards the spectator, and then took to the head of the corridor of glacier on its left, which in the view is left perfectly white. The slopes were steep and covered with new-fallen snow, flour-like and evil to tread upon. On the ascent we had reviled it, and had made our staircase with much caution, knowing full well that the disturbance of its base would bring down all that was above. In descending, the bolder spirits counselled trusting to luck and a glissade ; the cautious ones advocated avoiding the slopes and crossing to the rocks on their farther side. The advice of the latter prevailed, and we had half traversed the snow, to gain the

[1] The ascent of the Grandes Jorasses was made to obtain a view of the upper part of the Aiguille Verte, and upon that account the westernmost summit (overlooking the Mer de Glace) was selected in preference to the highest one. Both summits are shown upon the accompanying engraving. That on the right is (as it appears to be) the highest.

[*From Whymper's diary* : I directed Croz to cut along the arête, but it was found to be of ice, and I countermanded the order.]

That upon its left is the one which we ascended, and is about 100 feet lower than the other. A couple of days after our ascent, Julien Grange, Henri Grati, Jos. Mar. Perrod, Alexis Clusaz, and Daniel Gex (all of Courmayeur), followed our track to the summit in order to learn the way. As far as my observation extends, such things are seldom done by money-grasping or spiritless guides, and I have much pleasure in being able to mention their names. The highest point (13,797) was ascended on June 29–30, 1868, by Mr. Horace Walker, with the guides Julien Grange, Melchior Anderegg, and J. Jaun.

THE GRANDES JORASSES AND THE DOIRE TORRENT, VAL FERRET (D'ITALIE).

ridge, when the crust slipped and we went along with it. "Halt !" broke from all four, unanimously. The axe-heads flew round as we started on this involuntary glissade. It was useless, they slid over the underlying ice fruitlessly. "Halt !" thundered Croz, as he dashed his weapon in again with super-human energy. No halt could be made, and we slid down slowly, but with accelerating motion, driving up waves of snow in front, with streams of the nasty stuff hissing all around. Luckily, the slope eased off at one place, the leading men cleverly jumped aside out of the moving snow, we others followed, and the young avalanche which we had started, continuing to pour down, fell into a yawning crevasse, and showed us where our grave would have been if we had remained in its company five seconds longer. The whole affair did not occupy half a minute. It was the solitary incident of a long day, and at night-fall we re-entered the excellent house kept by the courteous Bertolini, well satisfied that we had not met with more incidents of a similar description.

CHAPTER XVI

THE FIRST PASSAGE OF THE COL DOLENT

" Men willingly believe what they wish."

CÆSAR.

FREETHINKING mountaineers have been latterly in the habit of going up one side of an alp and coming down the other, and calling the route a pass. In this confusion of ideas may be recognized the result of the looseness of thought which arises from the absence of technical education. The true believer abhors such heresies, and observes with satisfaction that Providence oftentimes punishes the offenders for their greediness by causing them to be benighted. The faithful know that passes must be made *between* mountains, and not over their tops. Their creed declares that between any two mountains there *must* be a pass, and they believe that the end for which big peaks were created—the office they are especially designed to fulfil—is to point out the way one should go. This is the true faith, and there is no other.

We set out upon the 26th of June to endeavour to add one more to the passes which are strictly orthodox. We hoped, rather than expected, to discover a quicker route from Courmayeur to Chamonix than the Col du Géant, which was the easiest, quickest, and most direct pass known at the time across the main chain of Mont Blanc.[1] The misgivings which I had as to the result caused us to start at the unusual hour of 12.40 a.m.

---

[1] The view of Mont Blanc from a gorge on the south of the Italian Val Ferret, mid-way between the villages of La Vachey and Praz Sec, and about 3,000 feet above them, is, in my opinion, the finest which can be obtained of that mountain range anywhere upon the Italian side.

THE SUMMIT OF THE COL DOLENT.

200 feet of rope again came to an end, and we again descended one by one. From this point we were able to clamber down by the rocks alone for about 300 feet. They then became sheer cliff, and we stopped for dinner, about 2.30 p.m., at the last place upon which we could sit. Four hours' incessant work had brought us rather more than half-way down the gully. We were now approaching, although we were still high above, the schrunds at its base, and the guides made out, in some way unknown to me, that Nature had perversely placed the only snow-bridge across the topmost one towards the centre of the gully. It was decided to cut diagonally across the gully to the point where the snow-bridge was supposed to be. Almer and Biener undertook the work, leaving Croz and myself firmly planted on the rocks to pay out the rope to them as they advanced.

It is generally admitted that veritable ice-slopes (understanding by *ice* something more than a crust of hard snow over soft snow) are only rarely met with in the Alps. They are frequently spoken of, but such as that to which I refer are *very* rarely seen, and still more seldom traversed. It is, however, always possible that they may be encountered, and on this account, if for no other, it is necessary for men who go mountaineering to be armed with ice-axes, and with good ones. The form is of more importance than might be supposed. Of course, if you intend to act as a simple amateur, and let others do the work, and only follow in their steps, it is not of much importance what kind of ice-axe you carry, so long as its head does not fall off, or otherwise behave itself improperly.[1] There is no better weapon for cutting steps in ice than a common pick-axe, and the form of ice-axe which is now usually employed by the best guides is very like a miniature pick. My own axe is copied from Melchior Anderegg's. It is of wrought iron, with point and edge steeled. Its weight, including spiked handle, is four pounds. For cutting

---

[1] This observation is not made without reason. I have seen the head of one tumble off at a slight tap, in consequence of its handle having been perforated by an ingenious but useless arrangement of nails.

steps in ice, the pointed end of the head is almost exclusively employed ; the adze end is handy for polishing them up, but is principally used for cutting in hard snow. Apart from its value as a cutting weapon, it is invaluable as a grapnel. It is naturally a rather awkward implement when it is not being employed for its legitimate purpose, and is likely to give rise to much strong language in crushes at railway termini, unless its head is protected with a leathern cap, or in some other way. Many attempts have been made, for the sake of convenience, to fashion an ice-axe with a movable head, but it seems difficult or impossible to produce one except at the expense of cutting qualities, and by increasing the weight.

MY ICE-AXE.

Mr. T. S. Kennedy (of the firm of Fairbairn & Co.), whose practical acquaintance with mountaineering, and with the use and manufacture of tools, makes his opinion particularly valuable, has contrived the best that I have seen ; but even it seems to me to be deficient in rigidity, and not to be so powerful a weapon as the more common kind with the fixed head. The simple instrument which is shown in the annexed diagram is the invention of Mr. Leslie Stephen, and it answers the purposes for which he devised it, namely, for giving better hold upon snow and ice than can be obtained

from the common alpenstock, and for cutting an occasional step. The amateur scarcely requires anything more imposing, but for serious ice-work a heavier weapon is indispensable. To persons armed with the proper tools, ice-slopes are not so dangerous as many places which appeal less to the imagination. Their ascent or descent is neces- KENNEDY ICE-AXE. sarily laborious (to those who do the work), and they may therefore be termed difficult. They *ought* not to be dangerous. Yet they always seem dangerous, for one is profoundly convinced that if he slips he will certainly go to the bottom.

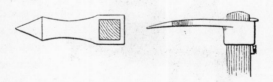

Hence, any man, who is not a fool, takes particular care to preserve his balance, and, in consequence, we have the noteworthy fact that accidents have seldom or never taken place upon ice-slopes.

The same slopes covered with snow are much less impressive, and *may* be much more dangerous. They may be less slippery, the balance may be more easily preserved, and if one man slips he may be stopped by his own personal efforts, provided the snow which overlies the ice is consolidated and of a reasonable depth. But if, as is more likely to be the case upon an angle of 50° (or anything approaching that angle), there is only a thin

stratum of snow which is not consolidated, the occurrence of a
slip will most likely take the entire party as low as possible, and
in addition to the chance of broken necks, there will be a strong
probability that some, at least, will be smothered by the dislodged snow. Such accidents are far too common, and their
occurrence, as a rule, may be traced to the want of caution
which is induced by the apparent absence of danger.

I do not believe that the use of the rope, in the ordinary way,
affords the least *real* security upon ice-slopes. Nor do I think
that any benefit is derived from the employment of crampons.
Mr. Kennedy was good enough to present me with a pair
some time ago, and one of these has been engraved. They are
the best variety I have seen of the species, but I only feel comfortable with them on my feet in places where they are not of
the slightest use (that is in situations where there is no possibility
of slipping), and would not wear them upon an ice-slope for

any consideration whatever.
All such adventitious aids
are useless if you have not
a good step in the ice to
stand upon, and if you have
got that, nothing more is
wanted except a few nails
in the boots.

Almer and Biener got to
the end of their tether ; the rope no longer assured their safety,
and they stopped work as we advanced and coiled it up.

[*From Whymper's diary :* At last Croz and myself had paid out
the whole 200 feet to them, and it was necessary to follow.
Now it so happened that I felt myself compelled to tie ; Croz
of course followed, about 15 feet behind. There was therefore
150 or 160 feet of rope hanging in a loop between Biener and
myself. It was simply an impossibility to gather it up into a
coil as I advanced, as I had all my work to do to hold on against

its weight. It was an exceedingly trying time. Almer was working powerfully and continuously, and fearfully hard work it was. At last he approached the bridge. He moves quicker, at last I see him turn round and kick. Can it be ? Yes, it is, —snow !]

Shortly afterwards they struck a streak of snow that proved to be just above the bridge of which they were in search. The slope steepened, and for 30 feet or so we descended face to the wall, making steps by kicking with the toes, and thrusting the arms well into the holes above, just as if they had been rounds in a ladder. At this time we were crossing the uppermost of the schrunds. Needless to say that the snow was of an admirable quality ; this performance would otherwise have been impossible. It was soon over, and we then found ourselves upon a huge rhomboidal mass of ice, and still separated from the Argentière Glacier by a gigantic crevasse. The only bridge over this lower schrund was at its eastern end, and we were obliged to double back to get to it. Cutting continued for half an hour after it was passed, and it was 5.35 p.m. before the axes stopped work, and we could at last turn back and look comfortably at the formidable slope upon which seven hours had been spent.[1]

The Col Dolent is not likely to compete with the Col du Géant, and I would recommend any person who starts to cross it to allow himself plenty of time, plenty of rope, and ample guide-power. There is no difficulty upon any part of the route, excepting upon the steep slopes immediately below the summit on each side. When we arrived upon the Glacier d'Argentière,

---

[1] It occupies about one-sixth of an inch upon the map. I estimate its height at 1,200 feet. The triangulation of Capt. Mieulet places the summit of the pass 11,624 feet above the sea.

So far as I am aware, the Col Dolent was not again crossed until 1878. On Sept. 2, of that year, Messrs. W. E. Davidson and J. W. Hartley, with the guides Johann Jaun and Laurent Lanier, traversed it in the reverse direction.

our work was as good as over.   We drove a straight track to the chalets of Lognan, and thence the way led over familiar ground.   Soon after dusk we got upon the high road at Les Tines, and at 10 p.m. arrived at Chamonix.   Our labours were duly rewarded.   Houris brought us champagne and the other drinks which are reserved for the faithful, but before my share was consumed I fell asleep in an arm-chair.   I slept soundly until daybreak, and then turned into bed and went to sleep again.

CHAPTER XVII

ASCENT OF THE AIGUILLE VERTE

" Few have the fortitude of soul to honour
A friend's success, without a touch of envy."
ÆSCHYLUS.

MICHEL CROZ now parted from us. His new employer had not
arrived at Chamonix, but Croz considered that he was bound
by honour to wait for him, and thus Christian Almer, of
Grindelwald, became my leading guide.

CHRISTIAN ALMER.[1]

Almer displayed aptitude for mountaineering at an early age.
Whilst still a very young man he was known as a crack chamois-

[1] Engraved, by permission, from a photograph by Mr. E. Edwards.

hunter, and he soon developed into an accomplished guide. Those who have read Mr. Wills' graphic account of the first ascent of the Wetterhorn [1] will remember that, when his party was approaching the top of the mountain, two stranger men were seen climbing by a slightly different route, one of whom carried upon his back a young fir-tree, branches, leaves, and all.

ICE PINNACLES ON THE MER DE GLACE.

Mr. Wills' guides were extremely indignant with these two strangers (who were evidently determined to be the first at the summit), and talked of giving them blows. Eventually they gave them a cake of chocolate instead, and declared that they were good fellows. "Thus the pipe of peace was smoked, and tranquillity reigned between the rival forces." Christian Almer was one of these two men.

[1] *Wanderings among the High Alps*, 1858.

This was in 1854. In 1857–8 he made the first ascents of the Mönch and the Eiger, the former with Dr. Porges, and the latter with Mr. Charles Barrington.[1] Since then he has wandered far and near, from Dauphiné to Tyrol.[2] With the exception of Melchior Anderegg, there is not, perhaps, another guide of such wide experience, or one who has been so invariably successful ;

ON THE MER DE GLACE.

and his numerous employers concur in saying that there is not a truer heart or a surer foot to be found amongst the Alps.

Before recrossing the chain to Courmayeur, we ascended the

[1] See the *Alpine Journal*, vol. xi., pp. 172–4.

[2] Most of his principal exploits are recorded in the publications of the Alpine Club.

Aiguille Verte.   In company with Mr. Reilly I inspected this mountain from every direction in 1864, and formed the opinion that an ascent could more easily be made from the south than upon any other side.   We set out upon the 28th from Chamonix to attack it ; minus Croz, and plus a porter (of whom I will speak more particularly presently), leaving our comrade very downcast at having to kick his heels in idleness, whilst we were about to scale the most celebrated of his native Aiguilles.

Our course led us over the old Mer de Glace—the glacier made famous by Saussure and Forbes.   The heat of the day was over, but the little rills and rivulets were still flowing along the surface of the ice ; cutting deep troughs where the gradients were small ; leaving ripple-marks where the water was with more difficulty confined to one channel ; and falling over the precipitous walls of the great crevasses, sometimes in bounding cascades, and sometimes in diffused streams, which marked the perpendicular faces with graceful sinuosities.[1]   As night came on, their music died away, the rivulets dwindled down to rills ; the rills ceased to murmur, and the sparkling drops, caught by the hand of frost, were bound to the ice, coating it with an enamelled film which lasted until the sun struck the glacier once more.

We camped on the Couvercle (7,800) under a great rock, and at 3.15 the next morning started for our Aiguille, leaving the porter in charge of the tent and of the food.   Two hours' walking over crisp snow brought us up more than 4,000 feet, and within about 1,600 feet of the summit.   From no other direction can it be approached so closely with equal facility.   Thence the mountain steepens.   After his late severe piece of ice-work, Almer had a natural inclination for rocks ; but the lower rocks of the final peak of the Aiguille Verte were not inviting, and he went on and on, looking for a way up them, until we arrived in front of a great snow couloir that led from the Glacier de Talèfre right up to the crest of the ridge connecting the summit

---

[1] Adn.   rendered in the accompanying drawing by Mr. Cyrus Johnson (p. 281).   The " ripple-marks " are seen in the engraving upon p. 280.

of the Verte with the mountain called Les Droites. This was the route which I intended to be taken ; but Almer pointed out that the gully narrowed at the lower part, and that, if stones fell, we should stand some chance of getting our heads broken ; and so we went on still more to the east of the summit, to another and smaller couloir which ran up side by side with the great one. At 5.30 we crossed the schrund which protected the final peak, and, a few minutes afterwards, saw the summit and the whole of the intervening route. " Oh ! Aiguille Verte," said my guide, stopping as he said it, " you are dead, you are dead " ; which, being translated into plain English, meant that he was cock-sure we should make its ascent.

Almer is a quiet man at all times. When climbing he is taciturn—and this is one of his great merits. A garrulous man is always a nuisance, and upon a mountain-side he may be a danger, for actual climbing requires a man's whole attention. Added to this, talkative men are hindrances ; they are usually thirsty, and a thirsty man is a drag.

Guide-books recommend mountain-walkers to suck pebbles, to prevent their throats from becoming parched. There is not much goodness to be got out of the pebbles ; but you cannot suck them and keep the mouth open at the same time, and hence the throat does not become dry. It answers just as well to keep the mouth shut, without any pebbles inside,—indeed, I think, better ; for if you have occasion to open your mouth, you can do so without swallowing any pebbles.[1] As a rule, amateurs, and particularly novices, *will not* keep their mouths shut. They attempt to " force the pace " ; they go faster than they can go without being compelled to open their mouths to breathe ; they pant ; their throats and tongues become parched, they drink and perspire copiously ; and, becoming exhausted, declare that the dryness of the air, or the rarefaction

---

[1] I have heard of two well-known mountaineers who, under the influence of sudden alarm, *swallowed their crystals*. I am happy to say that they were able to cough them up again.

of the air (everything is laid upon the air), is in fault.   On
several accounts, therefore, a mountain-climber does well to
hold his tongue when he is at work.

At the top of the small gully we crossed over the intervening
rocks into the large one, and followed it so long as it was filled
with snow.   At last ice replaced snow, and we turned over to
the rocks upon its left.   Charming rocks they were ; granitic
in texture,[1] gritty, holding the nails well.   At 9.45 we parted
from them, and completed the ascent by a little ridge of snow
which descended in the direction of the Aiguille du Moine.
At 10.15 we stood on the summit (13,541 feet), and devoured
our bread and cheese with a good appetite.

I have already spoken of the disappointing nature of purely
panoramic views.   That seen from Mont Blanc itself is notori-
ously unsatisfactory.   When you are upon that summit you look
down upon the rest of Europe.   There is nothing to look up
to ; all is below ; there is no one point for the eye to rest upon.
The man who is there is somewhat in the position of one who
has attained all that he desires,—he has nothing to aspire to ; his
position must needs be unsatisfactory.   Upon the summit of the
Verte there is not this objection.   You see valleys, villages,
fields ;   you see mountains interminable rolling away, lakes
resting in their hollows ;   you hear the tinkling of the sheep-
bells as it rises through the clear mountain air, and the roar of
the avalanches as they descend to the valleys : but above all
there is the great white dome, with its shining crest high above ;
with its sparkling glaciers that descend between buttresses which
support them : with its brilliant snows, purer and yet purer
the farther they are removed from this unclean world.[2]

[1] Hand specimens of the highest rocks of the Aiguille Verte cannot be distinguished from granite.   The rock is almost identical in quality with that
at the summit of Mont Dolent, and is probably a granitoid gneiss.

[2] The summit of the Aiguille Verte was a snowy dome, large enough for
a quadrille.   I was surprised to see the great height of Les Droites.   Capt.
Mieulet places its summit at 13,222 feet, but I think it is very slightly lower
than the Verte itself.

Even upon this mountain-top it was impossible to forget the world, for some vile wretch came to the Jardin and made hideous sounds by blowing through a horn. Whilst we were denouncing him a change came over the weather; cumulus clouds gathered in all directions, and we started off in hot haste. Snow began to fall heavily before we were off the summit-rocks, our track was obscured and frequently lost, and everything became so sloppy and slippery that the descent took as long as the ascent. The schrund was recrossed at 3.15 p.m., and thence we raced down to the Couvercle, intending to have a carouse there; but as we rounded our rock a howl broke simultaneously from all three of us, for the porter had taken down the tent, and was in the act of moving off with it. " Stop, there ! What are you doing ? " He observed that he had thought we were killed, or at least lost, and was going to Chamonix to communicate his ideas to the *guide chef*. " Unfasten the tent, and get out the food." Instead of doing so the porter fumbled in his pockets. " Get out the food," we roared, losing all patience. " Here it is," said our worthy friend, producing a dirty piece of bread about as big as a halfpenny roll. We three looked solemnly at the fluff-covered morsel. It was past a joke,—he had devoured everything. Mutton, loaves, cheese, wine, eggs, sausages—all was gone—past recovery. It was idle to grumble, and useless to wait. We were light, and could move quickly,—the porter was laden inside and out. We went our hardest,—he had to shuffle and trot. He streamed with perspiration ; the mutton and cheese oozed out in big drops,—he larded the glacier. We had our revenge, and dried our clothes at the same time, but when we arrived at the Montenvers the porter was as wet as we had been upon our arrival at the Couvercle. We halted at the inn to get a little food, and at a quarter past eight re-entered Chamonix, amidst firing of cannon, and other demonstrations of satisfaction on the part of the hotel-keepers.

One would have thought that the ascent of this mountain,

which had been frequently assailed before without success, would have afforded some gratification to a population whose chief support is derived from tourists ; and that the prospect of the perennial flow of francs which might be expected to result from it would have stifled any jealousy consequent on the success of foreigners.[1]

It was not so. Chamonix stood on its rights. A stranger had ignored their regulations, had imported two foreign guides, and, furthermore, he had added injury to that insult—he had not taken a single Chamonix guide. Chamonix would be revenged ! It would bully the foreign guides ; it would tell them they had lied,—that they had not made the ascent ! Where were their proofs ? Where was the flag upon the summit ?

Poor Almer and Biener were accordingly chivied from pillar to post, from one inn to another, and at length complained to me. Peter Perren, the Zermatt guide, said on the night that we returned that this was to happen, but the story seemed too absurd to be true. I now bade my men go out again, and followed them myself to see the sport. Chamonix was greatly excited. The *bureau* of the *guide chef* was thronged with clamouring men. Their ringleader—one Zacharie Cachat—a well-known guide, of no particular merit, though not a bad fellow, was haranguing the multitude. He met with more than his match. My friend Kennedy, who was on the spot, heard of the disturbance and rushed into the fray, confronted the burly guide, and thrust back his absurdities into his teeth.

There were the materials for a very pretty riot ; but they manage these things better in France than we do, and the gendarmes—three strong—came down and dispersed the crowd. The guides quailed before the cocked hats, and retired to cabarets to take little glasses of absinthe and other liquors more or less injurious to the human frame. Under the influence of these stimulants, they conceived an idea which combined revenge

[1] The Chamonix tariff price for the ascent of the Aiguille is now placed at £4 *per guide.*

with profit. " You have ascended the Aiguille Verte, you say. *We* say we don't believe it. *We* say, do it again ! Take three of us with you, and we will bet you two thousand francs to a thousand, that you won't make the ascent ! "

This proposition was formally notified to me, but I declined it, with thanks, and recommended Kennedy to go in and win. I accepted, however, a hundred-franc share in the bet, and calculated upon getting two hundred per cent on my investment. Alas ! how vain are human expectations ! Zacharie Cachat was put into confinement, and although Kennedy actually ascended the Aiguille a week later, with two Chamonix guides and Peter Perren, the bet came to nothing.[1]

The weather arranged itself just as this storm in a teapot blew over, and we left at once for the Montenvers, in order to show the Chamoniards the easiest way over the chain of Mont Blanc, in return for the civilities which we had received from them during the past three days.

---

[1] It should be said that we received the most polite apologies for this affair from the chief of the gendarmes, and an invitation to lodge a complaint against the ringleaders. We accepted his apologies, and declined his invitation. Needless to add, Michel Croz took no part in this demonstration.

Mr. Kennedy's ascent of the Aiguille Verte is described in the *Alpine Journal*, vol. iii., pp. 68–75.

WESTERN SIDE OF THE COL DE TALEFRE.

CHAPTER XVIII

THE FIRST PASSAGE OF THE COL DE TALEFRE

" 'Tis more by art than force of numerous strokes."

HOMER.

THE person who discovered the Col du Géant must have been a shrewd mountaineer. The pass was in use before any other was known across the main chain of Mont Blanc, and down to the present time it remains the easiest and quickest route from Chamonix to Courmayeur, with the single exception of the pass that we crossed upon the 3rd of July 1865,[1] for the first time, lying about mid-way between the Aiguille de Triolet and the Aiguille de Talèfre ; which, for want of a better name, I called the Col de Talèfre.

When one looks toward the upper end of the Glacier de Talèfre from the direction of the Jardin or of the Couvercle,

[1] [From this date there are no further entries in Whymper's diary for 1865. Apparently it was a frequent habit of his to write up the diary after a lapse of several days.]

the ridge that bounds the view seems to be of little elevation.
It is overpowered by the colossal Grandes Jorasses, and by the
almost equally magnificent Aiguille Verte. The ridge, notwithstanding, is by no means despicable. At no point is its elevation
less than 11,600 feet. It does not look anything like this height.
The Glacier de Talèfre mounts with a steady incline, and the
eye is completely deceived.

In 1864, when prowling about with Mr. Reilly, I instinctively
fixed upon a bent couloir which led up from the glacier to the
lowest part of the ridge ; and when, after crossing the Col de
Triolet, I saw that the other side presented no particular difficulty,
it seemed to me that this was the *one* point in the whole of the
range which would afford an easier passage than the Col du
Géant.

We set out from the Montenvers at 4 a.m. upon July 3, to
see whether this opinion was correct, and it fortunately happened
that the Rev. A. G. Girdlestone and a friend, with two Chamonix
guides, left the inn at the same hour as ourselves, to cross the
Col du Géant. We kept in company as far as our routes lay
together, and at 9.35 we arrived at the top of our pass, having
taken the route to the south of the Jardin. Description is unnecessary, as our track is laid down very clearly on the engraving at
the head of this chapter, and upon the map.

Much snow had fallen during the late bad weather, and as
we reposed upon the top of our pass (which was 11,430 feet
above the level of the sea, and 370 feet higher than the Col du
Géant), we saw that the descent of the rocks which intervened
between us and the Glacier de Triolet would require some
caution, for the sun's rays poured down directly upon them, and
the snow slipped away every now and then from ledge to
ledge just as if it had been water,—in cascades not large enough
to be imposing, although sufficient to knock us over if we got
in their way. This little bit of cliff consequently took a longer
time than it should have done, for when we heard the indescribable swishing, hissing sound which announced a coming fall,

we of necessity huddled under the lee of the rocks until the snow ceased to shoot over us.

We got to the level of the Glacier de Triolet without misadventure, then steered for its left bank to avoid the upper of its two formidable ice-falls, and after descending the requisite distance by some old snow lying between the glacier and the cliffs which border it, crossed directly to the right bank over the level ice between the two ice-falls.[1] The right bank was gained without any trouble, and we found there numerous beds of hard snow (avalanche débris) down which we could run or glissade as fast as we liked.

Glissading is a very pleasant employment when it is accomplished successfully, and I have never seen a place where it can be more safely indulged in than the snowy valley on the right bank of the Glacier de Triolet. In my dreams I glissade delightfully, but in practice I find that somehow the snow will not behave properly, and that my alpenstock *will* get between my legs. Then my legs go where my head should be, and I see the sky revolving at a rapid pace ; the snow rises up and smites me, and runs away ; and when it is at last overtaken it suddenly stops, and we come into violent collision. Those who are with me say that I tumble head over heels, and there may be some truth in what they say. Streaks of ice are apt to make the heels shoot away, and stray stones cause one to pitch headlong down.

[1] Below the second ice-fall the glacier is completely covered up with moraine matter, and if the *left* bank is followed, one is compelled either to traverse this howling waste or to lose much time upon the tedious and somewhat difficult rocks of Mont Rouge.

Somehow these things always seem to come in the way, so it is as well to glissade only when there is something soft to tumble into.[1]

Near the termination of the glacier we could not avoid traversing a portion of its abominable moraine, but at 1.30 p.m. we were clear of it, and threw ourselves upon some springy turf conscious that our day's work was over. An hour afterwards we resumed the march, crossed the Doire torrent by a bridge a little below Gruetta, and at five o'clock entered Courmayeur, having occupied somewhat less than ten hours on the way. Mr. Girdlestone's party came in, I believe, about four hours afterwards, so there was no doubt that we made a shorter pass than the Col du Géant ; and we perhaps discovered a quicker way of getting from Chamonix to Courmayeur, or *vice versa*, than will be found elsewhere, so long as the chain of Mont Blanc remains in its present condition.[2]

---

[1] In glissading an erect position should be maintained, and the point of the alpenstock allowed to trail over the snow. If it is necessary to stop, or to slacken speed, the point is pressed against the slope, as shown in the illustration.

[2] Comparison of the Col de Triolet with the Col de Talèfre will show what a great difference in ease there may be between tracks which are nearly identical. For a distance of several miles these routes are scarcely more than half a mile apart. Nearly every step of the former is difficult, whilst the latter has no difficulty whatever. The route we adopted over the Col de Talèfre may perhaps be improved. It may be possible to go directly from the head of the Glacier de Triolet to its right bank, and, if so, at least thirty minutes might be saved.

CHAPTER XIX

THE FIRST ASCENT OF THE RUINETTE—THE MATTERHORN

" In almost every art, experience is worth more than precepts."

QUINTILIAN.

ALL of the excursions that were set down in my programme had been carried out, with the exception of the ascent of the Matterhorn, and we now turned our faces in its direction, but instead of returning *via* the Valtournanche, we took a route across country, and bagged upon our way the summit of the Ruinette.

We passed the night of July 4 at Aosta, under the roof of the genial Tairraz, and on the 5th went by the Val d'Ollomont and the Col de Fenêtre (9,141 feet) to Chermontane.[1] We slept that night at the chalets of Chanrion (a foul spot, which should be avoided), left them at 3.50 the next morning, and after a short scramble over the slope above, and a little tramp on the Glacier de Breney, we crossed directly to the Ruinette (12,727 feet), and went almost straight up it. There is not, I suppose, another mountain in the Alps of the same height that can be ascended so easily. You have only to go ahead : upon its southern side one can walk about almost anywhere.

Though I speak thus slightingly of a very respectable peak, I will not do anything of the kind in regard to the view which it gives. It is happily placed in respect to the rest of the Pennine Alps, and as a standpoint it has not many superiors. You see mountains, and nothing but mountains. It is a solemn—some would say a dreary—view, but it is very grand. The great

[1] For routes, see the Map of the Valpelline.

Combin (14,164 feet), with its noble background of the whole range of Mont Blanc, never looks so big as it does from here. In the contrary direction, the Matterhorn overpowers all besides. The Dent d'Hérens, although closer, looks a mere outlier of its great neighbour, and the snows of Monte Rosa, behind, seem intended for no other purpose than to give relief to the crags in front. To the south there is an endless array of Bec's and Becca's, backed by the great Italian peaks, whilst to the north Mont Pleureur (12,159 feet) holds its own against the more distant Wildstrubel.

We gained the summit at 9.15,[1] and stayed there an hour and a half. My faithful guides then admonished me that Prarayé, whither we were bound, was still far away, and that we had yet to cross two lofty ridges. So we resumed our harness and departed ; not, however, before a huge cairn had been built out of the blocks of gneiss with which the summit is bestrewn. Then we trotted down the slopes of the Ruinette, over the Glacier de Breney, and across a pass which I called the Col des Portons, after the neighbouring peaks. Thence we proceeded across the great Otemma Glacier towards the Col d'Oren.

The part of the glacier that we traversed was overspread with snow which completely concealed its numerous pitfalls. We marched across it in single file, and, of course, roped together. All at once Almer dropped into a crevasse up to his shoulders. I pulled in the rope immediately, but the snow gave way as it was being done, and I had to spread out my arms to stop my descent. Biener held fast, but said afterwards that his feet went through as well, so, for a moment, all three were in the jaws of the crevasse. We now slightly altered our course, so as to take the fissures transversely, and after the centre of the glacier

[1] After crossing the Glacier de Breney, we ascended some débris, and then some cliffy ground, to the glacier which surrounds the peak upon the south ; bore to the left (that is to the west) and went up the edge of the glacier ; and lastly took to the arête of the ridge which descends towards the southwest, and followed it to the summit.

was passed changed it again and made directly for the summit of the Col d'Oren.

It is scarcely necessary to observe, that it is my invariable practice to employ a rope when traversing a snow-covered glacier. Many guides, even the best ones, object to be roped, more especially early in the morning when the snow is hard. They object, sometimes, because they think it is unnecessary. Crevasses that are bridged by snow are almost always more or less perceptible by undulations on the surface ; the snow droops down, and hollows mark the courses of the chasms beneath. An experienced guide usually notices these almost imperceptible wrinkles, steps on one side or the other, as the case may require, and rarely breaks through unawares. Guides think there is no occasion to employ a rope because they think that they will *not* be taken by surprise. Michel Croz was of this opinion, and used to say that only imbeciles and children required to be tied up in the morning. I told him that in this particular matter I was a child to him. " You see these things, my good Croz, and avoid them. I do not, except you point them out to me, and so that which is not a danger to you, *is* a danger to me." The sharper one's eyes get by use, the less is a rope required as a protective against these hidden pitfalls ; but, according to my experience, the sight never becomes so keen that they can be avoided with unvarying certainty, and I mentioned what occurred upon the Otemma Glacier to show that this is so.

I well remember my first passage of the Col Théodule—the easiest of the higher Alpine glacier passes. We had a rope, and my guide said it was not necessary to use it, as he knew all the crevasses. However, we did not go a quarter of a mile before he dropped through the snow into a crevasse up to his neck. He was a heavy man, and would scarcely have extricated himself alone ; anyhow, he was very glad of my assistance. When he got on to his legs again, he said, " Well, I had no idea that there was a crevasse there ! " He no longer objected to use the rope, and we proceeded ; upon my part, with greater peace of mind than before. I have crossed the pass eighteen times since then, and have invariably insisted upon being tied together.

Guides object to the use of the rope upon snow-covered glacier, because they are afraid of being laughed at by their comrades ; and this, perhaps, is the more common reason. To illustrate this, here is another Théodule experience. We arrived at the edge of the ice, and I required to be tied. My guide (a Zermatt man of repute) said that no one used a rope going across that pass. I declined to argue the matter, and we put on the rope ; though very much against the wish of my man, who protested that he should have to submit to perpetual ridicule if we met any of his acquaintances. We had not gone very far before we saw a train coming in the contrary direction. " Ah ! " cried my man, " there is Ritz (mentioning a guide who used to be kept at the Riffel hotel for the ascent of Monte Rosa) ; it will be as I said, I shall never hear the end of this."   The guide we met was followed by a string of tomfools, none of whom were tied together, and had his face covered by a mask to prevent it becoming blistered.   After we had passed, I said, " Now, should Ritz make any observations to you, ask him why he takes such extraordinary care to preserve the skin of his face, which will grow again in a week, when he neglects such an obvious precaution in regard to his life, which he can only lose once." This was quite a new idea to my guide, and he said nothing more against the use of the rope so long as we were together.

I believe that the unwillingness to use a rope upon snow-covered glacier which born mountaineers not unfrequently exhibit, arises—first, on the part of expert men, from the consciousness that they themselves incur little risk ; secondly, on the part of inferior men, from fear of ridicule, and from aping the ways of their superiors ; and, thirdly, from pure ignorance or laziness. Whatever may be the reason, I raise up my voice against the neglect of a precaution so simple and so effectual. In my opinion, the very first thing a glacier traveller requires is plenty of good rope.

Now, touching the *use* of the rope. There is a right way, and there are wrong ways of using it. I often meet, upon glacier passes, elegantly-got-up persons, who are clearly out of their element, with a guide stalking along in front, paying no attention to the innocents in his charge. They are tied together as a matter of form, but they evidently have no idea *why* they are tied up, for they walk side by side, or close together, with the rope trailing on the snow. If one tumbles into a crevasse, the rest stare, and say, " La ! what is the matter with Smith ? " unless, as is more likely, they all tumble in together. This is

the wrong way to use a rope. It is abuse of the rope.

It is of the first importance to keep the rope taut from man to man. If this is not done, the rope affords no real security and your risks *may* be considerably magnified. There is little difficulty in extricating one man who breaks through a bridged crevasse if the rope is taut ; but t⁓ ɔase may be very awkward if two break through at the same moment, close together, and there are only two others to aid, or perhaps only one other. Further, the rope ought not upon any account to graze over snow, ice, or rocks, otherwise the strands suffer, and the lives of the whole party may be endangered. Apart from this, it is extremely annoying to have a rope knocking about one's heels. If circumstances render it impossible for the rope to be kept taut by itself, the men behind should gather it up round their hands,[1] and not allow it to incommode those in advance. A man

[1] For example, when the leader suspects crevasses, and *sounds* for them, in the manner shown in the engraving, he usually loses half a step or more. The second man should take a turn of the rope round his hand to draw it back in case the leader goes through.

must either be incompetent, careless, or selfish, if he permits
the rope to dangle about the heels of the person in front of
him.

The distance from man to man must neither be too great nor
too small. About 12 feet between each is sufficient. If there
are only two or three persons, it is prudent to allow a little more
—say 15 feet. More than this is unnecessary, and less than
9 or 10 feet is not much good.

It is essential to examine your rope from time to time to see
that it is in good condition, and if you are wise you will do this
yourself every day. Latterly, I have examined every inch of

THE RIGHT WAY TO USE THE ROPE.

my rope overnight, and upon more than one occasion have
found the strands of the Manilla rope nearly half severed through
accidental grazes.

Thus far the rope has been supposed to be employed upon
level, snow-covered glacier, to prevent any risk from concealed
crevasses. On rocks and on slopes it is used for a different
purpose (namely, to guard against slips), and in these cases it is
equally important to keep it taut, and to preserve a reasonable
distance one from the other. It is much more troublesome to
keep the rope taut upon slopes than upon the level ; and upon
difficult rocks it is all but impossible, except by adopting the
plan of moving only one at a time (see p. 125).

There is no good reason for employing a rope upon easy
rocks, and I believe that its needless use is likely to promote
carelessness. On difficult rocks and on snow-slopes (frequently
improperly called ice-slopes) it is a great advantage to be tied

together, provided the rope is handled properly ; but upon actual ice-slopes, such as that on the Col Dolent (p. 276), or upon slopes in which ice is mingled with small and loose rocks, such as the upper part of the Pointe des Ecrins (p. 169), it is almost useless, because the slip of one person might upset the entire party.[1] I am not prepared to say, however, that men should not be tied together upon similar slopes. Being attached to others usually gives confidence, and confidence decidedly assists stability. It is more questionable whether men should be in such places at all. If a man can keep on his feet upon an *escalier* cut in an ice-slope, I see no reason why he should be debarred from making use of that particular form of staircase. If he cannot, let him keep clear of such places.

There would be no advantage in discoursing upon the use of the rope at greater length. A single day upon a mountain's side will give a clearer idea of the value of a good rope, and of the numerous purposes for which it may be employed, than anyone will obtain from reading all that has been written upon the subject ; but no one will become really expert in its management without much experience.

From the Col d'Oren we proceeded down the Combe of the same name to the chalets of Prarayé, and passed the night of the

[1] When several persons are descending such places, it is evident that the *last man* cannot derive any assistance from the rope, and so might as well be untied. Partly upon this account, it is usual to place one of the strongest and steadiest men last. Now, although this cannot be termed a senseless precaution, it is obvious that it is a perfectly useless one, if it is true that a single slip would upset the entire party. The best plan I know is that which we adopted on the descent of the Col Dolent, namely, to let one man go in advance until he reaches some secure point. This one then detaches himself, the rope is drawn up, and another man is sent down to join him, and so on until the last. The last man still occupies the most difficult post, and should be the steadiest man ; but he is not exposed to any risk from his comrades slipping, and they, of course, draw in the rope as he descends, so that his position is less hazardous than if he were to come down quite by himself.

6th under the roof of our old acquaintance, the wealthy herdsman. On the 7th we crossed the Valcournera pass, *en route* for
Breuil. My thoughts were fixed on the Matterhorn, and my
guides knew that I wished them to accompany me. They had
an aversion to the mountain, and repeatedly expressed their
belief that it was useless to try to ascend it. "*Anything* but
Matterhorn, dear sir!" said Almer; "*anything* but Matterhorn." He did not speak of difficulty or of danger, nor was he
shirking *work*. He offered to go *anywhere*; but he entreated
that the Matterhorn should be abandoned. Both men spoke
fairly enough. They did not think that an ascent could be
made; and for their own credit, as well as for my sake, they did
not wish to undertake a business which, in their opinion, would
only lead to loss of time and money.

I sent them by the short cut to Breuil, and walked down to
Valtournanche to look for Jean-Antoine Carrel. He was not
there. The villagers said that he, and three others, had started
on the 6th to try the Matterhorn by the old way, on their own
account. They will have no luck, I thought, for the clouds were
low down on the mountains; and I walked up to Breuil, fully
expecting to meet them. Nor was I disappointed. About half-
way up I saw a group of men clustered around a chalet upon
the other side of the torrent, and, crossing over, found that the
party had returned. Jean-Antoine and Cæsar were there, C. E.
Gorret, and J.-J. Maquignaz. They had had no success. The
weather, they said, had been horrible, and they had scarcely
reached the Glacier du Lion.

I explained the situation to Carrel, and proposed that we,
with Cæsar and another man, should cross the Théodule by
moonlight on the 9th, and that upon the 10th we should pitch
the tent as high as possible upon the east face. He was unwilling
to abandon the old route, and urged me to try it again. I
promised to do so provided the new route failed. This satisfied
him, and he agreed to my proposal. I then went up to Breuil,
and discharged Almer and Biener—with much regret, for no

two men ever served me more faithfully or more willingly.[1]
On the next day they crossed to Zermatt.

The 8th was occupied with preparations. The weather was
stormy ; and black, rainy vapours obscured the mountains.
Towards evening a young man came from Valtournanche, and
reported that an Englishman was lying there, extremely ill.
Now was the time for the performance of my vow [2] ; and on
the morning of Sunday the 9th I went down the valley to look
after the sick man.   On my way I passed a foreign gentleman,
with a mule and several porters laden with baggage.   Amongst
these men were Jean-Antoine and Cæsar, carrying some barometers.   " Hullo ! " I said, " what are you doing ? "   They
explained that the foreigner had arrived just as they were setting
out, and that they were assisting his porters.   " Very well ; go
on to Breuil, and await me there ; we start at midnight as
agreed."   Jean-Antoine then said that he should not be able
to serve me after Tuesday the 11th, as he was engaged to travel
" with a family of distinction " in the valley of Aosta.   " And
Cæsar ? "   " And Cæsar also."   " Why did you not say this
before ? "   " Because," said he, " it was not settled. The engagement is of long standing, but *the day* was not fixed. When
I got back to Valtournanche on Friday night, after leaving you,
I found a letter naming the day."   I could not object to the
answer ; still the prospect of being left guideless was provoking. They went up, and I down, the valley.

The sick man declared that he was better, though the exertion
of saying as much tumbled him over on to the floor in a fainting
fit. He was badly in want of medicine, and I tramped down to
Châtillon to get it. It was late before I returned to Valtournanche, for the weather was tempestuous, and rain fell in torrents.
A figure passed me under the church-porch.   " *Qui vive ?* "

---

[1] During the preceding eighteen days (I exclude Sundays and other non-
working days) we ascended more than 100,000 feet, and descended 98,000
feet.

[2] See p. 87.

" Jean-Antoine." " I thought you were at Breuil." " No, sir :
when the storms came on I knew we should not start to-night,
and so came down to sleep here." " Ha, Carrel ! " I said ;
" this is a great bore. If to-morrow is not fine we shall not be
able to do anything together. I have sent away my guides,
relying on you ; and now you are going to leave me to travel
with a party of ladies. That work is not fit for *you* (he smiled,
I supposed at the implied compliment) ; can't you send someone
else instead ? " " No, monsieur. I am sorry, but my word is
pledged. I should like to accompany you, but I can't break my
engagement." By this time we had arrived at the inn door.
" Well, it is no fault of yours. Come presently with Cæsar,
and have some wine." They came, and we sat up till midnight,
recounting our old adventures, in the inn of Valtournanche.

The weather continued bad upon the 10th, and I returned to
Breuil. The two Carrels were again hovering about the above-
mentioned chalet, and I bade them adieu. In the evening the
sick man crawled up, a good deal better ; but his was the only
arrival. The Monday crowd [1] did not cross the Théodule, on
account of the continued storms. The inn was lonely. I went
to bed early, and was awoke the next morning by the invalid
inquiring if I had " heard the news." " No ; what news ? "
" Why," said he, "a large party of guides went off this morning
to try the Matterhorn, taking with them a mule laden with
provisions."

I went to the door, and with a telescope saw the party upon
the lower slopes of the mountain. Favre, the landlord, stood by.
" What is all this about ? " I inquired. " Who is the leader of
this party ? " " Carrel." " What ! Jean-Antoine ? " " Yes ;
Jean-Antoine." " Is Cæsar there too ? " " Yes, he is there."
Then I saw in a moment that I had been bamboozled and hum-
bugged ; and learned, bit by bit, that the affair had been arranged
long beforehand. The start on the 6th had been for a preliminary

[1] Tourists congregate at Zermatt upon Sundays, and large gangs and droves
usually cross the Théodule pass on Mondays.

reconnaissance ; the mule, that I passed, was conveying stores for the attack ; the " family of distinction " was Signor F. Giordano, who had just despatched the party to facilitate the way to the summit, and who, when the facilitation was completed, was to be taken to the top along with Signor Sella ! [1]

I was greatly mortified. My plans were upset ; the Italians had clearly stolen a march upon me, and I saw that the astute Favre chuckled over my discomfiture, because the route by the eastern face, if successful, would not benefit his inn. What was to be done ? I retired to my room, and soothed by tobacco, re-studied my plans, to see if it was not possible to outmanœuvre the Italians. " They have taken a mule's load of provisions." " That is *one* point in my favour, for they will take two or three days to get through the food, and, until that is done, no work will be accomplished." " How is the weather ? " I went to the window. The mountain was smothered up in mist. " Another point in my favour." " They are to facilitate the· way. Well, if they do that to any purpose, it will be a long job." Altogether, I reckoned that they could not possibly ascend the mountain and come back to Breuil in less than seven days. I got cooler, for it was evident that the wily ones might be outwitted after all. There was time enough to go to Zermatt, to try the eastern face, and, should it prove impracticable, to come back to Breuil before the men returned ; and then, it seemed to me, as the mountain was not padlocked, one might start at the same time as the Messieurs, and yet get to the top before them.

The first thing to do was to go to Zermatt. Easier said than done. The seven guides upon the mountain included the ablest men in the valley, and none of the ordinary muleteer-guides were at Breuil. Two men, at least, were wanted for my baggage, but not a soul could be found. I ran about, and sent about in all directions, but not a single porter could be obtained. One

[1] The Italian Minister. Signor Giordano had undertaken the business arrangements for Signor Sella. [See Appendix B for Giordano's account.]

was with Carrel ; another was ill ; another was at Châtillon, and so forth. Even Meynet, the hunchback, could not be induced to come ; he was in the thick of some important cheese-making operations. I was in the position of a general without an army ; it was all very well to make plans, but there was no one to execute them. This did not much trouble me, for it was evident that so long as the weather stopped traffic over the Théodule, it would hinder the men equally upon the Matter-horn ; and I knew that directly it improved company would certainly arrive.

About midday on Tuesday the 11th a large party hove in sight from Zermatt, preceded by a nimble young Englishman, and one of old Peter Taugwalder's sons.[1] I went at once to this gentleman to learn if he could dispense with Taugwalder. He said that he could not, as they were going to recross to Zermatt on the morrow, but that the young man should assist in trans-porting my baggage, as he had nothing to carry. We naturally got into conversation. I told my story, and learned that the young Englishman was Lord Francis Douglas,[2] whose recent exploit—the ascent of the Gabel-horn—had excited my wonder and admiration. He brought good news. Old Peter had lately been beyond the Hörnli, and had re-ported that he thought an ascent of

LORD FRANCIS DOUGLAS.

the Matterhorn was possible upon that side. Almer had left

[1] Peter Taugwalder, the father, was called *old* Peter, to distinguish him from his eldest son, *young* Peter. In 1865 the father's age was about 45.

[2] Brother of the [then] Marquis of Queensberry. An account of his ascent of the Gabelhorn, on July 7, 1865 (the first made on the Zinal side), was found after his death amongst his papers, and was published in the *Alpine Journal*, vol. ii., pp. 221–2.

Zermatt, and could not be recovered, so I determined to seek for old Peter. Lord Francis Douglas expressed a warm desire to ascend the mountain, and before long it was determined that he should take part in the expedition.

Favre could no longer hinder our departure, and lent us one of his men. We crossed the Col Théodule on Wednesday

THE CHAPEL AT THE SCHWARZSEE (LAC NOIR) IN 1865.

morning the 12th of July, rounded the foot of the Ober Theodul Glacier, crossed the Furggen Glacier, and deposited tent, blankets, ropes, and other matters in the little chapel at the Schwarzsee.[1] All four were heavily laden, for we brought across the whole of my stores from Breuil. Of rope alone there was about 600 feet. There were three kinds. First, 200 feet of the Manilla rope ; second, 150 feet of a stouter, and probably stronger rope than the first ; and third, more than 200 feet of a lighter and weaker rope than the first, of a kind that I used formerly (stout sash-line).

[1] For route, and the others mentioned in the subsequent chapters, see the map of the Matterhorn and its glaciers.

We descended to Zermatt, sought and engaged old Peter, and gave him permission to choose another guide.[1] When we returned to the Monte Rosa hotel, whom should we see sitting upon the wall in front but my old *guide chef*, Michel Croz. I supposed that he had come with Mr. B——, but I learned that that gentleman had arrived in ill-health, at Chamonix, and had returned to England. Croz, thus left free, had been immediately engaged by the Rev. Charles Hudson, and they had come to Zermatt with the same object as ourselves—namely, to attempt the ascent of the Matterhorn !

Lord Francis Douglas and I dined at the Monte Rosa hotel, and had just finished when Mr. Hudson and a friend entered the *salle à manger*. They had returned from inspecting the mountain, and some idlers in the room demanded their intentions. We heard a confirmation of Croz's statement, and learned that Mr. Hudson intended to set out on the morrow at the same hour as ourselves. We left the room to consult, and agreed it was undesirable that two independent parties should be on the mountain at the same time with the same object. Mr. Hudson was therefore invited to join us, and he accepted our proposal. Before admitting his friend—Mr. Hadow—I took the precaution to inquire what he had done in the Alps, and, as well as I remember, Mr. Hudson's reply was, " Mr. Hadow has done Mont Blanc in less time than most men." [2] He then mentioned several other

[1] [In reply to a question put to him late in life by Mr. H. F. Montagnier, young Peter Taugwalder stated : " Neither Mr. Hudson nor Mr. Whymper engaged the two Taugwalders. It was Lord Douglas, though all these gentlemen united together in a single company under the command of the chief guide Michel Croz." (From a document in possession of the Alpine Club.) At the official inquiry of July 21st, 1865, however, old Peter Taugwalder states that he was " engaged by Lord Douglas and Whymper."]

[2] In the *Alpine Journal*, vol. iii., pp. 75–6, Mr. T. S. Kennedy, in speaking of this ascent (which was, I believe, made upon the 7th of July 1865), says that Mr. Hadow went from the Grands Mulets to the summit of Mont Blanc in less than four hours and a half, and descended from the summit to Chamonix in five hours.

excursions that were unknown to me, and added, in answer to a further question, " I consider he is a sufficiently good man to go with us." Mr. Hadow was admitted without any further question, and we then went into the matter of guides. Hudson thought that Croz and old Peter would be sufficient. The question was referred to the men themselves, and they made no objection.

So Croz and I became comrades once more ; and as I threw myself on my bed and tried to go to sleep, I wondered at the strange series of chances which had first separated us and then brought us together again. I thought of the mistake through which he had accepted the engagement to Mr. B—— ; of his unwillingness to adopt my route ; of his recommendation to transfer our energies to the chain of Mont Blanc ; of the retirement of Almer and Biener ; of the desertion of Carrel ; of the arrival of Lord Francis Douglas ; and, lastly, of our accidental meeting at Zermatt ; and as I pondered over these things I could not help asking, " What next ? " If any one of the links of this fatal chain of circumstances had been omitted, what a different story I should have to tell !

REV. CHARLES HUDSON.

CHAPTER XX

THE FIRST ASCENT OF THE MATTERHORN

> " Had we succeeded well,
> We had been reckoned 'mongst the wise : our minds
> Are so disposed to judge from the event."
>
> EURIPIDES.

> " It is a thoroughly unfair, ~~but~~ an ordinary custom, to praise or blame
> designs (which in themselves may be good or bad) just as they turn out
> well or ill. Hence the same actions are at one time attributed to earnestness
> and at another to vanity."
>
> PLINY MIN.

WE started from Zermatt on the 13th of July 1865, at half-past
five, on a brilliant and perfectly cloudless morning. We were
eight in number—Croz, old Peter and his two sons,[1] Lord F.
Douglas, Hadow, Hudson,[2] and I. To ensure steady motion,

---

[1] The two young Taugwalders were taken as porters, by desire of their
father, and carried provisions amply sufficient for three days, in case the ascent
should prove more troublesome than we anticipated.

[2] I remember speaking about pedestrianism to a well-known mountaineer
some years ago, and venturing to remark that a man who averaged thirty
miles a day might be considered a good walker. " A fair walker," he said,
" a *fair* walker." " What then would you consider *good* walking ? "
" Well," he replied, " I will tell you. Some time back a friend and I agreed
to go to Switzerland, but a short time afterwards he wrote to say he ought
to let me know that a young and delicate lad was going with him who would
not be equal to great things, in fact, he would not be able to do more than
fifty miles a day ! " " What became of the young and delicate lad ? "
" He lives." " And who was your extraordinary friend ? " " Charles
Hudson." I have every reason to believe that the gentlemen referred to *were*

one tourist and one native walked together. The youngest Taugwalder fell to my share, and the lad marched well, proud to be on the expedition, and happy to show his powers. The wine-bags also fell to my lot to carry, and throughout the day, after each drink, I replenished them secretly with water, so that at the next halt they were found fuller than before ! This was considered a good omen, and little short of miraculous.

equal to walking more than fifty miles a day, but they were exceptional, not *good* pedestrians.

Charles Hudson, Vicar of Skillington in Lincolnshire, was considered by the mountaineering fraternity to be the best amateur of his time. He was the organizer and leader of the party of Englishmen who ascended Mont Blanc by the Aiguille du Goûter, and descended by the Grands Mulets route, without guides, in 1855. His long practice made him surefooted, and in that respect he was not greatly inferior to a born mountaineer. I remember him as a well-made man of middle height and age, neither stout nor thin, with face pleasant—though grave, and with quiet unassuming manners. Although an athletic man, he would have been overlooked in a crowd ; and although he had done some of the greatest mountaineering feats which have been done, he was the last man to speak of his own doings. His friend Mr. Hadow was a young man of nineteen, who had the looks and manners of a greater age. He was a rapid walker, but 1865 was his first season in the Alps. Lord Francis Douglas was about the same age as Mr. Hadow. He had had the advantage of several seasons in the Alps. He was nimble as a deer, and was becoming an expert mountaineer. Just before our meeting he had ascended the Ober Gabelhorn (with old Peter Taugwalder and Jos. Viennin), and this gave me a high opinion of his powers ; for I had examined that mountain all round, a few weeks before, and had declined its ascent on account of its apparent difficulty.

My personal acquaintance with Mr. Hudson was very slight—still, I should have been content to have placed myself under his orders if he had chosen to claim the position to which he was entitled. Those who knew him will not be surprised to learn that, so far from doing this, he lost no opportunity of consulting the wishes and opinions of those around him. We deliberated together whenever there was occasion, and our authority was recognized by the others. Whatever responsibility there was devolved upon us. I recollect with satisfaction that there was no difference of opinion between us as to what should be done, and that the most perfect harmony existed between all of us so long as we were together.

On the first day we did not intend to ascend to any great height, and we mounted, accordingly, very leisurely ; picked up the things which were left in the chapel at the Schwarzsee at 8.20, and proceeded thence along the ridge connecting the Hörnli with the Matterhorn.[1] At half-past eleven we arrived at the base of the actual peak ; then quitted the ridge, and clambered round some ledges, on to the eastern face. We were now fairly upon the mountain, and were astonished to find that places which from the Riffel, or even from the Furggen Glacier, looked entirely impracticable, were so easy that we could *run about.*

Before twelve o'clock we had found a good position for the tent, at a height of 11,000 feet.[2] Croz and young Peter went on to see what was above, in order to save time on the following morning. They cut across the heads of the snow-slopes which descended towards the Furggen Glacier, and disappeared round a corner ; but shortly afterwards we saw them high up on the face, moving quickly. We others made a solid platform for the tent in a well-protected spot, and then watched eagerly for the return of the men. The stones which they upset told us that they were very high, and we supposed that the way must be easy. At length, just before 3 p.m., we saw them coming down,

[1] Arrived at the chapel 7.30 a.m. ; left it 8.20 ; halted to examine route 9.30 ; started again 10.25, and arrived at 11.20 at the cairn made by Mr. Kennedy in 1862 (see p. 66), marked 3,298 metres upon the map of the Matterhorn and its Glaciers. Stopped 10 min. here. From the Hörnli to this point we kept, when possible, to the crest of the ridge. The greater part of the way was excessively easy, but there were a few places where the axe had to be used.

[2] Thus far the guides did not once go to the front. Hudson or I led, and when any cutting was required we did it ourselves. This was done to spare the guides, and to show them that we were in earnest. The spot at which we camped was four hours' walking from Zermatt, and is marked upon the map—CAMP (1865). It was just upon a level with the Furggengrat, and its position is indicated upon the engraving facing p. 246 by a little circular white spot, in a line with the word CAMP.

evidently much excited. "What are they saying, Peter?" "Gentlemen, they say it is no good." But when they came near we heard a different story. "Nothing but what was good; not a difficulty, not a single difficulty! We could have gone to the summit and returned to-day easily!"

We passed the remaining hours of daylight—some basking in the sunshine, some sketching or collecting; and when the sun went down, giving, as it departed, a glorious promise for the morrow, we returned to the tent to arrange for the night. Hudson made tea, I coffee, and we then retired each one to his blanket bag; the Taugwalders, Lord Francis Douglas, and myself, occupying the tent, the others remaining, by preference, outside. Long after dusk the cliffs above echoed with our laughter and with the songs of the guides, for we were happy that night in camp, and feared no evil.

We assembled together outside the tent before dawn on the morning of the 14th, and started directly it was light enough to move. Young Peter came on with us as a guide, and his brother returned to Zermatt.[1] We followed the route which had been taken on the previous day, and in a few minutes turned the rib which had intercepted the view of the eastern face from our tent platform. The whole of this great slope was now revealed, rising for 3,000 feet like a huge natural staircase.[2] Some parts were more, and others were less, easy; but we were not once brought to a halt by any serious impediment, for when an obstruction was met in front it could always be turned to the right or to the left. For the greater part of the way there was, indeed, no occasion for the rope, and sometimes Hudson led, sometimes myself. At 6.20 we had attained a height of 12,800 feet, and halted for half an hour; we then continued the ascent without a break until 9.55, when we stopped for fifty minutes, at a height of 14,000 feet. Twice we struck the north-east ridge

---

[1] It was originally intended to leave both of the young men behind. We found it difficult to divide the food, and so the new arrangement was made.

[2] See pp. 245–248.

and followed it for some little distance,—to no advantage, for it was usually more rotten and steep, and always more difficult than the face.[1] Still, we kept near to it, lest stones perchance might fall.[2]

We had now arrived at the foot of that part which, from the Riffelberg or from Zermatt, seems perpendicular or overhanging, and could no longer continue upon the eastern side. For a little distance we ascended by snow upon the arête—that is, the ridge—descending towards Zermatt, and then, by common consent, turned over to the right, or to the northern side. Before doing so, we made a change in the order of ascent. Croz went first, I followed, Hudson came third ; Hadow and old Peter were last. " Now," said Croz, as he led off, " now for some-

[1] See remarks on arêtes and faces on pp. 223, 224. There is very little to choose between in the arêtes leading from the summit towards the Hörnli (N.E. ridge) and towards the Col du Lion (S.W. ridge). Both are jagged, serrated ridges, which any experienced climber would willingly avoid if he could find another route. On the northern (Zermatt) side the eastern face affords another route, or any number of routes, since there is hardly a part of it which cannot be traversed ! On the southern (Breuil) side the ridge alone, generally speaking, can be followed ; and when it becomes impracticable, and the climber is forced to bear down to the right or to the left, the work is generally of the most difficult character.

[2] Very few stones fell during the two days I was on the mountain, and none came near us. Others who have followed the same route have not been so fortunate ; they may not, perhaps, have taken the same precautions. It is a noteworthy fact, that the lateral moraine of the left bank of the Furrgen Glacier is scarcely larger than that of the right bank, although the former receives all the débris that falls from the 4,000 feet of cliffs which form the eastern side of the Matterhorn, whilst the latter is fed by perfectly insignificant slopes. Neither of these moraines is large. This is strong evidence that stones do *not* fall to any great extent from the eastern face. The inward dip of the beds retains the detritus in place. Hence the eastern face appears, when one is upon it, to be undergoing more rapid disintegration than the other sides : in reality, the mantle of ruin spares the mountain from further waste. Upon the southern side, rocks fall as they are rent off ; " each day's work is cleared away " every day ; and hence the faces and ridges are left naked, and are exposed to fresh attacks.

thing altogether different." The work became difficult and required caution. In some places there was little to hold, and it was desirable that those should be in front who were least likely to slip. The general slope of the mountain at this part was *less* than 40°, and snow had accumulated in, and had filled up, the interstices of the rock-face, leaving only occasional fragments projecting here and there. These were at times covered with a thin film of ice, produced from the melting and refreezing of the snow. It was the counterpart, on a small scale, of the upper 700 feet of the Pointe des Ecrins,—only there was this material difference ; the face of the Ecrins was about, or exceeded, an angle of 50°, and the Matterhorn face was less than 40°.[1] It was a place over which any fair mountaineer might pass in safety, and Mr. Hudson ascended this part, and, as far as I know, the entire mountain, without having the slightest assistance rendered to him upon any occasion. Sometimes, after I had taken a hand from Croz, or received a pull, I turned to offer the same to Hudson ; but he invariably declined, saying it was not necessary. Mr. Hadow, however, was not accustomed to this kind of work, and required continual assistance. It is only fair to say that the difficulty which he found at this part arose simply and entirely from want of experience.

This solitary difficult part was of no great extent.[2] We bore away over it at first, nearly horizontally, for a distance of about 400 feet ; then ascended directly towards the summit for about 60 feet ; and then doubled back to the ridge which descends towards Zermatt. A long stride round a rather awkward corner brought us to snow once more. The last doubt vanished ! The Matterhorn was ours ! Nothing but 200 feet of easy snow remained to be surmounted !

You must now carry your thoughts back to the seven Italians who started from Breuil on the 11th of July. Four days had

[1] This part was less steeply inclined than the whole of the eastern face.
[2] I have no memorandum of the time that it occupied. It must have taken about an hour and a half.

passed since their departure, and we were tormented with anxiety lest they should arrive on the top before us. All the way up we had talked of them, and many false alarms of " men on the summit " had been raised. The higher we rose, the more

" CROZ ! CROZ ! ! COME HERE ! "

intense became the excitement. What if we should be beaten at the last moment ? The slope eased off, at length we could be detached, and Croz and I, dashing away, ran a neck-and-neck race, which ended in a dead heat. At 1.40 p.m. the world was at our feet, and the Matterhorn was conquered. Hurrah ! Not a footstep could be seen.

It was not yet certain that we had not been beaten. The

summit of the Matterhorn was formed of a rudely level ridge, about 350 feet long,[1] and the Italians might have been at its farther extremity. I hastened to the southern end, scanning the snow right and left eagerly. Hurrah ! again ; it was untrodden. " Where were the men ? " I peered over the cliff, half doubting, half expectant, and saw them immediately—mere dots on the ridge, at an immense distance below. Up went my arms and my hat. " Croz ! Croz ! ! come here ! " " Where are they, Monsieur ? " " There, don't you see them, down there ? " " Ah ! the *coquins*, they are low down." " Croz, we must make those fellows hear us." We yelled until we were hoarse. The Italians seemed to regard us—we could not be certain. "Croz, we *must* make them hear us ; they *shall* hear us ! " I seized a block of rock and hurled it down, and called upon my companion, in the name of friendship, to do the same. We drove our sticks in, and prized away the crags, and soon a torrent of stones poured down the cliffs. There was no mistake about it this time. The Italians turned and fled.[2]

Still, I would that the leader of that party could have stood with us at that moment, for our victorious shouts conveyed to him the disappointment of the ambition of a lifetime. He was *the* man, of all those who attempted the ascent of the Matterhorn, who most deserved to be the first upon its summit. He was the first to doubt its inaccessibility, and he was the only man who

[1] The highest points are towards the two ends. In 1865 the northern end was slightly higher than the southern one. In bygone years Carrel and I often suggested to each other that we might one day arrive upon the top, and find ourselves cut off from the very highest point by a notch in the summit-ridge which is seen from the Théodule and from Breuil (marked **D** on the outline on p. 94). This notch is very conspicuous from below, but when one is actually upon the summit it is hardly noticed, and it can be passed without the least difficulty.

[2] I learnt afterwards from J.-A. Carrel that they heard our first cries. They were then upon the south-west ridge, close to the Cravate, and *twelve hundred and fifty feet* below us ; or, as the crow flies, at a distance of about one-third of a mile.

persisted in believing that its ascent would be accomplished. It was the aim of his life to make the ascent from the side of Italy, for the honour of his native valley. For a time he had the game in his hands : he played it as he thought best ; but he made a false move, and he lost it.

The others had arrived, so we went back to the northern end

THE SUMMIT OF THE MATTERHORN IN 1865 (NORTHERN END).

of the ridge. Croz now took the tent-pole,[1] and planted it in the highest snow. " Yes," we said, " there is the flag-staff, but where is the flag ? " " Here it is," he answered, pulling off his blouse and fixing it to the stick. It made a poor flag, and there was no wind to float it out, yet it was seen all around.

[1] At our departure the men were confident that the ascent would be made, and took one of the poles out of the tent. I protested that it was tempting Providence ; they took the pole nevertheless.

They saw it at Zermatt—at the Riffel—in the Val Tournanche. At Breuil, the watchers cried, " Victory is ours ! " They raised " bravos " for Carrel, and " vivas " for Italy, and hastened to put themselves *en fête*. On the morrow they were undeceived. " All was changed ; the explorers returned sad—cast down—disheartened—confounded—gloomy." " It is true," said the men. " We saw them ourselves—they hurled stones at us ! The old traditions *are* true,—there are spirits on the top of the Matterhorn ! " [1]

[1] Signor Giordano was naturally disappointed at the result, and wished the men to start again. *They all refused to do so, with the exception of Jean-Antoine.* Upon the 16th of July he set out again with three others, and upon the 17th gained the summit by passing (at first) up the south-west ridge, and (afterwards) by turning over to the Z'Mutt, or north-western side. On the 18th he returned to Breuil.

Whilst we were upon the southern end of the summit-ridge, we paid some attention to the portion of the mountain which intervened between ourselves and the Italian guides. It seemed as if there would not be the least chance for them if they should attempt to storm the final peak directly from the end of the " shoulder." In that direction cliffs fell sheer down from the summit, and we were unable to see beyond a certain distance. There remained the route about which Carrel and I had often talked, namely, to ascend directly at first from the end of the " shoulder," and afterwards to swerve to the left —that is, to the Tiefenmatten side—and to complete the ascent from the north-west. When we were upon the summit we laughed at this idea. The part of the mountain that I have described upon p. 312 was not easy, although its inclination was moderate. If that slope were made only ten degrees steeper, its difficulty would be greatly increased. To double its inclination would be to make it impracticable. The slope at the southern end of the summit-ridge, falling towards the north-west, was *much* steeper than that over which we passed, and we ridiculed the idea that any person should attempt to ascend in that direction, when the northern route was so easy. Nevertheless, the summit was reached by that route by the undaunted Carrel. From knowing the final slope over which he passed, and from the account of Mr. F. C. Grove, I do not hesitate to term the ascent of Carrel and Bich in 1865 the most desperate piece of mountain-scrambling upon record. In 1869 I asked Carrel if he had ever done anything more difficult. His reply was, " Man cannot do anything much more difficult than that ! " See Appendix C.

We returned to the southern end of the ridge to build a cairn, and then paid homage to the view.[1]   The day was one of those superlatively calm and clear ones which usually precede bad weather.   The atmosphere was perfectly still, and free from all clouds or vapours.   Mountains fifty—nay a hundred—miles off, looked sharp and near.   All their details—ridge and crag, snow and glacier—stood out with faultless definition.   Pleasant thoughts of happy days in bygone years came up unbidden, as we recognized the old, familiar forms.   All were revealed— not one of the principal peaks of the Alps was hidden.   I see them clearly now—the great inner circles of giants, backed by the ranges, chains, and *massifs*.   First came the Dent Blanche, hoary and grand ;   the Gabelhorn and pointed Rothorn ;   and then the peerless Weisshorn :   the towering Mischabelhörner, flanked by the Allalinhorn, Strahlhorn, and Rimpfischhorn ; then Monte Rosa—with its many Spitzes—the Lyskamm and the Breithorn.   Behind were the Bernese Oberland, governed by the Finsteraarhorn ;   the Simplon and St. Gotthard groups ; the Disgrazia and the Ortler.   Towards the south we looked down to Chivasso on the plain of Piedmont, and far beyond. The Viso—one hundred miles away—seemed close upon us ; the Maritime Alps—one hundred and thirty miles distant— were free from haze.   Then came my first love—the Pelvoux ; the Ecrins and the Meije ;   the clusters of the Graians ;   and lastly, in the west, glowing in full sunlight, rose the monarch of all —Mont Blanc.   Ten thousand feet beneath us were the green fields of Zermatt, dotted with chalets, from which blue smoke rose lazily.   Eight thousand feet below, on the other side, were the pastures of Breuil.   There were forests black and gloomy, and meadows bright and lively ;   bounding waterfalls

[1] The summit-ridge was much shattered, although not so extensively as the south-west and north-east ridges.   The highest rock, in 1865, was a block of mica-schist, and the fragment I broke off it not only possesses, in a remarkable degree, the *character* of the peak, but mimics, in an astonishing manner, the details of its form.   (See illustration on page 319.)

and tranquil lakes ; fertile lands and savage wastes ; sunny plains and frigid *plateaux*. There were the most rugged forms, and the most graceful outlines—bold, perpendicular cliffs, and gentle undulating slopes ; rocky mountains and snowy mountains, sombre and solemn, or glittering and white, with walls— turrets — pinnacles — pyramids — domes — cones — and spires ! There was every combination that the world can give, and every contrast that the heart could desire.

We remained on the summit for one hour—

> " One crowded hour of glorious life."

It passed away too quickly, and we began to prepare for the descent.

THE ACTUAL SUMMIT OF THE MATTERHORN IN 1865.

CHAPTER XXI

DESCENT OF THE MATTERHORN [1]

HUDSON and I again consulted as to the best and safest arrangement of the party. We agreed that it would be best for Croz

[1] The substance of Chapter XXI appeared in a letter in *The Times*, August
8, 1865.   A few paragraphs have now been added, and a few corrections have
been made.   The former will help to make clear that which was obscure in
the original account, and the latter are, mostly, unimportant.

[On July 26th, 1865, Whymper addressed a letter from Interlaken to Herr
von Fellenberg, describing the ascent and descent.   In all material particulars
it agrees with his letter to *The Times* of August 8th, 1865.   In a covering
letter he writes : " I cannot bring myself to write to the newspapers respecting this sad affair ; but, it seems to me, there is no impropriety in addressing
this letter to you, and in its being published by you.   It is, I am sure you will
feel with me, highly desirable that a correct account of it should be made
known to the public."]

to go first,[1] and Hadow second ; Hudson, who was almost equal to a born mountaineer in sureness of foot, wished to be third ; Lord Francis Douglas was placed next, and old Peter, the strongest of the remainder, after him.   I suggested to Hudson that we should attach a rope to the rocks on our arrival at the difficult bit, and hold it as we descended, as an additional protection.   He approved the idea, but it was not definitely settled that it should be done.   The party was being arranged in the above order whilst I was sketching the summit, and they had finished, and were waiting for me to be tied in line, when someone remembered that our names had not been left in a bottle.   They requested me to write them down, and moved off while it was being done.

A few minutes afterwards I tied myself to young Peter, ran down after the others, and caught them just as they were commencing the descent of the difficult part.[2]   Great care was being taken.   Only one man was moving at a time ; when he was firmly planted the next advanced, and so on.   They had not, however, attached the additional rope to rocks, and nothing was said about it.   The suggestion was not made for my own sake, and I am not sure that it even occurred to me again.   For some little distance we two followed the others, detached from them, and should have continued so had not Lord Francis Douglas asked me, about 3 p.m., to tie on to old Peter, as he feared, he said, that Taugwalder would not be able to hold his ground if a slip occurred.

A few minutes later, a sharp-eyed lad ran into the Monte Rosa Hotel, to Seiler, saying that he had seen an avalanche fall

[1] If the members of the party had been more equally efficient, Croz would have been placed *last*.

[2] Described upon pp. 311, 312.

[In his letter to Fellenberg, Whymper states that they " caught them before they had descended any great distance, and I then tied myself in line behind old Taugwalder.   On arrival at the difficult part, the greatest care was taken . . ."]

from the summit of the Matterhorn on to the Matterhorn Glacier. The boy was reproved for telling idle stories ; he was right, nevertheless, and this was what he saw.

Michel Croz had laid aside his axe, and in order to give Mr. Hadow greater security, was absolutely taking hold of his legs, and putting his feet, one by one, into their proper positions.[1] So far as I know, no one was actually descending. I cannot speak with certainty, because the two leading men were partially hidden from my sight by an intervening mass of rock, but it is my belief, from the movements of their shoulders, that Croz, having done as I have said, was in the act of turning round, to go down a step or two himself ; at this moment Mr. Hadow slipped, fell against him, and knocked him over. I heard one startled exclamation from Croz, then saw him and Mr. Hadow flying downwards ; in another moment Hudson was dragged from his steps, and Lord Francis Douglas immediately after him.[2]

[1] Not at all an unusual proceeding, even between born mountaineers. I wish to convey the impression that Croz was using all pains, rather than to indicate inability on the part of Mr. Hadow. The insertion of the word " absolutely " makes the passage, perhaps, rather ambiguous. I retain it now, in order to offer the above explanation.

[2] At the moment of the accident, Croz, Hadow, and Hudson, were close together. Between Hudson and Lord F. Douglas the rope was all but taut, and the same between all the others who were *above*. Croz was standing by the side of a rock which afforded good hold, and if he had been aware, or had suspected, that anything was about to occur, he might and would have gripped it, and would have prevented any mischief. He was taken totally by surprise. Mr. Hadow slipped off his feet on to his back, his feet struck Croz in the small of the back, and knocked him right over, head first. Croz's axe was out of his reach, and without it he managed to get his head uppermost before he disappeared from our sight. If it had been in his hand I have no doubt that he would have stopped himself and Mr. Hadow.

Mr. Hadow, at the moment of the slip, was not occupying a bad position. He could have moved either up or down, and could touch with his hand the rock of which I have spoken. Hudson was not so well placed, but he had liberty of motion. The rope was not taut from him to Hadow, and the two men fell ten or twelve feet before the jerk came upon him. Lord F. Douglas

All this was the work of a moment. Immediately we heard Croz's exclamation, old Peter and I planted ourselves as firmly as the rocks would permit [1] : the rope was taut between us, and the jerk came on us both as on one man. We held ; but the rope broke midway between Taugwalder and Lord Francis Douglas.[2] For a few seconds we saw our unfortunate companions sliding downwards on their backs, and spreading out their hands, endeavouring to save themselves. They passed from our sight uninjured, disappeared one by one, and fell from precipice to precipice on the Matterhorn Glacier below, a distance of nearly 4,000 feet in height. From the moment the rope broke it was impossible to help them.

So perished our comrades ! For the space of half an hour we remained on the spot without moving a single step. The two men, paralysed by terror, cried like infants, and trembled in such a manner as to threaten us with the fate of the others. Old Peter rent the air with exclamations of " Chamonix ! Oh, what will Chamonix say ? " He meant, Who would believe that Croz could fall ? The young man did nothing but scream

was not favourably placed, and could neither move up nor down. Old Peter was firmly planted, and stood just beneath a large rock which he hugged with both arms. I enter into these details to make it more apparent that the position occupied by the party at the moment of the accident was not by any means excessively trying. We were compelled to pass over the exact spot where the slip occurred, and we found—even with shaken nerves—that *it* was not a difficult place to pass. I have described the *slope generally* as difficult, and it is so undoubtedly to most persons ; but it must be distinctly understood that Mr. Hadow slipped at a comparatively easy part.

[1] Or, more correctly, we held on as tightly as possible. There was no time to change our position.

[2] [In his letter to Fellenberg, Whymper writes : " It has been stated that it broke in consequence of its fraying over a rock ; this is not the case, it broke in mid-air, and the end does not show any traces of its having been previously injured. . . . No blame can be attached to any of the guides, they all did their duty manfully ; but I cannot but think that had the rope been tight between those who fell as it was between myself and Taugwalder, that the whole of this frightful calamity might have been averted."]

or sob, " We are lost ! we are lost ! " Fixed between the two, I could neither move up nor down. I begged young Peter to descend, but he dared not. Unless he did, we could not advance. Old Peter became alive to the danger, and swelled the cry, " We are lost ! we are lost ! " The father's fear was natural— he trembled for his son ; the young man's fear was cowardly— he thought of self alone. At last old Peter summoned up courage, and changed his position to a rock to which he could fix the rope ; the young man then descended, and we all stood together. Immediately we did so, I asked for the rope which had given way, and found, to my surprise—indeed, to my horror—that it was the weakest of the three ropes. It was not brought, and should not have been employed, for the purpose for which it was used. It was old rope, and, compared with the others, was feeble. It was intended as a reserve, in case we had to leave much rope behind, attached to rocks. I saw at once that a serious question was involved, and made him give me the end. It had broken in mid-

ROPE BROKEN ON THE MATTERHORN.

air, and it did not appear to have sustained previous injury.[1]

For more than two hours afterwards I thought almost every moment that the next would be my last ; for the Taugwalders, utterly unnerved, were not only incapable of giving assistance,

[1] [Late in life, young Peter Taugwalder was asked by Mr. H. F. Montagnier, " Did old Peter choose the rope used to attach himself, his son and Mr. Whymper to the rest of the party ? " He replied, " Old Peter said the rope would not be strong enough, but Michel Croz wanted to have it so and attached Mr. Whymper between the two Taugwalders, for Michel Croz acted as commander of the party." (Document in possession of the Alpine Club.)]

but were in such a state that a slip might have been expected from them at any moment.   After a time, we were able to do that which should have been done at first, and fixed rope to firm rocks, in addition to being tied together.   These ropes were cut from time to time, and were left behind.[1]   Even with their assurance the men were afraid to proceed, and several times old Peter turned with ashy face and faltering limbs, and said, with terrible emphasis, " *I cannot !* "

About 6 p.m. we arrived at the snow upon the ridge descending towards Zermatt, and all peril was over.   We frequently looked, but in vain, for traces of our unfortunate companions ; we bent over the ridge and cried to them, but no sound returned.   Convinced at last that they were neither within sight nor hearing, we ceased from our useless efforts ; and, too cast down for speech, silently gathered up our things, and the little effects of those who were lost, preparatory to continuing the descent.   When, lo ! a mighty arch appeared, rising above the Lyskamm, high into the sky.   Pale, colourless, and noiseless, but perfectly sharp and defined, except where it was lost in the clouds, this unearthly apparition seemed like a vision from another world ; and, almost appalled, we watched with amazement the gradual development of two vast crosses, one on either side.   If the Taugwalders had not been the first to perceive it, I should have doubted my senses.   They thought it had some connection with the accident, and I, after a while, that it might bear some relation to ourselves.   But our movements had no effect upon it.   The spectral forms remained motionless.   It was a fearful and wonderful sight ; unique in my experience, and impressive beyond description, coming at such a moment.[2]

[1] These ends, until recently, were still attached to the rocks, and marked our line of ascent and descent.

[2] See illustration facing page 325.   I paid very little attention to this remarkable phenomenon, and was glad when it disappeared, as it distracted our attention.   Under ordinary circumstances I should have felt vexed afterwards at not having observed with greater precision an occurrence so rare and so wonderful.

FOG-BOW, SEEN FROM THE MATTERHORN ON JULY 14, 1865.

"THE TAUGWALDERS THOUGHT THAT IT HAD SOME CONNECTION WITH THE ACCIDENT."

I was ready to leave, and waiting for the others. They had recovered their appetites and the use of their tongues. They spoke in patois, which I did not understand. At length the son said in French, " Monsieur." " Yes." " We are poor men ; we have lost our Herr ; we shall not get paid ; we can ill afford this."[1] " Stop ! " I said, interrupting him, " that is nonsense ; I shall pay you, of course, just as if your Herr were

I can add very little about it to that which is said above. The sun was directly at our backs ; that is to say, the fog-bow was opposite to the sun. The time was 6.30 p.m. The forms were at once tender and sharp ; neutral in tone ; were developed gradually, and disappeared suddenly. The mists were light (that is, not dense), and were dissipated in the course of the evening.

It has been suggested that the crosses are incorrectly figured in the illustration, and that they were probably formed by the intersection of other circles or ellipses, as shown in the annexed diagram. I think this suggestion is very likely correct ; but I have preferred to follow my original memorandum.

In Parry's *Narrative of an Attempt to reach the North Pole*, 4to, 1828, there is, at pp. 99–100, an account of the occurrence of a phenomenon analogous to the above-mentioned one. " At half-past five p.m. we witnessed a very beautiful natural phenomenon. A broad white fog-bow first appeared opposite to the sun, as was very commonly the case," etc. I follow Parry in using the term fog-bow.

It may be observed that, upon the descent of the Italian guides (whose expedition is noticed in the note upon p. 314, and again in the Appendix), upon July 17th, 1865, the phenomenon commonly termed the Brocken was observed. The following is the account given by the Abbé Amé Gorret in the *Feuille d'Aoste*, October 31, 1865 :—" Nous étions sur l'épaule " (the " shoulder ") " quand nous remarquâmes un phénomène qui nous fit plaisir ; le nuage était très-dense du côté de Valtornanche, c'était serein en Suisse ; nous nous vîmes au milieu d'un cercle aux couleurs de l'arc-en-ciel ; ce mirage nous formait à tous une couronne au milieu de laquelle nous voyions notre ombre." This occurred at about 6.30 to 7 p.m., and the Italians in mention were at about the same height as ourselves—namely, 14,000 feet.

[1] They had been travelling with, and had been engaged by, Lord F. Douglas, and so considered him their employer, and responsible to them.

here." They talked together in their patois for a short time, and then the son spoke again. " We don't wish you to pay us. We wish you to write in the hotel-book at Zermatt, and to your journals, that we have not been paid." " What nonsense are you talking ? I don't understand you. What do you mean ? " He proceeded—" Why, next year there will be many travellers at Zermatt, and we shall get more *voyageurs*." [1]

Who would answer such a proposition ? I made them no reply in words,[2] but they knew very well the indignation that I felt. They filled the cup of bitterness to overflowing, and I tore down the cliff, madly and recklessly, in a way that caused them, more than once, to inquire if I wished to kill them. Night fell ; and for an hour the descent was continued in the darkness. At half-past nine a resting-place was found, and upon a wretched slab, barely large enough to hold the three, we passed six miserable hours. At daybreak the descent was

MONSIEUR ALEX. SEILER.

resumed, and from the Hörnli ridge we ran down to the chalets of Buhl, and on to Zermatt. Seiler met me at his door, and followed in silence to my room. " What is the matter ? " " The Taugwalders and I have returned." He did not need more, and burst into tears ; but lost no time in useless lamentations, and set to work to arouse the village. Ere long a score of men had started to ascend the Hohlicht heights, above Kalbermatt and Z'Mutt, which commanded the plateau of the Matterhorn Glacier. They returned after six hours, and reported that they had seen the bodies lying motionless on the snow. This was on Saturday ; and they proposed that we should leave on

[1] Transcribed from the original memorandum.
[2] Nor did I speak to them afterwards, unless it was absolutely necessary, so long as we were together.

Sunday evening, so as to arrive upon the plateau at daybreak on Monday. Unwilling to lose the slightest chance, the Rev. J. M'Cormick and I resolved to start on Sunday morning. The Zermatt men, threatened with excommunication by their priests if they failed to attend the early mass, were unable to accompany us. To several of them, at least, this was a severe trial. Peter Perren declared with tears that nothing else would have prevented him from joining in the search for his old comrades. Englishmen came to our aid. The Rev. J. Robertson and Mr. J. Phillpotts offered themselves, and their guide Franz Andermatten ;[1] another Englishman lent us Joseph Marie and Alexandre Lochmatter. Frédéric Payot, and Jean Tairraz, of Chamonix, also volunteered.

We started at 2 a.m. on Sunday the 16th, and followed the route that we had taken on the previous Thursday as far as the Hörnli. Thence we went down to the right of the ridge,[2] and mounted through the *séracs* of the Matterhorn Glacier. By 8.30 we had got to the plateau at the top of the glacier, and within sight of the corner in which we knew my companions must be.[3] As we saw one weather-beaten man after another raise the telescope, turn deadly pale, and pass it on without a word to the next, we knew that all hope was gone. We approached. They had fallen below as they had fallen above— Croz a little in advance, Hadow near him, and Hudson some distance behind ; but of Lord Francis Douglas we could see nothing.[4] We left them where they fell ; buried in snow at the base of the grandest cliff of the most majestic mountain of the Alps.

[1] A portrait of Franz Andermatten is given in the engraving facing p. 218.
[2] To the point marked **Z** on the map.
[3] Marked with a cross on the map.
[4] A pair of gloves, a belt, and boot that had belonged to him were found. This, somehow, became publicly known, and gave rise to wild notions, which would not have been entertained had it been also known that the *whole* of the boots of those who had fallen *were off*, and were lying upon the snow near the bodies.

All those who had fallen had been tied with the Manilla, or with the second and equally strong rope, and, consequently, there had been only one link—that between old Peter and Lord Francis Douglas — where the weaker rope had been used. This had a very ugly look for Taugwalder, for it was not possible to suppose that the others would have sanctioned the employment of a rope so greatly inferior in strength when there were more than two hundred and fifty feet of the better qualities still remaining out of use.[1] For the sake of the old guide (who bore a good reputation), and upon all other accounts, it was desirable that this matter should be cleared up ; and after my examination before the court of inquiry which was instituted by the Government was over, I handed in a number of questions which were framed so as to afford old Peter an opportunity of exculpating himself from the grave suspicions which at once fell upon him. The questions, I was told, were put and

THE MANILLA ROPE.[2]

[1] I was 100 feet or more from the others whilst they were being tied up, and am unable to throw any light on the matter. Croz and old Peter no doubt tied up the others.

[2] The three ropes have been reduced by photography to the same scale.

answered ; but the answers, although promised, have never reached me.[1]

Meanwhile, the administration sent strict injunctions to recover

THE ENGLISH CHURCH AT ZERMATT.

the bodies, and upon the 19th of July, twenty-one men of

[1] This was not the only occasion upon which M. Clemenz (who presided over the inquiry) failed to give up answers that he promised. It is greatly to be regretted that he did not feel that the suppression of the truth was equally against the interests of travellers and of the guides. If the men were untrustworthy, the public should have been warned of the fact ; but if they were blameless, why allow them to remain under unmerited suspicion ?

Old Peter Taugwalder laboured for a long time under an unjust accusation. Notwithstanding repeated denials, even his comrades and neighbours at Zermatt persisted in asserting or insinuating that he *cut* the rope which led from him to Lord Francis Douglas. In regard to this infamous charge, I say that he *could* not do so at the moment of the slip, and that the end of the rope in my possession shows that he did not do so beforehand. There remains,

Zermatt accomplished that sad and dangerous task.[1] Of the
body of Lord Francis Douglas they, too, saw nothing ; it was
probably still arrested on the rocks above.[2] The remains of
Hudson and Hadow were interred upon the north side of the
Zermatt Church, in the presence of a reverent crowd of sym-
pathizing friends. The body of Michel Croz lies upon the
other side, under a simpler tomb ; whose inscription bears
honourable testimony to his rectitude, to his courage, and to
his devotion.[3]

So the traditional inaccessibility of the Matterhorn was
vanquished, and was replaced by legends of a more real character. Others will essay to scale its proud cliffs, but to none
will it be the mountain that it was to its early explorers. Others

however, the suspicious fact that the rope which broke was the thinnest and
weakest one that we had. It is suspicious, because it is unlikely that any of
the four men in front would have selected an old and weak rope when there
was abundance of new, and much stronger, rope to spare ; and, on the other
hand, because if Taugwalder thought that an accident was likely to happen,
it was to his interest to have the weaker rope where it was placed.

I should rejoice to learn that his answers to the questions which were put
to him were satisfactory. Not only was his act at the critical moment wonderful as a feat of strength, but it was admirable in its performance at the right
time. He left Zermatt, and lived for several years in retirement in the United
States ; but ultimately returned to his native valley, and died suddenly on
July 11, 1888, at the Lac Noir (Schwarzsee).

[The questions, with old Peter's answers, are shown in Appendix H.]

[1] They followed the route laid down upon the map, and on their descent
were in great peril from the fall of a *sérac*. The character of the work they
undertook may be gathered from a reference to p. 110.

[2] This, or a subsequent, party discovered a sleeve. No other traces have
been found.

[3] At the instance of Mr. Alfred (now Mr. Justice) Wills, a subscription list
was opened for the benefit of the sisters of Michel Croz, who had been partly
dependent upon his earnings. In a short time more than £280 were raised.
This was considered sufficient, and the list was closed. The proceeds were
invested in French Rentes (by Mr. William Mathews), at the recommendation
of M. Dupui, at that time Maire of Chamonix.

may tread its summit-snows, but none will ever know the feelings of those who first gazed upon its marvellous panorama ; and none, I trust, will ever be compelled to tell of joy turned into grief, and of laughter into mourning. It proved to be a stubborn foe ; it resisted long, and gave many a hard blow ; it was defeated at last with an ease that none could have anticipated, but, like a relentless enemy—conquered but not crushed—it took terrible vengeance. The time may come when the Matterhorn shall have passed away, and nothing, save a heap of shapeless fragments, will mark the spot where the great mountain stood ; for, atom by atom, inch by inch, and yard by yard, it yields to forces which nothing can withstand. That time is far distant ; and, ages hence, generations unborn will gaze upon its awful precipices, and wonder at its unique form. However exalted may be their ideas, and

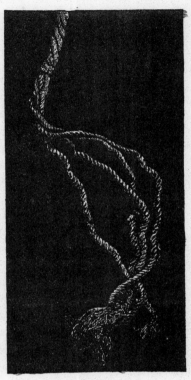

THE SECOND ROPE.

however exaggerated their expectations, none will come to return disappointed !

The play is over, and the curtain is about to fall. Before we part, a word upon the graver teachings of the mountains. See yonder height ! 'Tis far away—unbidden comes the word " Impossible ! " " Not so," says the mountaineer. " The way is long, I know ; it's difficult—it may be—dangerous. It's possible, I'm sure ; I'll seek the way ; take counsel of my brother mountaineers, and find how they have gained similar heights, and learned to avoid the dangers." He starts (all slumbering down below) ; the path is slippery—may be laborious, too. Caution and perseverance gain the day—the height is reached ! and those beneath cry, " Incredible ; 'tis superhuman ! "

We who go mountain-scrambling have constantly set before us the superiority of fixed purpose or perseverance to brute-force. We know that each height, each step, must be gained by patient, laborious toil, and that wishing cannot take the place of working ; we know the benefits of mutual aid ; that many a difficulty must be encountered, and many an obstacle must be grappled with or turned, but we know that where there's a will there's a way ; and we come back to our daily occupations better fitted to fight the battle of life, and to overcome the impediments which obstruct our paths, strengthened and cheered by the recollection of past labours, and by the memories of victories gained in other fields.

I have not made myself either an advocate or an apologist for mountaineering, nor do I now intend to usurp the functions of a moralist ; but my task would have been ill performed if it had been concluded without one reference to the more serious lessons of the mountaineer. We glory in the physical regeneration which is the product of our exertions ; we exult over the grandeur of the scenes that are brought before our eyes, the splendours of sunrise and sunset, and the beauties of hill, dale, lake, wood, and waterfall ; but we value more highly the development of manliness, and the evolution, under combat with difficulties, of those noble qualities of human nature— courage, patience, endurance, and fortitude.

Some hold these virtues in less estimation, and assign base and contemptible motives to those who indulge in our innocent sport. " Be thou chaste as ice, as pure as snow, thou shalt not escape calumny."

Others, again, who are not detractors, find mountaineering, as a sport, to be wholly unintelligible. It is not greatly to be wondered at—we are not all constituted alike. Mountaineering is a pursuit essentially adapted to the young or vigorous, and not to the old or feeble. To the latter, toil may be no pleasure ; and it is often said by such persons, " This man is making a toil of pleasure." Let the motto on the title-page be an answer, if an answer be required. Toil he must who goes mountaineering ; but out of the toil comes strength (not merely muscular energy— more than that), an awakening of all the faculties ; and from the strength arises pleasure. Then, again, it is often asked, in tones which seem to imply that the answer must, at least, be doubtful, " But does it repay you ? " Well, we cannot estimate our enjoyment as you measure your wine, or weigh your lead,— it is real, nevertheless. If I could blot out every reminiscence, or erase every memory, still I should say that my scrambles amongst the Alps have repaid me, for they have given me two of the best things a man can possess—health and friends.

The recollections of past pleasures cannot be effaced. Even now as I write they crowd up before me. First comes an endless series of pictures, magnificent in form, effect, and colour. I see the great peaks, with clouded tops, seeming to mount up for ever and ever ; I hear the music of the distant herds, the peasant's *jodel*, and the solemn church-bells ; and I scent the fragrant breath of the pines : and after these have passed away, another train of thoughts succeeds—of those who have been upright, brave, and true ; of kind hearts and bold deeds ; and of courtesies received at stranger hands, trifles in themselves, but expressive of that good will towards men which is the essence of charity.

Still, the last, sad memory hovers round, and sometimes drifts across like floating mist, cutting off sunshine, and chilling the remembrance of happier times. There have been joys too great to be described in words, and there have been griefs upon which I have not dared to dwell ; and with these in mind I say, Climb if you will, but remember that courage and strength are nought without prudence, and that a momentary negligence may destroy the happiness of a lifetime. Do nothing in haste ; look well to each step ; and from the beginning think what may be the end.

APPENDIX

A. THE DEATH OF BENNEN [1]

On February 28, 1864, Mr. P. C. Gosset and Mr. B—— started from the village of Ardon (about mid-way between Sion and Martigny), to make the ascent of the Haut de Cry (9,744 feet), with the guides J. J. Nance, F. Rebot, A. Bevard, and J. J. Bennen. They arrived within a few hundred feet of the summit before midday, and deter-mined to complete the ascent by following the crest of a ridge leading towards the east. Before this could be done it was necessary to cross some steep snow ; and, while passing this, an avalanche was unfor-tunately started. Bennen and Mr. B—— perished ; the others happily escaped. The following narrative, from the pen of Mr. Gosset, illustrates, in a very impressive manner, the danger of traversing new-fallen snow at considerable inclinations :

" We had to go up a steep snow-field, about 800 feet high, as well as I remember. It was about 150 feet broad at the top, and 400 or 500 at the bottom. It was a sort of couloir on a large scale. During the ascent we sank about one foot deep at every step. Bennen did not seem to like the look of the snow very much. He asked the local guides whether avalanches ever came down this couloir, to which they answered that our position was perfectly safe. We had mounted on the northern side of the couloir, and having arrived at 150 feet from the top, we began crossing it on a horizontal curve, so as to gain the E. arête. The inflexion or dip of the couloir was slight, not above 25 feet, the inclination near 35°. We were walking in the following order :—Bevard, Nance, Bennen, myself, B., and Rebot. Having crossed over about three-quarters of the breadth of the couloir, the two leading men suddenly sank considerably above their waists. Bennen tightened the rope. The snow was too deep to think of

[1] See p. 54.

335

getting out of the hole they had made, so they advanced one or two steps, dividing the snow with their bodies. Bennen turned round and told us he was afraid of starting an avalanche ; we asked whether it would not be better to return and cross the couloir higher up. To this the three Ardon men opposed themselves ; they mistook the proposed precaution for fear, and the two leading men continued their work. After three or four steps gained in the aforesaid manner, the snow became hard again. Bennen had not moved—he was evidently undecided what he should do ; as soon, however, as he saw hard snow again, he advanced and crossed parallel to, but above the furrow the Ardon men had made. Strange to say, the snow supported him. While he was passing I observed that the leader, Bevard, had ten or twelve feet of rope coiled round his shoulder. I of course at once told him to uncoil it and get on the arête, from which he was not more than fifteen feet distant. Bennen then told me to follow. I tried his steps, but sank up to my waist in the very first. So I went through the furrows, holding my elbows close to my body, so as not to touch the sides. This furrow was about twelve feet long, and as the snow was good on the other side, we had all come to the false conclusion that the snow was accidentally softer there than else-where. Bennen advanced ; he had made but a few steps when we heard a deep, cutting sound. The snow-field split in two about fourteen or fifteen feet above us. The cleft was at first quite narrow, not more than an inch broad. An awful silence ensued ; it lasted but a few seconds, and then it was broken by Bennen's voice, ' We are all lost.' His words were slow and solemn, and those who knew him felt what they really meant when spoken by such a man as Bennen. They were his last words. I drove my alpenstock into the snow, and brought the weight of my body to bear on it. I then waited. It was an awful moment of suspense. I turned my head towards Bennen to see whether he had done the same thing. To my astonishment I saw him turn round, face the valley, and stretch out both arms. The snow on which we stood began to move slowly, and I felt the utter uselessness of any alpenstock. I soon sank up to my shoulders, and began descending backwards. From this moment I saw nothing of what had happened to the rest of the party. With a good deal of trouble I succeeded in turning round. The speed of the avalanche increased rapidly, and before long I was covered up with

snow. I was suffocating when I suddenly came to the surface again.
I was on a wave of the avalanche, and saw it before me as I was
carried down. It was the most awful sight I ever saw. The head
of the avalanche was already at the spot where we had made our last
halt. The head alone was preceded by a thick cloud of snow-dust ;
the rest of the avalanche was clear. Around me I heard the horrid
hissing of the snow, and far before me the thundering of the foremost
part of the avalanche. To prevent myself sinking again, I made use
of my arms much in the same way as when swimming in a standing
position. At last I noticed that I was moving slower ; then I saw
the pieces of snow in front of me stop at some yards' distance ; then
the snow straight before me stopped, and I heard on a large scale the
same creaking sound that is produced when a heavy cart passes over
frozen snow in winter. I felt that I also had stopped, and instantly
threw up both arms to protect my head in case I should again be
covered up. I had stopped, but the snow behind me was still in
motion ; its pressure on my body was so strong, that I thought I
should be crushed to death. This tremendous pressure lasted but a
short time ; I was covered up by snow coming from behind me.
My first impulse was to try and uncover my head—but this I could
not do, the avalanche had frozen by pressure the moment it stopped,
and I was frozen in. Whilst trying vainly to move my arms, I suddenly became aware that the hands as far as the wrist had the faculty
of motion. The conclusion was easy, they must be above the snow.
I set to work as well as I could ; it was time, for I could not have
held out much longer. At last I saw a faint glimmer of light. The
crust above my head was getting thinner, but I could not reach it any
more with my hands ; the idea struck me that I might pierce it with
my breath. After several efforts I succeeded in doing so, and felt
suddenly a rush of air towards my mouth. I saw the sky again
through a little round hole. A dead silence reigned around me ; I
was so surprised to be still alive, and so persuaded at the first moment
that none of my fellow-sufferers had survived, that I did not even
think of shouting for them. I then made vain efforts to extricate my
arms, but found it impossible ; the most I could do was to join the
ends of my fingers, but they could not reach the snow any longer.
After a few minutes I heard a man shouting ; what a relief it was to
know that I was not the sole survivor ! to know that perhaps he was

not frozen in and could come to my assistance ! I answered ; the voice approached, but seemed uncertain where to go, and yet it was now quite near. A sudden exclamation of surprise ! Rebot had seen my hands. He cleared my head in an instant, and was about to try and cut me out completely, when I saw a foot above the snow, and so near to me that I could touch it with my arms, although they were not quite free yet. I at once tried to move the foot ; it was my poor friend's. A pang of agony shot through me as I saw that the foot did not move. Poor B. had lost sensation, and was perhaps already dead. Rebot did his best : after some time he wished me to help him, so he freed my arms a little more so that I could make use of them. I could do but little, for Rebot had torn the axe from my shoulder as soon as he had cleared my head (I generally carry an axe separate from my alpenstock—the blade tied to the belt, and the handle attached to the left shoulder). Before coming to me Rebot had helped Nance out of the snow ; he was lying nearly horizontally, and was not much covered over. Nance found Bevard, who was upright in the snow, but covered up to the head. After about twenty minutes the two last-named guides came up. I was at length taken out ; the snow had to be cut with the axe down to my feet before I could be pulled out. A few minutes after one o'clock P.M. we came to my poor friend's face. . . . I wished the body to be taken out completely, but nothing could induce the three guides to work any longer, from the moment they saw that it was too late to save him. I acknowledge that they were nearly as incapable of doing anything as I was. When I was taken out of the snow the cord had to be cut. We tried the end going towards Bennen, but could not move it ; it went nearly straight down, and showed us that there was the grave of the bravest guide the Valais ever had, and ever will have. The cold had done its work on us ; we could stand it no longer, and began the descent."

[B. THE MATTERHORN FROM BREUIL

THE following letters from Signor Giordano to Signor Quintino Sella deal with plans to ascend the Matterhorn from Breuil. The translation is by Mr. J. E. C. Eaton, from Cav. Guido Rey's *The Matterhorn*.

' *Turin, July* 7, 1865.

' DEAR QUINTINO,—I am starting off, heavily armed for the destination you wot of. I sent off the day before yesterday the first tent, 300 metres of rope, and some iron hoops and rings, besides various kinds of provisions for ourselves, a spirit-lamp for heating water, tea, &c. All these things together weigh about 100 kilos. I have also sent Carrel 200 fcs., in order that he may meet these articles at Châtillon and transport them to Valtournanche and Breuil at once. I shall be up there myself to-morrow evening, to superintend the work.

' I am taking with me a second tent, three barometers, your own among them, and the " Annuaire du Bureau des Longitudes." As soon as I reach the scene of operations I will write to you again.

' You need only trouble about your own personal requirements, viz., your headgear, a few rugs, &c., and some good cigars ; if possible, also a little good wine and a few shekels, because I have only been able to bring about 3,000 fcs. with me.

' Let us, then, set out to attack this Devil's mountain, and let us see that we succeed, if only Whymper has not been beforehand with us.'

' *Breuil Hotel, at the foot of the Théodule.*
' *July* 11*th, evening.*

' DEAR QUINTINO,—It is high time for me to send you news from here. I reached Valtournanche on Saturday at midday. There I found Carrel, who had just returned from a reconnoitring expedition of the Matterhorn, which had proved a failure owing to bad weather.

' Whymper had arrived two or three days before ; as usual, he wished to make the ascent, and had engaged Carrel, who, not having yet had my letters, had agreed, but for a few days only. Fortunately the weather turned bad. Whymper was unable to make his fresh attempt, and Carrel left him and came with me, together with five other picked men who are the best guides in the valley. We immediately sent off our advance guard, with Carrel at its head. In order not to excite remark we took the rope and other materials to Avouil, a hamlet which is very remote and close to the Matterhorn, and this is to be our lower base. Out of six men, four are to work up above, and two will act continuously as porters, a task which is at least as difficult as the other.

' I have taken up my quarters at Breuil for the time being. The weather, the god whom we fear and on whom all will depend, has been hitherto very changeable and rather bad. As lately as yesterday morning it was snowing on the Matterhorn, but yesterday evening it cleared. In the night (10th–11th) the men started with the tents, and I hope that by this time they will have reached a great height ; but the weather is turning misty again, and the Matterhorn is still covered ; I hope the mists will soon disperse. Weather permitting, I hope in three or four days to know how I stand. Carrel told me not to come up yet, until he should send me word ; naturally he wishes personally to make sure of the last bits. As seen from here they do not seem to me to be absolutely inaccessible, but before saying that one must try them ; and it is also necessary to ascertain whether we can bivouac at a point much higher than Whymper's highest. As soon as I have any good news I will send a message to St. Vincent, the nearest telegraph office, with a telegram containing a few words ; and do you then come at once. Meanwhile, on receipt of the present, please send me a few lines in reply, with some advice, because I am head over ears in difficulty here, what with the weather, the expense, and Whymper.

' I have tried to keep everything secret, but that fellow, whose life seems to depend on the Matterhorn, is here, suspiciously prying into everything. I have taken all the competent men away from him, and yet he is so enamoured of this mountain that he may go up with others and make a scene. He is here, in this hotel, and I try to avoid speaking to him.

' In short, I will do my best to succeed, and I have hopes. Provided Aeolus be on our side !

' I will write no more at present, hoping soon to send you a favourable sign. I trust this news from the Alps will refresh you somewhat in the heat of Turin and the oppression of ministerial affairs.'

' *Breuil Hotel, July* 14*th.*

' DEAR QUINTINO,—I am sending a telegram for you by express to St. Vincent, seven hours' walk from here ; at the same time, to make assurance double sure, I send you this letter.

' At 2 p.m. to-day I saw Carrel and Co. on the top peak of the Matterhorn ; many others saw them as well as I ; so success seems certain, notwithstanding that the day before yesterday the weather was very bad, so that the mountain was covered with snow. So start at once if you can, or else telegraph to me at St. Vincent. Fancy, I do not even know whether you are at Turin ! I have had no news from there for a week ; so I am just writing on the chance. If you do not come or telegraph by to-morrow evening I shall go and plant our flag up there, that it may be the first. This is essential. I will, however, do all I can to wait for you, so that you may come your-self. Whymper has gone off to make an attempt on the other side, but I think in vain.'

' *Breuil, July* 15*th.*

' DEAR QUINTINO,—Yesterday was a bad day, and Whymper, after all, gained the victory over the unfortunate Carrel. Whymper, as I told you, was desperate, and seeing Carrel climbing the mountain, tried his fortune on the Zermatt slope. Every one here, and Carrel above all, considered the ascent absolutely impossible on that side ; so we were all easy in our minds. On the 11th Carrel was at work on the mountain, and pitched his tent at a certain height. On the night between the 11th and 12th, and the whole of the 12th, the weather was horrible, and snow on the Matterhorn ; on the 13th weather fair, and yesterday the 14th fine. On the 13th little work was done, and yesterday Carrel might have reached the top, and was perhaps only about 500 or 600 feet below, when suddenly, at about 2 p.m., he saw Whymper and the others already on the summit. Whymper must have promised a considerable sum to various Swiss guides if they could take him up, and having been favoured with an exceptionally fine day, he succeeded. I had, it is true, sent Carrel word of Whymper's proposed attempt, and had enjoined on him to get up at any cost, without loss of time to prepare the way, but my warning did not reach him in time, and moreover Carrel did not believe the ascent from the north to be possible. However, yesterday, as I saw some men on the Matterhorn, and was assured by every one that they were our party, I sent off the telegram to you, bidding you come up. Poor Carrel, when he saw that he had been forestalled, had not the courage to proceed, and beat a retreat with his weapons and his baggage. He arrived here late this morning, and it was then that I sent off another telegram by express to stop you from coming. As you see, although every man did his duty, it is a lost battle, and I am in great grief.

' I think, however, that we can play a counter-stroke by some one's making the ascent at once on this side, thus proving at any rate that the ascent is feasible this way ; Carrel still thinks it possible. I was only vexed with him for bringing down the tents, the ropes, and all the other things that had been carried up with so much labour to a point so near the summit. He puts the blame on the party, who had completely lost heart, and on his fear that I should be unwilling to go to any further expense.

' At any rate, in order not to return ridiculous as well as unsuccessful, I think that we ought at least to plant our flag on the summit. I at once tried to organize a fresh expedition, but hitherto, with the exception of Carrel and another, I have not found any men of courage whom I can trust. Some others might, perhaps, be found if I paid them extravagantly, but I do not think it wise to go to such expense ; and then, if their courage is deficient, there would be no certainty of success.

' I am therefore trying to fit out the expedition cheaply and will only give up if this one is unsuccessful. Now I shall not even have the satisfaction of going up myself, because Carrel says that, for the sake of quickness and in order to make the best of the short time we have at our disposal, it will be better that they should not have any traveller with them.

' We must also remember that we are threatened by the weather, which is doubtful.

' Just see how annoying it all is !

' Yesterday the Val Tournanche was already *en fête* thinking that we were victorious : to-day we were disillusioned. Poor Carrel is to be pitied, the more so as part of the delay was due to his idea that Whymper would not be able to ascend from Zermatt. I am trying to act like Terentius Varro after the battle of Cannae.

' P.S.—Notwithstanding what has happened, you might still make the first ascent from the Italian side, if you had the time ; but till now Carrel has not assured me that the way is feasible right to the top. That is why I have not telegraphed to you again ; perhaps I shall come to Turin myself in a couple of days.']

C. SUBSEQUENT HISTORY OF THE MATTERHORN [1]

THE Val Tournanche natives who started to facilitate the way up the south-west ridge of the Matterhorn for MM. Giordano and Sella, pitched their tent upon my third platform, at the foot of the Great Tower (12,992 feet), and enjoyed several days of bad weather under its shelter. On the first fine day (13th of July) they began their work, and about midday on the 14th got on to the " shoulder," and arrived at the base of the final peak (the point where Bennen stopped on July 28, 1862). The counsels of the party were then divided. Two —Jean-Antoine Carrel and J.-Joseph Maquignaz—wished to go on ; the others were not eager about it. A discussion took place, and the result was they all commenced to descend, and whilst upon the Cravate (13,524 feet) they heard our cries from the summit.[2] Upon the 15th they went down to Breuil and reported their ill-success to M. Giordano (see p. 316). That gentleman was naturally much disappointed, and pressed the men to set out again.[3] Said he, " Until now I have striven for the honour of making the first ascent,—fate has decided against me,—I am beaten. Patience ! Now, if I go to any further expense, it will be on your account, for your honour, and for your interests. Will you start again to settle the question, or, at least, to let there be no more uncertainty ? " The majority of the men (in fact the whole of them with the exception of Jean-Antoine) refused point-blank to have anything more to do with the mountain. Carrel, however, stepped forward, saying, " As for me, I have not given it up ; if you (turning to the Abbé Gorret) or the others will

[1] We resume here the account of the proceedings of the Italians who started from Breuil on the 11th of July 1865. See p. 301.

[2] The foregoing particulars were related to me by J.-A. Carrel.

[3] The following details are taken from the account of the Abbé Amé Gorret (published in the *Feuille d'Aoste*, Oct. 1865), who was at Breuil when the men returned.

come, I will start again immediately." "Not I!" said one. "No more for me," cried a second. "If you would give me a thousand francs I would not go back," said a third. The Abbé Gorret alone volunteered. This plucky priest was concerned in the very first attempts upon the mountain,[1] and is an enthusiastic mountaineer. Carrel and the Abbé would have set out by themselves had not J. B. Bich and J.-A. Meynet (two men in the employ of Favre the inn-keeper) come forward at the last moment. M. Giordano also wished to accompany them, but the men knew the nature of the work they had to undertake, and positively declined to be accompanied by an amateur.

These four men left Breuil at 6.30 a.m. on July 16, at 1 p.m. arrived at the third tent-platform, and there passed the night. At daybreak on the 17th they continued the ascent by the route which had been taken before ; passed successively the Great Tower, the Crête du Coq, the Cravate, and the "shoulder,"[2] and at 10 a.m. gained the point at the foot of the final peak from which the explorers had turned back on the 14th.[3] They had then about 800 feet to accomplish, and, says the Abbé, "nous allions entrer en pays inconnu, aucun n'étant jamais allé aussi loin."

The passage of the cleft which stopped Bennen was accomplished, and then the party proceeded directly towards the summit, over rocks which for some distance were not particularly difficult. The steep cliffs down which we had hurled stones (on the 14th) then stopped their way, and Carrel led round to the left or Tiefenmatten side. The work at this part was of the very greatest difficulty, and stones and icicles which fell rendered the position of the party very precarious ; [4] so much so that they preferred to turn up directly towards

[1] See Appendix G, attempt No. 1.

[2] These terms, as well as the others, Great Staircase, Col du Lion, Tête du Lion, Chimney, and so forth, were applied by Carrel and myself to the various points, in consequence of real or supposed resemblances in the rocks to other things. A few of the terms originated with the author, but they were chiefly due to the inventive genius of J.-A. Carrel.

[3] This point is marked by the red letter **E** upon the lower of the two outlines facing p. 53.

[4] I have seen icicles more than a hundred feet long hanging from the rocks near the summit of the Matterhorn.

the summit, and climb by rocks that the Abbé termed " almost perpendicular." He added, " This part occupied the most time, and gave us the greatest trouble." At length they arrived at a fault in the rocks which formed a roughly horizontal gallery. They crept along this in the direction of a ridge that descended towards the north-west, or thereabouts, and when close to the ridge, found that they could not climb on to it ; but they perceived that, by descending a gully with perpendicular sides, they could reach the ridge at a lower point. The bold Abbé was the heaviest and the strongest of the four, and he was sacrificed for the success of the expedition. He and Meynet remained behind, and lowered the others, one by one, into the gully. Carrel and Bich clambered up the other side, attained the ridge descending towards the north-west, shortly after-

J. B. BICH, IN 1892.

wards gained an " easy route,[1] they galloped," and in a few minutes reached the southern end of the summit-ridge.

The time of their arrival does not appear to have been noticed. It was late in the day, I believe about 3 p.m. Carrel and his comrade only waited long enough to plant a flag by the side of the cairn that we had built three days previously, then descended at once, rejoined the others, and all four hurried down as fast as possible to the tent. They were so pressed for time that they could not eat ! and it was 9 p.m. before they arrived at their camp at the foot of the Great Tower. In descending they followed the gallery above mentioned throughout its entire length, and so avoided the very difficult rocks over which they had passed on the ascent. As they were traversing the length of the " shoulder " they witnessed the phenomenon to which I have already adverted at the foot of p. 325.

When Carrel and Bich were near the summit they saw our traces upon the Matterhorn Glacier, and suspected that an accident had

[1] The words of the Abbé. I imagine that he meant *comparatively* easy.

occurred ; they did not, however, hear of the Matterhorn catastrophe until their return to Breuil, at 3 p.m. upon the 18th. The details of that sad event were in the mouths of all, and it was not unnaturally supposed, in the absence of correct information, that the accident was a proof that the northern side was frightfully dangerous. The safe return of the four Italians was regarded, on the other hand, as evidence that the Breuil route was the best. Those who were interested (either personally or otherwise) in the Val Tournanche made the most of the circumstances, and trumpeted the praises of the southern route. Some went further, and instituted comparisons between the two routes to the disadvantage of the northern one, and were pleased to term our expedition on the 13–14th of July precipitate, and so forth. Considering the circumstances which caused us to leave the Val Tournanche on the 12th of July, these remarks were not in the best possible taste, but I have no feeling regarding them. There may be some, however, who may be interested in a comparison of the two routes, and for their sakes I will place the essential points in juxtaposition. We (that is the Taugwalders and myself) were absent from Zermatt 53 hours. Excluding halts and stoppages of one sort or another, the ascent and descent occupied us 23 hours. Zermatt is 5,315 feet above the level of the sea, and the Matterhorn is 14,780 ; we had therefore to ascend 9,465 feet. As far as the point marked 10,820 feet the way was known, so we had to find the way over only 3,960 feet. The members of our party (I now include all) were very unequal in ability, and none of us could for a moment be compared as cragsmen with Jean-Antoine Carrel. The four Italians who started from Breuil on the 16th of July were absent during 56½ hours, and as far as I can gather from the published account, and from conversation with the men, excluding halts, they took for the ascent and descent 23¾ hours. The hotel at Giomein is 6,890 feet above the sea, so they had to ascend 7,890 feet. As far as the end of the " shoulder " the way was known to Carrel, and he had to find the way over only about 800 feet. All four men were born mountaineers, good climbers, and they were led by the most expert cragsman I have seen. The weather in each instance was fine. It is seen, therefore, that these four nearly equally matched men took a *longer* time to ascend 1,500 feet *less* height than ourselves, although we had to find the way over more than four times as much untrodden ground as they. This alone would lead any mountaineer to suppose that their route must have been more difficult than ours.[1] I know the greater part of the ground over which they passed, and from my knowledge, and from the account of Mr. Grove, I am sure that their route was not only more difficult, but that it was *much* more difficult, than ours.

This was not the opinion in the Val Tournanche at the end of 1865, and the natives confidently reckoned that tourists would flock to their side in preference to the other. It was, I believe, the late Canon Carrel of Aosta (who always took great interest in such matters) who first proposed the construction of a *cabane* upon the southern side of the Matterhorn. The project was taken up with spirit, and funds for its execution were speed-ily provided—principally by the members of the Italian Alpine Club, or by their friends. The indefatigable Carrel found a natural hole upon the ledge called the Cravate (13,524 feet), and this, in course of time, was turned, under his direction, into a respectable little hut. Its position is superb, and gives a view of the most magnificent character.

THE LATE CANON CARREL, OF AOSTA.

Whilst this work was being carried out, my friend Mr. F. Craufurd Grove consulted me respecting the ascent of the Matterhorn. I recommended him to ascend by the northern route, and to place himself in the hands of Jean-Antoine Carrel. Mr. Grove found, however, that Carrel distinctly preferred the southern side, and they ascended accordingly by the Breuil route. Mr. Grove has been good enough to supply the following account of his expedition. He carries on my description of the southern route from the highest point I attained on that side (a little below the Cravate) to the summit, and thus renders complete my descriptions of the two sides.

"In August 1867 I ascended the Matterhorn from Breuil, taking

[1] The pace of a party is ruled by that of its least efficient member.

as guides three mountaineers of the Val Tournanche—J.-A. Carrel, J. Bich, and S. Meynet,—Carrel being the leader. At that time the Matterhorn had not been scaled since the famous expedition of the Italian guides mentioned above.

" Our route was identical with that which they followed in their descent when, as will be seen, they struck out on one part of the mountain a different line from that which they had taken in ascending. After gaining the Col du Lion, we climbed the south-western or Breuil arête by the route which has been described in these pages, passing the night at the then unfinished hut constructed by the Italian Alpine Club on the Cravate. Starting from the hut at daylight, we reached at an early hour the summit of the ' shoulder,' and then traversed its arête to the final peak of the Matterhorn. The passage of this arête was perhaps the most enjoyable part of the whole expedition. The ridge, worn by slow irregular decay into monstrous and rugged battlements, and guarded on each side by tremendous precipices, is grand beyond all description, but does not, strange to say, present any remarkable difficulty to the climber, save that it is exceedingly trying to the head. Great care is of course necessary, but the scramble is by no means of so arduous a nature as entirely to absorb the attention ; so that a fine climb, and rock scenery, of grandeur perhaps unparalleled in the Alps, can both be appreciated.

" It was near the end of this arête, close to the place where it abuts against the final peak, that Professor Tyndall's party turned in 1862,[1] arrested by a cleft in the ridge. From the point where they stopped the main tower of the Matterhorn rises in front of the climber, abrupt, magnificent, and apparently inaccessible. The summit is fully 750 feet in vertical height above this spot, and certainly, to my eye, appeared to be separated from me by a yet more considerable interval ; for I remember, when at the end of the arête, looking upward at the crest of the mountain, and thinking that it must be a good 1,000 feet above me.

" When the Italian guides made their splendid ascent, they traversed the arête of the shoulder to the main peak, passed the cleft which has been mentioned (p. 100), clambered on to the tremendous northwestern face of the mountain (described by Mr. Whymper at pp. 312 and 316), and then endeavoured to cross this face so as to get on

[1] See p. 94, and pp. 100, 101.

to the Z'Mutt arête.[1] The passage of this slope proved a work of great difficulty and danger. I saw it from very near the place which they traversed, and was unable to conceive how any human creatures managed to crawl over rocks so steep and so treacherous. After they had got about half-way across, they found the difficulties of the route and the danger from falling stones so great, that they struck straight up the mountain, in the hope of finding some safer way. They were to a certain extent successful, for they came presently to a small ledge, caused by a sort of fault in the rock, running horizontally across the north-western face of the mountain a little distance below the summit. Traversing this ledge, the Italians found themselves close to the Z'Mutt arête, but still separated from it by a barrier, to outflank which it was necessary to descend a perpendicular gully. Carrel and Bich were lowered down this, the other two men remaining at the top to haul up their companions on their return, as otherwise they could not have got up again. Passing on to the Z'Mutt arête without further difficulty, Carrel and Bich climbed by that ridge to the summit of the mountain. In returning, the Italians kept to the ledge for the whole distance across the north-western face, and descended to the place where the arête of the shoulder abuts against the main peak by a sort of rough ridge of rocks between the north-western and southern faces. When I ascended in 1867, we followed this route in the ascent and in the descent. I thought the ledge difficult, in some places decidedly dangerous, and should not care to set foot on it again ; but assuredly it is neither so difficult nor so continuously dangerous as those gaunt and pitiless rock-slopes which the Italians crossed in their upward route.

" The credit of making the *Italian* ascent of the Matterhorn belongs undoubtedly to J.-A. Carrel and to the other mountaineers who accompanied him. Bennen led his party bravely and skilfully to a point some 750 feet below the top. From this point, however, good guide though he was, Bennen had to retire defeated ; and it was reserved for the better mountain-craft of the Val Tournanche guide to win the difficult way to the summit of the Matterhorn."

Mr. Craufurd Grove was the first traveller who ascended the Matterhorn after the accident, and the natives of Val Tournanche

---

[1] A ridge descending towards the Z'Mutt Glacier.

were, of course, greatly delighted that his ascent was made upon their side. Some of them, however, were by no means well pleased that J.-A. Carrel was so much regarded. They feared, perhaps, that he would acquire the monopoly of the mountain. Just a month after Mr. Grove's ascent, six Valtournanchians set out to see whether they could not learn the route, and so come in for a share of the good things which were expected to arrive. They were three Maquignaz, Cæsar Carrel (my old guide), J.-B. Carrel, and a daughter of the last named ! They left Breuil at 5 a.m. on Sept. 12, and at 3 p.m. arrived

J.-JOSEPH MAQUIGNAZ.[1]

at the hut, where they passed the night. At 7 a.m. the next day they started again (leaving J.-B. Carrel behind), and proceeded along the "shoulder" to the final peak ; passed the cleft which had stopped Bennen, and clambered up the comparatively easy rocks on the other side until they arrived at the base of the last precipice, down which we had hurled stones on July 14, 1865. They (young woman and all) were then about 350 feet from the summit ! Then, instead of turning to the left, as Carrel and Mr. Grove had done, J.-Joseph and J.-Pierre Maquignaz paid attention to the cliff in front of them, and managed to find a means of passing up, by clefts, ledges, and gullies, to the summit. This was a shorter (and it appears to be an easier) route than that taken by Carrel and Grove, and it has been followed by all those who have since then ascended the mountain from the side of Breuil.[2] Subsequently, ropes were fixed over the most difficult portions of the final climb.

[1] By permission, from a photograph by Signor Sella.

[2] J.-Joseph and J.-Pierre Maquignaz alone ascended ; the others had had enough and returned. It should be observed that ropes had been fixed, by J.-A. Carrel and others, over *all* the difficult parts of the mountain as high as the shoulder, *before* the ascent of these persons. This explains the facility with

In the meantime they had not been idle upon the other side. A hut was constructed upon the eastern face, at a height of 12,526 feet

THE SUMMIT OF THE MATTERHORN IN 1874 (NORTHERN END).

which they moved over ground which had been found very trying in earlier times. The young woman declared that the ascent (as far as she went) was a trifle, or used words to that effect ; if she had tried to get to the same height before 1862, she would probably have been of a different opinion.

above the sea, near to the crest of the ridge which descends towards Zermatt (north-east ridge).[1] The erection was undertaken by the Knubels, of St. Niklaus, at the expense of Monsieur Alex. Seiler and of the Swiss Alpine Club. This hut upon the east face is placed in an insecure position, and is now seldom used, as another hut or *cabane* has been built upon the Hörnli ridge,[2] a few yards to the east of, and

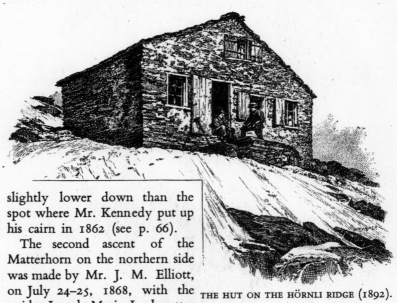

THE HUT ON THE HÖRNLI RIDGE (1892).

slightly lower down than the spot where Mr. Kennedy put up his cairn in 1862 (see p. 66).

The second ascent of the Matterhorn on the northern side was made by Mr. J. M. Elliott, on July 24–25, 1868, with the guides Joseph Marie Lochmatter and Peter Knubel. Since then very numerous ascents have been made both upon the Swiss and upon the Italian side. Down to the end of 1871 they were equally divided between the northern (or Zermatt) and the southern (or Breuil) route. Until that time, neither guides nor tourists had got clear of the idea that the Swiss route was more difficult and dangerous than the Italian one. In 1872 (the year following the publication of *Scrambles amongst the*

[1] This is marked on the Map of the Matterhorn and its Glaciers (*Cab. S.A.C.*). A view of it was given in *The Ascent of the Matterhorn*.

[2] The position of the hut on the Hörnli ridge is marked by the word *Cabane* on the Map of the Matterhorn and its Glaciers.

Alps) the Zermatt side found more favour, and it has continued to be the popular route to the present time.

The first of the following ascents which calls for notice is that by Signor F. Giordano. This gentleman came to Breuil several times after his visit in 1865, but he was always baffled by the weather. In July 1866, he got as high as the Cravate with Jean-Antoine Carrel and other men, and was detained there *five days and nights unable to move either up or down* ! At last, on Sept. 3–5, 1868, he was able to gratify his desire, and accomplished the feat of ascending the mountain upon one side and descending it upon the other. Signor Giordano spent a considerable time in examining the structure of the Matterhorn, and became benighted upon its eastern face in consequence.

Questions having been frequently put to me respecting the immediate summit of the Matterhorn, and difficulties having been expressed as to recognition of the two views given upon pp. 313 and 315, I made an ascent of the mountain in 1874, to photograph the summit, and to see what changes had occurred since our visit nine years before. The summits of most high mountains vary from time to time, and the Matterhorn is no exception to the general rule. It was sharper and narrower in 1874 than in 1865. Instead of being able " to run about," every step had to be cut with the axe ; and the immediate summit, instead of being a blunt and rounded eminence, was a little cone of snow which went to a sharp point. In consequence of a strong north wind which was blowing at the time, we had to work down upon the edge of the cliff overlooking Breuil, to get protection for the camera, and eventually we gained a position which gave a good view of the summit ; but our ledge was so small that we could not venture to unrope, and Jean-Antoine had to squat down whilst I photographed over his head. The engraving upon p. 351 has been made from the photograph which was taken on this occasion. The nearest of the lower peaks, on the left, is the summit of the Dent d'Hérens.

Carrel and I stopped a second night at the *cabane* on the east face, and whilst there we had the insecurity of its position forcibly impressed upon us by seeing a huge block break away from the rock at its side, and go crashing down over the very route which is commonly pursued by tourists. The view from this hut extends from the Bietschhorn in the north to the Grand Tournalin in the south, and includes the Mischabelhörner group, the Allalinhorn, Alphubel, Rimpfischhorn and Strahlhorn, Monte Rosa, the Lyskamm and the Breithorn. The uppermost 800 feet of the Matterhorn can be seen from the hut, but the rest of the intervening part of the mountain is not visible, being hidden by a small ridge which projects from the face.

Many persons have talked at different times about the possibility of finding a way up the Matterhorn from the side of the Z'Mutt Glacier ; but it was not until the year 1879 that a way was discovered. On September 2–3, Mr. A. F. Mummery with the guides Alexander Burgener, Petrus, and Gentinetta succeeded in gaining the summit by first going up the long snow-buttress which runs out from the mountain towards the north-west, and then up the rocks above. When nearing the top, they joined the routes taken by Carrel and Mr. Grove upon the first ascents which were made on the Italian side.[1]

At the very time that Mr. Mummery was engaged in his expedition, Mr. W. Penhall with the guides Ferdinand Imseng and Louis Zurbrücken, was occupied on a similar enterprise, and also ascended the Matterhorn from the direction of the Stockje. Mr. Penhall, however, at first took a course slightly more to the south than Mr. Mummery, though he, at last, like the others, got on to the main Z'Mutt arête, and completed the ascent by following a portion of the old Italian route.[2]

Three days afterwards (Sept. 5–6), Mr. J. Baumann followed in Mr. Mummery's footsteps. "I found it," he said, "an interesting rock-climb, presenting no extraordinary difficulties. . . . I am of opinion that this ascent by the Z'Mutt *arête* will in future become the favourite way of crossing the Matterhorn."[3] As yet, Mr. Baumann's anticipation has not been realized.

In 1899, Sig. Guido Rey, of Turin, undertook a very bold and enterprising exploration of the Furggen ridge—that which leads from the Furggengrat towards the summit of the Matterhorn.

"I started from Breuil with Antoine Maquignaz and a porter on

---

[1] Mr. Mummery's description will be found in the *Alpine Journal*, vol. ix., pp. 458–62.

[2] See *Alpine Journal*, vol. ix., pp. 449–58.

[3] *Alpine Journal*, vol. ix., p. 366.

Aug. 24, 1899, at one o'clock in the night, and went to the Breuiljoch, and thence directly up the Furggen ridge, as far as the point reached by Mummery,—which may be called ' l'Epaule de Furggen.' At this point real difficulty begins.

" Meanwhile Daniel Maquignaz, with two porters and a large amount of rope, had reached the summit of the Matterhorn by the usual way ; and descended about 85 metres " [280 feet] " down the Furggen ridge, until he came to a place where the rocks became overhanging. There he stopped, and fixed a rope, and let the same down to the spot where we were standing, which was about 10 metres higher than l'Epaule de Furggen. By means of this rope, I and my men ascended about 80 metres, with great difficulty, the rocks being smooth and nearly vertical. After two hours of *grimpade* " [scrambling] " we thus arrived at the base of some overhanging rock upon which stood Daniel and his men. We were separated 12 or 15 metres from Daniel, and tried to pull ourselves up ; but this was impossible on account of the great oscillation of the rope, and from there being no means of laying hold of the rock either with hands or feet. At 5 p.m. we gave up our attempts, and returned the way we had come ; and, walking down the whole night, arrived at Breuil on the morning of the 25th of August. The point reached on this attempt was distant from the summit about 105 metres " [344 feet].

" I again left Breuil on the 28th, and ascended the Matterhorn by the usual Italian route. Daniel, Antoine, and porters were with me, carrying a rope ladder about 15 metres long. I descended from the summit to the Furggen ridge as far as the point previously attained by Daniel's party, and found means of getting a few metres lower. There I fixed the ladder, and let it down the overhanging wall. Descending it, I reached the point where we arrived on the 25th of August. Having completely explored the ridge, and touched every part of it, I returned immediately to the summit, and descended, in very bad weather, by the Hörnli route."

[The Furggen ridge was first climbed on September 4, 1911, by Signor Mario Piacenza, with the guides Joseph Carrel and J. Gaspard. The north face, between the Hörnli and Z'Mutt ridges, was first climbed by the brothers Franz and Toni Schmid of Munich, July 31–August 1, 1932. The south face was climbed on October 15, 1931, by Signor E. Benedetti, with the guides Louis Carrel and Maurice Bich ; this party made the second ascent of the Furggen ridge on September 2, 1930, taking three hours from the final shoulder to the summit. The east face was climbed on September 18–19, 1932, by Signori E. Benedetti and G. Mazzotti, with the guides Louis and Lucien Carrel, Maurice Bich and Antoine Gaspard. The final step of approximately 1,000 feet took 11 hours.]

[D. LETTERS FROM SIR EDWARD DAVIDSON, PRESIDENT OF THE ALPINE CLUB 1911–13, CONCERNING THE GALERIE CARREL

Christmas Eve/95.

' MY DEAR WHYMPER :

' I have waited to answer your note until I could find time to look up a few notes as to " times " and " dates."

' After the jovial night of $\frac{\text{Saturday} \quad \text{Aug} : 24}{\text{Sunday} \quad \text{Aug} : 25}$ which we spent together in the Cabane de la Tour with the snow falling outside, I, as you will remember, returned over the Furggenjoch to the Riffel Alp. On Tuesday August 27th I re-crossed the Furggenjoch from the Riffel Alp to the Cabane de la Tour accompanied by Daniel Maquignaz and Christan Klucker and a porter whom we sent back from someway below the hut with a party whom we met on their way down the Italian side of the mountain. We had a tremendous gale all night ; and at daylight on Wednesday August 28th, a violent icy north wind was blowing which would have frozen us as soon as we reached the Tyndallgrat. As however the weather looked otherwise fine, and as Daniel predicted that the north wind would blow itself out in 24 hours, we decided to stop another day. Daniel went down to Breuil after breakfast to see his family and to get some more wine and provisions and returned about seven o'clock that evening. I may say " en passant," as I knew you are a connoisseur of " times," that he took only 1¾ hours to go from the hut to the inn at Breuil. At about one o'clock in the night the wind entirely ceased and the sun rose on Thursday August 29th on a day so perfect in all respects that I have rarely seen its like.

' We left the Cabane at 5.15 a.m., reached the Pic Tyndall at

7.20 a.m. and the Enjambée which separates the Tyndallgrat from the final peak or " dernier mamelon " at 8.5 a.m. Five minutes above the Enjambée we stopped for breakfast from 8.10 a.m. to 8.55 a.m. The guides here went off to reconnoitre and actually went some little way on the Z'Mutt side of the ridge to see for the best road. We eventually climbed a quarter of an hour higher up by the ordinary route on the " dernier mamelon " (the climbing being here of course extremely easy) and at a point just twenty minutes above the Enjambée and, at the same rate of walking, about 25 or 30 minutes from the foot of " l'Echelle Jordan " we committed ourselves finally to the Z'Mutt face at 9.10 a.m. At first we went transversely *downwards* for about a hundred feet and next we climbed transversely upwards for about fifty minutes, arriving at the end (say) of 50 minutes at a place whence a ribbon of snow stretched, pretty continuously, along a band of rock, running towards the Z'Mutt arête. At this spot we found the cork of a wine tin. About 30 minutes after we had started on the Z'Mutt face and just beyond the hardest bit of the climb—as we made it—we came across an iron piton driven into the rock and shortly afterwards we found two more similar iron-spikes.

' Up to the place where we found the first piton there was nothing at all resembling a " galerie," " corridor," or ledge in the rock—but beyond that, even before we got to the snow, there was enough of a ledge at any rate to swear by. From the snow there was a distinct ledge. The first half-hour of the traverse was exceedingly difficult and with guides even *almost* as good as the two magnificent companions I had with me I think " excessively and unjustifiably dangerous " would not be too strong an expression to apply to *this* part of the climb. The rocks sloped downwards *quâ* stratification—the angle of the slope was very steep—there was very little hand or foothold and the stone was rotten and came away. We *crawled* with the greatest care, only one moving at a time. In fact I remember that at one moment the thought *did* cross my mind that perhaps we ought not to force the matter further.

' However, the going was obviously easier when once the snow patch was reached, and shortly afterwards the discovery of the piton showed us that we had at any rate now got to where some one had been before us. From the first piton to the snow patch was also very hard climbing, but decidedly not so difficult as the first half-hour of the traverse.

'From the snow patch to the Z'Mutt arête was *comparatively* easy, though still requiring great care as all traverses on a face must needs do. The snow patch was about halfway across the face in distance and considerably more than that in time. At the "fault," where on the occasion of the first and also, I believe, of the second ascent two men stopped behind to pull their companions up on their return from the summit, we drove in an iron peg which Klucker had brought with him and doubled over it an extra rope which we had also brought for contingencies. By this rope we descended and, as we did not intend to come back the same way, we pulled it off the peg when we were all down. I am sure that either Klucker or Maquignaz, with the help of the other, could have climbed *up* this place without a hanging rope, but I am not so certain about the climbing down. Klucker practically did come down last without trusting to the rope *physically*, but he had its moral support and we were moreover well placed down below. I also think that the place could be turned ; and Mummery's first ascent of the peak from Z'Mutt when he undoubtedly climbed up as high as the "Galerie" goes to prove this to be a correct conjecture.

'From the spot where we struck the Z'Mutt arête, to the Italian summit, we took just half an hour fastish going. The place where the Z'Mutt arête is *usually* gained when the Matterhorn is ascended from the Z'Mutt side is about a quarter of an hour lower down on the arête.

'The finding of the three iron pitons was a great surprise to all of us as neither Daniel, who is undoubtedly a head and shoulders the first of the Val Tournanche guides, nor Klucker, who has read everything, nor myself had the slightest idea that any spikes had been fixed. Daniel told me later on that he had spoken to *Salomon* Meynet (who accompanied Grove's party in 1867) *not* J. A. Meynet (who was with Carrel in 1865) and that Salomon declared that there were *five* such spikes when he made the ascent, and that they were put in by Carrel. I could not make out whether Carrel had put them in to aid the *descent* of the first party or—on the second occasion—to facilitate subsequent expected ascents, the route by l'Echelle Jordan not having been then discovered. Salomon also said that the cork we found was undoubtedly the cork of a wine tin belonging to Grove's party in 1867, who (he stated) had partaken of refreshment at the spot where we found it.

' At any rate we only saw *three* spikes, and if there had been more of them to be seen by the route we took, I don't think we should have missed them. Moreover I am sure that anyone who had had spikes with him would have begun fixing them on the earlier part of our route if he had followed it. I am disposed to think therefore that we most probably followed Carrel's original 1865 ascending route, and struck into his 1865 *descending* route somewhere about the first piton we found. Possibly the other 2 pitons may be fixed on the portion of Carrel's descending route 1865, and Grove's route of 1867 which we did not (if my assumption be correct) follow. After this lapse of time possibly Grove might not be very clear as to his exact route, but the expedition on the other hand was such a grand one, and so remarkable, that even small incidents may have made a stronger impression on him than they would have done on an ordinary mountaineering day.

' It was to me one of the most interesting days I ever had. As a *route* up the Matterhorn however, it is not recommendable—being not only longer but far harder than either of the remaining two routes on the Italian side. The somewhat corresponding traverse over the Breuil face of the final peak to " l'Enjambée des trois Jean Baptiste " is not to compare with it in difficulty, though between the " big Stretch of the Three " and the summit this route is far from easy.

' If you would like any more details of this or any other of my six ascents of the Matterhorn, they are always at your service, as is any other information which I possess. I have been obliged to write " currente calamo " and to express myself consequently in a style not fit, without correction, for further use. But I think I have explained as clearly (though more clumsily than I like) as in me lies what we did last Aug : 29th.

' Ever yours sincerely,
' W. E. DAVIDSON.

' I see I haven't mentioned that the first part of our route was exposed to falling stones and bits of ice to some extent, while the latter part was protected by cliffs which overhang. I didn't however notice that the rocks over which we crawled were very *much* redder than their neighbours. There is a good deal of reddish rock on the upper part of the peak. However the first part of our traverse was certainly over reddish rock.'

February 10th, 1896.

' MY DEAR WHYMPER,

' I ought to have written before now to thank you for your note enclosing Grove's very interesting observations on the ascent of the Matterhorn by Carrel's " Galerie." I have twice sat down to do so but have been interrupted.

' It is quite clear that we followed Grove's route for the greater part of the way across the face ; it is not clear to me whether for the first half-hour on the N.W. face (i.e. before we came to the first of the three iron pitons which we found) we did go the same way as he did ; but from the first piton onwards it is beyond all doubt that our ways were identical.

' My impression was that we took to the N.W. face too soon, and that we had in consequence to traverse obliquely and upwards till we struck into Grove's route at this first piton, and that he did not leave the Breuil arête until somewhat higher up—i.e., at the foot of the long cord leading to the " Echelle Jordan "—from which spot he probably traversed almost horizontally, and between which spot and the first piton which we came across, the other pitons which we did not find were possibly fixed.

' But if, as Grove seems to say in his letter to you, he got on to the N.W. face of the mountain at the point where the arête Tyndall (or the " Spalla " rather) abuts against the final peak, i.e., immediately after he passed l'Enjambée—there he took to the N.W. face from 20 minutes to half an hour earlier than we did.

' Apart, however, from Grove's positive recollection on this point, my impression would be that as Carrel, the leader of the party, knew from his previous experience that the lower part of the final peak was comparatively easy, he would have continued to climb up the Breuil ridge as far as the Col Félicité where he struck it on his descent in 1865, by following the whole length of the " Galerie."

' I gather that Carrel fixed these pitons when he ascended with Grove in 1867, and not in 1865 ? Where exactly he (Carrel) went in 1865, before he reached the " Galerie," in his desperate scramble over some red rocks, had always been rather a puzzle to me, and I confess (unless he went the way we did or thereabouts) it is still rather a riddle.

' On the other hand Grove was evidently convinced when he wrote his account for your *Scrambles amongst the Alps* that he did not take exactly the same route in 1867 as Carrel took in his *ascent* in 1865, and I expect that during the ascent in 1867 Carrel probably pointed out to Grove his original route over the red rocks in 1865.

' From the place where we found the cork of the wine tin (i.e., about half way across the face where the ledge began to be clearly defined by a ribbon of snow) there can be no doubt that all three parties followed step by step the same route to the summit. From this place to the first piton we found there is no doubt also that Grove's party and mine followed the same route, for the two other pitons we saw were fixed between the first we found and the place of the cork.

' I'm afraid we shall never entirely clear the matter up to our satisfaction, as it is improbable that either Grove or myself will repeat the ascent, and I think it is exceedingly unlikely that my guides will do so, unless *perhaps* with Farrar, if affairs at Johannesburg permit of his climbing this season.

' I considered the first half-hour of the route until we got to the first piton *excessively* difficult, indeed, the extreme of what a steady traveller with a couple of such magnificent guides as I had might do with reasonable safety. The rock was friable, the angle of the slope was very high, the strata sloped downwards and the utmost care and caution were required.

' I understand that Mummery, who had surveyed the " Galerie " from near the " fault " in the ledge close to the Z'Mutt arête, told Farrar that it was so easy that one could stroll across it with an old umbrella ! If he had tried he would, I fear, with unexpected precipitation, have arrived at a very different conclusion.

' As to the " gully " I quite agree with Grove, that anybody who had an extra rope with him would most certainly employ it as a " corde supplémentaire " for the descent. But I think that either Klucker or Daniel *could* with the help of the other from below, have climbed it at a pinch.

' Moreover it is possible, as Mummery's original ascent in 1879 from Z'Mutt showed, to climb up into the "Galerie" from below and to reach a point between the "gully" and the Breuil arête, from a place on the Z'Mutt face, whence the Z'Mutt arête can easily be reached. The proper route from the Z'Mutt side hits the Z'Mutt arête off at a point lower down by a quarter of an hour's good going than the point at which the Z'Mutt arête is reached by the "Galerie" and gully ; but on the first occasion the party kept climbing up the Z'Mutt face until they hit the "Galerie" at a point where they found a rusty iron hook. (See the account in Mummery's book.)

'Please don't trouble Grove about these matters until he is well enough to enjoy their consideration, which I sincerely hope on his account may be very soon. If then any further matters of interest should occur to him, as arising out of this letter, no doubt he will mention them.

'The only direct question which occurs to me is that already suggested, i.e., were the iron pitons already fixed in 1867, (that is to say, had they been fixed by Carrel's party in 1865) or were they taken up and fixed in 1867.

'Yours very truly,
'W. E. Davidson.

'P.S. By the way, have you heard that when in 1894 Farrar was returning to the Staffel Alp after *descending* the Z'Mutt ridge of the Matterhorn, and was passing just under the cliffs which support the Matterhorn Glacier, his porter Maquignaz saw an axe sticking in a patch of snow at the base of these cliffs. He went off and recovered it, and it proved to be an axe of very ancient pattern, which Daniel Maquignaz believes to have been Lord Francis Douglas'. Daniel told me this year that young Peter Taugwalder (I mean him who took part in the ascent in 1865) had seen the axe which Daniel purchased of his cousin for 20 francs, and said it was Douglas'. I saw the place where it was found, and it is possible that Douglas' axe might have got there.

'Some confusion has arisen owing to *another* old axe having been found on the side of the mountain last year. This axe I have myself seen, and Daniel recognized it as having belonged to his uncle Jean-Joseph Maquignaz. It was being exhibited last summer at the Riffel Alp as Douglas' axe, and some person wrote to the Alpine Post about it.

' But this was not at all the same axe that Farrar's porter found, but was one which Jean-Joseph dropped many years ago as he was going along the summit ridge between the Italian and the Swiss summits.

' W. E. D.'].

E. THE DEATH OF CARREL

WHEN telegrams came in, at the beginning of September 1890, stating that Jean-Antoine Carrel had died from fatigue on the south side of the Matterhorn, those who knew the man scarcely credited the report. It was not likely that this tough and hardy mountaineer would die from fatigue anywhere, still less that he would succumb upon " his own mountain." But it was true. Jean-Antoine perished from the combined effects of cold, hunger, and fatigue upon his own side of his own mountain, almost within sight of his own home. He started on the 23rd of August from Breuil, with an Italian gentleman and Charles Gorret (brother of the Abbé Gorret), with the intention of crossing the Matterhorn in one day. The weather at the time of their departure was the very best, and it changed in the course of the day to the very worst. They were shut up in the *cabane* at the foot of the Great Tower during the 24th, with scarcely any food, and on the 25th retreated to Breuil. Although Jean-Antoine (upon whom, as leading guide, the chief labour and responsibility naturally devolved) ultimately succeeded in getting his party safely off the mountain, he himself was so overcome by fatigue, cold, and want of food that he died on the spot.

Jean-Antoine Carrel entered his sixty-second year in January 1890,[1] and was in the field throughout the summer. On 21st August, having just returned from an ascent of Mont Blanc, he was engaged at Courmayeur by Signor Leone Sinigaglia, of Turin, for an ascent of the Matterhorn. He proceeded to the Val Tournanche, and on the 23rd set out with him and Charles Gorret, for the last time, to ascend his own mountain by his own route. A long and clear account of what happened was communicated by Signor Sinigaglia to the Italian Alpine Club, and from this the following relation is condensed :

[1] The exact date of his birth does not seem to be known. He was christened at the Church of St. Antoine, Valtournanche, on January 17, 1829.

" We started for the Matterhorn at 2.15 a.m. on the 23rd, in splendid
weather, with the intention of descending the same night to the hut at
the Hörnli on the Swiss side.   We proceeded pretty well, but the glaze
of ice on the rocks near the Col du Lion retarded our march somewhat,
and when we arrived at the hut at the foot of the Great Tower,
prudence counselled the postponement of the ascent until the next
day, for the sky was becoming overcast.   We decided upon this, and
stopped.

" Here I ought to mention that both I and Gorret noticed with un-
easiness that Carrel showed signs of fatigue upon leaving the Col du
Lion.   I attributed this to temporary weakness.   As soon as we reached
the hut he lay down and slept profoundly for two hours, and awoke
much restored.   In the meantime the weather was rapidly changing.
Storm clouds coming from the direction of Mont Blanc hung over the
Dent d'Hérens, but we regarded them as transitory, and trusted to the
north wind, which was still continuing to blow.   Meanwhile, three
of the Maquignaz and Edward Bich, whom we found at the hut,
returning from looking after the ropes, started downwards for Breuil,
at parting wishing us a happy ascent, and holding out hopes of a
splendid day for the morrow.

" But, after their departure, the weather grew worse very rapidly ;
the wind changed, and towards evening there broke upon us a most
violent hurricane of hail and snow, accompanied by frequent flashes of
lightning.   The air was so charged with electricity that for two consecutive hours in the night one could see in the hut as in broad daylight.
The storm continued to rage all night, and the day and night following,
continuously, with incredible violence.   The temperature in the hut
fell to — 3 degrees.

" The situation was becoming somewhat alarming, for the provisions
were getting low, and we had already begun to use the seats of the hut
as firewood.   The rocks were in an extremely bad state, and we were
afraid that if we stopped longer, and the storm continued, we should
be blocked up in the hut for several days.   This being the state of
affairs, it was decided among the guides that if the wind should abate
we should descend on the following morning ; and, as the wind did
abate somewhat, on the morning of the 25th (the weather, however,
still remaining very bad), it was unanimously settled to make a retreat.

" At 9 a.m. we left the hut.   I will not speak of the difficulties and

dangers in descending the arête to the Col du Lion, which we reached at
2.30 p.m. The ropes were half frozen ; the rocks were covered with a
glaze of ice, and fresh snow hid all points of support. Some spots were
really as bad as could be, and I owe much to the prudence and coolness
of the two guides that we got over them without mishap.

" At the Col du Lion, where we hoped the wind would moderate, a
dreadful hurricane recommenced, and in crossing the snowy passages
we were nearly *suffocated* by the wind and snow which attacked us on
all sides.[1] Through the loss of a glove, Gorret, half an hour after
leaving the hut, had already got a hand frost-bitten. The cold was
terrible here. Every moment we had to remove the ice from our
eyes, and it was with the utmost difficulty that we could speak so as
to understand one another.

" Nevertheless, Carrel continued to direct the descent in a most
admirable manner, with a coolness, ability, and energy above all praise.
I was delighted to see the change, and Gorret assisted him splendidly.
This part of the descent presented unexpected difficulties, and at
several points great dangers, the more so because the *tourmente* prevented Carrel from being sure of the right direction, in spite of his
consummate knowledge of the Matterhorn. At 11 p.m. (or thereabouts—it was impossible to look at our watches, as all our clothes
were half frozen) we were still toiling down the rocks. The guides
sometimes asked each other where they were ; then we went forward
again—to stop indeed would have been impossible. Carrel at last,
by marvellous instinct, discovered the passage up which we had come,
and in a sort of grotto we stopped a minute to take some brandy.

" While crossing some snow we saw Carrel slacken his pace, and then
fall two or three times to the ground. Gorret asked him what was the
matter, and he said ' nothing,' but he went on with difficulty. Attri-
buting this to fatigue through the excessive toil, Gorret put himself at
the head of the caravan, and Carrel, after the change, seemed better,
and walked well, though with more circumspection than usual. From
this place a short and steep passage takes one down to the pastures,
where there is safety. Gorret descended first, and I after him. We
were nearly at the bottom when I felt the rope pulled. We stopped,

---

[1] Signor Peraldo, the innkeeper at Breuil, stated that a relief party was in
readiness during the whole of August 25 (the day on which the descent was
made), and was prevented from starting by the violence of the tempest.

awkwardly placed as we were, and cried out to Carrel several times to come down, but we received no answer. Alarmed, we went up a little way, and heard him say, in a faint voice, ' Come up and fetch me, I have no strength left.'

" We went up and found that he was lying with his stomach to the ground, holding on to a rock, in a semi-conscious state, and unable to get up or to move a step. With extreme difficulty we carried him up to a safe place and asked him what was the matter. His only answer was, ' I know no longer where I am.' His hands were getting colder and colder, his speech weaker and more broken, and his body more still. We did all we could for him, putting with great difficulty the rest of the cognac into his mouth. He said something, and appeared to revive, but this did not last long. We tried rubbing him with snow, and shaking him, and calling to him continually ; but he could only answer with moans.

" We tried to lift him, but it was impossible—he was getting stiff. We stooped down, and asked in his ear if he wished to commend his soul to God. With a last effort he answered ' Yes,' and then fell on his back, dead, upon the snow."

Such was the end of Jean-Antoine Carrel,—a man who was possessed with a pure and genuine love of mountains ; a man of originality and resource, courage and determination, who delighted in exploration. His special qualities marked him out as a fit person to take part in new enterprises, and I preferred him to all others as a companion and assistant upon my journey amongst the Great Andes of the Equator. Going to a new country, on a new continent, he encountered much that was strange and unforeseen ; yet when he turned his face home-wards he had the satisfaction of knowing that he left no failures behind him.[1] After parting at Guayaquil in 1880, we did not meet again. In his latter years, I am told, he showed signs of age, and from information which has been communicated to me it is clear that he had arrived at a time when it would have been prudent to retire—if he could have done so. It was not in his nature to spare himself, and he worked to the very last. The manner of his death strikes a chord in hearts he never knew. He recognized to the fullest extent the duties of his position, and in the closing act of his life set a brilliant example of

[1] See *Travels amongst the Great Andes of the Equator*, 1892.

fidelity and devotion. For it cannot be doubted that, enfeebled as he was, he could have saved himself had he given his attention to self-preservation. He took a nobler course ; and, accepting his responsibility, devoted his whole soul to the welfare of his comrades, until, utterly exhausted, he fell staggering on the snow. He was already dying. Life was flickering, yet the brave spirit said " It is *nothing*." They placed him in the rear to ease his work. He was no longer able even to support himself ; he dropped to the ground, and in a few minutes expired.[1]

[F. A MODERN VIEW OF THE 1865 ACCIDENT

THE following critique is taken from the *Alpine Journal*, vol. xxxii. It is written by the late Capt. J. P. Farrar, President of the Alpine Club 1917–19.[2]

'. . . Whymper and Douglas cross to Zermatt on July 12th, seek and engage the elder Peter Taugwalder [3] It would appear that it

[1] Signor Sinigaglia wrote in a letter to a friend, from which I am permitted to quote, " I don't try to tell you of my intense pain for Carrel's death. He fell after having saved me, and no guide could have done more than he did." Charles Gorret, through his brother the Abbé, wrote to me that he entirely endorsed what had been said by Sig. Sinigaglia, and added, " We would have given our own lives to have saved his."

Jean-Antoine died at the foot of " the little staircase." On the 26th of August his body was brought to Breuil, and upon the 29th it was interred at Valtournanche. At the beginning of July 1893, an iron cross was placed on the spot where he expired, at the expense of Sig. Sinigaglia, who went in person along with Charles Gorret to superintend its erection.

[2] [The references here given are to the *present* edition.]

[3] Peter Taugwalder, *père*, was in my judgement most improperly and wrongfully prejudiced by the accident that occurred a few days later. He was certainly at the time one of the boldest guides in the Alps, and probably much the best of the Zermatt men. Many references to him are to be found. He was employed by Tuckett (P.P.G. iii, 259) ; he was one of the guides in Kennedy's winter attempt on the E. face of the Matterhorn in 1862, and later in the same year was the leading guide, his son, Peter, being second, when Kennedy (starting from Bricolla) got within an hour of the top of the Dent Blanche. A few days previous to the accident he had, after two attempts from the Zermatt side, made the first ascent of the Gabelhorn from Zinal.

was Douglas's service that he resumed,[1] since immediately after the accident the Taugwalders are reported as saying " We have lost our *Herr* ; we shall not get paid." At Zermatt, to their surprise, they find Hudson, with a young friend, Hadow, and Croz " come to Zermatt to attempt the ascent of the Matterhorn. . . . Mr. Hudson was . . . invited to join us, and he accepted our proposal " (p. 305).

' This compact sealed the fate of the greatest English mountaineer of the day and of his two younger companions. It was the closing chapter in the life of a great guide, the equal of Jakob Anderegg in daring, of Melchior and of Almer in executive ability ; of the one man who had gone far and would have gone further to redeem the Chamonix valley from the reproach, merited then and scarce removed even to-day, of having failed, with advantages unequalled in all the Alps, to produce its quota of great mountaineers.

' The death of Hudson and of Croz held up the tide of mountaineering for fully half a generation of man.

' Surely the first question that springs to one's mind is to account for this sudden change in the attitude of Croz. As late as June 21 we find him deliberately pass by the E. face and attempt instead the dangerous Furggen couloir with the object of gaining the E. face high up (*Scrambles*, p. 253). Nineteen days later he arrives at Zermatt with Hudson to attempt, as a matter in the course of his guide's business, the ascent by this very E. face. We can reasonably account for this change by the impress of the study, the experience, and the knowledge of his new employer. Hudson was then a man of thirty-six, of iron physique, indomitable, tireless, with twelve or thirteen years' mountaineering experience. We know that he had been certainly once, and probably several times, at Zermatt. We know his independence of mind—his trained study of new routes—his resolute skill, the fruit of long years of independent experience, and of apprenticeship to good guides.

' We are justified in assuming that he had worked and studied for

In describing this, Lord Francis Douglas writes : " Peter Taugwalder acted admirably, and really showed himself a first-rate guide." He was one of the very few men—indeed one might say the only guide—free of the spell of inaccessibility which the Matterhorn at that day laid on men's minds.

[1] He had made with Lord Francis Douglas, six days earlier, the second ascent of the Gabelhorn.

this day. He was the one man, of all his generation, of mature judgement formed by much independent mountaineering experience —capable of impressing his views on his companions—upon whom the E. face of the great mountain, however apparently inaccessible, failed to lay a spell, leaving him, with all his burning enthusiasm, ever cool and critical. Croz, with his temperament, could not fail to feel the impress of the master-mind.

' Moreover, we know from Kennedy (*A.J.*, ii., 68) that " at Easter in 1865 I was visiting the Rev. C. Hudson, at Skillington, to arrange a Swiss tour, and we agreed . ·. to go to Zermatt to try if we could climb the Matterhorn by its northern arête. . . . This programme we could not carry out together from unforeseen circumstances." Thus to Hudson's own observations and indomitable character were added the actual experiences of Kennedy, and, on the successful attempt itself, of Taugwalder.

' The hour of the Matterhorn had struck.

' It is not necessary to deal at length with the actual details of the expedition. So far as they can ever be known they are recounted in the memorable chapters (xx. and xxi.) of Whymper's immortal *Scrambles*

' We have thus combined for the attempt three parties :

' (1) Hudson and Hadow with Croz.

' (2) Douglas with Taugwalder, *père et fils*.

' (3) Whymper, " fortuitously a member " of the expedition, as he terms himself (*Scrambles*, p. 226).

' Each of these parties with, of course, obvious additions to the third, was quite competent to make the ascent of the Matterhorn.

' Hudson was a tried mountaineer of many years' experience, generally recognized as the best amateur of his day ; of almost unequalled experience ; in the full strength of manhood. Hadow was one of those active young Englishmen capable, with experienced companions, of going anywhere.

' I say distinctly that Hudson and Croz were fully qualified to conduct him on the proposed expedition, and that the sum of the powers of the party was much above the average of half the parties that go mountain-climbing to-day.

' Lord Francis Douglas had in two or three seasons added sufficient experience to the traditional enterprise and daring of his race. His guide Taugwalder was thoroughly reliable ; his second man, the younger Taugwalder, far from a novice.

'Whymper, then about twenty-five, had four or five magnificent seasons behind him under the best guides of the day. He had persistently attacked the great mountain from another side. He had shown, and was to show, qualities that have made his name immortal. He of all men had a right to join in the final attack even if it were not of his own planning.

'The Matterhorn was no more difficult then than now. We can infer, from the work previously done that season, that the mountain was in that year in a very forward state ; the " going " up to the shoulder, even above it, was probably very much as in a good August when I have known the Matterhorn to be dusty ! (1892).

'Yet the three parties together formed a fatal combination.

'Which of us does not know the danger of a large party on a mountain ? There is always far too much talk, with its attendant absence of close attention ; there is usually, as in this case, no recognized head ; indeed in the presence of his new employer and of his old and tried Monsieur of many a triumphant campaign Croz must have felt a divided allegiance.

'There was every element of danger in this fatal compact.

'The details of the ascent, as given by Whymper, indicate a certain casualness, inherent in all large parties. It is, however, when the descent commences that these elements of danger instantly combine to a fatal issue.

'The great unwieldy party carried at least three ropes. (*Scrambles*, p. 304.)

'(1) " 200 feet of the Manila rope."

'(2) " 150 feet of a stouter and probably stronger rope."

'(3) " 200 feet of a lighter and weaker rope . . . (stout sash-line)."

'One of these ropes would in all probability fall to be carried by each guide.

'It is difficult to explain how the first or second rope with which, we are distinctly told (p. 320), the four men who fell were tied only sufficed for them ; for we cannot imagine Taugwalder's tying himself on with the thin rope [1] which must have been the one he carried —the third one being with young Taugwalder and Whymper, " one

---

[1] A bit of this thin rope may be seen in the Zermatt Museum. It bears, possibly shrunk through time, scant resemblance to the illustration, p. 323.

hundred feet or more " away—if any portion of the other rope remained. Lord Francis Douglas, the man immediately in front of him, would not be likely to wind any portion of the rope round his own shoulders.

' Taugwalder cannot properly be blamed for the use of this rope. Mr. Whymper, with the candour running throughout his book, is perfectly fair to him. The intention to use this rope only as a " spare " rope had not been explained to him. The ropes were not his, or he might well be blamed for the practice, still very prevalent among guides and amateurs alike, which, not long ago, cost the life of a very brilliant mountaineer, Louis Theytaz, of paying scant attention to the age and strength of the tackle.

' We next come to the order of roping for the descent. Whymper (*Scrambles*, p. 319) states that " Hudson and I again consulted as to the best and safest arrangement. We agreed that it would be best for Croz to go first [1] and Hadow second ; Hudson, who was almost equal to a born mountaineer in sureness of foot, wished to be third ; Lord Francis Douglas was placed next, and old Peter, the strongest of the remainder, after him." Whymper and young Taugwalder joined on shortly afterwards, tied together with the other of the stouter ropes, young Taugwalder doubtless being last man.

' Mr. Whymper undoubtedly realized later the fatal error of judgement in this order, since he adds a footnote (p. 320) : " if the members of the party had been more equally efficient, Croz would have been placed last." Few mountaineers will disagree with this. On the contrary, the more unequally efficient the party the greater reason

---

[1] It is disconcerting to find that J. B. Croz, the elder brother, and, to some extent, teacher of Michel, was not averse to descending first on the rope, leaving his two Messieurs and " a lad . . . as porter " to follow down as best they could. (" Ascent of the Dent Blanche," by T. S. Kennedy, *A.J.*, i., 38.) Michel also is found descending first on the Verte, while Hudson was last for most of the day. But the party was a very strong one, consisting of two strong guides besides Croz, of two Messieurs of the first flight—Hudson and T. S. Kennedy—and Hodgkinson, a good amateur, all on one rope. They had shown what they were worth by making the first ascent by the Moine ridge. (*A.J.*, iii., 73.) The sounder practice of the Oberlanders at that date was for the best man to descend last on the rope. Cf. *A.J.*, i., 43, " The Weisshorn," by Leslie Stephen, where Melchior comes down last.

for Croz being, when descending, in the rear, where alone he would be able to counteract a slip. Choosing the line of descent was a secondary matter.

'The fatal order of roping is again the consequence of the want of coherence in the party. Had the parties been separate, then it can hardly be doubted that the order of descent of Hudson's party would have been as follows :

' 1. Hudson, leading down.

' 2. Hadow.

' 3. Croz, last man.

'The order of the second party would in all probability have been :

' 1. Whymper, leading down.

' 2. Young Taugwalder.

' 3. Douglas.

' 4. Old Taugwalder, last man.

'Had this order been adopted we should, in all probability, have not had to chronicle any accident.

'For the whole party on one rope the most prudent order, in my opinion, would have been :

' 1. Hudson, leading down, since he had led on the way up to the shoulder and was used to going without guides.

' 2. Douglas.

' 3. Young Taugwalder.

' 4. Hadow.

' 5. Croz, who would here be not too far away to give Hudson any advice if required, while at the same time he would be in the best position to ensure the safety of the less experienced of his Messieurs.

' 6. Whymper.

' 7. Old Taugwalder, last man.

'Thus the most inexperienced man, Hadow, would have had a young guide [1] in front of him and the strongest guide behind him.

---

[1] Young Peter Taugwalder can scarcely have been the mere porter, since already three years previously, at nineteen years of age, he was considered quite good enough by a good judge like T. S. Kennedy to act as second man to his father " old " Peter on the attempt upon the Dent Blanche, and within a month after the accident we find him in the service of famous members of the A.C., making the first ascent of the Dôme route (*A.J.*, ii., 133). He became later a well-known guide, one of the greatest authorities on the E. face of the

G. TABLE OF ATTEMPTS MADE TO ASCEND THE MATTERHORN PREVIOUS TO THE FIRST ASCENT

No. of Attempt.	Date.	Names.	Side upon which the attempt was made, and place arrived at.	Greatest height attained.	REMARKS.
1	1858–9.	J.-Antoine Carrel. J.-Jacques Carrel. Victor Carrel. Gab. Maquignaz. Abbé Gorret.	Breuil side. . " Chimney."	12,650	Several attempts were made before this height was attained ; the men concerned cannot remember how many. See p. 52.
2	1860. July . .	Alfred Parker. Charles Parker. Sandbach Parker.	Zermatt side . East face.	11,500 ?	Without guides. pp. 52, 53.
3	August .	V. Hawkins. J. Tyndall.	Breuil side . Hawkins got to foot of " Great Tower," Tyndall a few feet higher.	12,992 13,050 ?	Guides—J. J. Bennen and J.-Jacques Carrel. pp. 53–55.
4	1861. July . .	Messrs. Parker	Zermatt side . East face.	11,700 ?	No guides. p. 55.
5	Aug. 29 .	J.-Antoine Carrel. J.-Jacques Carrel.	Breuil side. . " Crête du Coq."	13,230	See p. 63.
6	Aug. 29–30	Edward Whymper	Breuil side. . " Chimney."	12,650	Camped upon the mountain, with an Oberland guide. pp. 56–63.
7	1862. January .	T. S. Kennedy .	Zermatt side . East face.	11,000 ?	Winter attempt. pp. 65, 66.
8	July 7–8 .	R. J. S. Macdonald. Edward Whymper.	Breuil side. . Arête below " Chimney."	12,000	Guides—Johann zum Taugwald and Johann Kronig. pp. 71–73.
9	July 9–10	R. J. S. Macdonald. Edward Whymper.	Breuil side. . " Great Tower."	12,992	Guides—J.-A. Carrel and Pession. pp. 73, 74.
,,	July 18–19	,, ,,	Breuil side. . Somewhat higher than the lowest part of the " Cravate."	13,400	Alone. pp. 75–87.
10	July 23–24	,, ,,	Breuil side. . " Crête du Coq."	13,150	Guides—J.-A. Carrel, Cæsar Carrel, and Luc Meynet. p. 89.
11	July 25–26	,, ,,	Breuil side. . Nearly as high as the highest part of the " Cravate."	13,460	With Luc Meynet. pp. 91, 92.
12	July 27–28	J. Tyndall . .	Breuil side. . " The Shoulder," to foot of final peak.	13,970	Guides—J. J. Bennen and Anton Walter ; porters—J.-Antoine Carrel, Cæsar Carrel, and another. pp. 92–95, 99–101.
13	1863. Aug. 10–11	Edward Whymper.	Breuil side. . " Crête du Coq."	13,280	Guides—J.-A. Carrel, Cæsar Carrel, Luc Meynet, and two porters. pp. 124–131.
14	1865. June 21 .	,, ,,	South-east face.	11,200 ?	Guides—Michel Croz, Christian Almer, Franz Biener ; porter—Luc Meynet. pp. 251–255.

Douglas would have had the best amateur in front of him—a man absolutely safe for himself—and a young guide behind him. .

' Hudson may have been lulled into false security by the long string behind him. The one point, however, in which the amateur is frequently inferior even to a moderate guide is in intuitively realizing when a sudden slip is likely to occur and in resistance to the consequent shock; indeed the moderate guide is often as quick as the best in this respect, inasmuch as indifferent and incapable climbers are usually his care.

' But the real cause of the accident was not the slip made by Hadow, not the breaking of the rope, but the want of coherence in the " fortuitously " formed party.

' A great lesson to be learned from the occurrence is to undertake no serious expedition with a large party. Even among good men it engenders a false sense of security and, most certainly, inattention and irresponsibility. It tends to irregularity of pace and loss of valuable time.']

[H. INTERROGATION OF OLD PETER TAUGWALDER

AT Whymper's request, the following questions were put by M. Clemenz to old Peter Taugwalder at Zermatt on July 21, 1865. The answers are appended, the numbers being those given in the official report, which is reproduced in the *Alpine Journal*, vol. xxxiii., pp. 234 *et seq.*

22. Have you made excursions with Lord Douglas before the ascent of the Matterhorn ?

Yes, I accompanied Lord Douglas as guide to Zinal and on the Gabelhorn.

23. Were you told before starting of whom the party was to

Matterhorn. Some of his expeditions, e.g. the S.E. arête of the Disgrazia (Colonel Strutt's *Bernina*, i., 210), have found few if any followers, although in that expedition his share was a bit discounted by the fact that his companion was Jakob Anderegg, then at his zenith. Whatever may be said about him there is no denying that he became a mighty man on his own mountain, and at the age of twenty-two must already have been a very useful member of any party.

consist, and did you make any objection to any of those proposed, or to the proportion of guides to travellers?

I was certainly informed how many people composed the party. I made no remark in criticism at its composition. Nevertheless, I remarked that in proportion to the number of tourists, there were too few guides. Messrs. Whymper and Hudson replied that they climbed as well as guides, whereupon I said nothing more.

24. Who tied the men up on leaving the summit?

The first four men of the party, namely Croz, Hadow, Hudson and Lord Douglas, were tied up by the guide Croz, and I tied myself on to Lord Douglas by a special rope.

25. Who was tied up first?

I cannot properly recall who was tied up first by Croz.

26. What rope was used?

The rope to which Croz and the three tourists were tied was quite new and strong.

27. Who tied you to Lord Douglas?

Myself.

28. Why was another rope [1] used between Lord Douglas and yourself?

Because the first rope was not long enough to enable me to attach myself.

29. Was the rope used between yourself and Lord Douglas, in your opinion, sufficiently strong for the purpose?

If I had found that the rope used between Lord Douglas and myself was not strong enough, I should have taken good care not to attach myself with it to Lord Douglas, and I should not have wished to endanger him any more than myself. If I had found this rope too weak, I should have recognized it as such before the ascent of the Matterhorn, and should have rejected it.

30. Describe the place at which the accident occurred.

Having descended about two to three hundred feet from the summit of the Matterhorn, we arrived at the second of the most dangerous places, where the mountain offers only smooth walls and where it is

---

[1] Whymper's phrase, in the questions forwarded to M. Clemenz, is "*une différente espèce de corde*." The question actually put by M. Clemenz substitutes for this phrase "ein anderes Seil": in the French translation "une autre corde."

very difficult to get a footing. It was there that the first tourist following Croz slipped and dragged off those behind him, and they in turn dragged off the guide Croz, after the rope between Lord Douglas and myself had broken.

31. In your opinion, was sufficient care used in the descent of that part ?

Yes. Nevertheless, it is to be regretted that the first man after Croz was a very bad climber.

32. How did the accident occur ?

I have already described it, but I add that after the rope broke between Lord Douglas and me, Mr. Whymper, myself and my son remained at this spot, from which we endeavoured to get clear as soon as possible. We descended in order to find a place where we could pass the night. Next morning we reached Zermatt safe and sound.

33. Was the rope tight, that is, not in loops, between the men at the time they fell ?

It was tight.

34. In your opinion, what was the cause of the rope breaking ?

I cannot say, but the weight of the three men with the force of their fall could have broken a strong rope.

35. Was it possible to have stopped the four falling men after the rope broke ?

Impossible.

M. Clemenz added :

36. If the rope between you and Lord Douglas had not broken, would you have been able to save the travellers ?

To which Taugwalder replied : I am convinced that if the rope had not broken between Lord Douglas and myself, I should, with the help of the guide Croz, have been able to save the travellers.

The examination was continued two days later, M. Clemenz putting his own questions.

53. Since your last deposition, have your recollections of the accident on the Matterhorn altered ? Have you anything to add or to modify in regard to your previous deposition ?

Nothing, except that I said to the guide Croz, before reaching the dangerous point, that one ought for greater safety to stretch a rope. Croz replied that it was not necessary.

54. Does your son know how the accident occurred ?

I do not think so, for he asked me at once : Are you still there, father ?

55. How was it that there were three tourists between Croz and yourself, while there was only one between yourself and your son ? The president of the court considers that this was not a reasonable division ; what do you say about it ?

Croz led the party, then came Hadow, then Hudson, who regarded himself as a guide ; they were followed by Lord Douglas, myself, Whymper and my son. If the president admits that Hudson was acting as guide, you will see that each tourist was between two guides.

56. Did the party regard Hudson as a guide ?

Hudson himself said he did not need a guide, and that he could act as a guide.

57. Who supplied the rope which attached you to Lord Douglas ? The rope was supplied by the tourists.

There follow certain questions concerning the engagement of his son and the times of departure, bivouacking, and arrival at the summit. The examination continues :

63. In his deposition, Mr. Whymper declared that Hadow slipped first and dragged Croz off, and that these two dragged off Hudson and Douglas in succession ; that during these moments, Whymper himself and the Taugwalders, father and son, had time to get their footing ; that at this instant the rope broke between Douglas and Taugwalder. In your reply to Question 30, you said that Hadow was the first to slip, then Hudson and Lord Douglas, and that Croz did not slip until after the others. As your deposition and Mr. Whymper's do not agree with each other, you are asked to declare whether you uphold your first answer.

As Mr. Whymper was above me, at a point from which he could take note [1] of this unfortunate accident, his deposition may be more correct, so that I cannot insist that Croz fell after the three tourists. Everything happened in a moment, and the surprise was so great that it was almost impossible to have exact knowledge of the accident.

64. Have you anything to add or to modify in regard to your previous depositions ?

I would add that for greater security I turned towards the rock,

[1] Compare Whymper's statement, p. 321.

and as the rope between Whymper and myself was not taut,[1] I was fortunately able to pass it round a projection of rock, which gave me the firmness needed for safety. The rope which attached me to Douglas and the others in front gave me such a shock at their fall that I am still in great pain at the place where the rope was round my body.]

[I. LETTERS FROM WHYMPER

THE following letters deal with Adams Reilly's proposed survey of the southern slopes of the Monte Rosa group, and with the aftermath of the 1865 accident :

20 Canterbury Place,
Lambeth Road, S.
Ap : 22, 1865.

DEAR REILLY,

' The only man I know of in the Val Tournanche who is at all near first-rate, is Jean-Antoine Carrel, and he lives at V.T. He is as good a rockman as I have ever seen, very strong, and very easily ruled. If you wanted a man for a new excursion in the V.T., he would do as well as Croz or any other man, and I would recommend you to take him, but his temper does not recommend him. He has another failing, he always quotes his relationship to the Chanoine Carrel at every halt, and endeavours on every opportunity to make you take a relative of his (another Carrel, also of V.T.) who is a hang-dog looking fellow, and is the man who went with Tyndall and Hawkins as related in " Vacation Tourists."

' There is yet another Carrel at or near V.T. named Cæsar. He is young, ugly, (well marked with smallpox, I think) but is very strong, a good mountaineer, and good tempered. He showed up very well on the Matterhorn.

' There is another man I have had living at or near V.T. who, as well as I remember, was named Walter or Walters ; I should class him with Cæsar Carrel, perhaps not quite so good, not having much experience.

' These are all the men about whom I know anything, except one

---

[1] Contrast Whymper's statement, p. 322.

or two duffers, who would not be any use to you, and I should say that of the lot, Luc Meynet or Cæsar Carrel would answer your purpose best. They both speak French and the local patois, a very polyglot lingo, and you must have a man who does this, to be any use to you.

' I have planned something about the Matterhorn, but Heaven knows if I shall carry it out, for my business in hand perplexes me, and *may* prevent my going out. Should I go, and be able to get a decent lot of guides, I shall go at the Matterhorn again, and it will decidedly increase my pleasure if you come too ; but of this more bye and bye when both of our plans are more matured. I have been very much annoyed by Croz throwing me up. I *suppose* he is tempted by more £ s. d., otherwise I cannot account for it, as it was a distinct understanding when we parted that he was engaged by me for the early part of the season ; but when I wrote a few weeks ago, he informed me that he was already engaged. I believe I have Almer for a space of about 10 days, and I have also written to Franz Biener, but have not had his answer. As I may find myself, after all, guideless, it is useless fixing anything at present, even if business allowed me.

' I am,

' dear Reilly,

' Yours very faithfully,

' EDWARD   WHYMPER.'

20, Canterbury Place,
Lambeth Road, S.
May 1, 1865.

' DEAR REILL.

' I think you would do well to wait a fortnight or so before writing to Meynet as the postal communication in the Val Tournanche is excessively limited, and I doubt is just now at a standstill. And indeed in writing I almost think it would be better to write to Favre, the landlord at Breuil, his address in full is :

M. Jean-Antoine Favre,
Hotel Giomein,
Breuil,
Val Tournanche.

He is a civil fellow, if he thinks he can make anything out of one, and being a man of some importance a letter is more likely to reach him quickly than Meynet.

' My plans are doubtful, but if I go, I shall try the Matterhorn in *June* ; I wish with all my heart you could be with me ; do if you possibly can. Charlet I decide *not* to have in any case.

' I do not think men will rise to the general appeal for the map, it requires special application I think.

' I am very glad you decided to do the Monte Rosa business. I have an idea of sketching all round the S. side myself, but abandon that as you will do it. My entering into competition with you is hopeless.

' My idea is, if business allows me, to have a short and stiff mountaineering campaign, and then, about the beginning of July, to set to work at serious sketching, which I have not had in the Alps since 1860. As I am entirely ruled by business, it is impossible for me to *fix* anything, but I hope to do as I have indicated, and leave England about the 8th of June.

' I am glad you think of reading an account of our M. Blanc doings ; the lot, with your additional ones, ought to be enough for a short paper. I don't believe you when you say it is a lame and impotent account of them. If there is anything you want from my note book about them, let me know by all means.

' I am, dear Reilly,
' Yours very faithfully,
' EDWARD WHYMPER.'

Breuil, June 20th, 1865.

' DEAR REILLY,

' I have directed the people here to let you have any properties just as I should have them myself, and I have told Luc Meynet, who lives at the bottom of the hill, that you will probably want him, at which he expressed delight. Should he want too much, cut him short and send for Cæsar Carrel at Valtournanche. I expect to be back here about the 10th of July, when I shall hope to meet you. I have had very bad luck as yet. Croz has become awfully bumptious, not to say fractious.

'Yours very faithfully,
'EDWARD WHYMPER.'

To the Rev. J. Robertson, Rugby.

Town House,
Haslemere,
Aug: 27, 1865.

'DEAR ROBERTSON,

'I am glad to see your handwriting, and gratefully acknowledge the receipt of your cheque for £2 towards the Croz fund.

'I was extremely sorry to miss you at Visp; I got in there very late (11.15) and was surprised to find my packet there although you were not. I did not like to call on you at the other place at midnight, and went off by the early diligence while, I suppose, you were still reposing. The manner in which I was persecuted by impertinent people on my way home passes all belief.

'You are right in supposing that letter was a difficult one to write. It appears to have given satisfaction to most people, but not to all, as I will show you one day. I would have stuck to the resolution I made at Zermatt had it been possible, but it was not; all kinds of pleasant rumours were propagated, and the amount of silly nonsense that was being written rendered it also desirable that I should write. Therefore after having rec^d two letters from Wills pressing me to write, two from the Ed. of *Times* and a score of others from friends whose opinion I value more or less, I gave way.

'I am,
'dear Robertson,
'yours very faithfully,
'EDWARD WHYMPER.'

20 Canterbury Place,
Lambeth Road, S.
Sept. 29, 1866.

'MY DEAR ROBERTSON,

'I want to ask your assistance and advice on these two points. And first as to the advice.

'Do you think the enclosed inscription can be taken exception to, either in taste or truthfulness ? or do you see any way in which it can be readily improved ? It is intended to go on a tomb that is erected in Zermatt churchyard in memory of poor Croz, and I want to send it out as soon as possible, as the mason is waiting at Zermatt to cut it.

'Now as to the assistance. I want to have it turned into French, and correct French. Of course I could do it myself, or get a translator in London to do it, but this won't do. I want it as well, and as elegantly (to use a word I detest) rendered as I can get it, and it has occurred to me that it might be accomplished by your intervention. I have a lively recollection of the kindness of M. Vecqueray, and I do not call to mind anyone who would be likely to do it so well as he, or who would take the pains that I think he would be likely to exercise.

'What I wish then, and I ask it with hesitation, is, that you will endeavour to obtain the translation of this epitaph by M. Vecqueray. It should be scarcely becoming for myself, almost a stranger, to prefer the request, or I would not trouble you in the matter, and it will be doing me a genuine favour if you will make it. I have already mentioned that I wish to send the inscription out as soon as possible ; therefore, should anything prevent the accomplishment of my wishes please to be so kind as to let me know without loss of time.

'I have not heard whether you went Alpwards this year. My own time was only sixteen days away from England, and almost every day was favoured with rain, wind and snow, each in excess. I did not go out wishing to make ascents or passes, having, as you may suppose, not quite so much appetite for this sort of thing as I had, but I went out nevertheless for definite objects, and I got as hard scrambling and walking as ever I have had. I have done with the Alps now and am getting rid of my properties, which looks as if I meant it.

'I am,
'my dear Robertson,
'Yours very faithfully,
'EDWARD WHYMPER.

' I shall be glad of an early answer as Seiler, who is looking after the matter, leaves Zermatt shortly.

' " Not far from here " will render better in French. I shall be glad to have any suggestion as to the disposition of the lines, which is always difficult.

A la Mémoire
de
MICHEL AUGUSTE CROZ
né a Le Tour (Vallée de Chamonix)
en témoignage de regret
à la perte d'un
homme brave et dévoué

———

aimé de ses compagnons
estimé des voyageurs
il périt non loin d'ici
en homme de coeur et guide fidèle.]

J. STRATIFICATION OF SNOW AND FORMATION OF GLACIER-ICE

IN the spring of 1866, the late Principal J. D. Forbes urged me to endeavour to find out more about the " veined structure " of glaciers, which he then, and, I believe, until his death, considered was very much in want of elucidation. After thinking the subject over, it seemed to me that its difficulties were so considerable that it would be useless to attempt to grapple with them except in a thorough manner, and that it would be necessary to scrutinize and to follow out the gradual transition of snow into glacier-ice, from beginning to end, in at least *one* glacier. Superficial examination was almost worthless, for it was known that the veined structure, or structures, existed in glacier-ice above the snow-line ; and hence it appeared that the only effectual procedure would be to sink a number of pits or trenches through the superincumbent snow, commencing at the very birthplace of the glacier, and to watch its growth and structural development as it descended to the lower regions. This opinion I still entertain.

I left England at the end of July, with the intention of sinking several pits in the Stock Glacier, which descends towards the north-east from the Col de Valpelline.[1] In the first instance it was desirable that a trench should be made in some position that was free from local interference, and in this respect the Col de Valpelline was an excellent station. It was a snowy plateau—almost a plain (without any protruding ridges or rocks)—which gave birth to two great glaciers— one (the Stock Glacier) descending gently towards the north-east, the second (the Valpelline Glacier) falling away rather more rapidly to the south-west.[2] Wretched weather and other troubles retarded the work, and only one pit was sunk in the time at my disposal. This was a little more than 22 feet in depth ; and, although it threw scarcely any light upon the veined structure, it yielded some information respecting stratification of snow and the formation of glacier-ice. I will describe, first of all, how the work was done ; and secondly, what we observed.

I arrived at Zermatt on the 30th of July, possessed of a pickaxe (one end of the head pointed and the other adze-shaped) and a couple of shovels ; engaged three common peasants as labourers, and Franz Biener as guide, and waited some days for the weather to improve. On the afternoon of August 2 we started, and camped on the rocks of the Stockje,[3] at a height of about 9,000 feet. It was a very gusty night, and snow fell heavily. Great avalanches poured down frequently from the surrounding slopes into the basin of the Tiefenmatten Glacier, and minor ones from the slopes of our tent. We left our camp at 9.20 a.m. on the 3rd, and proceeded to the summit of the col (11,650 feet) against a bitterly cold wind, and with the clouds embracing everything. I marked out a place for excavation, immediately at the summit of the pass,[4] 24 feet long by 5 wide, and the men soon threw out enough snow to protect themselves from the wind. Two walls of the pit were dressed smooth, a third was left rough, and the fourth was occupied by an inclined plane that led from the surface to the workers. Two men were always at work ; one hew-

[1] See Map of the Valpelline, etc.

[2] The glacier referred to above as the Valpelline Glacier is now called upon the Swiss Government Maps " Haut Glacier de Za-de-Zan."

[3] Marked on the Map of Matterhorn and its Glaciers, CAMP (1866).

[4] The pit was made about mid-way between the Tête Blanche and the point now called the Tête de Valpelline (3,813 metres).

ing with the pick, and the other throwing out with the shovel. The others rested, and relieved the workers about every fifteen minutes. For seven or eight feet down they got along rapidly, as the stuff could be thrown out ; but after a time the progress became much slower, for the snow had to be carried out in baskets.

After five hours' exposure to the wind and drifting snow I was half frozen, and in a worse state than the men, who kept themselves alive by their work. All our faces were massed with icicles. At length I beat a retreat, and descended to the tent with Biener. The mists were so dense that we dared not use either veils or spectacles, and I remained snow-blind in consequence for two days afterwards. On the morning of the 4th my eyelids refused to open, and the light was painful even when they were closed. The men started off at 6.45, leaving me with my head tied up in a handkerchief, unable to eat or even to smoke ! Biener came back at 4.30 p.m. and reported that the snow seemed to be getting softer rather than harder the farther they descended. On the 5th (Sunday) my condition was slightly improved, and on Monday morning I was able to make a start, and ascended to the col to see what the labourers had done in my absence. They did not appear to have overworked themselves ; for while on the first day they had got down more than 9 feet in 5 hours, they had, during the time I had been away, only accomplished 4 feet more. They accounted for this by saying that on Sunday night three feet of snow had drifted into the pit, and almost as much on Friday night. This, of course, had considerably added to the work. They were extremely anxious to get away ; which was not surprising, as the wind was blowing ferociously from the north-west, and was tearing away sheets of snow from the summit of the pass. Indeed, it was impossible to stand against it, and in a single hour we should have been all frozen if we had remained upon the surface. I told them that they had only to reach glacier, and the work would be over at that spot. This consoled them, and they promised to work hard during our absence.

Biener and I then crossed the Col de Valpelline and passed the night of the 6th at Prarayé. Upon the 7th we went down the Valpelline to Bionaz upon other business. On the 8th we returned to the summit of the col, and found all three men sitting on the nearest rocks smoking their pipes. They admitted that they had done nothing on that day, but excused themselves by saying that they had got down to glacier. I found that they had only gone down another foot during our thirty-six hours' absence. My wrath, however, was somewhat appeased when I went down into the pit. They had struck a layer of ice of much greater thickness than any which had been previously met with. It extended all round the floor of the pit to a depth of $6\frac{1}{4}$ inches. The men went to work again, and soon reached another stratum of ice of considerable thickness ; or, rather, three layers which were barely separated from each other. After this, the snow seemed to be no denser than it was above the great layer. I waited some time ; but my eyes were still very weak, and could not be exposed for many minutes together, so at length Biener and I went down to Zermatt through a terrific thunderstorm and very heavy rain.

On the 9th we returned again to the col, and whilst climbing the rocks of the Stockje, discovered the dead chamois which was mentioned upon p. 111. It rained as far as our camp, and thenceforward we had to fight our way up through continuously-falling snow, against an easterly gale. It blew dead in our teeth, and our progress was painfully slow. The snow was writhing all around, as if tormented ; or caught by whirlwinds, and sent eddying high aloft ; or seized by gusts and borne onwards in clouds which seemed to be driven right through us. The wind was appalling ; once I was fairly blown down, although tied to Biener, and many times we were sent staggering back for ten or a dozen paces against our will. Our track was obliterated at the summit, and we could not find the pit. We tried east, west, north, and south, to no purpose. At last we heard a shout ! We halted, panting for breath. Another ! It came with the wind, and we had to face the storm again. After a long search we arrived at the pit, which by this time was a huge hole twenty feet deep. The inclined plane had had to be abandoned, and a regular staircase led down to the bottom. The men had again struck work, having, they said, arrived at glacier ; the fact was, they were completely cowed by the weather, and had taken to shouting, expecting that we should be lost. I descended into the pit, and with two strokes of the pick went through their glacier, which was only another thick stratum of ice.

The last day had arrived, and the next was to see me *en route* for London. I drove the men to their work, and stood over them once

more. The stuff which came up in the baskets was different from
that which I had seen last ! It was not ice of a compact kind like
the horizontal layers, still it was not snow. Sometimes one could
say, This is snow ; but at others no one would have said that it was
snow. On inquiry, they said that it had been like this for several
feet. I went down, took the tools in my own hands, and hewed the
walls smooth. It was then apparent that vertical glacification (if I
may be permitted to use such an expression) had commenced (see
A A on section).[1]

The men were anxious to leave, for the weather was terrible. The
wind howled over our heads in a true hurricane. I was unwilling
to go until it was absolutely necessary. At length they refused to
work any longer ; I concluded the measurements ; we tied in line,
and floundered downwards, and at 9 p.m. arrived at Zermatt.

I will now proceed to describe what we saw. For 11 inches from
the surface the snow was soft and white, or what is usually termed
new snow. There was then a very decided increase in density, and
all the snow beneath had a slight bluish tint.[2] At 21 inches from the
surface the tone of the snow seemed somewhat deeper than that
which was above, but below this point there was little or no increase
in colour until the depth of 15 feet was passed. The density of the
snow naturally increased as we descended, although much less rapidly
than I expected. Down to the depth of $13\frac{1}{2}$ feet (or to just above
the broad blue band on the right-hand column of the section) the
mass was decidedly and unmistakably *snowy* ; that is to say, lumps
could readily be compressed between the hands. This was also the
case in some places *below* the depth of 15 feet. For example, at **B B**,
on the section, the snow was not perceptibly denser than it was six
or eight feet higher up. In other places, **A A**, it could not be termed
snowy ; it could not be readily compressed in the hands ; and it
looked and felt like an imperfect or wet and spongy form of ice.
The colour at **B B** was perceptibly lighter than at **A A**, but it should
be said that the colour here, and of the horizontal strata of ice, has been

[1] See the accompanying section, drawn to a scale of one inch to a foot from
actual measurement.

[2] Compared with the 11 inches of snow at the surface, that beneath seemed
dirty. I hesitate, however, to term it dirty. We did not anywhere detect
grit or sand.

intentionally exaggerated upon the section for the sake of clearness.

The entire mass was pervaded with horizontal strata of pure ice. In the 22 feet that we penetrated there were 75 such layers, varying from one-tenth of an inch in thickness to 6¼ inches, which amounted in the aggregate to 25⅝ inches of solid ice. These strata were approximately parallel to the surface of the snow, and to each other. Not perfectly so ; sometimes they approached, and sometimes receded from each other. Neither was their substance (thickness) constant. In some places they were more, and in others less thick. For example, the stratum which is between the brackets marked 1863–4 ? and 1864–5 ? was in some places an inch and a half thick, but in others scarcely an eighth of an inch. Upon the whole, the stouter strata were continued completely round the sides of the pit, and were tolerably uniform in thickness. The finer strata, on the other hand, frequently died out in short distances, and seldom or never could be traced completely round the walls. The finer strata also were much more numerous towards the surface than towards the bottom of the pit, and they were readily obscured by the drifting snow. It was obvious, yet important to observe, that the strata or layers of pure ice became fewer in number as one descended, and that upon the whole they became thicker.

I attempted to gain an idea of the temperature of the snow at different depths, but I do not care to quote my readings, as they were almost certainly falsified by the wind. I am not sure, moreover, that it is possible under any circumstances to obtain correct readings of snow temperature in the way that they were taken. The recorded temperatures, anyhow, must have been influenced by the surrounding air. If they were correct they proved that the lower strata were *warmer* than the upper ones.

We must now quit the region of facts, and descend to that of surmises and conjectures. The differences in the quality and in the tone of the snow of the first three feet below the surface were sufficiently marked to suggest that we saw in them snow belonging to three different *years*. The unanimous opinion of the four men was, that the uppermost 11 inches belonged to 1865–6, the next 10 inches to 1864–5, and the next 16 inches to 1863–4. In this matter they were not, perhaps, altogether incompetent judges. I am doubtful,

however, whether their opinion was correct, and incline to the idea
that the uppermost 11 inches had fallen during the summer of 1866,
and that the succeeding 10 inches *may* have been all that remained
of the preceding winter's snow. Whatever surprise may be felt at
so small a depth being considered as representing a year's fall, must
be modified when it is remembered that the position at which the
pit was sunk could scarcely have been more exposed. We had evidence while we were upon the summit that a mere fraction only of
the snow that fell remained *in situ*—the wind tore it away in sheets
and streams. It will be remembered, too, that no inconsiderable
amount passes off by evaporation. If other pits had been sunk to
the north and to the south of the pass, we should probably have found
in them a greater depth of snow between each of the horizontal layers
of pure ice. This is mere conjecture, and it may be taken for what
it is worth. It is more important to note—1. (*a*) That the fine layers
or strata of pure ice were *numerous* towards the surface ; (*b*) *disappeared* as we descended ; (*c*) and that the lower strata were, upon the
whole, much thicker than those towards the surface. 2. That the
thickness of these strata of pure ice amounted to nearly one-tenth of
the mass that we were able to penetrate. 3. That, below the depth
of 15 feet, vertical glacification began to show itself. Upon each
of these subjects I will now venture to offer a few remarks.

1. (*a*) *The fine horizontal layers or strata of pure ice were numerous
towards the surface*. All of these layers had been formed by weathering *at* the surface. It is usual, even during the winter, for considerable periods of fine weather to succeed heavy snowfalls ; and in these
periods the surface of the snow is alternately melted and refrozen,
and, at length, is glazed with a crust or film of pure ice. This, when
covered up by another snowfall, and exposed as in the section, appears
as a bluish horizontal line drawn through the whiter mass. The snow
between any two of these layers (near the surface) did not therefore
represent a year's snow, but it was the remnant, and only the remnant,
of a considerable fall, between whose deposition, and that of the next
stratum above, a considerable interval of time had probably elapsed.

(*b*) *The fine strata disappeared as we descended*. I imagine that this
was a result of pressure from the superincumbent mass, but I leave
to others to show the exact manner in which these finer strata were

got rid of. Is it possible to liquefy by steady pressure a plate of ice (say, one-tenth of an inch in thickness) placed in the interior of a mass of snow, without liquefaction of the snow ?

(c) *The lower strata of pure ice were, upon the whole, thicker than those towards the surface.* This, doubtless, was a result of vertical pressure. The ice-strata thickened under pressure. But why should some grow and others disappear ? I presume that the *finest* ones disappear, and that the stouter ones grow. Can it be shown experimentally that it is possible to liquefy by steady pressure a fine plate of ice placed in the interior of a mass of snow, and at the same time, under the same conditions, to thicken another and stouter plate of ice ?

2. *These horizontal strata of pure ice amounted in the aggregate to nearly one-tenth of the thickness of the mass that we penetrated.* It was perfectly well known prior to 1866 that the upper snows (which give birth to glaciers) were pervaded with strata of pure ice, and a number of observers had written before that date upon stratification of snow and of glacier. It may be questioned, however, whether any had an idea of the very important amount of glacification that is effected by superficial weathering, and subsequent thickening of the strata through vertical pressure. A search through the works of the principal writers on glaciers has failed to show me that any person imagined that one-tenth of the mass, or anything like that amount, may be composed of strata of pure ice.

There are two points in regard to these horizontal strata of pure ice that are worthy of consideration :—(a) Does not their existence, and especially the existence of the fine layers towards the surface, conclusively disprove the idea that the production of glacier-ice is greatly promoted by infiltration of water from the surface ? (b) Can these numerous strata of pure ice (some of which are of such considerable thickness, and extending over large areas) be *obliterated* in the subsequent progress of the glacier ? If so, how are they obliterated ? Or is it not reasonable to suppose that these thick strata of solid ice must continue to exist, must continue to thicken under pressure, and must supply many of those plates of pure ice which are seen in the imperfect ice of the glacier, and which have been referred to at different times and by various persons as the " veined structure " ?

3. *Below the depth of 15 feet the appearances which I have ventured to*

PINNACLES, NEAR SACHAS IN THE VALLEY OF THE DURANCE ; FORMED FROM AN OLD MORAINE.

term vertical glacification were first noticed. Were they accidental ? or will they be found at or about the same depth in all other places ? Into what would those appearances have developed at a greater depth ? What produced them ? These questions may perhaps be answered one day by future investigators. I cannot answer them except by guesses or conjectures. Most unwillingly I left the excavation just at the time when it promised to yield more valuable information than it had done previously ; and since then I have never been able to resume the work. I believe that the exposure of considerable sections of the interior of a glacier, at different parts of its course, would yield information of extreme interest ; and that more light would be thrown in such way upon the doubts and difficulties which attend the formation of glacier-ice and the " veined structure," than will ever be thrown upon those vexed subjects by wandering upon the surface of glaciers and by peering into crevasses.

K. DENUDATION IN THE VALLEY OF THE DURANCE

IN the summer of 1869, whilst walking up the valley of the Durance from Montdauphin to Briançon, I noticed, when about five kilometres from the latter place, some pinnacles on the mountain-slope to the west of the road. I scrambled up, and found the remarkable natural pillars which are represented in the annexed engraving.[1] They were formed out of an unstratified conglomerate of gritty earth, boulders, and stones. Some of them were more thickly studded with stones than a plum-pudding usually is with plums, whilst from others the stones projected like the spines from an echinoderm. The earth (or mud) was extremely hard and tenacious, and the stones, embedded in it, were extricated with considerable difficulty. The mud adhered very firmly to the stones that were got out, but it was

[1] They were 750 feet (by aneroid) above the road, and were not far from the village of Sachas. There were a dozen of about the size of those shown in the engraving, and also numerous *stumps* of other minor ones. There may have been more, and more considerable ones, farther behind. I was pressed for time, and could not proceed beyond the point shown in the illustration. I have thought the above imperfect account of these pinnacles worth recording, as I believe they have not been described or observed before.

readily washed away in a little stream near at hand.   In a few minutes I extracted fragments of syenite, mica-schist, several kinds of limestone and conglomerates, and some fossil plants characteristic of carboniferous strata.   Most of the fragments were covered with scratches, which told that they had travelled underneath a glacier.   The mud had all the character of glacier-mud, and the hill-side was covered with drift.   From these indications, and from the situation of the pinnacles, I concluded that they had been formed out of an old moraine.   The greatest of them were 60 to 70 feet high, and the moraine had therefore been at least that height.   I judged from appearances that the moraine was a frontal-terminal one of a glacier which had been an affluent of the great glacier that formerly occupied the valley of the Durance, and which, during retrogression, had made a stand upon this hill-side near Sachas.   This lateral glacier had flowed down a nameless *vallon* which descends towards the E.S.E. from the mountain called upon the French Government map Sommet de l'Eychouda (8,740 feet).

Only one of all the pinnacles that I saw was *capped* by a stone (a small one), and I did not notice any boulders lying in their immediate vicinity of a size sufficient to account for their production in the manner of the well-known pillars near Bozen.   The readers of Sir Charles Lyell's *Principles* (10th ed., vol. i., p. 338) will remember that he attributes the formation of the Bozen pillars chiefly to the protection which boulders have afforded to the underlying matter from the direct action of rain.   This is no doubt correct—the Bozen pinnacles are mostly capped by boulders of considerable dimensions. In the present instance this does not appear to have been exactly the case.   Running water has cut the moraine into ridges (shown upon the right hand of the engraving), and has evidently assisted in the work of denudation.   The group of pinnacles here figured, belonged, in all probability, to a ridge which had been formed in this way, whose crest, in course of time, became sharp, perhaps attenuated.   In such a condition, very small stones upon the crest of the ridge would originate little pinnacles ; whether these would develop into larger ones, would depend upon the quantity of stones embedded in the surrounding moraine-matter.   I imagine that the largest of the Sachas pinnacles owe their existence to the portions of the moraine out of which they are formed having been studded with a greater quantity of stones and small boulders than the portions of the moraine which formerly filled the gaps between them ; and, of course, primarily, to the fact that glacier-mud is extremely tenacious when dry, and is readily washed away. Thus, the present form of the pinnacles is chiefly due to the direct action of rain, but their production was assisted, in the first instance, by the action of running water.

INDEX

INDEX

D D*